Tyndale Old Testament Commentaries

Volume 28

TOTC

Haggai, Zechariah and Malachi

To our grandchildren
David, Neva, Samuel, Hudson (*in memoriam*), Christian and Lucy
'The city streets will be filled with boys and girls playing ...'
(Zech. 8:5)

Tyndale Old Testament Commentaries

Volume 28

Series Editor: David G. Firth
Consulting Editor: Tremper Longman III

Haggai, Zechariah and Malachi

An Introduction and Commentary

Andrew E. Hill

Inter-Varsity Press

IVP Academic
An imprint of InterVarsity Press
Downers Grove, Illinois

InterVarsity Press, USA
P.O. Box 1400
Downers Grove, IL 60515-1426, USA
Website: www.ivpress.com
Email: email@ivpress.com

Inter-Varsity Press, England
Norton Street
Nottingham NG7 3HR, England
Website: www.ivpbooks.com
Email: ivp@ivpbooks.com

InterVarsity Press®, USA, is the book-publishing division of InterVarsity Christian Fellowship/USA® <www.intervarsity.org> and a member movement of the International Fellowship of Evangelical Students.

Inter-Varsity Press, England, is closely linked with the Universities and Colleges Christian Fellowship, a student movement connecting Christian Unions in universities and colleges throughout Great Britain, and a member movement of the International Fellowship of Evangelical Students. Website: www.uccf.org.uk.

All Scripture quotations, unless otherwise indicated, are taken from the Holy Bible, New International Version®. NIV®. Copyright © 1973, 1978, 1984 by International Bible Society. Used by permission of Zondervan Publishing House. Distributed in the U.K. by permission of Hodder and Stoughton Ltd. All rights reserved. "NIV" is a registered trademark of International Bible Society. UK trademark number 1448790.

First published 2012

Image: © Erich Lessing/Art Resource, NY

USA ISBN 978-0-8308-4282-7
UK ISBN 978-1-84474-584-5

Set in Garamond MT 11/13pt
Typeset in Great Britain by Avocet Typeset, Chilton, Aylesbury, Bucks
Printed and bound in Great Britain by Ashford Colour Press Ltd

Library of Congress Cataloging-in-Publication Data

Hill, Andrew E.
  Haggai, Zechariah and Malachi : an introduction and commentary /
Andrew E. Hill.
      pages cm—(Tyndale Old Testament commentaries ; v. 28)
   Includes bibliographical references.
   ISBN 978-0-8308-4282-7 (pbk.: alk. paper)
   1. Bible. O.T. Haggai--Commentaries. 2. Bible. O.T.
Zechariah—Commentaries. 3. Bible. O.T. Malachi—Commentaries. I.
Title.
   BS1655.53.H55 2012
   224'.907—dc23

                                                                                    2012009669

British Library Cataloguing in Publication Data

A catalogue record of this book is available from the British Library.

| P | 18 | 17 | 16 | 15 | 14 | 13 | 12 | 11 | 10 | 9 | 8 | 7 | 6 | 5 | 4 | 3 | 2 | 1 |
| Y | 27 | 26 | 25 | 24 | 23 | 22 | 21 | 20 | 19 | 18 | 17 | 16 | 15 | 14 | 13 | 12 |

CONTENTS

ZECHARIAH

MALACHI

GENERAL PREFACE

The decision completely to revise the Tyndale Old Testament Commentaries is an indication of the important role that the series has played since its opening volumes were released in the mid-1960s. They represented at that time, and have continued to represent, commentary writing that was committed both to the importance of the text of the Bible as Scripture and a desire to engage with as full a range of interpretative issues as possible without being lost in the minutiae of scholarly debate. The commentaries aimed to explain the biblical text to a generation of readers confronting models of critical scholarship and new discoveries from the Ancient Near East, while remembering that the Old Testament is not simply another text from the ancient world. Although no uniform process of exegesis was required, all the original contributors were united in their conviction that the Old Testament remains the Word of God for us today. That the original volumes fulfilled this role is evident from the way in which they continue to be used in so many parts of the world.

A crucial element of the original series was that it should offer an up-to-date reading of the text, and it is precisely for this reason that new volumes are required. The questions confronting readers in the first half of the twenty-first century are not necessarily those from the second half of the twentieth. Discoveries from the Ancient Near East continue to shed new light on the Old Testament, whilst emphases in exegesis have changed markedly. Whilst remaining true to the goals of the initial volumes, the need for contemporary study of the text requires that the series as a whole be updated. This updating is not simply a matter of commissioning new volumes to replace the old. We have also taken the opportunity to update the format of the series to reflect a key emphasis from linguistics, which is that texts communicate in larger blocks rather than in shorter segments such as individual verses. Because of this, the treatment of each section of the text includes three segments. First, a short note on *Context* is offered, placing the passage under consideration in its literary setting within the book, as well as noting any historical issues crucial to interpretation. The *Comment* segment then follows the traditional structure of the commentary, offering exegesis of the various components of a passage. Finally, a brief comment is made on *Meaning*, by which is meant the message that the passage seeks to communicate within the book, highlighting its key theological themes. This section brings together the detail of the *Comment* to show how the passage under consideration seeks to communicate as a whole.

Our prayer is that these new volumes will continue the rich heritage of the Tyndale Old Testament Commentaries, and that they will continue to witness to the God who is made known in the text.

David G. Firth, Series Editor
Tremper Longman III, Consulting Editor

AUTHOR'S PREFACE

Haggai, Zechariah and Malachi preached to audiences who were jaded by the lack of relevance of organized religion to their daily economic and social life. They were self-absorbed, preoccupied with personal agendas, bent on comparing themselves with others, questioning the fairness of life, looking for an edge, pursuing material rather than spiritual things, morally ambivalent, apathetic with respect to civil responsibility, hypocritical with regard to religious practice, chasing much but grasping little – and the list goes on. Sound familiar?

The crisis of relevance persists today in numerous ways and at a variety of levels. Our three prophets sought to remedy the crisis of the relevance of the religion of YHWH for the people of God living in post-exilic Judah by calling them to *return to God* (Zech. 1:3; Mal. 3:7). Much of the teaching of Haggai, Zechariah and Malachi still has currency for the people of God dealing with the various crises of relevance in our contemporary culture. Their sermons remain an open invitation to *be still before the LORD* (Zech. 2:13), *to seek the LORD Almighty* (Zech. 8:22), and to come to understand and acknowledge that YHWH is *a great king* (Mal. 1:14). In short, they continue to call us to return to God – godly repentance is always relevant.

I am honoured to stand on the shoulders of such an able scholar as the late Joyce G. Baldwin. Over the years, I have personally and professionally benefited from her TOTC commentaries, first as a seminarian, later as a graduate student, and now as a professor of biblical studies. As a credit to her careful and insightful scholarship, I have intentionally made wide appeal to her analysis, where appropriate. I trust this iteration of the TOTC on the books of Haggai, Zechariah and Malachi will serve the next generation of students and pastor-teachers equally well.

The New International Version (NIV) is the baseline English translation used for the commentary, and quotations from this version are given in italics. Other English versions are referenced where helpful, including the NIV 2011 edition when pertinent. Bible translation is necessarily interpretive in many instances, so the broad engagement with an array of English versions brings both breadth of perspective and depth of understanding to the analysis of particular verses of Scripture. Numerous insightful and readable commentaries are available on the books of Haggai, Zechariah and Malachi. I have benefited from this excellent scholarship and have attempted to interact with these resources (cited in the Select bibliography for each book) in such a way that the reader gains an understanding of the biblical text, informed by a variety of voices.

Special attention is given to intertextual relationships in our analysis, since each of the three prophets often appeal (whether directly or indirectly) to the messages of their earlier counterparts. We read the Bible as theology (the *revelation* of God and his redemptive plan for humanity), history (the *record* of God's dealings with humanity, and especially Israel) and literature (the *story* of God and human experience). All three lenses are employed in our analysis of Haggai, Zechariah and Malachi. Emphasis is given to literary analysis of our three prophetic books, since each is a hybrid of sorts, combining a distinctive mix of genres and literary features in their sermons and visions to post-exilic Judah. This approach also assumes the books of Haggai, Zechariah and Malachi have some inherent relationship by way of theme(s) and message, since they arise out of the same general period of history and address the same constituency. This reading of the three post-exilic prophets also recognizes that they belong to a larger collection of prophetic books, the Book of the Twelve (or Minor Prophets), which may tell a more extended story about God and his people Israel.

By way of acknowledgments, I would like to thank my graduate assistants, Brett Blum and Jordan Brown, for their work in the process of compiling the manuscript for this commentary. I am indebted to the staff of IVP UK for their good work in seeing the volume through to publication. I would especially like to recognize Philip Duce (Senior Commissioning Editor) for the opportunity to contribute to this venerable commentary series. I offer my thanks as well to David Firth (Series Editor) for ably bringing this instalment of the TOTC to completion. I am grateful to both for their patience, professionalism and scholarly insight as overseers of the project.

I remain grateful for Teri, the wife of my youth. Thanks to her partnership, I am coming to understand more clearly, and practise more intentionally, the prophetic call to do justice and to love mercy. We look forward to the realization of Zechariah's vision of streets filled with boys and girls playing in safety – for our three (now grown-up) children, our several grandchildren, and for all children (Zech. 8:4–5).

To the reader, listen and learn from the preaching of these last three voices of the OT prophetic movement. Haggai reminds us to 'think carefully about our behaviour' (Hag. 1:5, 7; 2:15, 18, NJB). Zechariah exhorts us not to despise 'small beginnings' (Zech. 4:10, NLT), since *it is not by might nor by power, but by the Spirit* that the LORD Almighty accomplishes his purposes (Zech. 4:6). And finally, Malachi encourages the people of God by affirming that, '"I have always loved you," says the LORD' (Mal. 1:2, NLT).

Andrew E. Hill
Wheaton College
Wheaton, Illinois
Advent 2011

CHIEF ABBREVIATIONS

AB	Anchor Bible
ABD	D. N. Freedman et al. (eds.), *The Anchor Bible Dictionary*, 6 vols. (Garden City, New York: Doubleday, 1992)
AD	Anno Domini
anc.	ancient
ANE	Ancient Near East
ANEP	J. B. Pritchard, *The Ancient Near East in Pictures*, 2nd edn with suppl. (Princeton: Princeton University Press, 1969)
ANET	J. B. Pritchard, (ed.), *Ancient Near Eastern Texts Relating to the Old Testament*, 3rd edn with suppl. (Princeton: Princeton University Press, 1969)
AOTC	Abingdon Old Testament Commentaries
Aram.	Aramaic
b. (*Talm.*)	Babylonian (*Talmud*)
BBCOT	J. H. Walton et al. (eds.), *IVP Bible Background Commentary: Old Testament* (Downers Grove, Ill.: InterVarsity Press, 2000)
BC	Before Christ
BHQ	A. Gelston, *Biblia Hebraica Quinta 13: The Twelve Minor Prophets* (Stuttgart: Deutsche Bibelgesellschaft, 2010)
BHS	K. Elliger and W. Rudolf (eds.), *Biblia Hebraica Stuttgartensia* (Stuttgart: Deutsche Bibelgesellschaft, 1984)

BibSem	Biblical Seminar
BZAW	Beiheft zur ZAW
CAT	Commentaire de l'Ancien Testament
CBC	Cambridge Bible Commentary
CBQ	*Catholic Biblical Quarterly*
ch.	chapter(s)
CorBC	Cornerstone Biblical Commentary
CTR	*Criswell Theological Review*
CurTM	*Currents in Theology and Mission*
DOTPen	T. D. Alexander and D. W. Baker (eds.), *Dictionary of the Old Testament Pentateuch* (Downers Grove, Ill.: InterVarsity Press, 2003)
DSBOT	Daily Study Bible (Old Testament)
EB	English Bible
EBC	*Expositor's Bible Commentary* (Revised)
ed(s).	editor(s)
edn	edition
EncJud	*Encyclopaedia Judaica*
Eng.	English
esp.	especially
EvBC	Everyman's Bible Commentary
EVV	English versions
Fig.	Figure
FOTL	Forms of Old Testament Literature
FRLANT	Forschungen zur Religion und Literatur des Alten und Neuen Testaments
Gk	Greek
GKC	E. Kautzsch (ed.), *Gesenius' Hebrew Grammar* (Oxford: Clarendon Press, 1910).
Hag-Zech-Mal corpus	The books of Haggai, Zechariah and Malachi understood as a related literary collection
HAR	*Hebrew Annual Review*
HB	Hebrew Bible
Heb.	Hebrew
HolOTC	Holman Old Testament Commentary
HSM	Harvard Semitic Monographs
IBHS	B. K. Waltke and M. O'Connor, *An Introduction to Biblical Hebrew Syntax* (Winona Lake, IN:

	Eisenbrauns, 1990)
ICC	International Critical Commentary
Int	*Interpretation*
Int	Interpretation Commentary Series
ITC	International Theological Commentary
JAOS	*Journal of the American Oriental Society*
JETS	*Journal of the Evangelical Theological Society*
JPSV	Jewish Publication Society of America Version
JSOT	*Journal for the Study of the Old Testament*
JSOTSup	Journal for the Study of the Old Testament Supplementary series
KAT	Kommentar zum Alten Testament
Lat.	Latin
lit.	literally
LXX	Septuagint (pre-Christian Greek version of the Old Testament)
LXX A	Codex Alexandrinus
LXX B	Codex Vaticanus
LXX Q	Codex Marchallianus
MT	Massoretic Text (the standard Hebrew text of the Old Testament)
Mur	Wadi Murabba'at
n.	note
NAC	New American Commentary
NCBC	New Century Bible Commentary
NDBT	T. D. Alexander, B. S. Rosner, D. A. Carson, G. Goldsworthy (eds.), *New Dictionary of Biblical Theology* (Leicester: Inter-Varsity Press, 2000)
NETS	A. Pietersman and B. C. Wright, (eds.), *A New English Translation of the Septuagint* (New York: Oxford University Press, 2007)
NIB	L. E. Keck (ed.), *The New Interpreter's Bible* (Nashville: Abingdon Press, 1994–), 12 vols.
NICOT	New International Commentary on the Old Testament
NIDB	*New Interpreter's Dictionary of the Bible*
NIDOTTE	W. A. VanGemeren (gen. ed.), *New International Dictionary of Old Testament Theology and Exegesis*

	(Grand Rapids: Zondervan, 1997), 5 vols.
NIrV	New International Reader's Version, 1994
NIVAC	NIV Application Commentary
NJPS	New Jewish Publication Society, 1985
NSBT	New Studies in Biblical Theology
NT	New Testament
OT	Old Testament
OTL	Old Testament Library
para.	paragraph
pl	plural
Q	Qumran
repr.	reprint
RevExp	*Review and Expositor*
SBLDS	Society of Biblical Literature Dissertation Series
SBLMS	Society of Biblical Literature Monograph Series
sing.	singular
ST	*Studia Theologica*
suppl.	supplement
Symp	Symposium
Syr.	Syriac
Targ.	Targum
TBT	*The Bible Today*
TDOT	G. J. Botterweck and H. Ringgren (eds.), *Theological Dictionary of the Old Testament* (Grand Rapids: Eerdmans, 1974–)
TOTC	Tyndale Old Testament Commentaries
trans.	translator
TynB	*Tyndale Bulletin*
UBS	United Bible Societies
v./vv.	verse/verses
vers.	version(s)
vol(s).	volume(s)
VT	*Vetus Testamentum*
VTSup	Vetus Testamentum Supplement
Vulg.	Vulgate
WBC	Word Biblical Commentary
ZAW	*Zeitschrift für die Alttestamentliche Wissenschaft*
ZIBBCOT	J. H. Walton (gen. ed.), *Zondervan Illustrated Bible*

Backgrounds Commentary (Grand Rapids: Zondervan, 2009), 5 vols.

Bible Versions

CEV	Contemporary English Version, copyright © 1995 American Bible Society
ESV	English Standard Version, published by HarperCollins Publishers © 2001 by Crossway Bibles, a division of Good News Publishers
HCSB	Holman Christian Standard Bible, © copyright 1999 [2004] by Holman Bible Publishers
KJV	King James Version
NAB	New American Bible, copyright © 1995 by Oxford University Press, Inc. New York
NEB	New English Bible, copyright © Oxford University Press and Cambridge University Press 1961, 1970
NIV	New International Version, copyright © 1973, 1978, 1984
NIV 2011	New International Version 2011, copyright © 1973, 1978. 1984, 2011 by Biblica, Inc.
NJB	New Jerusalem Bible, copyright © 1985 by Darton, Longman & Todd Ltd and Doubleday, a division of Bantam Doubleday Dell Publishing Group, Inc.
NKJV	New King James Version, copyright © 1982 by Thomas Nelson, Inc.
NLT	New Living Translation, copyright © 1996 [2004, 2007]. Anglicized version, copyright © 2000.
NRSV	New Revised Standard Version, Anglicized edition, copyright © 1989, 1995 by the Division of Christian Education of the National Council of the Churches of Christ in the USA
RV	Revised English Version, 1881
TEV	Today's English Version (Good News Translation), copyright © 1992 American Bible Society
TNIV	Today's New International Version, copyright © 2001 [2005] by International Bible Society

SELECT BIBLIOGRAPHIES

General introduction to Haggai, Zechariah and Malachi

Baldwin, J. G. (1972), *Haggai, Zechariah and Malachi*, TOTC 28 (London/Downers Grove: IVP).

Berquist, J. L. (1995), *Judaism in Persia's Shadow* (Minneapolis: Fortress).

Collins, T. (1993), 'The Scroll of the Twelve', in *The Mantle of Elijah*, BibSem 20 (Sheffield: Sheffield Academic Press).

Dumbrell, W. J. (2002), *The Faith of Israel*, 2nd edn (Grand Rapids: Baker).

Firth, D. G. and Paul D. Wegner (eds.) (2011), *Presence, Power and Promise: The Role of the Spirit of God in the Old Testament* (Nottingham: Apollos; Downers Grove: IVP Academic).

Gottwald, N. K. (1985), 'Tragedy and Comedy in the Latter Prophets', *Semeia* 32: 83–96.

Hanson, P. D. (1992), 'Messiahs and Messianic Figures in Proto-Apocalypticism', in J. H. Charlesworth (ed.), *The Messiah: Developments in Earliest Judaism and Christianity* (Minneapolis: Fortress).

Hill, A. E. (1998), *Malachi*, AB 25D (New York: Doubleday).

House, P. (1990), *The Unity of the Twelve*, JSOTSup 97 (Sheffield: Sheffield Academic Press).

Merrill, E. H. (1994), *Haggai, Zechariah, Malachi* (Chicago: Moody).

Patterson, R. D. and A. E. Hill (2008), *Minor Prophets: Hosea – Malachi*, CorBC 10 (Wheaton, Ill.: Tyndale House).

Petersen, D. L. (2000), 'A Book of the Twelve?', in J. D. Nogalski and M. A. Sweeney (eds.), *Reading and Hearing the Book of the Twelve*, Symp 15 (Atlanta: SBL).

Redditt, P. L. and A. Schart (2003), *Thematic Threads in the Book of the Twelve*, BZAW 325 (Berlin: de Gruyter).

Rose, W. H. (2000), *Zemah and Zerubbabel: Messianic Expectations in the Early Postexilic Period*, JSOTSup 304 (Sheffield: Sheffield Academic Press).

Tollington, J. E. (1993), *Tradition and Innovation in Haggai and Zechariah 1 – 8*, JSOTSup 150 (Sheffield: JSOT Press).

Walton, J. H. and A. E. Hill (2004), *Old Testament Today* (Grand Rapids: Zondervan).

Haggai

Achtemeier, E. (1986), *Nahum – Malachi*, Int (Atlanta: John Knox).

Baldwin, J. G. (1972), *Haggai, Zechariah, Malachi*, TOTC 28 (London/Downers Grove: IVP).

Berquist, J. L. (1995), *Judaism in Persia's Shadow* (Minneapolis: Fortress).

Boda, M. J. (2000), 'Haggai: Master Rhetorician', *TynB* 51: 295–304.

—— (2004), *Haggai, Zechariah*, NIVAC (Grand Rapids: Zondervan).

—— (2007), 'Messengers of Hope in Haggai – Malachi', *JSOT* 32: 113–131.

Briant, P. (2002), *From Cyrus to Alexander: A History of the Persian Empire*, trans. P. T. Daniels (Winona Lake: Eisenbrauns).

Christensen, D. L. (1992), 'Impulse and Design in the Book of Haggai', *JETS* 35: 445–456.

Clements, R. E. (1965), *God and Temple* (Philadelphia: Fortress).

Coats, G. W. and B. O. Long (eds.) (1977), *Canon and Authority* (Philadelphia: Fortress).

Craig, K. M. (1996), 'Interrogatives in Haggai – Zechariah: A Literary Thread?', in *Forming Prophetic Literature: Essays on Isaiah and the Twelve in Honor of John D. W. Watts*, JSOTSup 235 (Sheffield: Sheffield Academic Press), 224–244.

Craigie, P. C. (1985), *The Twelve Prophets*, DSBOT, vol. 2 (Philadelphia: Westminster).

Dumbrell, W. J. (2002), *The Faith of Israel*, 2nd edn (Grand

Rapids: Baker; Leicester: Apollos).

Ferreiro, A. (ed.) (2003), *Ancient Christian Commentary on Scripture*, vol. 14 (Downers Grove: IVP).

Floyd, M. H. (2000), *Minor Prophets: Part 2*, FOTL XXII (Grand Rapids: Eerdmans).

Goldingay, J. (2006), *Old Testament Theology: Israel's Faith* (Downers Grove: IVP).

Gowan, D. E. (1986), *Eschatology in the Old Testament* (Philadelphia: Fortress).

Hildebrand, D. R. (1989), 'Temple Ritual: A Paradigm for Moral Holiness in Haggai II 10–19', *VT* 39: 154–168.

Hill, A. E. (1998), *Malachi*, AB 25D (New York: Doubleday).

—— (2003), *1 & 2 Chronicles*, NIVAC (Grand Rapids: Zondervan).

Jones, B. A. (1995), *The Formation of the Book of the Twelve: A Study in Text and Canon*, SBLDS 149 (Atlanta: Scholars Press).

Kaiser, W. C. (1995), *The Messiah in the Old Testament* (Grand Rapids: Zondervan).

Kessler, J. A. (2002), *The Book of Haggai: Prophecy and Society in Early Persian Yehud*, VTSup 91 (Leiden: Brill).

March, W. E. (1996), in L. E. Keck (ed.), *The New Interpreter's Bible*, vol. 7 (Nashville: Abingdon), 707–732.

Martens, E. A. (1994), *God's Design: A Focus on Old Testament Theology*, 2nd edn (Grand Rapids: Baker).

Mason, R. (1977), *The Books of Haggai, Zechariah and Malachi* (Cambridge: Cambridge University Press).

Merrill, E. H. (1994), *Haggai, Zechariah, Malachi: An Exegetical Commentary* (Chicago: Moody).

—— (2008), 'Haggai', in T. Longman and D. Garland (eds.), *The Expositor's Bible Commentary*, rev. edn, vol. 8 (Grand Rapids: Zondervan), 699–720.

Meyers, E. M. and C. L. Meyers (1987), *Haggai, Zechariah 1 – 8*, AB 25B (New York: Doubleday).

Motyer, J. A. (1998), 'Haggai', in T. E. McComiskey (ed.), *The Minor Prophets*, vol. 3 (Grand Rapids: Baker), 963–1002.

Neusner, J. (2007), *Zephaniah, Haggai, Zechariah and Malachi in Talmud and Midrash* (New York: University of America Press).

Nogalski, J. (1993), *Literary Precursors to the Book of the Twelve*, BZAW 217 (Berlin: Walter de Gruyter).

Patrick, F. Y. (2008), 'Time and Tradition in the Book of Haggai',
    in M. J. Boda and M. H. Floyd (eds.), *Tradition in Transition:
    Haggai and Zechariah 1 – 8 in the Trajectory of Hebrew Theology* (New
    York: T. & T. Clark), 40–55.
Petersen, D. L. (1984), *Haggai and Zechariah 1 – 8*, OTL
    (Philadelphia: Westminster).
Pierce, R. W. (1984), 'Literary Connectors and a
    Haggai/Zechariah/Malachi Corpus', *JETS* 27: 277–289.
—— (1984), 'A Thematic Development in the
    Haggai/Zechariah/Malachi Corpus', *JETS* 27: 401–411.
Redditt, P. L. (1995), *Haggai, Zechariah, Malachi*, NCBC (London:
    Marshall Pickering).
—— (2007), 'Themes in Haggai, Zechariah, Malachi', *Int* 61:
    184–197.
Rose, W. H. (2000), *Zemah and Zerubbabel: Messianic Expectations in
    the Early Postexilic Period*, JSOTSup 304 (Sheffield: Sheffield
    Academic Press).
Smith, J. M. P. in H. G. Mitchell, J. M. P. Smith and J. A. Bewer
    (1912), *Haggai, Zechariah, Malachi and Jonah*, ICC (Edinburgh:
    T. & T. Clark).
Smith, R. L. (1984), *Micah – Malachi*, WBC 32 (Waco: Word).
Stuhlmueller, C. (1988), *Haggai & Zechariah: Rebuilding with Hope*,
    ITC (Grand Rapids: Eerdmans).
Sweeney, M. A. (2000), *The Twelve Prophets*, Berit Olam, vol. 2
    (Collegeville, Minn.: Liturgical Press).
Taylor, R. A. and E. R. Clendenen (2004), *Haggai, Malachi*, NAC
    21A (Nashville: Broadman & Holman).
Terrien, S. (1978), *The Elusive Presence* (New York: Harper & Row).
Thomas, D. W. (1956), 'Haggai', in G. A. Buttrick (ed.), *The
    Interpreter's Bible*, vol. 6 (Nashville: Abingdon), 1036–1049.
Tucker, G. M. (1977), 'Prophetic Superscriptions and the Growth
    of a Canon', in G. W. Coats and B. O. Long (eds.), *Canon and
    Authority* (Philadelphia: Fortress), 56–70.
Verhoef, P. A. (1987), *Haggai and Malachi*, NICOT (Grand Rapids:
    Eerdmans).
Wolf, H. (1976), *Haggai and Malachi*, EvBC (Chicago: Moody).
Wolff, H. W. (1988), *Haggai: A Commentary*, trans. M. Kohl
    (Minneapolis: Augsburg).

Yamauchi, E. M. (1990), *Persia and the Bible* (Grand Rapids: Baker).

Zechariah

Achtemeier, E. (1986), *Nahum – Malachi*, Int (Atlanta: John Knox).

Andersen, F. I. and D. N. Freedman (1980), *Hosea*, AB 24 (New York: Doubleday).

Bahat, D. (1990), *The Illustrated Atlas of Jerusalem*, trans. S. Ketko (Jerusalem: CARTA).

Baldwin, J. G. (1972), *Haggai, Zechariah, Malachi*, TOTC 28 (London/Downers Grove: IVP).

Baly, D. (1974), *The Geography of the Bible*, rev. edn (New York: Harper & Row).

Barker, K. L. (2008), 'Zechariah', in T. Longman and D. E. Garland (eds.), *The Expositor's Bible Commentary*, rev. edn, vol. 8 (Grand Rapids: Zondervan), 723–833.

Blenkinsopp, J. (1998), 'The Judean Priesthood During the Neo-Babylonian and Achaemenid Periods: A Hypothetical Reconstruction', *CBQ* 60: 25–43.

Boda, M. J. (2004), *Haggai, Zechariah*, NIVAC (Grand Rapids: Zondervan).

Brosius, M. (1998), *Women In Ancient Persia (559–331 BC)* (Oxford: Clarendon Press).

Butterworth, M. (1992), *The Structure of Zechariah*, JSOTSup 130 (Sheffield: Sheffield Academic Press).

Calvin, J. (1979), *Commentaries on the Twelve Minor Prophets* (repr.), trans. J. Owen, vol. 15 (Grand Rapids: Baker).

Cathcart, K. J. and R. P. Gordon (1989), *The Targum of the Minor Prophets*, The Aramaic Bible 14 (Wilmington, Del.: Michael Glazier).

Childs, B. S. (1979), *Introduction to the Old Testament as Scripture* (Philadelphia: Fortress).

Clifford, R. J. (1972), *The Cosmic Mountain in Canaan and in the Old Testament*, HSM 4 (Cambridge: Harvard University Press).

Cook, S. L. (1995), *Prophecy & Apocalypticism: The Postexilic Social Setting* (Minneapolis: Fortress).

Craigie, P. C. (1985), *Twelve Prophets*, DSBOT, vol. 2 (Philadelphia: Westminster).

Dorsey, D. A. (1999), *The Literary Structure of the Old Testament* (Grand Rapids: Baker).

Eichrodt, W. (1967), *Theology of the Old Testament*, OTL, vol. 1 (Philadelphia: Westminster).

Fishbane, M. (1985), *Biblical Interpretation in Ancient Israel* (Oxford: Clarendon Press).

Frost, S. B. (1952), *Old Testament Apocalyptic, Its Origins and Growth* (London: Epworth).

Hanson, P. D. (1979), *The Dawn of Apocalyptic*, rev. edn (Philadelphia: Fortress).

—— (1987), *Old Testament Apocalyptic* (Nashville: Abingdon).

Harrington, H. K. (2002), 'Zechariah', in C. C. Kroeger and M. J. Evans (eds.), *The IVP Women's Bible Commentary* (Downers Grove: IVP), 491–500.

Hill, A. E. (1982), 'Dating "Second Zechariah": A Linguistic Reexamination', *HAR* 6: 105–134.

—— (1998), *Malachi*, AB 25D (New York: Doubleday).

—— (2008), *Hosea – Malachi*, CBC 10 (Wheaton: Tyndale).

Jeremias, C. (1977), *Die Nachtgesichte des Sacharja: Untersuchungen zu ihrer Stellung im Zusammenhand der Visionsberichte im Alten Testament und zu ihrem Bildmaterial*, FRLANT 117 (Göttingen: Vandenhoeck & Ruprecht).

Jones, B. A. (1995), *The Formation of the Book of the Twelve: A Study in Text and Canon*, SBLDS 149 (Atlanta: Scholars Press).

Jones, D. R. (1962), 'A Fresh Interpretation of Zechariah IX–XI', *VT* 12: 241–259.

Kaiser, W. C. (1995), *The Messiah in the Old Testament* (Grand Rapids: Zondervan).

—— (2000), *Mission in the Old Testament* (Grand Rapids: Baker Books).

Lacocque, A. (1981), *Zacharie 9 – 14*, CAT XIc (Neuchâtel/Paris: Delachaux & Niestlé).

Larkin, K. (1994), *The Eschatology of Second Zechariah* (Kampen: Kok Pharos).

Lind, M. C. (1980), *Yahweh Is a Warrior* (Scottdale, Penn.: Herald Press).

Longman, T. and R. B. Dillard (2006), *Introduction to the Old Testament*, 2nd edn (Grand Rapids: Zondervan;

Nottingham: Apollos).

Longman, T. and D. G. Reid (1995), *God Is a Warrior* (Grand Rapids: Zondervan).

Luther, M. (1973), *Lectures on Minor Prophets: Zechariah*, in H. C. Oswald (ed.), trans. R. J. Dinda, vol. 20 (St Louis: Concordia).

Mason, R. (1977), *The Books of Haggai, Zechariah and Malachi* (Cambridge: Cambridge University Press).

—— (1984), 'Some Echoes of the Preaching in the Second Temple? Tradition Elements in Zechariah 1 – 8', *ZAW* 96: 221–235.

—— (1990), *Preaching the Tradition: Homily and Hermeneutics after the Exile* (Cambridge: Cambridge University Press).

—— (2003), 'The Use of Earlier Biblical Material in Zechariah 9 – 14: A Study in Inner Biblical Exegesis', in M. J. Boda and M. H. Floyd (eds.), *Bringing Out the Treasure: Inner Biblical Allusion and Zechariah 9 – 14*, JSOTSup 304 (Sheffield: Sheffield Academic Press), 7–208.

McComiskey, T. E. (1998), 'Zechariah', in T. E. McComiskey (ed.), *The Minor Prophets*, vol. 3 (Grand Rapids: Baker), 1003–1244.

Merrill, E. H. (1994), *Haggai, Zechariah, Malachi* (Chicago: Moody Press).

Meyers, C. L. and E. M. Meyers (1987), *Haggai, Zechariah 1 – 8*, AB 25B (New York: Doubleday).

—— (1993), *Zechariah 9 – 14*, AB 25C (New York: Doubleday).

—— (1994), 'Demography and Diatribes: Yehud's Population and the Prophecy of Second Zechariah', in M. D. Coogan et al. (eds.), *Scripture and Other Artifacts: Essays in Honor of Philip J. King* (Louisville: Westminster John Knox), 268–285.

Miller, P. D. (1973), *The Divine Warrior in Early Israel* (Cambridge: Harvard University Press).

Moo, D. J. (1998), *The Epistle to the Romans*, NICNT (Grand Rapids: Eerdmans).

Nurmela, R. (1996), *Prophets in Dialogue: Inner-Biblical Allusions in Zechariah 1 – 8 and 9 – 14* (Åbo: Åbo Akademi University).

O'Brien, J. M. (2004), *Nahum, Habakkuk, Zephaniah, Haggai, Zechariah, Malachi*, AOTC (Nashville: Abingdon).

Ollenburger, B. C. (1996), 'Zechariah', in L. E. Keck (ed.), *The New Interpreter's Bible*, vol. 7 (Nashville: Abingdon), 735–840.

Petersen, D. L. (1984), *Haggai and Zechariah 1 – 8*, OTL
    (Philadelphia: Westminster).
—— (1995), *Zechariah 9 – 14 and Malachi*, OTL (Louisville:
    Westminster John Knox Press).
Pierce, R. W. (1984), 'Literary Connectors and a Haggai-
    Zechariah-Malachi Corpus', *JETS* 27: 277–289.
Radday, Y. T. and D. Wickman (1975), 'The Unity of Zechariah
    Examined in Light of Statistical Linguistics', *ZAW* 87: 30–55.
Redditt, P. L. (1995), *Haggai, Zechariah, Malachi*, NCBC (Grand
    Rapids: Eerdmans).
Rose, W. H. (2000), *Zemah and Zerubbabel: Messianic Expectation in the
    Early Postexilic Period*, JSOTSup 304 (Sheffield: Sheffield
    Academic Press).
Routledge, R. (2008), *Old Testament Theology: A Thematic Approach*
    (Nottingham: Apollos; Downers Grove: IVP Academic).
Rudolph, W. (1976), *Haggai – Sacharja 1–8/9–14 – Maleachi*, KAT
    XIII/4 (Gütersloh: Gütersloher Verlagshaus Mohn).
Ryken, L. (1984), *How to Read the Bible as Literature* (Grand Rapids:
    Zondervan).
Scott, R. B. Y. (1971), *The Way of Wisdom* (New York: Macmillan).
Sellin, E. and G. Fohrer (1968), *Introduction to the Old Testament*,
    trans. D. E. Green (Nashville: Abingdon Press).
Smith, J. M. P. in H. G. Mitchell, J. M. P. Smith and J. A. Bewer
    (1912), *Haggai, Zechariah, Malachi and Jonah*, ICC (Edinburgh:
    T. & T. Clark).
Smith, R. L. (1984), *Micah – Malachi*, WBC 32 (Waco: Word).
Stead, M. R. (2009), *Intertextuality of Zechariah 1 – 8*, Library of
    Hebrew Bible/Old Testament Studies 506 (New York: T. & T.
    Clark).
Stuhlmueller, C. (1988), *Haggai & Zechariah: Rebuilding with Hope*,
    ITC (Grand Rapids: Eerdmans).
Sweeney, M. A. (2000), *The Twelve Prophets*, Berit Olam, vol. 2
    (Collegeville, Minn.: Liturgical Press).
Tucker, G. M. (1977), 'Prophetic Superscriptions and the Growth
    of a Canon', in G. W. Coats and B. O. Long (eds.), *Canon and
    Authority* (Philadelphia: Fortress), 56–70.
Ulrich, E. et al. (1997), *Discoveries in the Judaean Desert (Vol. XV):
    Qumran Cave 4 (The Prophets)* (Oxford: Clarendon Press).

Van der Toorn, K. et al. (eds.) (1999), *The Dictionary of Deities and Demons in the Bible*, 2nd edn (Grand Rapids: Eerdmans).

Webb, B. G. (2003), *The Message of Zechariah* (Leicester/Downers Grove, Ill.: IVP).

Wenzel, H. (2011), *Reading Zechariah with Zechariah 1:1–6 as the Introduction to the Entire Book*, Contribution to Biblical Exegesis & Theology, 59 (Leuven: Peeters).

Westermann, C. (1991), *Prophetic Oracles of Salvation in the Old Testament*, trans. K. Crim (Louisville: Westminster John Knox).

Malachi

Achtemeier, E. (1986), *Nahum – Malachi*, Int (Atlanta: John Knox).

Andersen, F. I. and D. N. Freedman (1980), *Hosea*, AB 24 (New York: Doubleday).

—— (1989), *Amos*, AB 24A (New York: Doubleday).

Baker, D. W. (2006), *Joel, Obadiah, Malachi*, NIVAC (Grand Rapids: Zondervan).

Baldwin, J. G. (1972), *Haggai, Zechariah, Malachi*, TOTC 28 (London/Downers Grove: IVP).

Bartlett, J. R. (1989), *Edom and the Edomites*, JSOTSup 77 (Sheffield: Sheffield Academic Press).

Beale, G. K. (2004), *The Temple and the Church's Mission*, NSBT 17 (Leicester: Apollos; Downers Grove: IVP).

Berlin, A. (1994), *Zephaniah*, AB 25A (New York: Doubleday).

Bienkowski, P. (2001), 'New Evidence on Edom in the Neo-Babylonian and Persian Periods', in J. A. Dearman and M. P. Graham (eds.), *The Land That I Will Show You: Essays in Honor of J. Maxwell Miller*, JSOTSup 343, (Sheffield: Sheffield Academic Press), 198–213.

Brueggemann, W. (1982), *The Creative Word: Canon as a Model for Biblical Education* (Philadelphia: Fortress).

Calvin, J. (1979), *Commentaries on the Twelve Minor Prophets* (repr.), trans. J. Owen (Grand Rapids: Baker).

Cathcart, K. J. and R. P. Gordon (1989), *The Targum of the Minor Prophets*, The Aramaic Bible 14 (Wilmington, Del.: Michael Glazier).

Clark, D. J. and H. A. Hatton (2002), *A Handbook on Haggai,
Zechariah, and Malachi*, UBS Handbook Series (New York:
United Bible Societies).

Collins, J. J. (1984), 'The Message of Malachi', *TBT*: 209–215.

Craigie, P. C. (1985), *Twelve Prophets*, DSBOT, vol. 2 (Philadelphia:
Westminster).

Dentan, R. C. and W. L. Sperry (1956), 'Malachi', in G. A. Buttrick
(ed.), *The Interpreter's Bible*, vol. 6 (New York: Abingdon), 1121–
1144.

Durham, J. I. (1987), *Exodus*, WBC 3 (Waco: Word).

Ferreiro, A. (ed.) (2003), *Ancient Christian Commentary on Scripture:
The Twelve Prophets*, vol. 14 (Downers Grove, Ill.: IVP).

Fishbane, M. (1983), 'Form and Reformulation of the Biblical
Priestly Blessing', *JAOS* 103: 115–121.

—— (1985), *Biblical Interpretation in Ancient Israel* (Oxford:
Clarendon Press).

Fuller, R. E. (1991), 'Text-Critical Problems in Malachi 2:10–16',
JBL 110: 47–57.

Garland, D. E. (1987), 'A Biblical View of Divorce', *RevExp* 84:
419–432.

Glazier-McDonald, B. (1987), *Malachi: The Divine Messenger*, SBLDS
98 (Atlanta: Scholars Press).

Gordon, R. P. (1994), *Studies in the Targum of the Twelve Prophets*,
VTSup 51 (Sheffield: JSOT Press).

Hanson, P. D. (1986), *The People Called: The Growth of Community in
the Bible* (San Francisco: Harper & Row).

Hill, A. E. (1998), *Malachi*, AB 25D (New York: Doubleday).

Hoglund, K. (1994), 'Edomites', in A. J. Hoerth, G. L. Mattingly
and E. M. Yamauchi (eds.), *Peoples of the Old Testament World*
(Grand Rapids: Baker), 335–347.

Hugenberger, G. P. (1998), *Marriage as a Covenant* (Grand Rapids:
Baker), first published as *Marriage as Covenant: A Study of Biblical
Law and Ethics Governing Marriage, Developed from the Perspective of
Malachi*, VTSup 52 (Leiden: Brill, 1994).

Isbell, C. D. (1980), *Malachi* (Grand Rapids: Zondervan).

Jones, D. R. (1962), *Haggai, Zechariah and Malachi*, Torch Bible
Commentaries (London: SCM).

Keil, C. F. (1975), *Commentary on the Twelve Prophets* (repr.), trans.

J. Martin (Grand Rapids: Eerdmans).

Klein, R. W. (1986), 'A Valentine for Those Who Fear Yahweh: The Book of Malachi', *CurTM* 13: 143–152.

Kruse-Blinkenberg, L. (1967), 'The Book of Malachi According to Codex Syro-Hexaplaris Ambrosianus', *ST*: 95–119.

Levine, B. A. (1993), *Numbers 1 – 20*, AB 4 (New York: Doubleday).

Mallone, G. (1981), *The Furnace of Renewal* (Downers Grove: IVP).

Mason, R. (1977), *The Books of Haggai, Zechariah and Malachi*, CBC (Cambridge: Cambridge University Press).

—— (1990), *Preaching the Tradition: Homily and Hermeneutics after the Exile* (Cambridge: Cambridge University Press).

McKenzie, J. L. (1968), *Second Isaiah*, AB 20 (New York: Doubleday).

McKenzie, S. L. and H. W. Wallace (1983), 'Covenant Themes in Malachi', *CBQ* 45: 549–563.

Merrill, E. H. (1994), *Haggai, Zechariah, Malachi* (Chicago: Moody Press).

Meyers, C. L. and E. M. Meyers (1987), *Haggai, Zechariah 1–8*, AB 25B (New York: Doubleday).

—— (1993), *Zechariah 9 – 14*, AB 25C (New York: Doubleday).

O'Brien, J. M. (1990), *Priest and Levite in Malachi*, SBLDS 121 (Atlanta: Scholars Press).

—— (2004), *Nahum, Habakkuk, Zephaniah, Haggai, Zechariah, Malachi*, AOTC (Nashville: Abingdon).

Ogden, G. S. and R. R. Deutsch (1987), *Joel & Malachi: A Promise of Hope – A Call to Obedience*, ITC (Grand Rapids: Eerdmans).

Patterson, R. D. (1993), 'Old Testament Prophecy', in L. Ryken and T. Longman (eds.), *A Complete Literary Guide to the Bible* (Grand Rapids: Baker), 296–309.

Petersen, D. L. (1977), *Late Israelite Prophecy: Studies in Deutero-Prophetic Literature and in Chronicles*, SBLMS 23 (Missoula, Mont.: Scholars Press).

—— (1995), *Zechariah 9 – 14 and Malachi*, OTL (Louisville: Westminster John Knox Press).

Pilch, J. J. and B. J. Malina (eds.) (1998), *A Handbook of Biblical Social Values* (Peabody, Mass.: Hendrickson).

Redditt, P. L. (1995), *Haggai, Zechariah, Malachi*, NCBC (Grand Rapids: Eerdmans).

Rudolph, W. (1976), *Haggai-Sacharja-Maleachi*, KAT, XIII/4 (Gütersloh: Gütersloher Verlagshaus Mohn).

Schuller, E. M. (1996), 'The Book of Malachi', in L. E. Keck (ed.), *New Interpreter's Bible*, vol. 7 (Nashville: Abingdon), 843–877.

Smith, G. A. (1943), *The Book of the Twelve Prophets*, The Expositor's Bible (repr.) (Grand Rapids: Baker).

Smith, J. M. P. in H. G. Mitchell, J. M. P. Smith and J. A. Bewer (1912), *Haggai, Zechariah, Malachi and Jonah*, ICC (Edinburgh: T. & T. Clark).

Smith, R. L. (1984), *Micah – Malachi*, WBC 32 (Waco: Word).

Stuart, D. (1998), 'Malachi', in T. E. McComiskey (ed.), *The Minor Prophets*, vol. 3 (Grand Rapids: Baker), 1245–1396.

Sweeney, M. A. (2000), *The Twelve Prophets*, Berit Olam, vol. 2 (Collegeville, Minn.: Liturgical Press).

Tate, M. E. (1987), 'Questions for Priests and People in Malachi 1:2 – 2:16', *RevExp*: 391–407.

Taylor, R. A. and E. R. Clendenen (2004), *Haggai, Malachi*, NAC 21A (Nashville: Broadman & Holman).

Tucker, G. M. (1977), 'Prophetic Superscriptions and the Growth of a Canon', in G. W. Coats and B. O. Long (eds.), *Canon and Authority* (Philadelphia: Fortress), 56–70.

Ulrich, E. et al. (1997), *Discoveries in the Judaean Desert (Vol. XV): Qumran Cave 4 (The Prophets)* (Oxford: Clarendon Press).

VanGemeren, W. A. (1990), *Interpreting the Prophetic Word* (Grand Rapids: Zondervan).

Verhoef, P. A. (1987), *The Books of Haggai and Malachi*, NICOT (Grand Rapids: Eerdmans).

Watts, J. D. W. (1987), 'Introduction to the Book of Malachi', *RevExp* 84: 873–881.

Wells, C. R. (1987), 'The Subtle Crisis of Secularism: Preaching the Burden of Israel', *CTR*: 39–61.

Westermann, C. (1969), *Isaiah 40 – 66*, OTL, trans. D. M. G. Stalker (Philadelphia: Westminster).

—— (1991), *Basic Forms of Prophet Speech*, trans. H. C. White (Louisville: Westminster John Knox Press).

Wolf, H. (1976), *Haggai and Malachi*, EvBC (Chicago: Moody).

GENERAL INTRODUCTION

1. Historical background

The backdrop for the books of Haggai, Zechariah and Malachi is the Persian period of Ancient Near Eastern history (539–330 BC). Cyrus the Great had consolidated his power base by defeating the Medes in 549 BC, and he was welcomed into Babylon as king of Persia in 539 BC. Over a span of twenty years (c. 559–539 BC), Cyrus built an empire that sprawled across the Ancient Near East, from the Nile to the Indus Rivers. According to the Cyrus Cylinder, a decree issued in 538 BC permitted conquered people groups who had been deported by the Babylonians to return to their homelands. Naturally, this included the Jews, although they are not named in the decree.

The first wave of emigrants to Jerusalem numbered 42,360 (plus 7,337 servants; cf. Ezra 2:64–65). They were led by Sheshbazzar, a Judean prince and the first (Persian-appointed) governor of the Hebrew restoration community (Ezra 1:5–11). The foundation for a Second Temple was laid in Jerusalem during the early stages of Sheshbazzar's administration (Ezra 5:16). The meagre project was soon abandoned, however, as the vision of Ezekiel's temple-state (Ezek. 40 – 48) and Jeremiah's promise of a new covenant (Jer. 31) quickly faded amid the stark reality of Persian domination. In addition, the problems of survival in Jerusalem and Judah for the former Hebrew captives were compounded by the resistance of surrounding hostile foreigners (Ezra 4:4–5), an agrarian society plagued by drought and crop failure (Hag. 1:6, 11), and economic recession and widespread lawlessness (Zech. 8:9–11).

A second group of returnees arrived in Jerusalem under the leadership of Zerubbabel and Joshua about 522 BC. Zerubbabel, the new Persian-appointed governor, and the priest Joshua were inspired by the prophets Haggai and Zechariah to mobilize the Hebrew community in 520 BC in another attempt to rebuild the Jerusalem temple (Ezra 5:11–12). The Second Temple was completed in 515 BC (Ezra 6:15; cf. 3:8–13), some seventeen years after the failed initiative under the supervision of Sheshbazzar.

More specifically, the books of Haggai and Zechariah are dated to the reign of King Darius I of Persia (521–486 BC). Haggai delivered his messages during a four-month period in 520 BC, while Zechariah's ministry is dated between 520 and 518 BC (and probably extended for some time beyond this). Both Haggai and Zechariah are mentioned as the prophets who sparked the building of the Second Temple (Ezra 5:1).

The book of Malachi is undated. The prophet refers to an unnamed governor of Persian-controlled Judah (Mal. 1:8), and no kings or priests are mentioned by name. The Second Temple had been completed, but the achievement did not usher in the awaited messianic age (Mal. 3:6–12; cf. Zech. 8:9–23). Instead, the apathy and disillusionment that had delayed the reconstruction of the temple for nearly twenty years persisted in post-exilic Judah. Malachi preached in Jerusalem during this pre-Ezra era of decline (c. 500–450 BC, assuming the traditional date of 458 BC is correct for Ezra's journey to Jerusalem). It is possible that the Persian wars with the Greeks prompted Malachi's message (perhaps the Battle of Marathon in 490 BC), and the prophet interpreted the titanic clash between East and West as the shaking of the nations prophesied by Haggai (Hag. 2:20–22).[1]

2. The Book of the Twelve

The title, 'Book of the Twelve', is a designation for the books known as the Minor Prophets in the HB/OT (cf. Sir. 49:10; and Josephus [*Antiquities* 10.2.2]). Jewish tradition, based upon the interpretive approach known as *midrash halakah* (i.e. story-telling exegesis), assumed that the collection of Twelve Prophets was arranged to tell a particular 'story' about Israel.

The ancient Hebrew and Greek manuscript traditions reveal that most, if not all, of the Twelve Minor Prophets were written on a single scroll (although scribal practice does not explicitly indicate that these books were considered a literary unity). This has led some scholars to postulate that the Twelve Prophets are a book, or a collection of prophetic books, organized into a unified composition with discernible literary structure and plot movement.[2] Such imposed literary structure tends to cloud rather than reveal, so that the whole reads as much less than the sum of its parts.

A better approach may be simply to regard the Twelve Prophets as a scroll unified by the prophetic genre, with an implied narrative and a central theme (or themes?).[3] The plot-line (i.e. the message) of the Book of the Twelve, from a negative perspective, is one of

---

1. See further the commentary introductions for the Hag-Zech-Mal corpus that follow, and fuller discussions of the historical background of the Hag-Zech-Mal corpus in Baldwin (1972: 15–21); Merrill (1994: 3–10); and Berquist (1995: 51–73).
2. House (1990). See the assessment in Hill (1998: 15).
3. E.g. Petersen (2000: 9–10) identifies the prophetic concept of the Day of the Lord as the dominant theme of the Minor Prophets. Collins (1993: 65) recognizes several principal themes in the Scroll of the Twelve, including covenant-election, fidelity and infidelity, fertility and infertility, turning and returning, God's justice and mercy, God's kingship, the temple, and nations as enemies and as allies. See further Gottwald (1985: 83–96) and Redditt and Schart (2003).

covenant failure, as both the pre-exilic Hebrew kingdoms of Israel and Judah are conquered and exiled by the Assyrians and Babylonians respectively. From a positive point of view, the plot-line of the Book of the Twelve is one of worship renewal and the return of a remnant of the Hebrew community to YHWH, since there was a repatriation of Judah and the rebuilding of the Second Temple by the Jews returning from Babylonia during the restoration period. Placed in this larger literary context, the Hag-Zech-Mal corpus is foundational to this latter understanding of the message of the Twelve.

Additionally, the Twelve Prophets are framed by the prophetic call to repentance. Notably, the first two books, Hosea and Joel (cf. Hos. 6:1; 7:10; 14:1–2; Joel 2:12–14), and the last two books of the collection, Zechariah and Malachi (cf. Zech. 1:3–4; Mal. 3:7), admonish the Hebrews to turn back to God and restore faithful covenant relationship with him. The wider context for covenant renewal with YHWH in each case is *that day*, the eschatological Day of the Lord. Thus, the Twelve begin and end with a call to repentance, the threat of judgment and the promise of blessing in the Day of the Lord. Again, the Hag-Zech-Mal corpus contributes significantly to the themes of *repentance* and the *Day of the Lord* in the Twelve.

3. The theology of Haggai, Zechariah and Malachi

The Bible records God's progressive plan of redemption for humanity and all creation, culminating in the person and work of Jesus the Messiah (cf. Gal. 4:4–5). As such, the thrust of the OT is theological. 'The big picture is God ... In the end, the plotline [of the OT] offers us a worldview – an understanding of God and ourselves.'[4] The books of Haggai, Zechariah and Malachi contribute much to our understanding of God, what we are to believe, and how we are to live as the people of God.

The repeated use of the divine title, *the LORD Almighty*, by our three prophets summarizes an important theological tenet – God

---

4. Walton and Hill (2004: 11).

is sovereign. More specifically, God is sovereign over the nations (Zech. 1:18–21; Mal. 1:3–4), accomplishing his purposes for judgment of sin and the redemption of those who are obedient to him (Zech. 8:14–15; Mal. 3:2–4; 4:1–2). He is sovereign over the created order, he controls the world of nature, and even the agricultural cycles are subject to his rule (Hag. 1:11; Mal. 3:10–11). God's sovereignty extends to Israel as his covenant people and their destiny as his elect nation (Zech. 1:14–17; 2:10–13; Mal. 1:2–3). The sovereignty of God assures his faithfulness to his Word: YHWH is both covenant maker and covenant keeper (Mal. 3:6). God's sovereignty only serves to accentuate both his compassion and his justice (Mal. 3:17–18).[5]

The Second Temple is the central theme of the Hag-Zech-Mal corpus. Haggai rallied the Hebrew people to rebuild the sanctuary (Hag. 1:14). Zechariah further encouraged the building project (Zech. 6:9–12) and witnessed the vision of cleansing and investiture for the High Priest Joshua who would oversee temple worship (Zech. 3; 6:9–15). Later, the prophet Malachi advocated the renewal of proper temple worship and the reform of a corrupt priesthood (Mal. 1 – 2).

The re-establishment of YHWH's temple in Jerusalem was a testimony to God's glory and holiness (Hag. 2:7–9; Zech. 14:20). It was also significant as a witness of his reputation among the nations as the one true God (Mal. 1:11, 14), and the eventual locus of worship for Israel and the nations in the eschaton (Zech. 14:17). Related to the temple theme is the return of God's presence to Jerusalem and Mount Zion. Each of the Persian-period prophets emphasizes the re-entry of the divine presence to the temple, and the reality of God living with his people in renewed covenant relationship (Hag. 1:13; Zech. 1:16; 8:3; Mal. 3:1–2).

The call to repentance unifies the three prophets of post-exilic Judah. The notion of repentance is implicit in Haggai's report that the people *obeyed* and *feared* the Lord (Hag. 1:12). Both Zechariah

---

5. On the theological message of Haggai, Zechariah and Malachi, see further: Dumbrell (2002: 226–244); and Patterson and Hill (2008: 493–643).

(Zech. 1:3) and Malachi (Mal. 3:7) formally call their audiences to repentance, to *return* to God. But it appears that only Haggai's preaching was successful in turning the Hebrew people to God in obedience.

A topic related to repentance, which is somewhat overlooked, is the role of the Holy Spirit in the theology of the post-exilic prophets.[6] Haggai assured his audience that God's Spirit remained among them, even as the Holy Spirit rested on Moses and the seventy elders of Israel after the exodus from Egypt to enable them to lead the Hebrew people (Hag. 2:5; cf. Num. 11:16–17). Zechariah reminded Zerubbabel that God accomplishes his purposes by his Spirit, not by human might or power (Zech. 4:6). He also acknowledged (somewhat cryptically) that God's Spirit was allowed to rest as a result of an angelic being dispatched to the north country (Zech. 6:8), and that the Word of God spoken by the earlier prophets had been sent by the Spirit (Zech. 7:12). There is some question as to whether the *spirit of grace* poured out on Israel in the eschaton is a reference to the Holy Spirit (Zech. 12:10; see commentary, p. 245ff.). God's Spirit is not mentioned in Malachi, but may be implicitly understood in the obscure reference to the 'residue of the spirit' (Mal. 2:15, KJV). More generally, the NT indicates that the Spirit of God convicts the human heart of sin and prompts repentance (John 16:8; Eph. 4:30). As noted above, the message of repentance is shared by our three prophets. At one level, then, perhaps the Hag-Zech-Mal corpus anticipates the more robust doctrine of the Holy Spirit in the new covenant.

Zechariah and Malachi are concerned with the application of the precepts of the Mosaic covenant to daily life, including the demonstration of social justice (Zech. 7:8–10; 8:16–17; Mal. 3:5). The emphasis on the twin themes of the proper worship of God and the practice of social justice as prescribed by the Mosaic covenant anticipates the double love command (or 'Jesus creed') of the NT (cf. Matt. 22:34–40). Implicit in the first great commandment to love the Lord God completely is the response of appropriate personal and corporate worship. To love one's neighbour as oneself fulfils

----

6. See further D. G. Firth and P. D. Wegner (eds.) (2011).

the law of love (Deut. 6:4–5) and is the mark of true religion as taught in Scripture (cf. Isa. 1:17; Jas 1:27).

The theme of the *Day of the LORD* also unifies the messages of Haggai, Zechariah and Malachi. Each prophet makes a contribution to the overall understanding of this future sequence of history-ending events. For example, Haggai intimates the restoration of Davidic kingship of Israel (Hag. 2:23; cf. Zech. 3 – 4; 6:9–15 on the issue of leadership in post-exilic Judah and beyond). Zechariah makes reference to an outpouring of a spirit of compassion that prompts mourning in Israel over the enigmatic figure – the pierced one (Zech. 12:10–14). He also speaks cryptically of a humble king who brings peace (Zech. 9:9–10), and the striking of God's shepherd and the scattering of God's flock, Israel (Zech. 13:7–9). According to Tollington, the promises of a new idealized David in Haggai and Zechariah led to the gradual development of messianic hope in Second Temple Judaism.[7] The role of YHWH as divine warrior for Israel (Zech. 12:7–9), and the universal rule of YHWH as king over all the earth (Zech. 14:9), is noted as well.

Finally, Malachi warns the people that the *day of YHWH* is not only retribution for the wicked, but also refining that brings purification to the people of God (Mal. 3:3–4). Malachi makes unique contributions to OT eschatology with his reference to the scroll of remembrance in which the righteous are enrolled, and the Elijah figure who is the forerunner to 'the great and terrible day of the LORD' (Mal. 4:5, NRSV). Malachi's admonition remains pertinent: *Who can stand when he appears?* (Mal. 3:2).

As noted above, all three prophets reference the Day of the Lord. This is the day of God's visitation when he suddenly appears in his temple, to bring judgment to the wicked and vindication to the righteous (Mal. 3:1–2; 4:1–3). This eschatological day is usually couched in the language of the imminent future (e.g. 'See, I am about to …', Zech. 12:2, NRSV), suggesting a 'theology of waiting'. Yet it would be another four centuries before the Lord, in the person of Jesus the

---

7. Tollington (1993: 181). On messianic expectations in post-exilic Judah, see further Baldwin (1972: 24–27); Hanson (1992: 67–75); and Rose (2000).

Messiah, would appear in the Jerusalem temple (Luke 2:22–38). The prophets' understanding of God's ultimate theophany in the imminent future may have been rooted in Daniel's teaching regarding the four great empires that would rise and fall (including Babylonian and Persian) before the kingdom of God breaks into history (cf. Dan. 2:36–45; 8:15–26). The theology of waiting is still ours, as the church anticipates the second advent of Jesus the Messiah (Matt. 24:29–31; Acts 1:6–11), and the realization of all things made new (Rev. 21:5).

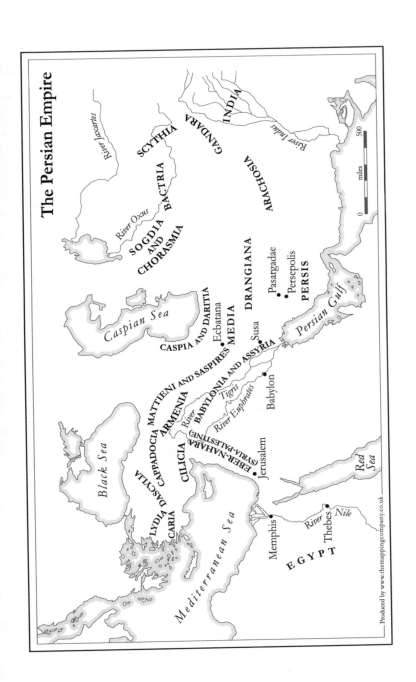

The Persian Empire

River Jacartes

SCYTHIA

GANDARA

INDIA

River Indus

SOGDIA AND CHORASMIA

BACTRIA

River Oxus

ARACHOSIA

Caspian Sea

DRANGIANA

Pasargadae
Persepolis
PERSIS

CASPIA AND DARITIA

Ecbatana
MEDIA

Susa

MATTIENI AND SASPIRES

ARMENIA

CAPPADOCIA

Persian Gulf

BABYLONIA AND ASSYRIA

River Tigris

Babylon

River Euphrates

LYDIA

DASCYLIA

CARIA

CILICIA

EBER-NAHARA (SYRIA-PALESTINE)

Jerusalem

Black Sea

Red Sea

Mediterranean Sea

Memphis

River Nile

Thebes

EGYPT

0   500   miles

Produced by www.themappingcompany.co.uk

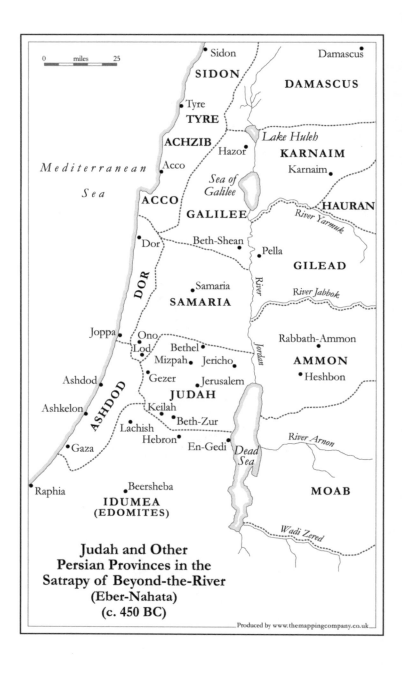

Judah and Other
Persian Provinces in the
Satrapy of Beyond-the-River
(Eber-Nahata)
(c. 450 BC)

Produced by www.themappingcompany.co.uk

HAGGAI

INTRODUCTION

1. Title and text

The book takes its title from the name of the prophet Haggai, identified in the superscription (1:1) as the bearer of God's message to the leaders of post-exilic Judah. Jewish tradition deemed Haggai, Zechariah and Malachi to be the only prophets belonging to the Second Temple era, so these books were naturally placed at the end of the collection also known as the 'Twelve Prophets'.[1] Haggai is the tenth book in the collection known as the Minor Prophets (or the Book of the Twelve in the Hebrew Bible). The Twelve Prophets are usually grouped with the Latter (or Major) Prophets, and without exception are found in the earliest delineations of the Old Testament canon. These twelve books were usually copied on one scroll in the ancient Hebrew manuscript tradition. The order of the Twelve Prophets does vary in some renditions of the canon

---

1. See *EncJud* 11: 50.

of the Hebrew Bible, but the sequence of books from Nahum to Malachi seems quite stable in the various canon lists.[2]

The Hebrew or Masoretic text (MT) of Haggai is in an excellent state of preservation.[3] Portions of Haggai are attested by fragments from the Dead Sea caves of Qumran (4QXII^B: Hag. 1:1–2; 2:2–4; 4QXII^C: Hag. 2:18–19, 20–21) and from the caves of Wadi Murabba'at (MurXII) for 1:12 – 2:10; 2:12–23 (dated to the second century AD). Verhoef cites only two minor variations in the extant Dead Sea manuscripts (which include 289 out of a total of 600 words in Haggai).[4]

The Septuagint (or LXX) largely corresponds to the MT, although it does rearrange several verses (e.g. 1:9 and 10 are spliced together; 1:15 becomes 2:1, affecting versification for all of ch. 2). Generally speaking, the LXX is marked by both expansionist (e.g. 2:9, 14, 21, 22) and harmonizing tendencies (e.g. 2:17, 21). The Lat. Vulg., Syr. and the Aram. Targ. are essentially faithful witnesses to the MT (granting some influence of the LXX on the Syr. and the Targ.).[5]

2. The prophet Haggai

The Hebrew name Haggai means 'festal' and is related to the Hebrew word (*ḥag*), meaning 'procession, festival'. This is a fitting name for the prophet who called the Hebrews to rebuild the temple of God (which had been destroyed by the Babylonians) and to re-instate the festal worship of Yahweh in Jerusalem.

---

2. See Jones (1995: 43–54).

3. Meyers and Meyers (1987: lxvii).

4. Verhoef (1987: 18). The Dead Sea caves fragments of Haggai support the verse order of the MT and yield only two minor divergences from the MT: 2:1 MurXII reads, 'the word of the LORD came *to* [Heb. *'el*] Haggai …', instead of '*by* [Heb. *běyad*] Haggai'; and in 2:3 MurXII reads, 'are you seeing *with him* [Heb. *'ittô*] now?', instead of 'seeing *it* [Heb. *'ōtô*] now?'

5. See further the discussions of the text of Haggai in Verhoef (1987: 18–20); and Merrill (1994: 17–18). For an original translation of Haggai's oracles and a thorough discussion of pertinent textual criticism, see Kessler (2002: 103–242).

The Bible records no biographical information for Haggai, but his prophetic ministry in post-exilic Jerusalem is attested by Ezra (Ezra 6:14). Two expressions identify Haggai as God's agent. He is called *the prophet* (Heb. *nābî*, 1:1; 2:10–11; Ezra 6:14), and he is labelled *the LORD's messenger* (Heb. *mal'ak*, Hag. 1:13). Both titles verify the prophet's divine commission.

According to Jewish tradition, the prophets Haggai, Zechariah and Malachi were among the founders of The Great Synagogue.[6] This body of Jewish leaders is alleged to have played a major role in post-exilic times in preserving Scripture and passing on the traditional precepts and lore. It is further believed by the rabbis that after these three prophets died the Holy Spirit departed from Israel.[7]

The LXX includes the names of Haggai and Zechariah in the preface to Psalms 138 (MT 139) and 145 – 148 (MT 146 – 149), suggesting they were responsible for the Hebrew recension from which the Greek version was translated.

3. Historical background

A decree issued in 538 BC by Cyrus the Great, the first of the Persian kings, permitted conquered people groups who had been deported to Mesopotamia by the Babylonians to return to their homelands (Ezra 1:1–4; cf. 2 Chr. 36:22–23). The royal edict was issued on a clay barrel, the famous Cylinder of King Cyrus, discovered in 1879 at the Esagila temple in ancient Babylon (now held by the British Museum). This pronouncement naturally included the Jews, although they are not actually named on the cylinder.

The first wave of Hebrew emigrants to Jerusalem left soon after the Cyrus edict and numbered 42,360, along with 7,337 servants (Ezra 2:64–65). They were led by Sheshbazzar, a prince of Judah and the first governor of the restoration community in post-exilic Judah (Ezra 1:5–11; cf. 5:14–16). The foundation for a new temple was laid during the early stages of his administration, some time in 538 or 537 BC (Ezra 5:16). The meagre project was soon abandoned,

---

6. E.g. *Aboth Rabbi Nathan* 1; *b. (Talm.) Baba Bathra* 15a.

7. See Neusner (2007: 41, 77, 208).

and the construction site lay neglected for nearly two decades, due to the problems of sheer survival in a ruined city surrounded by hostile foreigners and plagued by drought and crop failure. Not until the preaching of Haggai in August 520 BC did the initiative to rebuild the Jerusalem temple resume under the leadership of Zerubbabel, governor of Judah (Hag. 1:14).[8] The Second Temple was completed some four and a half years later in March 515 BC, under the auspices of the Persian king, Darius I (cf. Ezra 6:6–12). The monies granted for the rebuilding of the Second Temple probably took the form of 'rebates' returned to Judah from satrapy, and provincial taxes paid to the Persian royal treasury (cf. Ezra 6:5; Neh. 5:4, 15).[9]

4. Author

The book is silent on the issue of authorship, although it is assumed that the prophet Haggai penned his own oracles on the basis of the prophetic word formula: *the word of the LORD came through the prophet Haggai* (1:1).[10]

5. Date and occasion of writing

The date formula serves to root the speeches of Haggai in a specific historical context: the early years of the great Persian Empire (539–330 BC). The speeches are dated precisely to the day, month and year of the rule of Darius I, king of Persia. King Darius I (Hystaspes) ruled Persia from 522 to 486 BC. The equivalents for the date formulas are listed below:

---

8. On Persian rule and the early history of post-exilic Judah (or Yehud), see Meyers and Meyers (1987: xxix–xl); and Kessler (2002: 63–96).
9. See *ABD* 5, p. 85; cf. Meyers and Meyers (1987: xxxix); and Berquist (1995: 63).
10. On the genitive of authorship, a particular form of agency involving speaking and writing, see *IBHS* §9.5.1c, p. 143.

1:1	Year 2	month 6	day 1	= 29 August 520 BC
2:1	Year 2	month 7	day 21	= 17 October 520 BC
2:10	Year 2	month 9	day 24	= 18 December 520 BC
2:20	Year 2	month 9	day 24	= 18 December 520 BC

The post-exilic prophets Haggai and Zechariah dated their prophecies exactly during the days of Persian rule, because earlier Isaiah
had foreseen the importance of King Cyrus and the Persians to the
fortunes of elect Israel (Isa. 45:1–13). It seems likely that both
Haggai and Zechariah were influenced by Ezekiel's temple vision
(Ezek. 40 – 48), as well as his tendency to date his oracles. The
rebuilding of the Jerusalem temple was understood as the cornerstone event of the long-awaited messianic age. The chronological
precision attached to their oracles served as important reminders
of YHWH's faithfulness to his covenant promises (Ps. 111:9) and
his good intentions to restore unified kingship in Israel with David
as their prince (cf. Ezek. 37:15–28).

It seems likely that the book was written some time between
Haggai's challenge to rebuild the temple (520 BC) and its completion (515 BC), since the prophet does not mention the latter event.
The immediate occasion that prompted the speeches of Haggai was
probably a severe drought affecting the province of post-exilic
Judah (1:11). It is this event that permits God's messenger to address
the more important occasion for his oracles, the continued desolation of YHWH's temple, despite the return of the Hebrews from
Babylonian captivity (1:4). A second issue related to the prophet's
concern for the rebuilding of the temple is the public affirmation of
the leadership of the Judean state in the blessing of Joshua (2:4) and
Zerubbabel (2:23).

6. Audience

Haggai's first two oracles (1:1–15 and 2:1–9) are specifically addressed
to Zerubbabel the governor and Joshua the high priest – the two
leaders of post-exilic Jerusalem. As a part of these pronouncements,
the prophet also spoke a word of encouragement to the people of
Judah (1:13; 2:5). Haggai's third speech is directed to the priests (2:10–
19), while the fourth prophecy is spoken exclusively to Zerubbabel the

governor of Judah (2:20–23). We also learn that Zerubbabel, Joshua and the people obeyed the words of Haggai and applied themselves to rebuilding God's temple (1:14).

7. Form and structure

The book of Haggai is a literary hybrid that combines elements of historiography (e.g. date formulas and historical reports) with oracular speech (e.g. exhortation, admonition and prediction), yielding a type of prophetic narrative with a plot-line that progresses from a beginning (a temple in ruins) towards an end (a rebuilt Second Temple in Jerusalem). The brief account is complete with theme (the restoration of Judah), character development (as seen in the response of the leaders, Zerubbabel and Joshua, and the people in obeying the prophet's call to work) and dramatic movement (eschatological implications with cosmic impact). According to Kessler, 'The book reads somewhat like a story.'[11]

The book is comprised of four oracles or sermon-like speeches. Each of Haggai's four messages is dated precisely to a day and a month of the second year of the rule of King Darius of Persia. Baldwin identifies a paired pattern of accusation (1:1–11 and 2:10–17), response (1:12–14 and 2:18–19), and assurance of success (2:1–9 and 2:20–23) in the macro-structure of the book.[12] Kessler prefers to divide the book into four units or scenes, following the pattern of the four sermons, with each scene containing an introductory formula, a dramatic conflict, a divine response and a declaration of promise.[13]

Whether one structures Haggai into three, four or even five literary units, the book is clearly marked by chronological sequencing and narrative progression that features problem and resolution.[14]

---

11. Kessler (2002: 244); on the literary synthesis of Haggai see further pp. 251–257.

12. Baldwin (1972: 34).

13. Kessler (2002: 247–251).

14. Ibid., p. 251: 'In the course of the book we move from failure (1:4–11; 2:15–18) to blessing (2:18–19), from humiliation (1:4–11; 2:15–17) to exaltation (2:6–9, 20–23), and from alienation and rejection (1:2) to

Some biblical commentators confidently identify significant redactional activity in the book of Haggai. For example, Wolff postulates a complex editorial process that shapes Haggai's sermon fragments into the book as it now stands.[15] He identifies several growth rings framing Haggai's five original proclamations (1:4–11; 2:15–19 [considered a separate sermon and relocated earlier in the work]; 2:3–9; 2:14; 2:21b–23), and even these are assigned to a disciple of Haggai. The next stage of development witnessed the addition of historical introductions to Haggai's sermons, with the final stage of redaction accounting for the various interpolations to the book. It should be noted that the location of 2:15–19 with respect to 2:3–9 is still debated (see commentary below). The observation that: 'The book is so brief that it seems almost ridiculous to suspect its unity' is still apropos.[16] Yet this reality does not preclude the fact that the final form of the book of Haggai was probably the result of a limited editorial process. The superscription (1:1) and the historical introductions (1:15; 2:1, 10, 20) indicate that the prophet's sermons were organized chronologically and framed within a particular historical context. The slight variation in the historical introductions ('the word of the LORD came *through* the prophet Haggai', 1:1; 2:1 vs 'the word of the LORD came *to* the prophet Haggai', 2:10, 20) may suggest that the book went through multiple editions or that the final editor drew from diverse sources.[17] It is impossible to ascertain when such editorial activity took place, whether for the publication of Haggai's sermons as part of the temple dedication ceremony, or at the compilation of

---

acceptance and restoration (1:13–14; 2:5, 18, 23).' See further on the structure and unity of Haggai, Taylor and Clendenen (2004: 59–66); and Christensen (1992: 445–456), who understands Haggai as a prosodic composition and divides the book into three major cantos. On the more form-critical structuring of the book, see Floyd (2000: 53–257); and the commentary by R. L. Smith (1984: 146–163).

15. Wolff (1988: 17–20); Nogalski (1993: 216–237); and Redditt (1995: 11–12).

16. J. M. P. Smith (1912: 28).

17. Boda (2004: 38).

Haggai into the Book of The Twelve Prophets, or in stages between the two events.[18]

The literary relationship of Haggai and Zechariah 1 – 8 is part of a broader discussion that seeks to ascertain whether or not the post-exilic books of Haggai, Zechariah and Malachi form a distinct prophetic corpus. Haggai-Zechariah 1 – 8 is probably 'a single compendious work, published in anticipation of the auspicious event of the temple's rededication'.[19] Supporting evidence adduced for this literary unity includes the congruencies of message and historical context, similarities in style and theme, and the interlocking chronological headings. A related question is the broader relationship of Haggai with Zechariah and Malachi, and whether or not the three books constitute a literary corpus. Others have noted the use of the interrogative (especially the rhetorical question) as literary threads unifying the post-exilic prophets, as well as a storyline (i.e. a spiritual history of the restoration community) and common themes that tie the works together.[20]

Naturally, there are dissenting voices raising legitimate questions in response to reading Haggai-Zechariah 1 – 8 as a composite work and reading the three post-exilic prophets (Hag-Zech-Mal) as a corpus. For example, Kessler notes differences of style, vocabulary, historical emphasis and genre (especially the vision experience) between Haggai and Zechariah, to the degree that he prefers reading Haggai as a discrete literary unit.[21] Likewise, Nogalski questions treating Zechariah 9 – 14 on the same level as the remaining material, since it differs by way of genre and lacks the interrogative style central to Pierce's thesis for reading Hag-Zech-Mal as a corpus.[22]

---

18. Nogalski (1993: 234) observes only minimal alteration in Haggai in the editorial process of appropriating the book into the larger corpus of the Book of the Twelve.

19. See Meyers and Meyers (1987: xlvii).

20. E.g. Pierce (1984a: 277–289; 1984b: 401–411); Craig (1996: 224–244); Boda (2007: 127); and Redditt (2007: 188, 191–195).

21. Kessler (2002: 56–57).

22. Nogalski (1993: 238–240).

Despite these objections, the commonalities of interlocking chrono-logical markers, the congruencies of message and historical context, the rhetorical use of the interrogative, and the overarching theme of God's restoration of post-exilic Judah, at the very least, commend an integrated canonical reading of the three prophets of the Second Temple.[23]

8. Literary style

The speeches of Haggai are essentially prose summaries set in the third person. The messages are oracular in nature: that is, they repre-sent authoritative prophetic speech motivated or inspired by God himself. The speeches are also sermons, a type of hortatory discourse intended to motivate the audience to take some course of action. This kind of prophetic speech is often characterized by formulaic language. Several of these stylized expressions occur in Haggai, including the date formula (*the second year of King Darius*, 1:1; 2:1, 10, 20), the prophetic word formula (*the word of the LORD came*, 1:1; 2:1, 10, 20), the messenger formula (*this is what the LORD Almighty says* [or variations], e.g. 1:7; 13; 2:4 [found 29 times in the book]), and the covenant relationship formula (*for I am with you*, e.g. 2:4–5). The book of Haggai, although not an artistic masterpiece like Isaiah or Jeremiah, does demonstrate literary polish.[24]

This is especially the case in the use of a rhetorical question to emphasize a point in three of the four messages (e.g. 1:4; 2:3, 19), the repetition of words or phrases to set a tone or mood (e.g. the repeated imperative, *give careful thought to* [or variations] in 1:5, 7; 2:15, 18), and even wordplay on occasion – for instance, the similar sounds of the words 'ruin' (*ḥārēb*, 1:4) and 'drought' (*ḥōreb*, 1:11).

---

23. See further 'The Book of the Twelve' in the General Introduction
     (pp. 35–36).
24. On the impressive rhetorical strategies in Haggai, including the use of
     interjections, interrogatives, repetition and dialogical speech, see Boda
     (2000: 295–304).

9. Intertextuality

Like other OT authors, Haggai was familiar with earlier and contemporary biblical texts. Similarities in the use of words, phrases and wider literary, thematic and theological contexts suggest Haggai's interdependence with these portions of the HB/OT.

The listing of verses containing shared words, phrases and clauses does not necessarily presuppose the reliance of the book of Haggai upon the corresponding citation, nor does it attempt to distinguish categorically between an intertextual allusion and a quotation.[25]

Hag. 1:4//Jer. 33:10–12
Hag. 1:6, 10–11//Deut. 7:13; 11:13–17; 28:18, 22–24, 38–40, 51
Hag. 2:4//Jer. 30:11; Ezek. 34:30; 37:27
Hag. 2:4–5//Josh. 1:6–9
Hag. 2:5//Exod. 12:51; 13:3
Hag. 2:6–7, 21// Isa. 13:13; Joel 3:16 [MT 4:16]
Hag. 2:10–15//Zech. 8:9–23
Hag. 2:12//Lev. 6:26–27
Hag. 2:13//Lev. 11:28; 22:4–7
Hag. 2:17//Deut. 28:22; 1 Kgs 8:37; 2 Chr. 6:28; Amos 4:9
Hag. 2:19//Gen. 12:2
Hag. 2:22//Exod. 15:1, 4
Hag. 2:23//Exod. 6:7; Jer. 22:24

The NT directly cites the book of Haggai but once:
Heb. 12:26//Hag. 2:6, 21

10. Message

The prophet Haggai was a champion for the 'homeless' – in this case, the 'homeless' God of the Hebrew people. He was a prophet on a solitary mission – to stir the post-exilic Jewish community to

---

25. See further the discussion of intertextuality in Haggai in Taylor and Clendenen (2004: 83–89).

action in rebuilding the Jerusalem temple. Yet Haggai is a book with more than one single theme. Certainly the *primary* message of Haggai's preaching is the call to post-exilic Judah to rebuild the temple of God, which had been sacked and plundered nearly seventy years earlier by the Babylonians. His four related speeches were designed to awaken the residents of post-exilic Jerusalem to the responsibilities, obligations, privileges and promises of their covenant heritage. The prophet's charge to rebuild the temple is part of the broader theme of Haggai and the other post-exilic prophets (Zechariah and Malachi) – namely, God's restoration of Judah after the Babylonian exile.

Haggai also emphasizes the abiding presence of God's Spirit (1:13; 2:4–5), a theme shared with the book of Zechariah (cf. Zech. 1:16; 8:23). This pronouncement sparked the enthusiasm of the leadership and the people so that they began the work of rebuilding the temple (1:14). It is possible that Haggai intends his message concerning the restored presence of God in the post-exilic community of Judah as a fulfilment of Ezekiel's earlier promise that God would again make his home among his people (Ezek. 37:27–28).

The book presents two additional themes in a minor key: the divine blessing of spiritual and material prosperity bestowed upon the post-exilic Hebrew community, resulting in the restoration of glory to the Jerusalem temple (2:7–9, 19); and the overthrow of the nations (2:20–22). Both connect the message of Haggai with the larger eschatological themes of OT prophetic literature: God's promise of blessing to Israel, and God's threat of judgment upon the nations. According to Ezra, post-exilic Judah did realize a partial fulfilment of God's blessing as a result of the ministry of Haggai and Zechariah (cf. Ezra 6:14). Post-exilic Judah may have felt the tremors of God shaking the nations in the great wars between the Persians and the Greeks (during the reigns of Darius I and Xerxes). But apart from the relative peace and political stability the people of Judah enjoyed under Persian rule, Haggai's promise of great glory and of the wealth of the nations pouring into the rebuilt Jerusalem temple remained just that – a promise of a glorious future for God's earthly sanctuary.

11. Theological concerns

Each of Haggai's four messages highlights a different theological concern the prophet has for post-exilic Judah. The first (1:1–15) is the call to the people of Jerusalem to reprioritize community life. Haggai directs the leadership of the Judean province to focus on the restoration of proper worship of God, instead of the ease and security of their own *panelled houses* (1:4). This restoration of proper worship will be accomplished by rebuilding the Jerusalem temple for a homeless YHWH, reinstalling the Levitical priesthood, and reinstating the festival calendar and the sacrificial liturgy.

The second message (2:1–9) assures the post-exilic Hebrew community that God has not forgotten those previous promises of blessing and restoration made by earlier prophets like Isaiah (e.g. Isa. 61), Jeremiah (e.g. Jer. 32:36–44) and Ezekiel (e.g. Ezek. 37). It was important for community morale to understand that Haggai stood in the revered train of those prophetic predecessors. By his word of blessing and promise of restoration, he confirmed the continuity of his message with previous prophetic utterances concerning God's plan for the restoration of Israel after the Babylonian exile. These were not just more empty words of hope deferred to bolster a beleaguered remnant; these were the words of God's promise to his chosen people.

Ritual purity (for both the priests and the people) is the dominant theme of the third message (2:10–19). Haggai reminds his audience that the injunctions of the law of Moses are still operative. God expects his people to be holy, even as he is holy (Lev. 11:44–45).

Haggai's final, and perhaps most important, message re-establishes the prominence of the Davidic line in the religious and political life of the nation of Israel (2:20–23). The Davidic dynasty was singled out as the key to the restoration of the Hebrew people after the Babylonian exile (cf. Jer. 23:5; 31:15; Ezek. 37:24). Tragically, God was forced to pronounce the curse of judgment upon King Jehoiachin (and the line of David) at the time of the exile (Jer. 22:24–30). Haggai's last speech overturns that curse of judgment upon Jehoiachin (and the lineage of David) and reinstates that ancient covenant of David as the vehicle by which God intends to make good his promises of blessing and restoration to Israel (note especially the echo of the *signet ring* in Jer. 22:24 and Hag. 2:23).[26]

---

26. On messianism in Hag. 2:20–23, see the discussions in Taylor and Clendenen (2004: 195–201); Kaiser (1995: 205–211); and Wolf (1976: 54–55). On the theology of Haggai more broadly, see *NIDOTTE* 4: 691–693; *NDBT*: 255–257; and Dumbrell (2002: 226–229).

ANALYSIS

I. FIRST MESSAGE: HAGGAI'S CHALLENGE TO COVENANT RENEWAL (1:1–15)

A. Superscription (1:1)

B. The call to reconsider priorities (1:2–6)

    i. Excuse of the people (1:2)

    ii. God's response: Consider the current conditions (1:3–6)

C. The call to rebuild the temple (1:7–11)

    i. Go to work (1:7–8)

    ii. Failure to rebuild the temple tied to current distress (1:9–11)

D. The response of the people (1:12–15)

    i. The people obey and fear the Lord (1:12)

    ii. Reassurance of God's presence and renewed commitment by the people to rebuild the temple (1:13–15)

2. **SECOND MESSAGE: THE PROMISE OF RESTORATION (2:1–9)**
   A. Introduction (2:1–2)
      i. Date and prophetic word formulas (2:1)
      ii. Origin and audience of message (2:2)
   B. Present condition of the temple (2:3–5)
      i. Gone is the glory of Solomon's temple (2:3)
      ii. Exhortation to take courage and work (2:4–5)
   C. Promise of future glory for the temple (2:6–9)
      i. Warning of divine judgment against the nations (2:6–7)
      ii. Wealth, splendour and peace mark the rebuilt temple (2:8–9)

3. **THIRD MESSAGE: THE CALL TO HOLINESS (2:10–19)**
   A. Introduction: Date and prophetic word formulas (2:10)
   B. Haggai requests Torah instructions from the priests (2:11–14)
      i. A question about transferring ritual holiness (2:11–12)
      ii. A question about transferring ritual impurity (2:13)
      iii. Assessment of the people (2:14)
   C. The call to reflect upon current conditions (2:15–19)
      i. Effects of disobedience (2:15–17)
      ii. Promise of blessing (2:18–19)

4. **FOURTH MESSAGE: ZERUBBABEL, DAVIDIC SERVANT AND SIGNET RING (2:20–23)**
   A. Introduction: Date and prophetic word formulas (2:20)
   B. Warning of divine judgment against the nations (2:21–22)
   C. God's appointment of Zerubbabel as leader (2:23)

COMMENTARY

1. FIRST MESSAGE: HAGGAI'S CHALLENGE TO COVENANT RENEWAL (1:1–15)

A. Superscription (1:1)

Context

The literary form of the opening verse is that of superscription, a formal statement of taxonomy prefixed to a literary work that serves to classify the literature by genre (in this case as an oracular or prophetic text) and to identify the author, audience, date and sometimes the occasion prompting the message from God, as well as the source of the prophetic revelation – God himself. It is understood as distinct from an introduction, in that the superscription stands outside the body of literature it prefaces.[1] It is unclear whether these superscriptions were added by the author or by later editors during the process of collecting and arranging the contents of the OT canon.

---

1. On the contents and purpose of the superscription in prophetic literature, see G. M. Tucker, 'Prophetic Superscriptions and the Growth of a Canon' in Coats and Long (1977: 56–70, esp. pp. 57–58).

Comment

The date formula of the superscription to Haggai assigns the speech to the precise day and month: *In the second year of King Darius* of Persia (or 520 BC). The post-exilic prophets Haggai and Zechariah dated their prophecies with precision during the days of Persian rule, because earlier Isaiah had foreseen the importance of King Cyrus and the Persians to the fortunes of elect Israel (Isa. 45:1–13; see further Date and occasion of writing, pp. 46–47). *The first day* of the month was the day of the new moon in the lunar calendar, and it was a feast day or holy day for the Hebrews (Num. 10:10; cf. Isa. 1:13, 14; 66:23; Hos. 2:11; Amos 8:5). This was a time of Sabbath-like celebration for the people of God, as they both remembered God's past provision and anticipated even greater things ahead as they trusted in the Lord their Provider (cf. Ezek. 46:1, 3). The date was also a momentous occasion simply from the standpoint of a word from God breaking into the Hebrew community after the catastrophe of the Babylonian exile. Assuming a Hebrew calendar system with the new year beginning in the spring season (cf. Exod. 23:16; 34:22), the *sixth month* places Haggai's first message in the autumn harvest season (equivalent to our August/September).[2] By way of modern calendar equivalents, Haggai's first message was delivered on 29 August 520 BC.

The prophetic word formula, *the word of the LORD came*, introduces a prophetic revelation in the OT and classifies the book of Haggai as prophetic or oracular literature (cf. Hag. 1:1, 3; 2:1, 10, 20). The formula serves both to legitimate the recipient of the divine revelation and to lend authority to the prophet's message as the revealed 'word of God'. The frequent use of the speech formula in Haggai (and the Hag-Zech-Mal corpus) is intended to demonstrate the continuity of the message of the post-exilic prophets with earlier Hebrew prophetic tradition. The word *through* translates the literal

---

2. The historical development of the Hebrew calendar within its Ancient Near Eastern context remains a topic of debate in OT studies. See further the discussions in Baldwin (1972: 40, n. 1); Verhoef (1987: 49–50); cf. 'Ancient Israelite and Early Jewish Calendars', *ABD* 1:814–820; 'Calendar' in *NIDB* 3:521–527; and 'Festivals and Feasts' in *DOTPen*: 300–313.

expression 'by the hand of' (ESV), a phrase linking Haggai and Malachi. The phrase denotes writing or speaking, understood grammatically as a genitive of authorship.[3]

Next, *the prophet Haggai* is introduced. His name is fittingly related to the word for 'festival, procession' (Heb. *ḥag*). The term *prophet* (Heb. *nābî*) designates Haggai as an emissary, one who speaks with the authority of the commissioning agent (see the discussion of The prophet Haggai, pp. 44–45).

Finally, the recipients of Haggai's first message are identified, namely the two leaders of the post-exilic Hebrew community. *Zerubbabel* (whose name means 'seed, shoot of Babylon') was the governor of post-exilic Judah, and *Joshua* was the successor to the office of the high priest. The expression *governor of Judah* is applied to Zerubbabel only by the prophet Haggai (1:1, 14; 2:2, 21). The term *governor* (Heb. *peḥâ*) is an Assyrian loan word and is a rather vague title describing a governmental official during both the pre-exilic and post-exilic periods of Hebrew history (cf. 2 Kgs 18:24; Esth. 8:9; Jer. 51:23; Ezek. 23:6). What is clear is that Zerubbabel was appointed governor by the Persian king, and Judah was a rather insignificant provincial territory firmly under the jurisdiction of the Persian Empire. Zerubbabel is mentioned in Haggai's second message (2:2, 4), and he is the subject of the prophet's fourth sermon, linking the governor to the line of David and hinting at the restoration of Davidic kingship in the reference to Zerubbabel as the Lord's *signet ring* (2:20–23). Zerubbabel is identified as the son of Shealtiel, the eldest son of the exiled King Jehoiachin (Ezra 3:2, 8; cf. 2 Kgs 24:12–17), and thus his lineage can be traced to the family of David as Jehoiachin's grandson. The Chronicler, however, lists Zerubbabel as the descendant of Jehoiachin's third son, Pedaiah (1 Chr. 3:19). Commentators speculate as to whether Shealtiel adopted his eldest nephew, or if he was born to Shealtiel's widow by levirate marriage.[4]

---

3. See *IBHS* §9.5.1c, p. 143.

4. E.g. Baldwin (1972: 41); cf. Meyers and Meyers (1987: 10–11) who conclude that the confusion over Shealtiel's lineage cannot be satisfactorily resolved, yet they recognize Zerubbabel as his legitimate heir.

Zerubbabel is also mentioned in Zechariah (4:6, 7, 9, 10) and then mysteriously disappears from biblical record. Significantly, each leader is introduced with a brief genealogical record designed to recall the Babylonian exile and God's faithfulness in preserving and bringing back a remnant of his people to the land of covenant promise.

Joshua was a descendant of Levi and the son of Jehozadak, who was taken captive and deported to Babylonia when King Nebuchadnezzar sacked Jerusalem in 587 BC (cf. 1 Chr. 6:15; alternately spelled Jeshua in 1 Chr., Ezra and Neh.). Joshua is also mentioned in Zechariah (3:1; 6:11), and later records indicate some of his descendants were listed among those who married foreign women in the time of Ezra (Ezra 10:18). It is unclear whether Zerubbabel and Joshua were in the first wave of Hebrew emigrants who returned to Jerusalem soon after the decree of King Cyrus under the leadership of Sheshbazzar (Ezra 1:5–11; cf. 1:1–4), or if they led another caravan of Hebrew returnees to Jerusalem some time around 522 BC (Ezra 2:2, 64–65; 3:1–13). It seems likely that Ezra 2 presents a composite emigration record spanning the years from the edict of Cyrus to the completion of the Second Temple. If so, then Zerubbabel and Joshua probably led a mass emigration of Hebrews back to Judah, prompted by the ascension of Darius I to the Persian throne in 522 BC.[5] This may explain the enthusiasm and vigour of the restoration community for the temple construction project (vv. 12–15), since those more recent emigrants would not have been jaded by the previous two decades of failure to rebuild the temple.

Meaning
The superscription to Haggai legitimizes the prophet as a divine messenger and validates the authority of his message as the word of God to post-exilic Judah.

---

5. See Hill (1998: 69).

B. The call to reconsider priorities (1:2–6)

Context

Haggai's audience had assumed that the time had not yet come to rebuild the Lord's temple (1:2). The restoration community in Jerusalem was still struggling to establish itself politically and economically after the Babylonian exile. The degree of self-sufficiency attained was understood to be below expectations, at least to the extent that the people considered it unwise to divert their already meagre resources for the sake of investing in a high-profile campaign such as rebuilding YHWH's temple. Yet the prophet rebuked his audience for their preoccupation with their own standard of living (v. 4). Haggai's contemporary, Zechariah, also discerned that the real issue was one of self-interest, when he queried, 'Were you not eating and drinking for your own sake?' (Zech. 7:6, NJB). Those who argued for fiscal responsibility knew that the realities of an economic recession meant it was not the time to take on the funding of 'special projects' (cf. Zech. 8:10). Yet Haggai knew, like Hosea, that now was the time to seek the Lord (Hos. 10:12, NLT) – the gist of his first sermon to leaders and people of post-exilic Jerusalem.

Comment

2. The messenger formula, *This is what the* LORD *Almighty says*, is another common prophetic speech form (e.g. vv. 5, 7; 2:6). The construction signifies the oral transmission of a message by a third party. The expression suggests the divine assembly or council of the gods in Ancient Near Eastern thought. The messenger stands as an observer in the divine sessions and then reports what he has heard as an envoy of the council to others.[6] Since the verb form technically represents past action, the formula is more precisely translated, 'This is what the LORD Almighty said', indicating the prophet only conveys the message he has already heard from God.

The messenger formula occurs eight times in Haggai and ninety-one times in total in the Hag-Zech-Mal corpus. The expression

---

6. On the divine council motif in the ANE and OT see *ABD* 2:214–217.

places emphasis on the divine source and authority of the message, and the heavy repetition of the formula in the post-exilic prophets may have served to connect their ministries and messages to the earlier Hebrew prophetic tradition. Calling attention to such continuity may have been helpful in defusing a possible crisis concerning the prophetic word in the minds of some in Haggai's audience. The people had returned to the land of Judah more than twenty years earlier, and yet the promises of Jeremiah and Ezekiel regarding Israel's restoration after the Babylonian exile remained unfulfilled (cf. Jer. 31:31–33; 33:14–16; Ezek. 34:23–24; 37:24–28).

The divine title, LORD Almighty, is prominent in prophetic literature and is Haggai's favourite designation for God (found 14 times: 1:2, 5, 7, 9, 14; 2:4, 6, 7, 8, 9 [twice], 11, 23 [twice]). The expression is often understood as a construct-genitive relationship: 'the LORD of Hosts' (e.g. NAB, NRSV; the Heb. word ṣĕbā'ôt meaning 'host, army, warrior'). More precisely, the construction is one of absolute nouns in apposition, perhaps conveying a verbal force: 'Yahweh creates [angel] armies.'[7] In either case, the epithet emphasizes 'the invincible might behind the Lord's commands'.[8]

The prophet addresses these people (lit. 'this people'), perhaps a rebuke in itself, since he does not identify them with the possessive pronoun ('my [i.e. God's] people'). The NIV (The time has not yet come) follows the LXX here, reading the word time in the MT construction as the adverb yet. The repetition of time in the clause is awkward (lit. 'The time is not come, the time that the LORD's house should be built', KJV). The repetition may function rhetorically, perhaps reflecting the words of objection posed by Haggai's audience or simply injecting a sense of urgency into the prophet's message (since the word time is used in v. 4). The malaise of the people with respect to the rebuilding of the temple was due, in part, to their understanding that their current plight was a continuation of the divine judgment associated with the Babylonian exile.[9]

4. The rhetorical question is an emphatic speech device in

---

7. TDOT 5: 515.

8. Baldwin (1972: 42).

9. Patrick (2008: 5).

prophetic literature, requiring agreement with the expected answer to the question, rather than a formal reply (cf. 2:3, 19). The repetition of the pronoun (*you yourselves*) adds emphasis to the prophet's indictment of the people's self-interest.

The phrase *panelled houses* is probably better understood in the sense of 'roofed' or 'completed' houses, in contrast to YHWH's 'unfinished' house – lacking even a roof! The word *panelled* (Heb. *sāpan*) is quite rare, occurring only in 1 Kings 6:9, 15; 7:3 and Haggai 1:4, and can mean 'to cover, roof' or 'to panel'. The contrast expressed by the prophet is not one of elaborate adornment with lack of decoration, but rather the comparison of the habitable dwellings of the people complete with roofs with Yahweh's uninhabitable temple precinct.[10] The reference to the *ruin* of the temple seems to be a deliberate echo of Jeremiah 33:10–12, using the same word found in the promise of restoration for the *ruins* of Jerusalem.

5. The idiom *give careful thought to* (lit. 'set your heart toward') is a favourite expression of Haggai, occurring in 1:5, 7; 2:15, 18 (twice). The repetition of this clause in the imperative mood calls attention to the human will or volition. The people must choose to reflect and act upon the prophet's message. The imperative form of the exhortation further stresses the urgency of the hour and demands an immediate and specific response on the part of the addressee(s).[11]

6. The prophet first addresses the independent farmer who has *planted much*, but *harvested little*. The OT prophets often interpreted current events affecting the corporate life of the Hebrews through the lens of covenant blessings and curses (cf. Deut. 28:22–24). Haggai is no exception, as he understood the calamity of drought (or perhaps blight?) as the hand of the Lord Almighty at work in the realm of nature.[12]

---

10. See *BBCOT*: 797; and *ZIBBCOT* 5: 196.

11. See *IBHS* §34.4a, p. 571.

12. Merrill (2008: 709–710) notes that Haggai's 'list of disasters is not random ...', but reflects the curse section of Deuteronomy (Deut. 28:16, 18, 19, 23–24, 38, 39, 44), so that 'now their self-centered disloyalty to the Lord is bringing further covenantal curses on them'.

You eat ... drink ... put on clothes. The form of the verb used in each case conveys continuous action (cf. *The Message*, 'you keep filling your plates ... you keep drinking and drinking ... you put on layer after layer of clothes' – without result!). The catalogue of divine punishments for disobedience in the Mosaic covenant included drought, such that 'all your work will be for nothing' (Lev. 26:19–20, NLT).

Next, the prophet addresses the one who *earns wages*, or the hired hand. The word belongs exclusively to the vocabulary of the post-exilic prophets and describes those who work for others to earn a living, or possibly a self-employed individual.[13] In either case, the poor standard of living experienced by the labour force of the post-exilic community was designed to instruct the people in the matter of priorities.

The word-picture of *a purse with holes* (lit. 'a pierced bag') empha-sizes the almost instantaneous loss (and ongoing trickle-out effect) of a significant portion of wages, apparently unawares! No doubt, inflation and rising prices were also complicating factors and eroding the earning power of the workforce. Although coinage was minted by the Persians in limited quantities at this time, it is unlikely that a labourer's wages were paid in coins. The moneybag most likely would have contained discs or wedges of copper, silver or the like, approximately defined in value by weight.[14]

Meaning

The poverty and poor harvests referenced by Haggai (1:6) were not just 'bad luck' for the Hebrew restoration community. The OT prophets often interpreted current events affecting the corporate life of Israel through the lens of covenant blessings and curses (cf. Deut. 28). Haggai proves no exception, as he understood the

---

13. See the discussion in Meyers and Meyers (1987: 26).

14. So Baldwin (1972: 44). Though Persian coinage is attested in the late sixth century BC, Taylor and Clendenen's (2004: 127) speculation that Haggai presupposes the use of coins for remuneration probably overstates the case, since the widespread use of Persian coins at this early date in the far western sectors of the empire is unlikely.

calamity of drought (or perhaps crop blight) as the hand of God at work in the realm of nature. God delivered a 'wake-up call' to his people through the economic circumstances of 'supply and demand'. The message was a call to restore them to right relationship, demonstrated in the tangible act of rebuilding the Jerusalem temple.

C. The call to rebuild the temple (1:7–11)

Context
Haggai challenged his audience to extend the idea of the sovereign rule of the Lord Almighty to the realm of nature. The people seemingly made no connection between their bleak agricultural situation and the rule of God in this sphere of their daily life. Yet such associations should have been obvious from the terms of YHWH's covenant with Israel. The blessings and curses attached to the Mosaic law specifically mention drought, crop blight and poor harvests as divine plagues for covenant disobedience (cf. Lev. 26:19–20; Deut. 28:22–23).

Comment
7. This verse is an exact repetition of verse 5, but without the introductory adverb *Now*. The context indicates this further admonition for careful self-reflection is warranted, since the prophet suggests a direct cause-and-effect relationship between the depressed economic conditions, drought and crop failure experienced by the restoration community and the ruins of the temple precinct (vv. 8–11).

8. The charge to secure lumber for the temple reconstruction project is an indirect call to repentance. By taking action to remedy their plight, the leaders and the people are rejecting the defeatism bred by apathy and indifference. It is unclear whether the local timber was intended for construction equipment such as ramps, ladders and scaffolds, or for use as structural reinforcement between the courses of stone masonry to help minimize earthquake damage (cf. Ezra 5:8). Given the precedent for Lebanon cedar used in Solomon's temple (1 Kgs 5:6, 10–12), and the presumed deforestation of the environs of Jerusalem as a result of the Babylonian siege

(2 Kgs 25:1–2), it is unlikely that this lumber would have been sufficient to meet the demands of the temple project.

The Lord takes delight in those who fear and reverence him (Ps.
147:11). This fear or reverence which God savours is demonstrated
in the act of willing obedience, in this case responding to the call to
rebuild the temple. God is honoured or glorified in the obedience
of his people, since this is one of the ways in which the name of the
God of Israel is known and exalted among the nations (cf. 1 Sam.
15:22; Mal. 1:11, 14; 2:2). The passive verb form (*be honoured*) possibly
preserves a rare subjunctive ending: 'that I may be glorified'.[15]

9. Verses 9–10 recapitulate the message of verses 4–6, with the
operative word being *little*: the people had little to show in propor-
tion to the investment of time, energy and capital. The use of the
infinitive form of the verb *expected* is an example of an excited style,
as the prophet hurries to deliver the crux of his message: *my house
… remains a ruin* (see comments below).

What you brought home, I blew away. This may refer to the bulk of the
grain harvest kept by the worshipper after the first-fruits sacrifices
had been made at the altar of burnt offering. This sacrificial altar
had been rebuilt and put to use immediately by the first wave of
Hebrew returnees to Judah during the reign of Cyrus (cf. Ezra 3:2–
3). Some commentators note the definiteness of the word *house*,
minus any possessive pronoun, and translate 'the house' with reference to the temple precinct.[16] This understands the expression as a
reference to the first-fruits offerings themselves. The context
favours the notion of disappointment among the people in the
harvest yields that they brought to their own homes.[17] The ambiguity may be intentional, indicating God's disdain for the sacrificial
worship given the ruined condition of the temple precinct, as well
as the disappointing reality of how quickly the scanty harvest disappeared when the people brought their portion of the crops home.

---

15. Based on the Qere or Masoretic reading of the form in the margin
    notes of the MT. See the discussion of the form in Meyers and Meyers
    (1987: 28).
16. Ibid., pp. 3, 29.
17. So Motyer (1998: 977–978).

The verb *blew away* is rather uncommon in the OT and may suggest the effect of wind in the process of winnowing grain,[18] or a more forceful gust of destructive wind (cf. NJB, 'I blasted it'), or even blowing in the sense of casting a curse (cf. NJPS, note c, 'cast a curse on'). The same verb is used in Malachi 1:13 to describe the contempt of the people for God and temple worship when they *sniff at* the sacrificial rituals.

The rhetorical question *Why?* introduces the punchline of the prophet's first oracle – the direct cause-and-effect relationship between the plight of the people and the disrepair of YHWH's temple. The expression combines preposition and interrogative (lit. 'on account of what?') and may be understood emphatically in the sense of 'reason being?'

The repetition of this clause, *my house … remains a ruin*, completes an *inclusio*, or envelope construction, linking 1:4 and 1:9. This is the core message of 1:2–10, the prophet's challenge to the people to reflect upon their situation in light of the reality that God's temple is still in shambles.

10. The NIV properly retains the MT *dew* (Heb. *ṭal*), while the *BHS* proposes 'rain' (Heb. *māṭār*; so NJB; cf. NJPS, 'moisture' [*BHQ* omits the conjectural emendation]). *Dew* is sometimes a symbol of God's blessing (e.g. Prov. 19:12; Hos. 14:5), but more practically the moisture of overnight dews was crucial in late summer and early autumn to prevent the ripening grain from withering in the heat. Baldwin observes that 'the heavens and earth obeyed their Creator's word but his people did not'.[19] Yet they were without excuse, given the known threat of covenant curse in Deuteronomy 28:24 and the earlier preaching of Amos associating similar calamities with the people's disobedience (Amos 4:6–10).

11. The wordplay with *drought* (Heb. *ḥōreb*) and *ruin* (Heb. *ḥārēb*; v. 4) reflects the oral culture of the biblical world and is a feature of prophetic speech. The device is one of the ways in which the orator keeps the audience engaged with the message, and on occasion heightens the rhetorical impact. The LXX misreads the word *sword*

---

18. Ibid., p. 978.
19. Baldwin (1972: 44).

(Heb. *ḥereb*) for *drought* (Heb. *ḥōreb*), translating, 'I will bring a sword' (NETS).

Meaning

Haggai's call to rebuild the temple of YHWH should not be construed as some kind of 'magical formula', holding the promise of a remedy for the numerous problems facing the post-exilic Hebrew community. God cannot be manipulated into showering material blessings upon his people because of their diligent work in the reconstruction of the Jerusalem temple (1:5–6).[20] Nor should Haggai's message be viewed as contradictory to the words of warning pronounced by Jeremiah concerning misplaced trust in the physical structure of the temple (Jer. 7:4). Rather, Haggai summoned the people to the proper worship of God in contrast to heartless faith in a 'sacred building'.

The appropriate attitudes of reverence and humility and a genuine posture of obedience to the law of God identified explicitly in Zechariah (e.g. Zech. 7:4–10) are implicit in Haggai. The prophet was familiar with the 'temple theology' of King Solomon's prayer of dedication – God does not dwell in houses made with human hands (1 Kgs 8:23ff.). Haggai also knew the 'worship theology' of his predecessors – God desires mercy, not sacrifice (Hos. 6:6; Mic. 6:8) – and he understood, without doubt, that reviving the flow of God's covenantal blessings to Israel was contingent upon the people's careful and heartfelt obedience to the commandments of YHWH's covenant, not the rebuilding of the Jerusalem sanctuary (cf. Deut. 28:1–2, 9, 13).

D. The response of the people (1:12–15)

Context

The passage simply reports the fact that the whole community responded to Haggai's preaching. This demonstration of unity of spirit and commonality of purpose was so striking that it merited recording. Often overlooked is the importance of the phrase 'of

---

20. Cf. Achtemeier (1986: 98–99).

God's people' (v. 12, NLT). The theological emphasis of the report of the people's response to Haggai's message is the faithfulness of God in preserving an element of his elect people and re-establishing them in the land of covenant promise. He is a God who *remembers his covenant for ever* (Ps. 111:5).

Comment

12. The repetition of the phrase, *the whole remnant of the people*, in 1:14 emphasizes the unity of purpose within the restoration community for the temple rebuilding project. Haggai's use of the word *remnant* has triggered considerable debate among biblical commentators as to the theological nuance intended by the prophet. Some understand the term to refer to a core of righteous people embedded within the larger Hebrew community. Others consider the expression as simply one of several designations used by Haggai for the entirety of the covenant people resident in Judah (e.g. *the/se people*, 1:2, 12; *all you people*, 2:4; *this people*, 2:14). The term as used here designates the entirety of the people and is simply a report that the whole community responded to the prophet's message.

The people *obeyed*, understanding Haggai's message as the *voice of the LORD*. The lone use of this verb in Haggai is significant, in that it is a measure of the prophet's success – more often the message of the OT prophets fell on deaf ears.

The word *feared* indicates a willing response to the prophetic message motivated by reverence for God, rather than a reluctant obedience prompted by terror and dread of divine punishment.[21] The people '*feared* in the sense that they had been startled wide awake by the voice of God'.[22]

13. This unusual prophetic title (*the LORD's messenger*) may be explained by the literary device of wordplay with *messenger* (Heb. *mal'ak*) and *message* (Heb. *mal'akût*) in the following clause.

---

21. Cf. Boda (2004: 107–108) who suggests that both 'the posture of reverent submission and trust in Yahweh' (e.g. Deut. 10:12, 20) and the response of 'trembling fear' to the awesome presence of God (e.g. Deut. 5:5; 13:11) are appropriate in this context.

22. Baldwin (1972: 45).

Elsewhere, the priests (2 Chr. 36:16; Mal. 2:7) and the prophets generally (cf. Isa. 42:19) are identified as God's messengers. The title legitimizes and ascribes distinctive authority to Haggai as YHWH's agent and validates his message as a true word from God.

The term *messenger* signifies an agent entrusted with a word of revelation from God. The expression is sometimes associated with the divine council or assembly of the gods motif common to the earliest mythical literature of the Ancient Near East.[23] By analogy, the Hebrew prophets are understood as couriers of the council of YHWH. As a member of the council, the prophet hears the proclamation of YHWH and is commissioned to report the exact word of revelation directly to the people. This helps explain the repetition of the numerous speech formulas in prophetic literature. YHWH's prophets uttered the appropriate speech formulas to validate their role as divine messengers and to clarify the source of the message, the fact of its transmission and the authority of its contents.

This covenant relationship formula (*I am with you*) assures the audience of God's personal presence and support in the temple rebuilding project (cf. Gen. 26:3; Isa. 41:10; 43:5; Jer. 30:11). Haggai may have had Isaiah's exhortation in mind when he announced God's vested interest in seeing the temple restoration through to completion (cf. Isa. 43:5).

14. The root of the verb *stirred* means 'to rouse, awaken, set in motion' and is frequently attributed to God's sovereign work in enlivening people to accomplish his purposes (e.g. Ezra 1:1; Isa. 13:17; 41:25; Jer. 51:1, 11). Like Zechariah, Haggai recognizes the dynamic relationship between the empowering presence of God's Spirit and the spirit of the people in rousing the community to action (2:5; cf. Zech. 4:6). The NIV understands the stirring of the people as a result of the affirmation of the covenant formula, *I am with you* (v. 13).

---

23. See the discussion of the divine council in Meyers and Meyers (1987: 35); cf. *ABD* 2: 214–217. Boda (2007: 129–131) sees a shift in emphasis from the earthly messenger (e.g. the prophet) in Hag-Zech 1 – 8 to more of an emphasis on heavenly messenger figures in Zech. 9 – 14 and Mal.

15. Haggai's first oracle concludes with a date formula (*the twenty-fourth day of the sixth month*), including the regnal year of King Darius (his second year). The opening verse of the prophet's second oracle (2:1–9) also records a date formula (*the twenty-first day of the seventh month*), but with no regnal year cited. Many biblical commentators assume that the reference to the second regnal year of King Darius has been lost in the MT due the scribal error of haplography.[24] Some EVV insert the regnal year formula of 1:15b in 2:1 to provide a consistent reading of the opening date formulas for each of Haggai's four oracles, assuming the verse division has been misplaced (e.g. NIV, NRSV). It is more likely that the single reference to the regnal year of King Darius serves double duty in both date formulas (i.e. 1:15 and 2:1).[25]

Baldwin accounts for the twenty-three-day delay between the prophet's original message (*the first day of the sixth month*, 1:1) and the resumption of the work on the temple (*the twenty-fourth day of the sixth month*, 1:15) by noting that the sixth month was the month of harvesting in the orchards and fields.[26] The twenty-three-day interim period provided time to complete that important task before the workers assembled at the temple site to commence the rebuilding effort.

Meaning

As we have noted, the OT prophets often interpreted current events affecting the corporate life of the Israelites through the lens of covenant blessings and curses (cf. Deut. 28). Here Haggai under-

---

24. J. M. P. Smith (1912: 58); cf. Meyers and Meyers (1987: 37) who mention the possibility of the scribal error of haplography causing the loss of one year. Mason (1977: 23) considers the date formula of Hag. 1:15a a gloss, perhaps inserted when the oracle was misplaced from the end of ch. 1 to bring it into line with 2:10–14. March (1996: 720) comments that no anc. manuscripts support such a radical rearrangement of the text.

25. See Meyers and Meyers (1987: 36–37); cf. NLT: 'This was on September 21 of the second year of King Darius' reign. Then on October 17 of that same year ...' (1:15 – 2:1a).

26. Baldwin (1972: 46).

stood the calamity of drought (or perhaps blight, 1:6) as the hand
of the Lord Almighty at work in the realm of nature (cf. Zech. 10:1,
the LORD ... makes the storm clouds). The law of Moses forecasts just
such a scenario for the people of Israel, should they violate
YHWH's covenant. The catalogue of divine punishments for
disobedience includes drought, such that 'all your work will be for
nothing' (Lev. 26:19–20, NLT).

The final section of the prophet's first sermon reporting the
response of the remnant to Haggai's message offers an interesting
sequence of verbal action. First, the people obeyed (1:12). Next, we
learn that the people feared the Lord (1:12). Finally, we are told that
the people began to work on the house of the Lord (1:14). This
ordering reinforces the biblical pattern of worship followed by
service. A similar model of response to God may be seen in the
post-exodus experience of Israel at Mount Sinai. There the obedience of the people to the directives of Moses included acts of
preparation necessary for entering God's presence (Exod. 19:14).
The subsequent experience of formal worship (Exod. 24:1)
prompted acts of service in the form of giving to the construction
of the tabernacle (Exod. 25:2–3).

2. SECOND MESSAGE: THE PROMISE OF RESTORATION (2:1–9)

Context

The prophet's reference to *Egypt* (2:5) sets the hortatory tone and establishes the covenant theme for Haggai's second sermon. The citation is clearly a deliberate appeal to the historical traditions connected with the Hebrew exodus from slavery under the pharaoh. Haggai is probably alluding to Isaiah's oracles announcing the second exodus and the restoration of the Hebrews from Babylonian captivity (e.g. Isa. 40:3–5; 41:17–20; 42:14–16).

A. Introduction (2:1–2)

Comment

1. Haggai delivered his second message on the seventh or last regular day of the Feast of Tabernacles (cf. Lev. 23:33–34). The first and eighth days of the festival were Sabbath-like sacred assemblies (Lev. 23:35, 39). The prophet's oracle no doubt served as a capstone to the week's ritual worship and community celebration of the exodus-event and the fall harvest. There's a twist of irony in the

sermon as well, since the prophet has called the people to address the matter of YHWH's homelessness, as they build and live in their temporary shelters in commemoration of their own homelessness during the exodus sojourn. (See p. 60, on the date formula in 2:1.)

2. *Remnant of the people.* This refers to the rest of the people, in addition to the leaders Zerubbabel and Joshua (see commentary on 1:12, p. 71).

Meaning

Haggai received his second message from the Lord less than two months after the first. To hear from God again within such a short period of time affirmed the people's response of obedience to the first message. The timing of the second message with the annual celebration of the Feast of Tabernacles sets the context for the prophet's sermon on the theme of divine presence in the following section.

B. Present condition of the temple (2:3–5)

Context

The clause, *when you came out of Egypt* (2:5), looks both back to the past and forward in anticipation of the future, in an effort to encourage those presently in despair. This flashback to the exodus from Egypt was designed to demonstrate the continuity of the Lord's activity in history for elect Israel. Haggai's audience could be assured that the presence and power of God who delivered the Hebrews from pharaoh would also deliver his people from Babylonia and restore them to the land of covenant promise. It is also notable that Haggai's second message from the Lord came at the end of a series of major holy days and festivals in the Hebrew calendar, since the first day of the seventh month was the Feast of Trumpets (New Year), the tenth day of the same month was the solemn Day of Atonement, and the Feast of Tabernacles was observed for eight days beginning on the fifteenth day of the seventh month (cf. Lev. 23:23–43).

Comment

3. Haggai's dialogical engagement with his audience by means of (often rhetorical) questions is a characteristic feature of the entire post-exilic prophetic corpus. (See the section on Literary style in the Introduction, p. 51.)

4. The threefold repetition of the imperative verb *be strong* marks the shift from rebuke and challenge to encouragement and affirmation in Haggai's message. The exhortation echoes that of Moses to the people of Israel and to Joshua, as the second generation of post-exodus Hebrews were poised to enter the land of covenant promise (Deut. 31:6, 7). God spoke similar words to Joshua as the campaign to conquer Canaan was about to begin (Josh. 1:6, 9), and David uttered the same charge to Solomon at the building of the first temple (1 Chr. 28:20).

The repetition of the covenant relationship formula (see 1:13) calls to mind the new covenant promises made to the Hebrews prior to the Babylonian exile by the prophets Jeremiah (Jer. 30:11) and Ezekiel (Ezek. 34:30; 37:27).

5. The combination of the verb 'cut' and the noun 'covenant' is the Hebrew idiom for covenant making (cf. Gen. 15:9–10). The alternate combination of the verb 'cut' and the noun form used here is exceptional. The variant phraseology may call attention to the continuity of YHWH's activity in delivering his people, first from Egypt and then from Babylonia (cf. NRSV, 'the promise I made with you'). The variation in the Hebrew syntax in the placement of the clause in the initial position in verse 5 heightens the authority and verity of the prophet's command.

The restatement of the reality that God's *Spirit remains among* his people is important (cf. 2:4). Such reassurance was necessary, given Ezekiel's earlier vision of the glory of the Lord abandoning the Jerusalem temple prior to the Babylonian exile (Ezek. 10:18). The restoration community needed to know that this tragic chapter of Hebrew history had now ended. The form of the verb *remains* denotes ongoing action. This use of the verb *remain* (lit. 'stands') has the effect of personifying *Spirit* and thus makes this 'a powerful expression of divine presence'.[1] Haggai makes reference to the function of God's Spirit after the manner of Isaiah's commentary

---

1. Meyers and Meyers (1987: 52).

on the exodus-event – the Spirit of power who works miracles in
Israel's history (Isa. 63:11).

The construction of the prohibition, *Do not fear*, can have the
force of halting an action in progress: hence 'Stop being afraid.'
God's presence among his people assures, encourages, inspires and
verifies his intentions to see his purposes accomplished.

Meaning

The prophets were also pastors for the people of Israel as God's
flock. The assurance formulas in Haggai's second sermon are
striking (2:4, 5). They serve to alleviate the apprehension and fear of
the leaders and the people by linking God's presence in the current
community of Hebrews with his future activity on behalf of his
elect.[2] Haggai's joining of the abiding presence of YHWH (2:4) with
the word of YHWH's covenant promise is especially significant.
The prophet may have had Isaiah 59:20–21 in mind, where the
combination of God's covenant word and the presence of his Spirit
are tokens of his unswerving commitment to the restoration of his
people. For some, this theme of God's presence with his people
constitutes one theological centre of the entire Bible. The concept
of 'Immanuel' or 'God-with-us' theology has its origins in the intimate fellowship with God that humanity enjoyed before the fall
(Gen. 3:8).[3]

C. Promise of future glory for the temple (2:6–9)

Context

Haggai announces a future day of divine judgment of the nations,
and a promise of glory for the Second Temple surpassing that of
Solomon's temple. This new divine activity concerns the rebuilt
temple as a metaphor for God's glory and sovereign rule and the
restoration of the community of faithful people gathered around

---

2. See Petersen (1984: 57–58).

3. On the theme of the divine presence in the OT, see Clements (1965);
   Terrien (1978); Hill (2003: 245–247, 654–658); and Goldingay
   (2006: 96–106).

the temple. God's former shaking of creation alluded to by the prophet may be a reference to the flood-event, or more likely to the exodus-event (where the Heb. verb *rā'aš* is used to describe his activity in delivering the Hebrews from slavery in Egypt; cf. Judg. 5:4; Pss 68:8; 77:18).

Comment

6. The Hebrew expression ('once again, in a little while') is difficult to convey in English. The phrase seems to connote both the sense of urgency or immediacy, as well as the indefiniteness of the moment of divine judgment. Baldwin renders, 'wait, just one little while', indicating that although the interval before the Lord begins to shake all creation is short, it still requires a time of waiting.[4]

The verb *shake* (Heb. *rā'aš*) is an onomatopoetic word and denotes quaking and violent upheaval in the natural order. The term is associated with the language of theophany in the OT, the convulsions of creation in reaction to the appearance of YHWH (Isa. 24:18; Ezek. 38:20; Joel 2:10; 3:16). Haggai, however, is speaking of more than earthquakes. He applies the traditional language of theophany not to a divine appearance, but to new activity of YHWH on behalf of his people. This is seen in the cosmic scope of the shaking, represented in the polar sets of heavens/earth and sea/dry land,[5] and in the shaking of the nations (v. 7), the only reference to God's eschatological shaking of creation applied directly to people.[6]

7. The word *desired* (Heb. *ḥemdat*) is actually singular in form and means 'treasure' (so NRSV) or 'valuable thing'. The LXX renders the word in the plural ('choice things'), in agreement with the plural verb ('[they] will come', NETS; assuming the noun is a variant spelling of the term, and reconfigures the form as *ḥămudôt*). The singular form

---

4. Baldwin (1972: 51).

5. Cf. Boda (2004: 124), who notes that the merism (the heavens and earth) refers to the entire cosmos (Gen. 1:1), perhaps placing YHWH's eschatological shaking of the nations in a wider creation−redemption context.

6. See Sweeney (2000: 548).

may also be construed as a collective or as a plural, given its grammatical relationship with the following plural noun (e.g. 'the treasures of all the nations will come in', NAB; cf. NJB, NLT, NRSV; 'precious
things', NJPS).[7] The term is related to the root word for coveting in
the tenth commandment (Exod. 20:17). Ironically, the treasures
coveted by the nations will be given back to God, the maker and
owner of all things.

Historically, the gold and silver treasures of the Lord's temple
were lost to the nations when Babylonians sacked Jerusalem and
exiled the Hebrews (2 Kgs 25:13–15). Later, a substantial portion of
these precious articles were returned to the Lord's temple by the
nations, when King Cyrus of Persia sent an inventory of temple
vessels back to Jerusalem with Sheshbazzar (Ezra 1:7–11). The
prophets Isaiah (Isa. 60:5; 66:12) and Zechariah (Zech. 14:14, 17)
have similar visions of the wealth of the nations flowing into
Jerusalem as acts of homage and worship to God.

Despite the longstanding tradition of associating the 'desire of
the nations' with the first or second advent of Jesus the Messiah,
nothing in the context of Haggai's second sermon points to the
phrase as a messianic title or prediction. Nor does the NT connect
the phrase with the life and ministry of Jesus.[8]

The prophet predicted that the future *glory* (Heb. *kābôd*, 'splendour, honour, distinction') of the Second Temple would outstrip
the past glory of Solomon's majestic temple (v. 9), and he bolstered
his claim by declaring that the wealth of the nations would flow into
Jerusalem (v. 7). The real glory of the Second Temple, however, will
not be the revenues of gold and silver bursting its coffers. Rather,

---

7. On singular nouns construed as collectives or plurals, see *IBHS* §7.2.1,
   2, pp. 113–115; and by using the plural of the *nomen rectum* (or genitive
   noun), see GKC §124r, p. 401.
8. *The desired of all nations will come* (NIV) implies a messianic understanding
   of the passage (note the revision in the NIV 2011: 'what is desired by all
   nations will come'). For a brief history of Christian interpretation of
   the passage, see Taylor and Clendenen (2004: 160–165) who conclude,
   '[T]here is no convincing exegetical reason for thinking that the verse
   has any Christological import' (p. 161).

the glory of God's temple will consist of his presence in it and among his people (vv. 4–5; Zech. 2:5; cf. 1 Kgs 6:11). Israel's worship of the God of glory (Ps. 29:3) who alone possesses glory (Isa. 42:8; 48:11), and the recognition of his splendour and majesty by those created for his glory (Isa. 43:7), also bring glory to YHWH's house (Ps. 96:8).

8. The prophet's declaration recalls Job 41:11, that everything under heaven belongs to God. The emphatic construction of the syntax in the original underscores this truth (lit. 'to me is the silver, to me is the gold'; cf. NAB, 'mine is the silver, mine is the gold'). The context suggests that the desire or treasure of the nations Haggai has in mind is material wealth, namely gold and silver. There is no hint of greed or covetousness here. Rather, the prophet boldly predicts the complete recognition of God's sovereignty over the entire world. In the eschaton, the treasures of the world, once withheld from their true purpose as the property of YHWH, will return to his exclusive control. Note the staggering amounts of gold and silver contributed by King David and the Israelites to the building of Solomon's temple (1 Chr. 29:3–4, 7). Interestingly, just as the wealth of the Egyptians contributed to the furnishings and adornment of the tabernacle (cf. Exod. 12:35–36; 35:5, 22), and the wealth of the nations plundered by David adorned Solomon's temple, so too Haggai envisions the wealth of the nations flowing into the coffers of the Second Temple (cf. Isa. 60:11; 61:6; 66:12).

9. The literal rendering of the MT, 'Great will be the glory of this house, the latter', is somewhat cryptic (*the glory of this present house*, NIV). The ambiguity of the modifier 'latter' permits the reading, 'the glory of this latter house' (so KJV, NJPS) or 'the latter glory of this house' (so NAB, NLT, NRSV). It seems more likely that Haggai speaks of the 'latter glory of this house', especially in light of the reference to the *former glory* of the temple in 2:3. It is possible that a more immediate fulfilment of Haggai's oracle, forecasting the shaking of the nations and the restoration of glory to YHWH's temple in Jerusalem, foreshadows the messianic interpretation of the passage. Berquist suggests that the shaking of the nations may have been partially realized in the staging and marching of military troops in and through Judah by King Darius in the Persian campaign against

the Egyptians (c. 518 BC).[9] If so, the initial glorification of
Zerubbabel's temple may have been achieved by the patronage of
the Persian Empire as a result of the need for a base for military
operations in Egypt.[10] Some interpreters understand a more distant
fulfilment of this 'latter glory' of YHWH's temple in the presence
of Jesus the Messiah during his first advent (Matt. 12:6; Luke 2:28–
32; John 2:19–22), and perhaps a more complete fulfilment in his
second advent (Rev. 21:22).[11] The NT, however, makes no reference
to this text by way of quotation or allusion to the life and ministry
of Jesus.

The word *peace* (Heb. *šālôm*) is a wordplay on the name 'Jerusalem'
('city of peace'), and echoes the promise of Isaiah for the peace of
Jerusalem in answer to the psalmist's prayer (Isa. 66:12; cf. Ps. 122:6).
This place is somewhat ambiguous, but is probably a reference to the
Jerusalem temple, since the word *place* (Heb. *māqôm*) has ritual and
cultic connotations in certain contexts (e.g. Deut. 12:5, 14; Jer. 17:12;
Ezek. 43:7). The Hebrew word *šālôm* not only means 'peace' in the
sense of absence of armed conflict and physical security, but also
'wholeness, well-being', even 'prosperity' broadly and holistically

---

9. Berquist (1995: 66–67); Boda (2004: 160, 162–163) sees the upheaval in
   the Persian Empire associated with the accession of Darius I after the
   death of Cambyses as the backdrop for Haggai's two messages
   forecasting God's subjugation of the nations in the eschaton
   (2:6–7; 2:21–22).

10. Details of Darius's campaign in Egypt are sketchy, and the date is
    uncertain. It is possible that Darius made an incursion into Egypt some
    time in 518 BC after his campaign against the Sacians of Skunkha (or
    Scythia, peoples and regions north of the Black Sea and east of the
    Caspian Sea); cf. Briant (2002: 140). There is speculation that the Persian
    King Darius may have even visited the Jerusalem temple he ordered to
    be built on one of his visits to Egypt, whether the military campaign of
    518 BC (?) or in 497–496 BC when he commissioned the building of a
    temple to the god Amon at Hibis (cf. Hill [1998: 55]). On Darius in
    Egypt see Briant (2002: 474–476); and Yamauchi (1990: 148–149).

11. E.g. Wolf (1976: 39–40); Verhoef (1987: 106); and Stuhlmueller
    (1988: 31–32).

construed (so NJPS, NRSV). The LXX includes a scribal addition at the end of 2:9, reflecting on this aspect of the promise of peace: 'and peace of mind for an acquisition to everyone who creates, to raise up this shrine' (NETS).

Echoes of covenant ideas and themes resound in the vocabulary of Haggai's second message (2:1–9). Specifically, the prophet alluded to YHWH's covenant ties with Israel by mentioning the land (2:2, 4; cf. Gen. 12:1, 7; Exod. 3:8), the temple (2:3, 7, 9; an implicit reference to that place where YHWH would establish his name; Deut. 12:11; 14:23; 16:2) and the inauguration of peace (2:9; a key element of the new covenant promises of Jeremiah [30:10; 32:37] and Ezekiel [34:25; 37:26]). More striking are the assurance formulas (*Be strong*, 2:4 [3 times]; and *Do not fear*, 2:5). Both are commonly found in covenantal contexts (e.g. Gen. 15:1; 26:24; Exod. 20:20; Isa. 57:15). According to Petersen (1984: 57–58), both serve to alleviate the apprehension and fear of the people by connecting YHWH's current presence in the community with his future activity on behalf of his elect. Perhaps most significant is Haggai's wedding of the abiding presence of YHWH (2:4) with the word of YHWH's covenant promise (2:5). The prophet may have had Isaiah 59:20–21 in mind, where the combination of God's covenant word and the presence of his Spirit are tokens of YHWH's unswerving commitment to the restoration of his people.

Meaning

The true glory of the Second Temple that Haggai calls the people to build will not be the gold and silver of the nations (v. 8). Rather, the stunning glory of God's temple will be God himself and his presence in the sanctuary and among his people (v. 4). The destination of biblical history is the residence of God with his people, a day when God and the Lamb are the temple of the new Jerusalem (Rev. 21:3, 22). An outcome of God's redemptive activity is peace (v. 9). This peace or shalom of God calls to mind Ezekiel's promise of a future covenant of peace with creation and creatures (Ezek. 34:25). This promise of peace foreshadows the ministry of Jesus the Messiah, who offered a supernatural peace to his disciples (cf. John 14:27; 16:33).

3. THIRD MESSAGE: THE CALL TO HOLINESS (2:10–19)

Context

Two months had elapsed since Haggai's second sermon (17 October, 2:1), and the community was now three months into the temple restoration project (21 September, 1:15). The ninth month of the Hebrew calendar (Kislev, overlapping the Julian months of November and December) was the time for sowing the late-season crops like wheat and barley (sesame, millet, lentils and garden vegetables were planted from January until early March). The early rains of the winter season (falling from mid-October to early November) would have prepared the soil for planting. The latter rains of the winter season (arriving in early April) provided the necessary moisture for the maturation of the cereal crops. Haggai hints that the seed for the winter crops had been planted (v. 19), and now the farming community must await with patience the latter rains to ripen the fields for harvest. It was during this time of uncertainty, especially given the fragile agricultural economy of Palestine, that God's messenger called his people to covenant faith by boldly predicting a bumper crop for the winter harvest.

Theologically, the prophet's third message assumes God's sovereignty over the realm of nature as Creator (perhaps recalling Habakkuk's prayer, 3:17–19). He also presumes the audience's knowledge of the agricultural blessings and curses associated with the 'penalty clause' of the Mosaic treaty (cf. Deut. 28:4–6, 11–12, 18, 22, 39–40).

The phraseology of the promise of blessing (*I will bless you*, 2:19) echoes the language of the covenant God established with Abraham (*I will bless you*, Gen. 12:2) and the affirmation of that covenant with Isaac (combining divine blessing with the land of covenant promise, Gen. 26:3). The construction emphasizes God as the source of this blessing and the fact that his grace is not subject to manipulation by human endeavour (cf. Mal. 3:14). The only condition attached to divine favour is the return to God in repentance, characterized by the fear of the Lord and obedience to his commands (2:17; cf. 1:12–13). The parallels between Haggai 2:10–15 and Zechariah 8:9ff. are well documented. The complementary message of Zechariah, Haggai's contemporary, outlines the benefits of God's blessing far surpassing the anticipated agricultural prosperity, including: peace (Zech. 8:12, 'a sowing of peace' [ESV, NRSV]), honour among the nations as a symbol and source of divine blessing (Zech. 8:13), joyous worship (Zech. 8:19), glory as the place where all peoples will worship the Lord Almighty (Zech. 8:20–22), and the very presence of God in the midst of his people Israel (Zech. 8:23; cf. Hag. 2:4–5).

A. Introduction: Date and prophetic word formulas (2:10)

Comment

10. Haggai's third message was delivered on 18 December 520 BC. Two months had elapsed since Haggai's second sermon (17 October, 2:1), and the community was now three months into the temple restoration project (21 September, 1:15). The prophet Zechariah, Haggai's contemporary, had begun his ministry in Jerusalem a few weeks earlier (November 520 BC, Zech. 1:1).

Meaning
There is a subtle shift in the prophetic word formulas of the histor-

ical introductions in 2:10, 20. Unlike the formulas in 1:1 and 2:1, where *the word of the LORD came through the prophet*, calling attention to the prophet as the conveyor of divine revelation, the latter two formulas utilize the preposition *to*. Petersen (1984: 72) notes that this marks a slight change in the process of communication, since it signifies Haggai as the receiver of the divine message. Interestingly, the audiences of the last two sermons are more discrete than those of the first two sermons. First, Haggai addresses the priests (2:10–19), and then he speaks directly to Zerubbabel (2:20–23).

B. Haggai requests Torah instructions from the priests (2:11–14)

Context

Haggai's third speech consists of a warning oracle (vv. 10–14) and an oracle of blessing (vv. 15–19).[1] The warning speech has a didactic thrust, in that the priests are asked to answer two questions related to ritual purity. The distillation of Haggai's exchange with the priests on the question of ritual purity is the theological truth that holiness is not transferable, while impurity is transferable. The prophet then draws the logical and disturbing conclusion that the work and the worship of the people are defiled by virtue of impurity contaminating the community (2:14). Haggai's audience assumed that their service and sacrificial offerings were made pure and acceptable to God as a result of 'contact' with the ordained

---

1. Previous literary-critical scholarship has posited that Hag. 2:10–19 consists of two unrelated sermons, and that scribal error separated 2:15–19 from 1:15 (where it fits more logically according to this redaction theory). Boda counters, however, that recent studies have overturned this earlier (faulty) consensus. Especially pertinent to the discussion is the absence of any textual evidence for scribal error in relocating the passage earlier in the book and the grammatical requirements governing the use of the emphatic adverb *Now* (Heb. *'attâ*) in 2:15. See Boda (2004: 141–142); see further Taylor and Clendenen (2004: 179–180).

priesthood and YHWH's holy temple. Here the prophet had to correct wrong thinking and bad theology!

Comment

11. The prophet is not seeking information. Rather, the warning speech (vv. 10–14) has a didactic thrust in that, by responding to questions related to ritual purity, the priests 'would learn from their answers more than they knew'.[2] Dialogical speech piques and engages audience interest and is typical of the prophetic method, because such exchanges prepare the audience to hear the prophetic message and receive divine instruction. The crux of the matter in each 'test case' is the principle of transferability, of either holiness or ritual impurity, to a third party or object. The Mosaic law is silent on such transferability to the third level. By logical inference, the priests answer Haggai's hypothetical questions correctly. Hildebrand (1989: 160) summarizes: 'The two questions contrast holiness and uncleanness, both concerning contact to the third degree. Uncleanness is passed on to the third degree, holiness is not. In a word, uncleanness is more contagious than holiness.'

The NIV understands the word *law* (Heb. *tôrâ*) as a body of precepts, a later application of the term to the broader collection of Mosaic statutes that came to be known as the Torah or the Pentateuch. Here the original use of *tôrâ*, a short instruction or teaching point, is more appropriate to the context (cf. NJPS, 'Seek a ruling from the priests'; NRSV, 'Ask the priests for a ruling').

12. Animal flesh was set apart or made holy (Heb. *qōdeš*) by means of the ritual sacrifices conducted by the priests (e.g. Lev. 6:17, 25; 7:1). Portions of the sacrificial animal were sometimes carried in the folds of the priestly robes for presentation to the Lord as a wave offering (Num. 6:20), as a meal for the priest(s) (Lev. 6:26), or as a fellowship meal (Lev. 7:15). The garment of the priest was made holy or consecrated by virtue of the contact with the sacrificial offering, but that holiness was not transferable should the priest's robe touch other objects (Lev. 6:27). The word *stew* (Heb. *nāzîd*) occurs elsewhere only in Genesis 25:29, 34 and 2 Kings 4:38–40,

---

2. Craigie (1985: 148).

where context suggests a boiled dish, something akin to lentil soup or vegetable stew.

13. Conversely, ritual defilement as a result of contact with a corpse was passed on by further touch, like a contagious disease (cf. Lev. 11:28; 22:4–7).

14. The issue was not one of ritual pollution due to contact with impure people groups (e.g. the Samaritans),[3] or even the unconsecrated temple site.[4] Rather, the real failure of the Hebrew community was refusing fully to return to YHWH (v. 17). Verhoef (1987: 120) observes that 'disobedience is the main reason for God's displeasure in their sacrifices'.[5] The impurity compromising Hebrew worship was made public and denounced in a message delivered by Zechariah (nearly two years after Haggai's warning speech): the failure to be honest and just, the failure to show mercy and kindness, and the ongoing practice of oppression targeting the socially disadvantaged (Zech. 7:8–11).

The words *people* (Heb. *'am*) and *nation* (Heb. *gôy*) are used somewhat synonymously, with the former denoting the internal social and covenantal relations of the Hebrews and the latter describing the nation-state of Israel as a political entity. Petersen's comment (1984: 95–96) on Haggai's third sermon as a success story is pertinent, since this oracle attests the prophet's ability effectively to engage the various segments of post-exilic Judahite society, including the high priest, the governor, the priests and the people.

Meaning
The distillation of Haggai's exchange with the priests on the question of ritual purity is the theological truth that holiness is not trans-

---

3. Thomas (1956: 1047).

4. Petersen (1984: 84–85;) and Meyers and Meyers (1987: 57). See further the discussion of the various interpretive options as to the source of the people's defilement in Verhoef (1987: 118–120).

5. Cf. Mason (1977: 22) who comments that the LXX seems to have understood the ritual impurity as a moral and ethical issue, since it adds a quotation from Amos 5:10 to v. 14 ('And you used to hate those who reprove in the gates'). On the LXX, see further Petersen (1984: 71, n. c).

ferable, while impurity is transferable. The prophet then draws the logical and disturbing conclusion that the work and the worship of the people are defiled by virtue of impurity contaminating the community (2:14). Haggai's audience assumed that their service and sacrificial offerings were made pure and acceptable to God as a result of 'contact' with the ordained priesthood and YHWH's holy temple. Here the prophet had to correct wrong thinking and bad theology!

C. The call to reflect upon current conditions (2:15–19)

Context
Previously, Haggai had called upon the leaders and people of Judah to reflect upon their current bleak situation (1:5, 7). He then charged his audience to remember the Hebrew exodus from Egypt (2:5). Now the prophet again calls his audience to reflect upon their more immediate past: the two decades prior to the start of the temple reconstruction project (2:15). The contrast between the present reality and the preceding promises of future divine glory for God's temple and his people was a jolt for Haggai's audience. But there was hope, as God vowed, *From this day on I will bless you* (2:19).

Comment
   15. *Now give careful thought to this.* Five times the prophet admonished his audience to *give careful thought* to the past or to assess their current situation (1:5, 7; 2:15, 18 [twice]), placing emphasis on the role of human will or volition in responding to God. Previously, Haggai had drawn attention to the Hebrew exodus from Egypt (2:5). This exhortation called the people to look back at the two decades prior to the commencement of the temple reconstruction project, and the appeal to the past even included a citation of a portion of the prophet Amos's message addressing a similar situation (vv. 16–17; cf. Amos 4:8–9). For the Hebrews, lessons learned from history motivated obedience to YHWH in the present (Zech. 1:4–6) and were vital to the success of the next generation (Deut. 4:9–14). (See further commentary on 1:5, p. 65.)
   The adverb *now* is an important structural marker in Haggai, signifying temporal and logical sequence in the prophet's oracles (cf. 1:5;

2:4). Here the word marks the transition from the warning oracle (vv. 10–14) to the oracle of blessing (vv. 15–18) in the third sermon.

The temporal reference, *from this day on*, hearkens back to the date formula situating the prophet's third sermon (v. 10). The repetition of the phrase in verse 18 brackets Haggai's oracle of blessing (vv. 15–18) in an envelope construction. The expression introduces a parenthetic glance backwards to the conditions in post-exilic Judah prior to the initiation of the temple rebuilding project (vv. 15b–17), before directing the audience's attention to the future (v. 18).

Consider how things were (NIV) is an interpretive rendering of the LXX expansion, 'How were you?' (Gk *tines ēte*), for the difficult expression of the MT in verse 16a (which combines the inf. form of the verb 'to be' with the preposition 'from'). Motyer (1998: 997) correctly notes that emending what he identifies as a Hebrew colloquialism ('when things were so') is unnecessary ('Before stone was laid on stone in the temple of the LORD – when things were so – one came …').

The clause, *before one stone was laid on another*, may refer generally to the masonry work that would have comprised a major portion of the temple reconstruction project. Alternatively, the phrase may be a technical expression referring to a formal refoundation ceremony, which involved setting a symbolic foundation stone and included a sacrificial liturgy for dedicating and purifying the temple site (cf. Zech. 4:4–6). The suggestion is intriguing, although Haggai makes no direct reference to any such foundation-stone ceremony.[6]

16. The MT distinguishes between the *wine vat* (Heb. *yeqeb*), the collecting unit or reservoir (i.e. the lower chamber of the wine press), and the wine press (Heb. *pûrâ*), the pressing chamber or the

---

6. See the discussions in Petersen (1984: 88–89) and Meyers and Meyers (1987: 59, 222–227). Boda (2004: 141, 159) also connects Hag. 2:15–19 with the building foundation ceremony of the ancient world (perhaps akin to the Mesopotamian *kalu* ceremony). He further notes that the audiences addressed by the prophet are appropriate to such ceremonial days in the Ancient Near East (i.e. the priests, 2:10–14; the people, 2:15–19; and the royal house, 2:20–23).

trough of the wine press (cf. NJPS, 'and if one came to the vat ...
the press would yield only twenty').

17. The prophets recognized that God's sovereignty included the
power to act for either harm or good, in keeping with the promise
of blessing and the threat of curse attached to his covenant with
Israel (Deut. 28). Such actions in Israel's history distinguished the
true God from the idols of the nations (Isa. 41:23). The entire clause
(*I struck ... with blight and mildew*) repeats Amos 4:9. The citation
serves both to validate Haggai's ministry by connecting him with
the earlier prophetic tradition and to remind the people that history
is the arena of God's redemptive activity and there are lessons for
Israel embedded in her past.

Two of the three natural disasters are listed in Deuteronomy
28:22: *blight*, scorching wind that withers (Heb. *šiddāpôn*) and *mildew*,
perhaps a rotting fungus spawned by excessive moisture (Heb.
yērāqôn). *Blight* and *mildew* are among the plagues that may be reme-
died by prayer, according to Solomon's dedicatory prayer for the
Jerusalem temple (1 Kgs 8:37; 2 Chr. 6:28). The polar word pair indicates that divine chastisement may take on varied forms, and the
allusions to the earlier words of Moses and Solomon further
heighten the covenant implications of Haggai's message.

Yet you did not turn to me. NIV follows the ancient versions (LXX, Targ.,
Vulg.) instead of the MT, which reads, 'but you are not with me'.[7]

19. The rhetorical question anticipates the answer 'No!', because
the seed has already been planted. The implied negative answer to
the prophet's question is deduced from the crop failure mentioned
in verse 17 and the timing of the third oracle. The prophet's message
is dated to the month of December, after the winter rains (Oct–
Nov) but prior to the early spring harvest. The previous summer
harvest must provide enough grain both for consumption and
autumn planting. The blighted summer harvest threatens famine,
and the seed for the spring grain crop is already in the ground. The
people of Judah must wait upon the promise of God for a bumper
crop that will provide sufficient grain for sustenance, as well as seed
grain to be stored for the next planting (cf. Hab. 3:17).

---

7. See the discussion in Petersen (1984: 87, n. e).

The phrasing of the promise of blessing echoes the language of the covenant God established with Abraham (Gen. 12:2) and the affirmation of that covenant with Isaac (Gen. 26:3, where the blessing is tied to the land of covenant promise).

Meaning
Haggai's third declaration revealed God's intentions to overthrow the nations and restore the fortunes of Israel. It served to encourage and unify the community in their initiative to rebuild the temple. The reminder that divine justice was still operative in human history both fortified the people in spirit and awakened dormant faith. The long-deferred hope of Zion's shame changed into praise was finally becoming a reality (cf. Zeph. 3:14–20, esp. v. 19). The message was also a reminder that history is the arena of God's redemptive activity (cf. Dan. 2:20–23). For the Hebrews, lessons learned from history were vital to the success of the next generation (cf. Deut. 4:9–14).

4. FOURTH MESSAGE: ZERUBBABEL, DAVIDIC SERVANT AND SIGNET RING (2:20–23)

Context

Haggai's last message to post-exilic Judah is the shortest of his four sermons. His first (1:1–15) and last messages are directed to individuals. Both Zerubbabel the governor of Judah and Joshua the high priest were addressed in the opening oracle (1:1). Zerubbabel alone is the recipient of the prophet's final speech (v. 21). Haggai's first sermon exhorted Zerubbabel and Joshua to rally the people and rebuild the Jerusalem temple (1:2). In his final sermon, the prophet promises that God will establish Zerubbabel as his very own signet ring (v. 23), rehearsing the sequence of the Davidic covenant in which King David desires to build a temple for YHWH, but YHWH counters that he will build David's house or dynasty (2 Sam. 7:1–6, 11).

Haggai's closing speech takes the form of a salvation oracle, announcing deliverance and restoration for post-exilic Judah primarily by raising up leadership rooted in the Davidic line. The prophet's final sermon includes a briefer version of the theophanic pronouncement found in the second sermon (vv. 21–22; cf. 2:6–9).

The three key elements of Haggai's eschatology are the restored glory of the Second Temple (2:6–9), divine judgment in the 'shaking of the nations' (2:6–9; 2:20–22), and the restoration of Davidic leadership for Israel (v. 23).

A. Introduction: Date and prophetic word formulas (2:20)

Comment

20. The prophet receives two divine revelations on the same auspicious day (see 2:10 above).

Meaning

Such an unusual occurrence underscores the significance of the day for the restoration community of Judah, further reinforcing the speculation that this was the occasion of the temple's refoundation ceremony (see commentary on 2:15, pp. 89–90 and Zech. 4:7, pp. 157–158).

B. Warning of divine judgment against the nations (2:21–22)

Context

The prophet's vision of God shaking the heavens and the earth (v. 21) has parallels in Isaiah 13:13 and Joel 3:16. The numerous allusions to significant events of earlier Hebrew history, most notably the exodus from Egypt, further establish continuity between pre-exilic and post-exilic Israel. First, Haggai's message reminds his post-exilic audience that they are the heirs of God's covenant legacy with Israel, including the restoration promises announced by Jeremiah (e.g. Jer. 31:1–6, 33–34, 38–40) and Ezekiel (e.g. Ezek. 34:20–31); and second, that they should expect continuity in God's actions. That is, what YHWH has done for his people Israel in the past by way of deliverance and blessing, he will do so, and more, in the future.

Comment

21. The verse repeats the language of cosmic judgment predicted previously in 2:6 (see commentary, p. 79). The shaking of the nations that brings their wealth to the Lord's temple (2:6–7) is part of God's cosmic shaking of creation in the end times. The two theophanies (2:6–7 and 2:21–22) share similar vocabulary and structure, and in each case the flow of words moves from the cosmos to the nations. The results differ, however: whereas the first cosmic disruption leads to the wealth of the nations streaming into the Jerusalem temple, the second cosmic disruption brings about the subjugation of the nations under YHWH's rule (Boda, 2004: 161). The construction of the independent pronoun and the participle indicates the imminent future ('I am about to shake …'; cf. 'I am going to shake …', NJB) and places emphasis on the Lord as the subject of the impending action.[1] The verb *shake* (Heb. *rā'aš*) echoes two earlier seismic events: the Hebrew exodus from Egypt (Pss 68:8; 77:18), and David's rise to kingship in Israel (Ps. 18:7). There are clear allusions to both in Haggai's final message: the reference to chariots (v. 22) recalls the destruction of Pharaoh's chariots at the sea crossing (Exod. 15:1, 4, 19, 21), and David's kingship is represented in the symbol of the signet ring (Jer. 22:24). The LXX adds 'and the sea and the dry land' (NETS), an insertion based on the phrasing of 2:6.

22. The verb *overturn* is used generally of divine judgment (e.g. Amos 4:11) and is specifically associated with God's judgment of Sodom and Gomorrah (Gen. 19:21, 25, 29). The term also has connections with the exodus, referencing the miraculous events surrounding the Hebrew deliverance from Egypt (Exod. 7:17, 20; Pss 66:6; 78:44). *Royal thrones* interprets the awkward phrase 'throne of kingdoms', perhaps an oblique reference to the Persian dynasty (i.e. the rulers or dynasty of an empire composed of numerous political entities).[2] The singular 'throne' may also be construed as a plural, given its grammatical relationship with the following plural noun (e.g. 'thrones of kingdoms', NJB).[3] Motyer notes that the word

---

1. On the *futurum instans* (imminent future) use of the participle see *IBHS* §37.6f., pp. 627–628; GKC §116p, pp. 359–360. Boda (2004: 160) ventures that Haggai's message predicting the cosmic shaking of the nations may have had currency among the Jews who had witnessed the recent vulnerability of the Persian hegemony in the political unrest that followed the death of Cambyses and the accession of Darius.

2. See Meyers and Meyers (1987: 67).

3. On singular nouns construed as collectives or plurals, see *IBHS* §7.2.1,

thrones 'signifies the world without reference to God'.[4]

The verb *shatter* often refers generally to God's prerogative and power to destroy those who transgress his decrees, whether Hebrew or non-Hebrew (Deut. 4:3; Ps. 37:38; Prov. 14:11). More specifically, the word is associated with God's command (including his divine enablement) to Israel to destroy the Canaanite people groups occupying the land of the covenant promise, lest they ensnare the Israelites in their web of idolatry (Deut. 7:23–24; Josh. 9:24; 24:8). Ironically, the term for *power* is used to describe the 'mighty hand' of God in delivering his people from slavery in Egypt (Exod. 13:3, 14, 16). God, the One enthroned in heaven, scoffs at the collective power of the nations (Ps. 2:4).

The reference to *foreign kingdoms* (lit. 'kingdoms of the nations') may serve as a complement to the previous reference to the 'throne of kingdoms', with the former accenting the constituent nation-states comprising the Gentile empires and kingdoms, and the latter calling attention to the individual rulers or dynasties of these earthly realms. More important is the affirmation of the universality of God's rule – and the election of Israel as God's holy nation represented in his election of Zerubbabel (v. 23; note the reference to the nations in 2:7 above).

The repetition of the word *overthrow* and the series of four verbs depicting the destructive power of God (*shake, overturn, shatter, overthrow*) underscore his supremacy as true king over the nations. The reference to *chariots* calls to mind the chariots of Pharaoh, swallowed up in the sea in their attempt to pursue the escaping Israelites (Exod. 15:4). God even secured deliverance for his people by causing the wheels to fall off Pharaoh's chariots (Exod. 14:25).

The *horse* was a symbol of royal power in the ancient world, and the cavalry was an important component of a king's arsenal. Yet the righteous were admonished not to put their trust in the strength of horses, but rather to trust in the strength of their Lord – the one who created horses and gave them their strength (Pss 20:7; 33:16–

2, pp. 113–115; and by using the plural of the *nomen rectum* (or genitive noun), see GKC §124r, p. 401.

4. Motyer (1998: 1001).

17; cf. Deut. 17; Job 39:19). The verb *fall* echoes Exodus 15:4 where the chariots of Pharaoh *sank to the depths like a stone*. The word *fall* is also a euphemism for death, with connotations of descent into the underworld.[5] The language of *chariot and driver, horse and rider* has affinities with Jeremiah 51:21, where the prophet described the destructive power of the Babylonian armies as YHWH's war club (but they too would experience divinely ordained destruction, Jer. 51:25).

Panic and confusion leading to infighting (so-called internecine strife) is a motif associated with YHWH's warfare on behalf of Israel (e.g. Judg. 7:22; 1 Sam. 14:20; 2 Chr. 20:23).[6]

Ultimately, all sin is self-destructive, since it alienates one from God, breeds selfishness and self-reliance, and leads to physical and spiritual death.

Meaning

The prediction of the shaking of the nations (vv. 21–22) was designed to convince the people that God was still sovereign and had not forsaken his justice. Haggai called his audience to what is described as 'zealous allegiance' to God and his covenant.[7] The prophet was holding out the hope of 'nothing less than a universal reordering of all things and the establishment of the Kingdom of God on earth'.[8] The God of Israel shook the earth once before at the exodus (2:5). This was proof enough for Haggai that God would again act with great power to judge the nations, and deliver and restore his people Israel.

---

5. See Boda (2004: 162, n. 10).

6. Ibid., pp. 162–163. Boda comments that God wreaks such confusion among his enemies that they ironically bring about judgment upon themselves, 'confirming the ineptitude of human political power and military prowess. Such ineptitude has been demonstrated to this Jewish community in the recent Persian upheaval at the accession of Darius.'

7. Baldwin (1972: 59).

8. Achtemeier (1986: 101).

C. God's appointment of Zerubbabel as leader (2:23)

Context

Haggai's final sermon should not be construed as a subversive manifesto for political insurrection against the Persian Empire.[9] Rather, it was a call to wait faithfully and expectantly for the ever-imminent Day of the Lord, that day of judgment and redemption inaugurating God's kingdom of righteousness (Isa. 32:1–2, 15–20; 65:17–25). Zerubbabel was indeed instrumental in the rebuilding of the Second Temple, but much of what Haggai envisioned was never realized under his leadership. This does not represent a failure of the prophetic word, but rather is another example of the pattern in OT prophetic literature of predictions having both near and distant fulfilments. It also suggests that Zerubbabel may be a representative figure (like Moses [cf. Deut. 18:18], David [cf. Ezek. 34:23–24] and Elijah [Mal. 4:5–6]) who finds his ultimate expression in a greater Zerubbabel who is to come – namely, Jesus the Messiah.[10]

Comment

23. The phrase *on that day* is typical prophetic language for some indefinite future time, that is, eschatological time (e.g. Hos. 2:18; Amos 9:11; Zech. 12:3; 13:2). Petersen (1984: 102) recognizes the formula as an important transition point from the more general reference of divine judgment of the nations (vv. 21–22) to a more (immediate?) and concrete promise in which the prophet envisions a day when Judah will once again enjoy political autonomy under the rule of Zerubbabel, a Davidic descendant (perhaps anticipating the fulfilment of Ezekiel's restoration vision? [Ezek. 34:24; 37:24]). The reality that Haggai's vision for self-rule under the then governor of Judah, Zerubbabel, was never completely realized leaves open

---

9. Rose (2000: 251) summarizes with respect to the oracles of Haggai and Zechariah that it is 'difficult to read these prophets as announcing the restoration of the monarchy in the immediate future, let alone as promoting something like a revolt against the Persian empire'.

10. Taylor and Clendenen (2004: 199–201).

the question of later messianic fulfilment (see commentary on *signet ring* below, pp. 99–100).

The first-person verb forms continue the emphasis on God's agency in judging and ruling the nations, and in restoring his people Israel. The words *take* and *chosen* convey the sense of divine election in this context, the terminology recalling God *taking* Israel as his own people (Exod. 6:7), and King David to be his ruler over Israel (2 Sam. 7:8).[11] Likewise, God *chose* Abraham (Neh. 9:7) and Israel for special covenant relationship out of all the peoples of the earth (Deut. 7:6; 14:2). The prophet's reaffirmation of Israel's divine election was a much-needed exhortation, given the plight of God's people in the aftermath of the Babylonian exile.

Zerubbabel is identified as the son of Shealtiel, and thus a grandson of King Jehoiachin of Judah, and hence a Davidic descendant (Matt. 1:12; but note 1 Chr. 3:17–19 where Zerubbabel is identified as the son of Pedaiah; see further commentary on 1:1, pp. 61–62). The title *servant* indicates that Zerubbabel, like Moses (Mal. 4:4) and David (2 Sam. 7:5) before him, had been divinely chosen to fulfil a particular leadership role in God's plan for Israel and his redemptive mission in the world. Yet Zerubbabel, who played a strategic role as governor of post-exilic Judah, drops off the pages of OT history rather quickly and mysteriously, disappearing from the record after Zechariah's reference to his role in the building of the Second Temple (Zech. 4:6, 7, 9, 10). Both Ezra and Nehemiah remember Zerubbabel as a key figure in the restoration of Judah after the Babylonian exile (Ezra 3:2; Neh. 12:1), and he is esteemed as a member of the honour roll of Hebrew ancestors in later Jewish literature (Sir. 49:11).

The *signet ring* (Heb. *ḥôtām*) was a symbol of kingship and royal authority in the biblical world. The engraved stone set in the gold or silver finger ring was used to seal or endorse official documents.[12] Haggai employed the image to emphasize the divine

---

11. Boda (2004: 163) notes that the verb is often found in contexts where God changes the status of an individual (e.g. Abraham, Gen. 24:7; Josh. 24:3; David, 2 Sam. 7:8; Elijah, 2 Kgs 2:3).

12. See the discussion in Sweeney (2000: 554).

authority vested in Zerubbabel and to assure the people of God's continuing involvement in the restoration of Judah – even the political process.

The designation of Zerubbabel as the signet ring of the Lord no doubt rekindled messianic expectations among some in the post-exilic community, since he was a descendant of King David. But Haggai's expectations concerning the restoration of the Hebrew monarchy is more difficult to assess. Rose cautions against inter-preting Haggai's final oracle as messianic, while recognizing the identification of Zerubbabel as God's *signet ring* indicates a 'special protection for God's chosen servant at a time of substantial change in the political landscape'.[13] Boda articulates more fully that, while Haggai's message addresses future Davidic kingship, the words *servant* and *signet ring* are passive images of instrumentality. Thus Haggai's message is carefully phrased so as to define the role appro-priate for David's heirs: that is, the 'Davidic king was expected to fill the role of vice-regent on earth, executing Yahweh's authority and representing Yahweh's interests in the world'.[14] The blessing of Zerubbabel also has implications for Jeremiah's curse levied against King Jehoiachin (or Coniah) of Judah, a Davidic descendant (Jer. 22:24). Haggai's message overturns the earlier rejection of Jehoiachin and reinstates the election of the Davidic line and the promises of the Davidic covenant (using the language of royal adoption; cf. 2 Sam. 7:8, 14). Early on in church history, Christian interpreters understood the reference to the signet ring typologi-cally as a messianic title for Jesus the Messiah (e.g. Ambrose).[15] The

---

13. Rose (2000: 249–250); cf. March (1996: 731) who also understands the signet ring imagery as indicating a special relationship between God and Zerubbabel. On the signet ring in the ANE see further, *ZIBBCOT* 5: 199.

14. See Boda (2004: 165).

15. See '(Haggai 2:23) Zerubbabel, God's Servant' in Ferreiro (2003: 229); cf. Merrill (2008: 720) who regards the verse as a messianic text, but holding the idea that Jeremiah's earlier disqualification of Jehoiachin's descendants is still in force (requiring that Jesus' lineage be traced through David's son Nathan, Luke 3:31).

NT, however, makes no formal appeal to Haggai 2:23 as an OT text with Christological implications.

The threefold repetition of the divine utterance formula (*declares the LORD Almighty*) in verse 23 emphasizes the certain fulfilment of Yahweh's promise.

Meaning

Haggai's final sermon (2:20–23) completes the message he began in 2:10–19. The reflections on the Hebrews' past ritual impurity (2:14) give way to the promise of blessing – the reversal of the agricultural and economic woes currently experienced in post-exilic Judah in the aftermath of the Babylonian exile. The key elements of Haggai's eschatology are the restored glory of the Second Temple, the subjugation of the nations, and the reinstatement of Davidic leadership over Israel. The restoration of God's glory in the Jerusalem temple is a prophetic distinctive in Haggai, but certainly in keeping with the idea of 'the transformation of Zion' at the centre of OT eschatology.[16] Given the historical context, the vivid portrayal of God's power in subduing the nations was a most appropriate way to dispel the lingering doubt about God's sovereignty and justice after the cataclysm of Babylonian exile (cf. Mal. 2:17). Finally, Haggai's endorsement of Zerubbabel assured the people of God's continuing involvement in the political process, despite the failure of the Hebrew monarchies. Zerubbabel would complete the task God had assigned to him – the Second Temple would be built. No doubt, the reinstatement of the Davidic line rekindled hope for the Hebrews that God intended to keep his pledge about fulfilling the new covenant promises announced by Jeremiah and Ezekiel concerning the future shepherd-king David (cf. Jer. 22:17, 22, 26; Ezek. 37:24–25).

---

16. Gowan (1986: 4–20).

ZECHARIAH

INTRODUCTION

Zechariah is sometimes known as the 'little Isaiah', since this book has more to say about the messianic shepherd-king than any other OT prophetic book except Isaiah (see further Theological concerns, pp. 117–118). Zechariah's message was one of rebuke, exhortation and encouragement – a tract for troubled times. The Hebrews who had recently returned to Judah and Jerusalem after the Babylonian exile were confronted with numerous challenges. Not only were the people faced with the daunting task of rebuilding the city and temple of Jerusalem, they were still the pawn of a Mesopotamian superpower – now Persia instead of Babylonia. In addition, doubt and despair over the seeming failure of God's earlier promises for restoration after the exile, made by prophets like Jeremiah and Ezekiel, spawned disillusionment and apathy among the people.

The pastoral tone for the messages of Zechariah is set in his exchange with the angel commissioned to relay the *kind and comforting words* from the Lord (1:13). The hortatory character of his sermons is seen in words of encouragement, such as *be strong* and *do not be afraid* (8:9, 15). Zechariah's hope for his people was bound up in the

servant-deliverer. This coming shepherd-king would be of a humble
station in life (9:9; 13:7), serve as shepherd to a scattered and
wandering people (10:2), deliver Israel from her enemies and rule as
king in peace and righteousness in Jerusalem (9:9–10; 14:1–6, 9, 16).
Zechariah's repeated appeals to the words of the *earlier prophets*
authenticated his own ministry and assured his audience that they
had not misinterpreted God's previous revelations (1:4; 7:7, 12).
Mason (1990: 234) summarizes the ministry of all three of the post-
exilic prophets, Haggai, Zechariah and Malachi, as one of preaching
'the hopes of the [earlier] prophets to a people who could have
easily become cynical about their lack of fulfilment, assuring them
of both the present degree to which they had been and were being
fulfilled and the certainty of their ultimate triumph'.

1. Title and text

The book takes its title from the name of the prophet Zechariah,
identified in the superscription (1:1) as God's messenger to post-
exilic Judah. Jewish tradition deemed Haggai, Zechariah and Malachi
to be the only prophets belonging to the Second Temple era, so
these books were naturally placed at the end of the collection also
known as the Twelve Prophets.[1] Zechariah is the eleventh book in
the collection known as the Minor Prophets (or the Book of the
Twelve in the HB). The Twelve Prophets are usually grouped with
the Latter (or Major) Prophets, and without exception are found in
the earliest delineations of the OT canon. These twelve books were
usually copied on one scroll in the ancient Hebrew manuscript tradition. The order of the Twelve Prophets does vary in some renditions of the canon of the Hebrew Bible, but the sequence of books
from Nahum to Malachi seems quite stable in the various canon
lists.[2]

---

1. See *EncJud* 11: 50.
2. See further B. A. Jones (1995: 54). For example, Amos and Micah follow
   Hosea in the LXX, and one Qumran fragment places Jonah as the last
   book in the Twelve Prophets (4QXIIa). On the placement of Jonah at
   Qumran, see the discussion in Meyers and Meyers (1987: 51).

The books of Haggai, Zechariah and Malachi form a distinct sub-collection or literary corpus within the Book of the Twelve. All three prophets belong to the early Persian period of post-exilic Hebrew history and are unified by literary device (e.g. the rhetorical question) and theological themes (repentance leading to proper worship and the practice of social justice).[3]

The MT of Zechariah 1 – 8 and 9 – 14 is quite well preserved and relatively free of textual problems,[4] although, as Baldwin notes, this does not mean 'that there are no matters of dispute'.[5] The Hebrew of the MT is occasionally obscure and difficult to interpret (as evidenced by the textual footnotes in the EVV) due to unusual vocabulary or awkward syntax, ellipsis and the symbolic nature of the genre of prophetic and proto-apocalyptic literature. The LXX is generally a reliable (but at times an interpretive and expansive) witness to the MT of Zechariah.[6] Portions of the book are attested by fragments of the Dead Sea Scrolls or Qumran (Q) manuscripts, including: Zechariah 1:4–6, 9–10, 13–14; 2:10–14; 3:2–10; 4:1–4; 5:8–11; 6:1–5; 8:2–4, 6–7; 10:11–12; 11:1–2; 12:1–3, 7–12; 14:18.[7] Meyers and Meyers (1993: 50–51) note only three textual variations of significance between the MT and Q, and conclude that the Q manuscripts support the Hebrew text underlying the MT. Matters of textual variants and emendation are discussed in the commentary where pertinent.

The versification of the MT in Zechariah differs from the versification of the EB versions only at the beginning of the book. The Hebrew Bible begins chapter 2 at 1:18 (which means 2:1 in the EB vers. is 2:5 in the MT). The versification of the EB is used throughout this commentary on Zechariah.

---

3. Cf. Pierce (1984: 277–289).
4. Cf. Meyers and Meyers (1987: lxviii).
5. Baldwin (1972: 86–87).
6. See further the discussion in McComiskey (1998: 1099–1111).
7. See further Ulrich (1997: 220–318).

2. The prophet Zechariah

We learn from Ezra that Haggai and Zechariah were contemporary prophets of the early post-exilic period (Ezra 5:1). The date formulas in the two books indicate that Zechariah began preaching in Jerusalem about two months (Zech. 1:1) after Haggai's brief four-month ministry (Hag. 1:1; 2:20). Haggai and Zechariah were also complementary prophets, in that Haggai exhorted the people to rebuild the Jerusalem temple and Zechariah summoned the community to repentance and spiritual renewal (cf. 1 Esdras 6:1; 7:3; and 2 Esdras 1:40 which lists Zechariah among the Twelve Prophets). His task was to prepare the people for proper worship in the temple once the building project was completed.

The book's superscription (1:1) identifies Zechariah as the son of Berekiah and the grandson of Iddo. The records of Ezra confirm Zechariah as a descendant of Iddo (Ezra 5:1; 6:14 [the word 'son' in this context simply designates 'a descendant']). Nehemiah informs us that Zechariah's grandfather, Iddo, returned to Jerusalem from exile in Babylonia with Zerubbabel and Joshua (or Jeshua, Neh. 12:1, 4). Nehemiah also lists Zechariah as the head of the priestly family of Iddo (Neh. 12:16). This suggests that Zechariah was a member of the tribe of Levi and served in Jerusalem as both a priest and a prophet.

According to Jewish tradition, the prophets Haggai, Zechariah and Malachi were among the founders of The Great Synagogue.[8] This body of Jewish leaders is alleged to have played a major role in post-exilic times in preserving Scripture and handing on the traditional teaching and lore of Hebrew religion. It is further believed by the rabbis that after these three prophets had died the Holy Spirit departed from Israel.

3. Historical background

The setting for Zechariah's preaching, as for Haggai's, was the reign of Darius I, king of Persia (522–486 BC). Although the Hebrews

---

8. E.g. *Aboth Rabbi Nathan* 1; *b. (Talm.) Baba Bathra* 15a.

had returned to the land of Israel after the Babylonian captivity, the economic situation of the community was bleak, and spiritually the people languished in apathy, despair and hopelessness. (See further the discussion of the Historical background in the commentary on Haggai, p. 45–46.)

In response to this distress, God raised up two prophetic voices for the purpose of initiating programmes for the physical rebuilding and the spiritual renewal of post-exilic Jerusalem. The prophet Haggai was commissioned to exhort and challenge the Hebrew community to rebuild the Jerusalem temple. He preached for only four months, late in the year 520 BC. The people responded favourably to Haggai's message, and the reconstruction of the Lord's temple began that year (Hag. 1:12–15).

The prophet Zechariah complemented Haggai's message by calling for the spiritual renewal of God's people (Zech. 1:3–6; 7:8–14). His ministry began just two months after Haggai's, and Zechariah's last dated message was delivered in 518 BC. So Zechariah's ministry in post-exilic Jerusalem lasted at least two years. The reference to Haggai and Zechariah in Ezra 5:2 suggests that they both continued to support and encourage the people until the temple was completed and rededicated to the worship of YHWH with the celebration of the Passover Feast in 515 BC (Ezra 6:13–22). The undated oracles of Zechariah (chs. 9 – 14) may indicate that his prophetic ministry in post-exilic Jerusalem continued well beyond the completion of the Second Temple.

4. Author

The book is silent on the issue of authorship, although it is assumed that the prophetic word formula (*the word of the LORD came ...*, 1:1) signifies that Zechariah penned his own oracles.[9] By and large, Jewish and Christian scholarship has long recognized the tradition that Zechariah is responsible for the book that bears his name. The name Zechariah means 'YH(WH) has remembered.' This

---

9. On the genitive of authorship, a particular form of agency involving speaking and writing, see *IBHS* §9.5.1c, p. 143.

summarizes his basic message to post-exilic Judah – the Lord has remembered his covenant with Israel and plans to restore the fortunes of his people. The title *prophet* classifies Zechariah as a divinely commissioned spokesperson for God (1:1).

5. Date and occasion of writing

Three of Zechariah's speeches are precisely dated to the day, month and year of the reign of Darius I, king of Persia. The modern equivalents for the date formulas are listed below:

1:1–6	Year 2	month 8		= Oct/Nov 520 BC
1:7 – 6:8	Year 2	month 11	day 24	= 15 Feb 519 BC
7 – 8	Year 4	month 9	day 4	= 7 Dec 518 BC

It seems likely that this first portion of the book (chs. 1 – 8) was written sometime between 520 and 515 BC, since Zechariah makes no reference to the completion and dedication of the Jerusalem temple in 515 BC (cf. Ezra 6:13–22). Zechariah's preaching was prompted by the prophet Haggai's message to begin reconstruction of the Lord's temple, delivered to Jerusalem on 29 August 520 BC (Hag. 1:1).

Scholarly opinion is sharply divided over the authorship and date of the final two oracles in the book of Zechariah (chs. 9 – 11, 12 – 14). Some biblical scholars assign chapters 9 – 11 to a 'Second Zechariah', and chapters 12 – 14 to a 'Third Zechariah'. These hypothetical and anonymous writers were understood to have lived and prophesied in Jerusalem sometime during the fourth to the second centuries BC. It is often suggested that these two anonymous oracles, along with the book of Malachi, were added as an appendix to Zechariah 1 – 8 to complete the sacred number of the Twelve Prophets.[10] According to this view, the final written form of Zechariah is ascribed to the Maccabean period (c. 160 BC). The

---

10. E.g. Sellin and Fohrer (1968: 465); for the various views on the redaction of Zech. 9 – 14 and the canonical shaping of the Twelve Prophets, see the discussions in Childs (1979: 482–485); B. A. Jones (1995: 13–23); Petersen (1995: 2–3, 23–29); and Longman and Dillard (2006: 487–490).

evidence typically offered in support of a multiple-authorship hypothesis includes the perceived differences in style, tone, theology and historical situation between the two parts of the book (chs. 1 – 8 and chs. 9 – 14). Notable among the arguments are the reference to Greece (9:13, which is considered an allusion to the Hellenistic period), and the distinctively apocalyptic literary character of chapters 12 – 14.

More recent studies carefully analysing linguistic and grammatical features of Zechariah indicate remarkable literary continuity between chapters 1 – 8 and 9 – 14.[11] An examination of the literary features in light of archaeological discovery and socio-political considerations confirms an early Persian period date for Zechariah 9 – 14.[12] Finally, both Jewish and Christian tradition concerning the HB or OT clearly associate Zechariah 9 – 14 with the prophet Zechariah and chapters 1 – 8 of his book. Most likely the two undated oracles (chs. 9 – 11 and 12 – 14) were composed by the prophet Zechariah later in his life. Linguistic data retrieved from the Hebrew text of Zechariah suggest that the final draft of the book was probably completed sometime between 500 and 470 BC.[13]

6. Audience

As in the case of Haggai's prophecy, the messages of Zechariah originated in Judah and were intended for the people living in post-exilic Jerusalem and its environs (Zech. 1:3). Embedded within Zechariah's sermons and visions are words specifically addressed to Zerubbabel the governor and to Joshua the high priest, along with the rest of the Levitical priesthood (e.g. Zech. 3:8–9; 4:6–7; 7:4–5).

7. Literary style and structure

The book of Zechariah divides neatly into two major units. The first includes the introductory verse (or superscription) and the call

---

11. See Hill (1982: 105–134); and Radday and Wickman (1975: 30–55).
12. See Meyers and Meyers (1993: 52–55).
13. Cf. Hill (1982: 130–132).

to repentance (1:1–6), the seven night visions (1:7 – 6:15), and two sermons addressing the topic of fasting (chs. 7 – 8). The second part of the book consists of prophetic oracles, subdivided into two sections: the word of the Lord concerning the land of Hadrach (or Aram, chs. 9 – 11), and the word of the Lord concerning Israel (chs. 12 – 14).

Literary analysis of Zechariah's prophecy has identified an elaborate chiastic structure underlying the two parts of the book (see the chart below).[14] Although there is no overarching symmetrical or parallel design connecting the two halves of the book, repeated themes serve to unify Zechariah's visions, sermons and oracles. Prominent among these unifying themes are: the promise of divine presence in the midst of Israel, the enabling work of the Holy Spirit, God's judgment of the nations, the call for social justice, the establishment of divinely appointed leadership, and the ultimate triumph of righteousness and the blessing of peace for Jerusalem (see 10. Message, pp. 116–117).

The structure of the book of Zechariah

Adapted from Baldwin (1972: 89–90)

Part 1:

I. Prelude: Call to national repentance 1:1–6

II. Visions and postscripts

a   Vision 1: Patrol report of world at rest 1:7–17
  b   Vision 2: Horns and craftsmen (retribution for the nations) 1:18–21
  b¹   Vision 3: Measuring Jerusalem (the city protected by God) 2:1–5
      c   Postscript 1: Investiture of Joshua 2:6 – 3:10
        d Vision 4: Lampstand and olive trees 4:1–14
  b²   Vision 5: Flying scroll (retribution for evil) 5:1–4
  b³   Vision 6: Woman in *ephah* basket (Jerusalem purified by God) 5:5–11

---

14. See Baldwin (1972: 78–85); and Dorsey (1999: 317–320).

a¹   Vision 7: God's chariots patrol the earth 6:1–8
   c¹   Postscript 2: The crowning of Joshua 6:9–15

III. Messages on fasting
  a   The inquiry 7:1–3
    b   First sermon 7:4–14
      c   Covenant sayings 8:1–8
    b¹   Second sermon 8:9–17
  a¹   The response 8:18–19

IV. Postlude: Entreat and seek the Lord

Part 2:

I. Triumphant intervention of the Lord: His shepherd rejected
  a   The Lord triumphs from the north 9:1–8
    b   Arrival of the king 9:9–10
      c   Jubilation and prosperity 9:11 – 10:1
       d Rebuke for sham leaders 10:2–3
      c¹ Jubilation and restoration 10:4 – 11:3
    b¹   The fate of the good shepherd 11:4–17

II. Final intervention of the Lord: The suffering involved
      c² Jubilation in Jerusalem 12:1–9
    b²   Mourning for the pierced one 12:10 – 13:1
       d¹ Rejection of sham leaders 13:2–6
    b³   The shepherd slaughtered, the people scattered
          13:7–9
      c³ Cataclysm in Jerusalem 14:1–15
  a¹   The Lord worshipped as King over all 14:16–21

Building upon the literary analysis of Lamarche, Baldwin (1972: 78) has identified a chiastic structure underlying both halves of Zechariah's prophecy. While such patterns of inversion may be somewhat forced and artificial, they do provide some evidence of deliberate organization of themes, and argue for the unity of the entire literary work. It also may support the idea that Zechariah not only composed, but also arranged and edited, his own oracles.[15] Dorsey uncovers similar chiastic structures in Zechariah, and argues for the unity of the book on the basis of repeated themes. But he too admits that there is no overall structural scheme clearly tying the two halves of the book together.[16]

The approach that understands the prologue of Zechariah 1:1–6 as an introduction to the whole book, employed in combination with inner biblical exegesis, holds promise for demonstrating the literary unity of Zechariah.[17] This type of analysis seeks to tie both halves of Zechariah together lexically, thematically and theologically, by relating the message of Zechariah to the generalized call to repentance voiced in the earlier prophets in Zechariah 1:4.[18] More specifically, the dialogical relationship of the book of Zechariah to the words of the earlier prophets (Zech. 1:4), as seen in the numerous quotations and allusions to these prophets throughout Zechariah, demonstrates the literary coherence of the entire work.[19]

Like those of Haggai and Malachi, the sermons of Zechariah are basically prose sermon summaries in the third person. It is generally recognized that the post-exilic prophets display a tendency for rhetorical style, featuring instructional or catechetical content, and have a more devotional tone than their pre-exilic counterparts. The purpose of this preaching style was to establish continuity with the earlier prophetic tradition and reinforce the divine authority of their message, further evidenced by the multi-layered appeal to the oracles of their predecessors (e.g. Hag. 2:11–14; Zech. 1:1–6; Mal.

---

15. Baldwin (1972: 85).

16. See Dorsey (1999: 317–320); cf. Butterworth (1992: 304) who reaches a similar conclusion.

17. See Nurmela (1996: 39–42; 213–235); Boda (2004: 181); and Wenzel (2011: 55–58).

18. Zechariah probably draws from passages in Jeremiah calling the people of Judah to repentance, especially Jer. 25:5; cf. Jer.7:3, 5, 11; 18:11; 23:22; 35:15. E.g. Mason (1984: 227) considers Zech. 1:4 a 'near echo' of Jer. 25:4–5. See the full discussion in Wenzel (2011: 61–82), who concludes that Zech. 1:4 refers to Jer. 25:4–7.

19. See Wenzel (2011: 87–258).

3:1–4). The speeches may be formally classified as belonging to the genre of 'oracular prose'. The messages are oracular in nature because they represent authoritative prophetic speech, motivated or inspired by God himself. By prose, we mean that the literary texture of Zechariah is a blend of prosaic and rhetorical features distinctive of prophetic style.[20] This kind of prophetic speech is usually characterized by formulaic language. Examples of these stylized expressions in Zechariah include: the date formula and prophetic word formulas (1:1), the messenger formula (1:3), and the divine validation formula (2:9, 11).

In addition, Zechariah contains a number of literary forms that are rhetorical in nature, including: exhortation in the call to repentance (1:1–6), narrative in the form of a series of visions (1:7 – 6:8), prediction with revelation and interpretation formulas (5:1–4), inquiry with instructional response (6:1–8), symbolic actions (6:9–15), admonition with messenger and date formulas (7:1–7), and divine oracles of judgment and salvation (ch. 10).

Zechariah is sometimes classified as 'proto-apocalyptic' literature, in contrast to the apocalyptic literature that appears in later Jewish writings of the intertestamental period (e.g. 1 Esdras and 1 Enoch). It is true that the book exhibits certain features of apocalyptic writing, such as divine revelation cast in the form of visions, the presence of angelic messengers who both deliver and interpret the visions, the use of symbolism, and the themes of judgment for the nations and the deliverance of Israel. But other features of apocalyptic writing are notably absent, such as a rigid determinism (with regard to individual and national destinies) and pervasive pessimism (with regard to the prospects for humanity in the future), the rewriting of earlier Hebrew history (as if it were prophecy), and pseudonymity (or writing under a false name).

8. Understanding visionary literature

Biblical proto-apocalyptic literature (like its later offshoot, intertestamental Jewish apocalyptic literature) is a visionary genre

20. See the discussion in Andersen and Freedman (1980: 60–66).

given to interpretation of current events and prediction of future events in symbols, ciphers and codes – usually by means of angelic mediation (e.g. Zech. 1:9). As such, it represents a sub-category of the genre of prophecy in the larger scheme of hermeneutics or biblical interpretation.

Apocalyptic literature is crisis literature, typically conveying specific messages to particular groups of people caught up in a dire situation. Several basic questions are helpful in the interpretation of visionary literature in the Bible, including: Who is addressed? By whom? When? In what setting? For what reason? What is the relationship of the passage under investigation to the rest of the Bible?

Visionary literature announces an end to the way things are and opens up alternative possibilities to the audience as a result of God's impending intervention in human affairs. Three types of messages are usually associated with the visionary literature of the Bible. The first is a message of encouragement to the oppressed; the second, a warning to the oppressor; and the third, a call to faith for those wavering between God's truth and human wisdom.[21] Visionary literature portrays settings, characters and events in ways different from ordinary reality. While the visions depict literal events, the symbolic descriptions do not necessarily represent the events literally. Ryken offers helpful guidelines for reading and under-standing visionary literature:

- be ready for the reversal of the ordinary
- be prepared to use your imagination to picture a world that transcends earthly reality
- be prepared for a series of diverse, self-contained units that tend to be kaleidoscopic in nature (instead of looking for a smooth flow of narrative)
- seek to identify the historical event or theological reality in salvation history represented by the symbolism in the passage (observe the obvious, grasp the total scene, do not press every detail of the vision for hidden meaning)

---

21. Cf. Hanson (1987: 58–70).

- read widely in visionary literature (both biblical visionary literature and extra-biblical fantasy literature)
- recognize the element of mystery and the supernatural quality of the Bible (and be willing to admit humbly that an exact understanding of a given vision may be beyond us)[22]

9. Zechariah and typology

Zechariah has more to say about the messianic shepherd-king than any other OT prophetic book, except Isaiah. By means of typology, a method of biblical interpretation that establishes correspondence between OT events, persons, objects, ideas and similar NT items, the NT identifies an OT 'type' fulfilled in the NT 'antitype'. Specifically, the NT writers cite or allude to several passages in reference or application to the life and ministry of Jesus of Nazareth as the Messiah, including:[23]

- coming from a low and humble station of life (9:9; 13:7; cf. Matt. 21:5; 26:31, 56)
- restoring of Israel by the blood of his covenant (9:11; cf. Mark 14:24)
- serving as shepherd to a scattered and disoriented people (10:2; 13:7; cf. Matt. 9:36; 26:31)
- being betrayed for a payment of silver (11:11–12; cf. Matt. 26:14–16; 27:1–10)
- being pierced and struck down (12:10; 13:7; cf. Matt. 24:30; 26:31, 56; John 19:37)
- returning in glory and delivering Israel from her enemies (14:1–6; cf. Matt. 25:31)
- ruling as king in peace and righteousness in Jerusalem (9:9–10; 14:9, 16; cf. Rev. 11:15; 19:6)
- establishing a new world order (14:6–19; cf. Rev. 21:25; 22:1, 5).

---

22. From Ryken (1984: 165–174).
23. Cf. Kaiser (1995: 211–227). On the topic of intertextuality in Zechariah see further: Nurmela (1996), Mason (2003), Stead (2009) and Wenzel (2011).

10. Message

The prophetic ministries of Haggai and Zechariah in post-exilic Jerusalem overlapped chronologically and thematically. Haggai's primary message was a challenge to rebuild the temple of the Lord. Secondarily, he called for spiritual renewal among the people of God so that they might offer appropriate worship in the new sanctuary.

Zechariah's primary message, however, was an exhortation to repentance and spiritual renewal – a return to right relationship with God (Zech. 1:1–6). In fact, the central theme of Zechariah's sermons is encouragement, as he explicitly states his duty as one of comforting (1:13) and strengthening the people (8:9, 13, 15). As a complementary voice to Haggai, Zechariah also reinforced the summons to the people to rebuild the Jerusalem temple (8:9, 13). Yet his message extends beyond the material reconstruction of the Jerusalem temple to the moral and spiritual rebuilding of the Hebrew people, so that they might be holy unto the Lord and offer appropriate worship in the Second Temple (7:8–10; 8:14–17, 19; cf. 8:3). Boda finds links to the longstanding Hebrew tradition of penitential prayer in Zechariah's message, since such prayers set an agenda for spiritual renewal by focusing on repentance and forgiveness as a first step in overcoming the problems facing the supplicant (whether an individual or the community).[24] Zechariah's message of encouragement to a small and discouraged remnant of God's people (8:6) was cast in the form of visions of the future. This series of visions promised peace to Israel, divine judgment of the nations, the restoration of Jerusalem, responsible government as a result of divinely appointed leadership, and a covenant of righteousness in Zion (1:7 – 6:15). The theme of social justice is emphasized in lessons about fasting over the destruction of Solomon's temple and the Babylonian exile (7:8–12; 8:14–17).

Zechariah's last two messages are also visions designed to instil hope in God by focusing on the future restoration of the people of Israel (9 – 14). Specifically, the prophet forecasts the return of

---

24. Boda (2004: 174–175).

YHWH to his temple (9:8–10), the deliverance of Israel from her enemies (12:8–9), and the establishment of God's kingdom in Jerusalem (14:9–11).

11. Theological concerns

Behind Zechariah's call to repentance (1:3) was the concern for a right relationship with God, a renewal of the covenant established between YHWH and Israel at Mount Sinai (Exod. 19 – 24). This was a burden Zechariah shared with Haggai (Hag. 1:12) and Malachi (Mal. 3:7), and the OT prophets generally (e.g. Isa. 1:16–20; Hos. 6:1–3). The prophet's interest in Israel's covenant relationship with Yahweh extended to issues of social justice. Obedience to the stipulations of God's covenant led to justice, honesty, fairness, mercy and kindness (7:9–10; 8:16–17). Zechariah warned his audience not to repeat the past, because such covenant violations had sent an earlier generation into exile (7:11–14).

Closely related to Zechariah's concern for maintaining covenant relationship with Yahweh is his assurance that God will once again live among his people, and the glory of the Lord will rest in Jerusalem (Zech. 1:16; 2:5, 10–11; 8:3, 23; 14:16). Zechariah shares this vision of the Lord's return with other OT prophets (e.g. Isa. 52:8; Joel 3:21). The restoration of the divine presence in Israel promised by the prophet has both an immediate and an eschatological fulfilment. The immediate manifestation of the divine presence is associated with the rebuilt temple, a spiritually restored Israel, and the resurgence of agricultural production (Zech. 1:17; 4:8–9; 6:15; cf. Hag. 2:19). The future manifestation of the divine presence is associated with the deliverance of Jerusalem and the people of Israel from enemy nations, the enthronement of the Lord as King over all the earth, and the universal worship of YHWH (Zech. 9:16; 10:6; 12:9; 14:9). In each case, the return of the Lord's presence to Jerusalem is connected with the enabling work of God's Spirit (Zech. 4:6; 12:10; cf. Hag. 2:5).

Zechariah also addresses issues of theology proper, the knowledge of God. The emphasis on God's love for Jerusalem is evidence that he is a covenant-making and covenant-keeping God (1:14; 8:2, 15). The fact of God's sovereign rule over the nations and the reality of his compassion for Israel as his people mean that divine deliverance and divine judgment will be accomplished in the sphere of human history (11:6–12). Zechariah presents the mystery of the messiah as both a righteous king (9:9) and a suffering shepherd (13:7). This will result in a redeemed people who testify of their loyalty to God (13:9). The awesome holiness of God will transform the created order, and the long-awaited kingdom of the Lord will be established over all the earth (14:9). Consequently, all peoples will worship the King, the Lord Almighty (Zech. 14:9, 16, 21).

Yet Zechariah admonishes the people that God must be given the freedom to accomplish his purposes for the good of Israel in his own way and time. This is reflected in his exhortation to Zerubbabel not to 'despise small beginnings' (Zech. 4:10, NLT). Zechariah reminds his audience that God has acted in the past for the ultimate good of his people, even in the judgment of the Babylonian exile (7:12–14; cf. 14:3). The people of Israel can take courage in the present and have hope for the future, because God can be trusted to keep his word and fulfil his promises made through Zechariah the prophet (4:9). For this reason, all humanity is to be silent before the Lord, 'for he is springing into action from his holy dwelling' (2:13, NLT).

ANALYSIS

1. **PRELUDE: A CALL TO RETURN TO THE LORD (1:1–6)**
    A. Superscription (1:1)
    B. Prologue: The call to return to God ... for a change (1:2–6)

2. **ZECHARIAH'S VISIONS (1:7 – 6:15)**
    A. A man among the myrtle trees (1:7–17)
    B. Four horns and four blacksmiths (1:18–21)
    C. A man with a measuring line (2:1–5)
    D. The exiles are called home (2:6–13)
    E. Cleansing for the high priest (3:1–10)
    F. A gold lampstand and two olive trees (4:1–14)
    G. A flying scroll (5:1–4)
    H. A woman in a basket (5:5–11)
    I. Four chariots (6:1–8)
    J. The crowning of high priest Joshua (6:9–15)

3. **ZECHARIAH'S MESSAGES (7 – 8)**
   A. Zechariah receives a delegation from Bethel (7:1–7)
      i. The delegation raises a question about fasting (vv. 1–3)
      ii. The prophet's initial response (vv. 4–7)
   B. The call to covenant justice (7:8–14)
      i. The admonition for social justice rejected by the
         Hebrew ancestors (vv. 8–12)
      ii. God's punishment: exile (vv. 13–14)
   C. God's promise of restoration for Jerusalem (8:1–8)
      i. God's zeal for Zion (vv. 1–2)
      ii. God's return to Zion (v. 3)
      iii. God restores peace and safety to Jerusalem, (vv. 4–5)
      iv. God will bring his people back from exile and
          repopulate Jerusalem (vv. 6–8)
   D. God's promises to deliver and restore the remnant of Israel
      (8:9–23)
      i. The prophet's exhortation to rebuild the temple (vv. 9–
         13)
      ii. God's plans for Jerusalem (vv. 14–17)
      iii. Joyful fasting (vv. 18–19)
      iv. The nations will seek the Lord in Jerusalem (vv. 20–23)

4. **ZECHARIAH'S ORACLES (9 – 14)**
   A. First oracle (9 – 11)
      i. Judgment against Israel's enemies (9:1–8)
      ii. Zion's coming king (9:9–13)
      iii. The Lord will appear and deliver his people (9:14–17)
      iv. The Lord will restore his people (10:1 – 11:3)
         a. The Lord will care for his flock (10:1–5)
         b. The Lord will restore Israel (10:6–12)
         c. Lament over the destruction of Lebanon (11:1–3)
      v. The two shepherds (11:4–17)
         a. Zechariah's commission (vv. 4–6)
         b. The sign of the shepherds' staffs (vv. 7–14)
         c. Zechariah commissioned a second time (vv. 15–17)
   B. Second oracle (12 – 14)
      i. Future deliverance of Jerusalem (12:1–14)
         a. God defends Judah and Jerusalem (vv. 1–9)

COMMENTARY

1. PRELUDE: A CALL TO RETURN TO THE LORD (1:1–6)

A. Superscription (1:1)

Context
The literary form of the opening verse is that of superscription, a formal statement of taxonomy prefixed to a literary work that serves to classify the literature by genre (in this case as an oracular or a prophetic text) and to identify the author, audience, date and sometimes the occasion prompting the message from God, as well as the source of the prophetic revelation – God himself. It is understood as distinct from an introduction in that the superscription stands outside the body of literature it prefaces.[1] It is unclear whether these superscriptions were added by the author or by later editors during the process of collecting and arranging the contents of the OT canon.

---

1. On the contents and purpose of the superscription in prophetic literature, see Tucker (1977: 56–70, esp. 57–58).

The prelude to the book of Zechariah includes the superscription (1:1) and a prologue (1:2–6). The superscription highlights two important theological truths. First, the date formula roots the prophet's message in a particular time and space, and affirms God as the sovereign ruler of history. He is the one who determines the course of world events and removes and establishes kings (Dan. 2:21). The precision of the date formulas also serves as a touchstone for future messages from God announced by the prophet.

Secondly, we learn that God willingly communicates with humanity by giving messages to particular individuals who herald and publish this divine revelation through speeches and writings. God's ability to communicate with human beings sets him apart from the idols of false religions who cannot hear or speak (cf. Isa. 46:5–7). His omniscience makes him unique: alone as God and without rival (Isa. 43:10–13).

Comment

1. The date formula of the superscription to Zechariah assigns the first set of sermons to the *eighth month of the second year of Darius*, king of Persia (or roughly Oct–Nov of 520 BC). King Darius I (Hystaspes) ruled Persia from 522 to 486 BC. The post-exilic prophets Haggai and Zechariah dated their prophecies with precision during the days of Persian rule, because earlier Isaiah had foreseen the importance of King Cyrus and the Persians to the fortunes of elect Israel (Isa. 45:1–13). The two subsequent date formulas include the day of the month (1:7; 7:1). Since this is the only date in Zechariah that falls within Haggai's chronology, further specificity was unnecessary.[2]

The prophetic word formula, *the word of the LORD came*, introduces a prophetic revelation in the OT and classifies the book of Zechariah as prophetic or oracular literature (cf. 1:1, 7; 4:6, 8; 6:9; 7:1, 4, 8; 8:1). The formula serves both to legitimate the recipient of the divine revelation and to lend authority to the prophet's message as the revealed word of God. The frequent use of the speech formula

---

2. Meyers and Meyers (1987: 90–91).

in Zechariah (and the Hag-Zech-Mal corpus) is intended to demonstrate the continuity of the message of the post-exilic prophets with earlier Hebrew prophetic tradition.

Next, the recipient of this divine word is named, *the prophet Zechariah*. His name means 'YHWH remembers', and this is fitting, since he both encourages his audience with the truth that YHWH has remembered his covenant with Israel by restoring them in the land, and calls them to remember (and act upon) the words of God's previous prophetic messengers. The term *prophet* (Heb. *nābî*) designates Zechariah as an emissary, one who speaks with the authority of the commissioning agent – in this case God himself. The genealogy of Zechariah suggests that he was a member of the tribe of Levi and served in Jerusalem as both a priest and a prophet (see 2. The prophet Zechariah, p. 106).

Meaning
The superscription to Zechariah legitimizes the prophet as a divine messenger and validates the authority of his message as the word of God to post-exilic Judah.

B. Prologue: The call to return to God … for a change (1:2–6)

Context
The prologue (1:2–6) contains multiple layers of material from earlier OT prophets, either by way of quotation or allusion, in a pastiche of prophetic discourse.[3] This rather generalized appeal to the earlier prophetic tradition enables the audience to hear echoes of a similar message from several different OT prophets, depending upon their knowledge and familiarity with *the earlier prophets* (1:4). Boda (2004: 176) observes that 'although difficult to follow, it [the prologue] reflects a rhetorical trend in later prophecy in which Yahweh is emphasized as the source of prophetic speech, even if that is at the expense of flow'. The prelude to Zechariah (1:1–6) is widely recognized as an introduction to the first half of

---

3. See Petersen (1984: 110); Wenzel (2011: 46–60).

the book (chs. 1 – 8),[4] if not the entire book of Zechariah.[5]

Previously, Haggai's audience assumed the time had not yet come to rebuild the Lord's temple (Hag. 1:2). Apparently, the restoration community in Jerusalem was still struggling to establish itself politically and economically. Yet Zechariah, Haggai's contemporary, also discerned that the real issue was one of self-interest, when he proclaimed that the people were eating and drinking just to please themselves (Zech. 7:6; cf. Hag. 1:4). Zechariah was well aware of the economic austerity of the times (cf. Zech. 8:10, *Before that time* [i.e. before work had begun on the Second Temple] *there were no wages for man or beast*). Like Hosea, however, he knew that now *it is time to seek the LORD* (Hos. 10:12).

Comment

2. The OT prophets are not averse to ascribing anger and wrath to God (*The LORD was very angry with your forefathers*). God is a personal being, capable of instances of spontaneous love and anger. The emotion of God's anger is often described as an inward fire that erupts and burns with an unquenchable intensity (cf. Jer. 4:4; 23:19). God's anger issues out of his holiness, the essential attribute of his character (Ps. 93:5; Isa. 6:3; Rev. 4:8). The objects of God's wrath are those who oppose him, those travelling the path of wickedness (Ps. 1:4–6). Since God is also righteous, his anger is just (Ps. 11:7; Isa. 1:27; 5:16). Ultimately, God's wrath is divine retribution against the sins committed by humanity. This means his anger is not capricious or arbitrary, but rather it is a 'legitimate reaction to the transgression of known stipulations'.[6] The covenantal context of Zechariah's call to repentance alludes to the use of the word in Deuteronomy 29:28 and Jeremiah 21:5, where God's anger burned against the Israelites because they had broken faith with the Lord and had worshipped other gods. The Lord is a jealous God; he will not give his glory to

---

4. E.g. Baldwin (1972: 91).

5. Cf. Meyers and Meyers (1987: 98); Boda (2004: 181); and Wenzel (2011: 55–58). On intertextuality more generally in Zechariah 1 – 8, see Stead (2009).

6. Eichrodt (1967: 260).

another (Deut. 32:16, 21; Isa. 42:8; 48:11). Thankfully, the Lord is a merciful and gracious God, patient and slow to anger (Exod. 34:6; Nah. 1:3). It is worth noting, according to Zechariah, that the people acknowledged that they had received what they deserved (v. 6). The word *forefathers* (lit. 'fathers') is an inclusive reference to the Hebrew community of past generations ('ancestors', so NLT).

3. *This is what the LORD Almighty says.* The construction constitutes the *messenger formula* in prophetic speech and signifies the oral transmission of a message by a third party. The phrase suggests the divine assembly or council of the gods in Ancient Near Eastern thought. The messenger of the council stands as an observer in council sessions and then reports to others what he has heard as an envoy of the council.[7] For this reason, the verb of 'speaking' is better rendered according to its past-tense form: 'Thus said the LORD of Hosts' (so JPSV). The messenger formula occurs twenty times in Zechariah and ninety-one times in total in the Hag-Zech-Mal corpus. The expression places emphasis on the divine source and authority of the message, and the heavy repetition of the formula in the post-exilic prophets may have served to connect their ministries and messages to the earlier Hebrew prophetic tradition. Calling attention to such continuity may have been helpful in defusing a possible crisis concerning the prophetic word in the minds of some in Haggai's audience. The people had returned to the land of Judah more than twenty years earlier, and yet the promises of Jeremiah and Ezekiel regarding Israel's restoration after the Babylonian exile remained unfulfilled (cf. Jer. 31:31–33; 33:14–16; Ezek. 34:23–24; 37:24–28).

The divine title *LORD Almighty* is widely used in prophetic literature and occurs more than fifty times in Zechariah. The expression is often understood as a construct-genitive relationship: 'the LORD of Hosts' (KJV, the Heb. word *ṣĕbā'ôt*, meaning 'host, army, warrior'). More precisely, the construction is one of absolute nouns in apposition, perhaps conveying a verbal force: 'Yahweh *creates* [angel] armies.'[8] In either case, the epithet emphasizes 'the

---

7. See *ABD* 2: 214–217.

8. *TDOT* 5: 515.

invincible might behind the Lord's commands'.[9]

In contexts expressing covenant relationship, the word *return* (Heb. *šûb*, v. 3) is the OT term for repentance, and signifies an 'about-face' or a complete turnabout on the part of the person repenting. The expression connotes a change or shift in loyalty away from sin and self and towards God, a reorientation to YHWH and his covenant demands. The imperative form of the verb conveys a sense of urgency and places a demand for immediate and specific action on the part of those so addressed. The fourfold repetition of the word *return* or *turn* (in vv. 3–4) serves only to heighten this sense of urgency. The liturgical formula in the prophetic summons to repentance (*return to me and I will return to you*) is repeated in Malachi 3:7 and has a precursor in Isaiah's plea to Jerusalem to *return to me [God], for I have redeemed you* (Isa. 44:22). The language of the liturgical formula may be rooted in the penitential prayers of the Psalms (e.g. Pss 80:3, 7, 14, 19; 85:4–8).[10]

4. Zechariah refers generally to God's prophets who preceded him (*the earlier prophets*), but the historical context (the recent repatriation of Judah after the Babylonian exile) and the allusions in his messages to themes of repentance and covenant renewal suggest he has especially the prophets Isaiah (cf. Isa. 45:22), Jeremiah (cf. Jer. 18:11) and Ezekiel (cf. Ezek. 33:11) in mind.[11] The word pair *ways* and *practices* often signifies a lifestyle in prophetic literature. The dispositions of the hearts and minds of the people, as well as their deeds, were bent towards evil.[12]

The combination of the word pair *listen* and *pay attention*, in context with terms for God's law, connotes obedience, or in this case, the lack thereof ('but they would not listen to me or obey me', TEV).[13] Nehemiah rehearses the same summary of Israel's failure to *listen* and *pay attention* to the Lord's commands (Neh. 9:29, 34).

5. The two rhetorical questions of verse 5 reintroduce the two

---

9. Baldwin (1972: 42).
10. Cf. Petersen (1984: 131); and Boda (2004: 174–175).
11. See the discussion in Boda (2004: 181).
12. See Boda (2004: 179).
13. Cf. McComiskey (1998: 1030).

parties discussed previously, the *ancestors* and the *prophets*. The first question 'inspires at least two different possible answers – they are in exile or they are dead'.[14] Assuming the former, the word *ancestors* (see v. 2 above) is a reference to the people of Israel (2 Kgs 17:13–14) and Judah (2 Chr. 36:15–16) who were swept into exile because they were stubborn and refused to believe the word of the Lord. The same expression is found in King Hezekiah's 'Passover Letter' calling the people of Israel and Judah to return to the Lord (2 Chr. 30:7). Assuming the latter, the *ancestors* were those who *sinned and are no more* (Lam. 5:7). It is likely here that Zechariah's intentionally ambiguous speech is designed to prompt both responses in his audience.

The answer to the second rhetorical questions is: Indeed, no, 'the *prophets* were mortals'. Petersen (1984: 134) makes an important observation about the prophets who obeyed God and yet suffered the same fate as those who rejected God's word: 'Both obedient and disobedient humans belong together in one set when distinguished from the set of realia mentioned in v. 6 – "my words and my statutes".'

6. The word pair *words* and *decrees* alters slightly the language of Deuteronomy 28:15 which stands behind the statement. The substitution of the term *words* for the more common *commandments* (Heb. *miṣwâ*) 'has special force in this Call for Obedience', since it continues the linking of the law issued at Sinai and prophecy in later Hebrew tradition.[15] Like its earlier counterpart, the phrase concretizes the enduring power and authority of God's will.

The word *servant* was a title for Moses, the archetype of the OT prophet (Deut. 34:5; cf. Deut. 18:15; Mal. 4:4). The true servant obeys the instructions of the master or overlord. A key trait of the OT prophets was their obedience to God's word, making the story of Jonah all the more unusual (cf. Jon. 3:3). Jesus Christ, the ultimate Prophet, demonstrated this same relationship to his Father (John 5:19–20; 12:49–50).

The verb *overtake* alludes to the covenant curses of the Mosaic

---

14. Petersen (1984: 133).
15. Meyers and Meyers (1987: 96); cf. Boda (2004: 179).

law, pursuing and overtaking those who refuse to obey God's commands (Deut. 28:15, 45).

The repetition of the verb *repented* revisits the key theme of repentance established in the introduction (v. 3) and sets the tone for the book.

The resumption of the language of verse 4 lacks the adjective *evil*, perhaps suggesting 'the sins of the present era are less outrageous than those of the pre-exilic age'.[16] The admission that God's punishment of Israel's covenant disobedience was just reflects the genuine contrition of the Hebrews after the Babylonian exile, and is a feature of penitential prayers in the post-exilic period (cf. Lam. 1:18; Neh. 9:33).[17] The verb *determined* indicates that what God had 'purposed' (NEB) or 'planned to do' (NLT, NRSV) was accomplished, namely punishing Israel for violating his covenant with them. The curses of the Mosaic covenant did indeed overtake them (Deut. 28; cf. Jer. 4:28; Lam. 2:17). Yet Zechariah offers hope to his audience, because even as God had *determined* to bring disaster on Israel, he has also *determined* to do good again to Jerusalem and Judah (8:14–15).

Meaning

The prologue advances the thesis or theme of Zechariah's message, namely repentance: *Return to me* [the LORD Almighty], *and I will return to you* (v. 3). It also introduces an important theological tenet that undergirds the prophet's visions, sermons and oracles: God accomplishes what he *determines* to do (v. 6).

---

16. Meyers and Meyers (1987: 97).
17. Cf. Boda (2004: 180).

2. ZECHARIAH'S VISIONS (1:7 – 6:15)

Context

Zechariah's 'book of visions' (1:7 – 6:15) contains eight revelations from God, proclaiming a coming age of salvation and restoration for the Hebrew community in post-exilic Judah. The structure of the night visions follows a standard pattern for this form of visionary literature. The simple outline includes: (a) an introductory statement; (b) followed by a description of the vision the prophet sees; (c) the prophet then asks for an interpretation of the vision; and (d) an interpreting angel provides an explanation of the meaning of the vision. The date formula (1:7) indicates that Zechariah's series of eight visions occurred during a single night, two months after Haggai's final two oracles promising a return of the divine presence and a great shaking of the cosmos (Hag. 2:10–19, 20–23). The timing suggests that God is now advancing the programme of restoration announced by Haggai.

The first vision depicts God's concern for Jerusalem (vv. 7–15), and the supporting oracle of response (vv. 16–17) confirms God's intentions to rebuild his temple and restore the prosperity of the city. The vision opens with a scene of troops of riders upon horses of various colours patrolling the earth (vv. 8–11). There is some question as to the identity of the characters portrayed in the vision. The *man* on the red horse among the myrtle trees is later addressed as *the angel of the LORD* (v. 11). The unnamed *angel* (vv. 9, 13–14) is a divine messenger who guides Zechariah through the vision and interprets the symbolic action witnessed by the prophet. It is assumed that the troops of riders are also angelic beings of some unnamed sort or classification.

A. A man among the myrtle trees (1:7–17)

Comment

1:7. This second message to the prophet Zechariah occurs approximately three months after the date formula given in verse 1 (see commentary for 1:1, p. 124). This second *word of the LORD* takes the form of revelatory experiences in a series of night visions, apparently during a single evening (cf. 4:1). The date formula of verse 7 governs all eight of the visions given to Zechariah (1:7 – 6:15). *Shebat*, the eleventh month of the Jewish calendar, overlaps the months of January/February in our Julian calendar.

8. The clause (*During the night I had a vision*) is a technical expression that means 'to receive revelation from God' and implies more than mere human insight (cf. Isa. 30:10). Rather, this experience is the result of divine inspiration and indicates that the prophet actually saw and heard the communication from God in some sort of 'virtual reality'.

The participial form of the verb *riding* is better understood as 'mounted' (so NJPS, NIV 2011), since the horse and rider are stationary. Mason (1977: 36) connects the myrtle trees to the entrance of heaven, since *myrtle trees* represent the abode of the gods in Ancient Near Eastern mythology. Baldwin (1972: 101) is probably closer to a correct understanding in simply associating the myrtle tress with the Kidron valley outside Jerusalem. The Lord had returned to the outskirts of the city, symbolically speaking, but had not yet entered Jerusalem because the Second Temple was still under construction.

The specific colours of the horses (*red, brown and white horses*) are the subject of some debate, as we learn from visionary literature elsewhere in the Bible that the colours of horses sometimes convey symbolic meaning (cf. Rev. 6:1–18). The colours, however, are insignificant to the meaning of this vision. The patrolling of the earth by these angelic riders simply indicates that God is still concerned about Jerusalem.[1]

9. The unnamed interpreting *angel* is a divine messenger who guides Zechariah through the night visions and explains the symbolic actions of the various scenes the prophet witnesses. Daniel had a similar experience with an interpreting angel (cf. Dan. 8:15–19; 10:14).

10–11. *The man standing among the myrtle trees* explains the significance of the horses in response to the question posed by Zechariah. 'They are the ones the LORD has sent out to patrol the earth' (NLT). The particular form of the verb 'patrol' simply denotes movement back and forth. The expression suggests a relentless criss-crossing and ongoing scrutiny of the earth by these angelic sentinels (cf. Job 1:7; 2:2, where Satan is included among the angels who roam the earth and report back to the Lord).

And they reported to the angel of the LORD, who was standing among the myrtle trees (v. 11a). The unnamed man sitting on a red horse among the *myrtle trees* (v. 8) is given the title of *the angel of the LORD*. This person has the ability to reveal directly information ordinarily hidden to human beings, so it seems the word *angel* or *messenger* (Heb. *mal'āk*) signifies a heavenly being rather than a mortal. Often the appearance of *the angel of the LORD* in the OT is associated with action on behalf of the nation of Israel. At times this angel may be a manifestation of God himself (e.g. Gen. 16:13; Judg. 13:21–22), or at other times a divine being distinguished from God (perhaps Jesus Christ pre-incarnate, cf. Exod. 23:23; 32:34; 1 Chr. 21:27).

The report of the angelic sentinels is one of cosmic peace: 'the whole earth is tranquil and at rest' (v. 11b, NAB). This may mean that King Darius has quelled the revolts across the Persian Empire that greeted his succession to the throne. It may also signify that,

---

1. See the discussions in Baldwin (1972: 100, 146–149); Petersen (1984: 140–143); and Redditt (1995: 52–53).

although God has not yet done so, he will soon begin his campaign of 'eschatological reversal'.[2] Petersen (1984: 146) comments: '[T]here is no disturbance, whether by earthly or divine agents. For most Israelites at most times in their history, this message would have been utterly welcome. Not so this time.'

12–13. The direction of the discourse is somewhat circuitous, as *the angel of the LORD* addresses the *LORD Almighty* (v. 12a), who then responds to the interpreting angel accompanying Zechariah (v. 13). *'LORD Almighty, how long will you withhold mercy from Jerusalem and from the towns of Judah?'* (v. 12b). The divine title *LORD Almighty* identifies YHWH as 'the sovereign judge who remains in control of the discipline of his covenant people'.[3] The interrogative phrase *How long?* is a technical expression often found in Hebrew laments (e.g. Pss 6:3; 13:1–2; 79:5). It is used here as 'a rhetorical form that is designed to elicit a response from the deity and to call attention to the plight of the now incomplete … temple complex'.[4] The query laments the suspension of YHWH's *mercy* or 'compassion' (so NEB; 'withhold pardon', NJPS) for his chosen people (since this is one of his defining attributes, cf. Exod. 34:6–7). The question addresses the rationale behind the delay in realizing the promises of restoration for Israel after the Babylonian exile announced earlier by Jeremiah and Ezekiel (e.g. Jer. 33:6–11; Ezek. 36:24–36). The word pair *Jerusalem* and *towns of Judah* refers to those people inhabiting Jerusalem proper, and the cities of Judah point to 'a regional notion of community, not simply an exclusive urban focus on Jerusalem'.[5]

The *seventy years* of God's anger against Jerusalem and Judah (v. 12) is a reference to the duration of the Babylonian exile announced by Jeremiah (Jer. 25:11–12; 29:10). The precise reckoning of the seventy-year time period for the Babylonian exile is a matter of some debate. If Daniel was taken captive during the first Babylonian invasion of Judah (c. 605 BC), then the exile lasted approximately

---

2. So Redditt (1995: 51).

3. Boda (2004: 197).

4. Petersen (1984: 147).

5. Ibid., p. 149.

sixty-six years, and the number seventy is a round figure (placing the decree of Cyrus in 539 BC).

The *kind* or 'gracious' speech (so ESV, NRSV; lit. 'good words') are *comforting words* (v. 13), signalling that YHWH is about to act and again have compassion on his people. Presumably the encouraging message heard by the interpreting angel is the word Zechariah is commanded to proclaim (vv. 14–17).

14. The imperative verb *proclaim* means to 'shout' (NLT) or 'cry out' (KJV), after the manner of a herald or street preacher.[6] The word *jealous* (Heb. *qānā'*) is a highly emotive term (cf. NJB, 'burning with jealousy') signifying God's zeal, 'one of the basic elements of the OT conception of God'.[7] God's passionate love for Jerusalem can be traced to the promises he made through Moses to establish 'a place for his name' (Deut. 12:11; 14:23). As a result of King David's conquest of Jerusalem and his vision for a temple of YHWH to be built there, that city became the place where God's name was honoured (cf. 1 Kgs 8:29, 48). God loves Jerusalem because that is where he lives (Ps. 76:2). Mount Zion is his home on earth, because the symbol of his divine presence, the ark of the covenant, is housed in the temple (Ps. 74:2). This means that God maintained order in the cosmos and ruled over the nations of the earth from his holy city Jerusalem – the city he loves more than any other city (Pss 78:68; 87:2). The place names Jerusalem and Zion are distinct and complementary entities, with Jerusalem a broader term signifying the territories ruled by the Judean kings, and Zion the site of Yahweh's temple.[8]

15. Petersen associates the nations that 'enjoy their ease' (NEB) with *the whole world at rest and in peace* (v. 11, NIV): 'The nations as instruments of Yahweh's purpose have overstepped their bounds.'[9] Since God had already orchestrated the downfall of the nations of Assyria and Babylonia by Zechariah's time, the threat of divine

---

6. Cf. Redditt (1995: 55).

7. *NIDOTTE* 3: 938; see also the discussion of the word 'jealousy' in Baldwin (1972: 108–109).

8. Meyers and Meyers (1987: 121).

9. Petersen (1984: 154).

wrath against the 'complacent nations' (NAB) may be a warning to
Persia. By comparison, God was only 'mildly angry' (NJB) with
Israel's pre-exilic ancestors. His zeal for his people Israel is
evidenced in the degree of his anger against the nations, when
measured against the punishment he inflicted upon Israel and Judah.
The nations (especially Assyria and Babylonia) were excessive in
their destruction of the divided Hebrew kingdoms of Israel and
Judah ('but they overdid the punishment', NJPS; 'they heaped evil
on evil', NEB; cf. Isa. 10:5–19; 47:5–7; Jer. 51:24). 'The implication
was that they would be punished for making the disaster worse than
God intended, or Jerusalem deserved.'[10]

16. The re-entry of YHWH (presumably *the man among the myrtle
trees*, 1:8) into Jerusalem, and his habitation of the restored temple,
links the first vision to God's promise to return to his people if they
turn to him (1:3). The fact that YHWH returns with 'mercy' or
'compassion' (NEB, NJB) answers the question posed in 1:12 and
connects Zechariah's message with the future glory of Zion
envisioned by Isaiah (e.g. Isa. 54:7–8; 60:10) and Jeremiah (e.g. Jer.
30:18).

The declaration that YHWH's *house* or 'temple' (NJB) will be
rebuilt both echoes and complements Haggai's charge to commence
with the reconstruction of the Jerusalem sanctuary (cf. Hag. 1:13–
15). 'But Zechariah's message moves in new directions … He places
more emphasis on the divine and human inhabitants of the temple
structure.'[11] The return of the Divine Presence to Jerusalem marks
the end of the Babylonian exile (cf. Ezek. 43:5). Such a view permits
an understanding of the seventy years of Babylonian exile (cf. Jer.
25:11–12; 29:10) as both the length of time the Hebrews were exiled
from the land of covenant promise (c. 605–587 BC) and the period
that Israel is without the Jerusalem temple (c. 587–515 BC, assuming
the rededication of the Second Temple in c. 515 BC).

The *measuring line* was a string used to mark the foundation lines
of walls and buildings (cf. Ezek. 40:1–3). The stretching of the
builder's string refers to general layout and design more than to

---

10. Redditt (1995: 56).
11. Boda (2004: 56).

actual detailed measurements (cf. Job 38:5; Jer. 31:39). 'The word functions as a metonymy for the whole process of rebuilding. By speaking of the initial step, the prophet refers to the entire project.'[12]

17. The word *again* is repeated four times in verse 17. The repetition speaks to the certainty of God's intention to restore Jerusalem and 'the renewing of an already existing bond between God and the people'.[13] The verb *overflow* usually means 'to scatter' (e.g. Gen. 11:4) or 'disperse in defeat' (e.g. Num. 10:35). The use of the word in this context suggests the image found in Proverbs 5:16 of water spilling out of a spring. The term *prosperity* is literally 'good things' (NEB), and alludes to the blessings of the Mosaic covenant (cf. Deut. 28:11) and Jeremiah's promise of restoration (Jer. 32:42–44).

Zechariah promises the people *comfort*, a term that often connotes consolation and healing empathy during times of mourning and bereavement. It is a theme in biblical prophecy which sought to deal with the suffering and anguish of the destruction of Judah and Jerusalem by the Babylonians (cf. Isa. 40:1–2; 52:9; 66:13). The verb *choose* alludes to God's covenant with Abram (cf. Neh. 9:7), and is specifically 'linked to the function of the first temple as the place of God's presence'.[14] The post-exilic Hebrew community needed to know that the Babylonian exile had not rendered God's election of Israel null and void. The oracle concluding the first night vision (vv. 14–17) sets a tone of encouragement and a theme of hope for the rest of the book. The repetition of the messenger formula (*This is what the LORD Almighty says*, vv. 14, 16, 17) accents the divine authority invested in the prophet's message.

Meaning

The gist of the prophet's first vision is summarized in verses 16–17. The Lord will return to Jerusalem in mercy, his temple will be rebuilt, Jerusalem and its environs will be restored to prosperity, and

---

12. Ibid., p. 200.
13. Redditt (1995: 56).
14. Boda (2004: 201).

God's people will experience the comfort of reaffirmation of divine election.

B. Four horns and four blacksmiths (1:18–21 [MT 2:1–4])

Context

The second vision, using the symbols of animal horns and craftsmen, forecasts retribution for the nations that have waged war against and scattered Israel.

Comment

18. The expression *Then I looked up* (lit. 'I lifted my eyes and I saw') indicates that the prophet was 'engrossed in thinking over all he had been hearing until another vision caught his attention' (note the repetition of the phrase in Zech. 2:1; 5:1; 6:1).[15]

The *horn* (Heb. *qeren*) was a symbol of power and authority in the biblical world and may represent an individual (e.g. 1 Sam. 2:1), a dynasty (e.g. 1 Sam. 2:10) or a nation (as in v. 19). In prophetic visions, the *horn* is commonly used in biblical prophecy to designate a king or a leader of a nation (often represented by a horn attached to an animal, e.g. Dan. 7:8; 8:8). It would seem that Zechariah has animal horns in mind in the retelling of his vision, although the context suggests metal horns of some kind (rather than ivory), since blacksmiths are summoned to beat the horns down and destroy them (v. 20). It is possible that the horns of Zechariah's vision were horned crowns or even royal battle standards of some sort used as emblems for the nations.[16]

19. The four *horns* of Zechariah's vision may represent four specific nations, or the number may be used symbolically to signify the totality or complete roster of nations guilty of oppressing Israel. Of the four beasts of Daniel's vision, only the Babylonian Empire has come and gone at the time of Zechariah's preaching (cf. Dan. 2:36–39; 7:17). Persia, Daniel's two-horned ram (Dan. 8:20), was currently on the scene as the dominant power of the Ancient Near

15. Baldwin (1972: 110).
16. So Meyers and Meyers (1987: 136).

East.[17] It seems likely, then, that Zechariah makes reference to those nations responsible for the destruction of the kingdoms of Israel (finally in 722 BC) and Judah (finally in 587 BC) and the deportation of the Hebrew citizens from those kingdoms.

Naturally, Assyria and Babylonia were among the *four horns* to be cut down, since they conquered and exiled the Hebrew kingdoms of Israel and Judah respectively (cf. 2 Kgs 17:24–25; 25:1–2). Other nations oppressing the Hebrews included Egypt and Greece, both mentioned in Zechariah (9:13; 10:10–11). Babylonia overthrew Assyria, and Persia overthrew Babylonia, which points to the conclusion that the divine judgment of the nations accused of scattering and humbling Israel was already well underway. One wonders if the prophet Malachi had Zechariah 1:18–21 in mind in his reference to the overthrow of Edom, one of the nations condemned for allying with the Babylonians against the Judean kingdom (Mal. 1:4–5; cf. Ps. 137:7–8). God's use of the nations for the purpose of accomplishing both the punishment of the wicked and purification of the righteous is part of the mystery of his work as Sovereign Lord of history. God's rule of human history to accomplish his redemptive purposes is declared by Daniel (2:21) and acknowledged by the prophets (Isa. 14:24–27).

20. The word *craftsmen* ('smiths', NJPS, NJB; 'blacksmiths', NAB, NRSV) is used generally of an artisan of any sort (e.g. mason, carpenter, smith, etc.). If the horns representing the nations are made of metal (cf. 1 Kgs 22:11), then the blacksmith is the appropriate craftsman for the task of destroying the horns (cf. 2 Chr. 24:12; Isa. 44:12).

21. The word rendered *throw down* (NIV) is a unique form of a rare word in the OT. The word implies that the horns are cut off or cut down, and then thrown to the ground (cf. NJPS, 'these men have come to throw them into a panic, to hew down the horns of the nations'). Since *horns* were symbolic of the power and authority of nations in the biblical world, the hewing down and trampling of these horns depicts an end to their authority and rule.

---

17. Meyers and Meyers (1987: 136–37) argue against including Persia among those nations about to be overthrown.

Meaning

The meaning of the second vision is plainly stated: God plans to bring his judgment against the nations responsible for destroying Jerusalem and exiling Judah (1:21 [MT 2:4]). This declaration of retribution makes explicit the earlier threat of punishment voiced in God's anger with the nations enjoying peace and security at the expense of the Hebrews (1:15). In terms of the sequence of events, the vision suggests that the restoration of Jerusalem will follow the overthrow of these aggressor nations.

C. A man with a measuring line (2:1–5 [MT 2:5–9])

Context

The third vision injects two new developments in the sequence of Zechariah's visions. First, the scope of the vision narrows from the cosmos in vision one, to the nations in vision two, and finally to the city of Jerusalem. Second, the prophet moves from an observer on the sidelines to a participant in the action of the world of the vision (by addressing a question directly to the man with a measuring line, v. 2). The vision is another salvation message and consists of two parts: the vision itself (vv. 1–3) and the oracle of response explaining the meaning of the vision (vv. 4–5). Taken together, the second and third visions portray God as working in timely and significant ways to guarantee the protection of his people.[18]

Comment

2:1. It is unclear whether this *man with a measuring line in his hand* is another angel or a human being, although the word *man* suggests a human being. The word used here for *measuring line* is different from the one found in 1:16 above. This is the only occurrence of the two-word phrase in the OT. The function of this *measuring line* appears to be that of a surveyor's line used to delineate an area or divide tracts of land, rather than the 'builder's string' (1:16) used in the construction process.

2. The infinitive verbal forms (*to measure* and *to find out*) are

18. Baldwin (1972: 112).

ambiguous with respect to time and so may apply either to the then-present Jerusalem (*it is*, so NIV, NLT) or to the city in some indefinite future time ('it is to be', so JPSV). Marking out the boundaries of the city was logical, since the people were involved in a major rebuilding project with the restoration of the Jerusalem temple and the reconstruction of homes in the city precincts.[19] Given the Samaritan opposition to the Hebrew return to Judah after the Babylonian exile (Ezra 4:1–5), it would be natural to repair the defensive wall around the city in order to protect their renewed urban assets. Redditt's discussion of the purpose of the *measuring line* is cogent, since elsewhere the measuring line was a symbol of judgment (in the partitioning of Samaria by foreigners and in the destruction of Jerusalem; Amos 7:17; 2 Kgs 21:13).[20] Zechariah and his accompanying interpreting angel are soon assured by a second angelic being that the measuring line symbolizes blessing – not judgment (vv. 3–6).

3. The interpreting angel who was accompanying Zechariah through the series of visions (cf. 1:9) departed to greet another angelic being. Apparently the answer to the prophet's question by the man with the measuring line prompted an immediate response from the heavenly realm. The opening emphatic interjection (lit. 'behold' or 'see!') is usually rendered *then* in contemporary EVV (so NIV, NRSV; cf. ESV, 'And behold'). McComiskey (1998: 1051) rightly calls attention to the suspense created by this meeting of angelic figures and what it might bode for Zechariah and his people.

4. The sense of urgency attached to the message of the second angel is reflected in the pair of imperative verbs, *run* and *tell*. The reference to that *man* ('young man', NEB) is ambiguous. Merrill (1994: 115) identifies the *young man* with Zechariah the prophet. It seems more likely that the *young man* is the *man with a measuring line* (2:1), since Jerusalem will one day exist without walls: 'To measure it now would be premature and to measure it then would be impossible.'[21]

---

19. Boda (2004: 221).

20. Redditt (1995: 58).

21. McComiskey (1998: 1053); cf. Petersen (1984: 169); and Baldwin (1972: 112), who comments, 'The very understandable reasoning of the surveyor

The oracle of response (vv. 4–5) makes several startling claims, including: Jerusalem will exist without walls; a large number of people and animals will populate the city; the Lord will be a wall of fire around Jerusalem; and the glory of God will reside in the city. All this stood in stark contrast to the city as Zechariah knew it, with the temple reduced to a rubble heap, the city walls in disrepair and the people opting to live outside the confines of Jerusalem. The phrase 'as villages without walls' (ESV) translates the plural form of a rather rare word in the OT (lit. 'open, rural country'). While the syntax of the expression is awkward, the meaning is clear: 'Jerusalem won't have any boundaries. It will be too full of people and animals even to have a wall' (CEV).[22]

5. The final two claims of the oracle of response address the issue of the protection of Jerusalem, since walls were essential fortifications for cities of any size and importance in the ancient world. The symbolic representation of divine protection in the *wall of fire* calls to mind the pillar of fire that led the Hebrews in their exodus from Egypt (Exod. 13:21–22) and the ring of horses and chariots of fire that surrounded Elisha when the king of Aram sent troops to capture God's prophet (2 Kgs 6:17).[23] God's presence in the midst of his people is an OT theme that begins with the call to build the tabernacle (Exod. 25:8), finds expression in Ezekiel's vision of God's glory being restored in the Jerusalem temple (Ezek. 43:1–5), and is the focal point of Zechariah's first vision and a trajectory for the book as a whole (1:16; cf. 14:16). The association of divine

---

is not in keeping with God's purpose, which is declared by another angel … to Zechariah's interpreting angel.'

22. See the full discussion in Petersen (1984: 170–177).

23. Jeremias (1977: 174) (as cited in Petersen [1984: 171] links the wall of fire to the motif of the divine guardian of Eden. Petersen connects the image to the Persian unwalled royal city of Pasargadae, which was surrounded by fire altars representing the protective presence of their god Ahura Mazda; cf. Boda (2004: 224). Webb (2003: 81) associates the wall of fire with the protecting presence of God in the pillar of fire accompanying the Hebrews at the time of the exodus from Egypt (cf. Exod. 14:19–20).

presence in a city with protection by the deity (or deities) was found among the Sumerians and other people groups of the biblical world.[24]

Meaning
Zechariah envisions a day when a restored Jerusalem will experience God's presence in the form of a protecting *wall of fire* without and its very *glory* within (v. 5).

D. The exiles are called home (2:6–13 [MT 2:10–17])

Context
God's call for the return of the Hebrew exiles from Babylonia is one of two oracles accompanying the visions of Zechariah (see also 6:9–15). The prophetic exhortation divides neatly into two parts: the first promises a restoration of God's people to the land of Israel (vv. 6–9), and the second promises the restoration of God's presence with his people in Jerusalem (vv. 10–13).

The first message of the accompanying oracle continues the theme of divine protection emphasized in the third vision (v. 8; cf. 2:5). The reference to slaves plundering their oppressors echoes events associated with the Hebrew exodus from Egypt, when God predisposed the Egyptians to pay the Israelites to leave their land (v. 9; cf. Exod. 11:2–3; 12:35–36). The second message anticipates the fourth vision – the cleansing of the high priest as a necessary preparation for welcoming God's presence back to Jerusalem (3:1–10).

Comment
2:6. The repeated interjection (Heb. *hôy*) is translated variously as 'Ho!' (KJV), 'Up!' (NAB, NRSV), 'Away' (JPSV), *Come! Come!* (NIV), 'Come away!' (NLT). The emphatic construction, coupled with the divine oracle speech formula (*declares the LORD*), carries the force of a promise.

The *land of the north* is a metaphor for the 'far reaches of the earth'

---

24. *BBCOT*: 800.

as well as a literal statement, since one needed to travel north (following the Tigris and Euphrates river valleys) when moving from east to west (or vice versa) in the biblical world.[25] Military campaigns against the region of Syro-Palestine typically came from the *north*, which is why the prophets make reference to armies invading Israel from the north (cf. Isa. 41:25; Jer. 1:13–14; Ezek. 38:15). The *four winds of heaven* is a figure of speech for the four major points of the compass (cf. Ezek. 12:14; 37:9). The Hebrew exiles would return to Judah and Jerusalem from all directions.

7. Even as God *scattered* his people in the Babylonian exile (v. 6), the commands to *flee* (v. 6) and *escape* (v. 7) indicate that their return is his doing as well. The name *Zion* variously designates the Jerusalem temple, the Temple Mount, the city of Jerusalem, the land of Israel and the people of Israel. In the reference to the *Daughter of Zion* in verse 10, *Zion* here alludes to the people of Israel. The phrase *Daughter of Babylon* (lit. 'dweller in the daughter of Babylon') is a figure of speech for the collective inhabitants of a place.[26] The immediate context suggests the inhabitants addressed are the Hebrew exiles scattered throughout Babylonia.

8. The line, '(after his glory sent me) regarding the nations that plundered you' (NRSV), is especially difficult in Hebrew. It is possible that the word 'glory' refers to God ('since the Glory commissioned me', NJB; see 2:5), indicating that 'the Glory', or God himself, sent the prophet.[27] The cryptic phrase may also be construed in a temporal sense (*After he has honoured me and has sent me*, NIV; 'After a period of glory', NLT), or it may be descriptive of the prophet's commission ('when he sent me on a glorious mission', NEB; 'He who sent me after glory', JPSV). The gist of verse 8a speaks to the prophet's mission of pronouncing divine judgment against the nations who have plundered Israel, who are treasured by God.

The clause, *for whoever touches you touches the apple of his eye*, is sometimes translated 'the pupil of his eye' (so NJPS), since the word rendered *apple* or 'pupil' is related to the word group meaning (lit.)

---

25. See the discussion in Petersen (1984: 175).

26. Cf. Meyers and Meyers (1987: 164).

27. So Petersen (1984: 172, 173 n. d.); cf. Meyers and Meyers (1987: 162, 165).

'gate' (i.e. 'the gate of the eye' or the 'pupil').[28] The idiom may refer
to Israel as God's elect people and hence his 'precious possession'
(NLT). The expression may also refer to the one who harms Israel
('whoever touches you, touches the pupil of his own eye', NJPS)
and brings harm to himself in the form of divine judgment (i.e.
harming God's elect is equivalent to poking yourself in the eye!).

9. Zechariah envisions a day of reversal, when the oppressor and
plunderer will become the oppressed and plundered – a common
theme in the prophets (cf. Isa. 14:2; Jer. 14:12; Hab. 2:8). To 'wave
the hand' is a signal that will set in motion God's destructive 'action
against those who so much as touch his people'.[29]

The fulfilment of the prophetic word serves to legitimate the
prophet as God's true messenger (*Then you will know that the LORD
Almighty has sent me*; cf. Jer. 28:9).

10. The imperative verbs *shout* (or even 'Sing!', NAB, NJB) and *be
glad* (or 'Rejoice!' NEB, NLT) are both exclamations of triumphant
joy and expressions of worship (cf. Pss 67:4; 68:3; 92:4; 95:1). The
announcement of the imminent *coming* of the Lord is a repeated
theme in the post-exilic prophets (cf. Hag. 2:7; Mal. 3:1). Despite
his transcendent holiness, God desires to re-establish his 'address',
so to speak, among his people. The word *live* is the same verb used
in reference to God's intention to 'live' in the tabernacle (Exod.
25:8). This theme of the divine presence, showcasing the immanence of God, extends throughout Scripture, from the tabernacle of Moses (Exod. 25:8) to the restored creation (Rev. 21:3).
God's declaration to re-inhabit Jerusalem echoes the earlier promise
of 1:17. (On the divine oracle speech formula, *declares the LORD*, see
v. 6 above.)

11. The joining of the nations to the people of Israel in the Day
of the Lord is a repeated theme in the prophets (Isa. 66:18–21; Mic.
4:2), and in Zechariah 1 – 8 specifically (cf. Zech. 1:15, 21; 8:23). The
theme of YHWH's kingship over the nations frames the second half
of Zechariah (Zech. 9:10; 14:9). God's plan to bless all nations by
electing one nation as his special people is realized (cf. Gen. 12:1–3).

---

28. See McComiskey (1998: 1060–1061).
29. Meyers and Meyers (1987: 167).

The phrase *my people* is covenant terminology and speaks to the universalization of YHWH's covenant (cf. Isa. 56:6–7).[30] The joining of the nations to Israel informs the third night vision of the unwalled city of Jerusalem due to the numerous inhabitants.[31]

12. The verb 'possess' can mean *inherit* (so NIV, NRSV), or more appropriately in this context, 'take possession' ('The LORD will once again claim Judah as his own possession', NEB). Redditt (1995: 62) comments that the verb ('possess') and the noun *portion* 'were characteristically used of Israel, who would inherit the land from God as her portion, so Zechariah was employing conventional thinking with an ironic twist'. This is the only reference in the OT to the land of Israel as *the holy land*. The *land* was made *holy* by virtue of the association of God's glory and presence within the Jerusalem temple (cf. Pss 11:4; 15:1). God's abandonment and rejection of Jerusalem witnessed by Ezekiel is reversed, as 'he will again choose Jerusalem' (NAB; cf. Ezek. 10:18–22; 43:1–5). The verb *choose* reaffirms God's choosing or election of Abraham (cf. Gen. 12:1–3).

13. Like the English word 'hush', the imperative 'Be silent!' (Heb. *has*) is an onomatopoetic word 'and suits the rhetorical nature of prophetic oracles'.[32] The term denotes a reverent silence in God's presence, and connotes a call to be alert and discerning since God is about to act (cf. Hab. 2:20; Zeph. 1:7).

Meaning
God will regather his people scattered by the Babylonian exile (v. 6). Indeed, that second exodus has already begun, as remnants of the Hebrew people returned from exile have lived in Judah for two decades. More importantly, the Lord Almighty comes to *live among* his people (vv. 10–11) and restore Jerusalem (v. 12).

---

30. Meyers and Meyers (1987: 169).
31. Boda (2004: 238).
32. Meyers and Meyers (1987: 171).

E. Cleansing for the high priest (3:1–10)

Context

The fourth night vision depicts a heavenly courtroom, with the 'prosecuting attorney' (or *Satan*) accusing the defendant (*Joshua the high priest*) of being unfit for his priestly duties. The Lord is both 'defence attorney' and 'judge', and he censures the arguments of the prosecution, dismisses the case, and declares Joshua innocent by virtue of his divine election and cleansing. The *angel of the LORD* (v. 1) and *the LORD* (v. 2) seem to one and the same divine being (see commentary on 1:11, pp. 133–134). The vision unfolds in three movements: the removal of the high priest's filthy clothes (vv. 1–4); the dressing of the high priest in clean clothes (vv. 5–7); and the interpretation of the symbolic actions (vv. 8–10).

Comment

3:1. *Joshua the high priest* was a descendant of Levi and the son of Jehozadak, who was taken captive and deported to Babylonia when King Nebuchadnezzar sacked Jerusalem in 587 BC (cf. 1 Chr. 6:15). Joshua is also mentioned in Zechariah (3:1; 6:11), and later records indicate that some of his descendants were listed among those who married foreign women in the time of Ezra (Ezra 10:18). It is unclear whether Zerubbabel and Joshua were in the first wave of Hebrew emigrants who returned to Jerusalem soon after the decree of King Cyrus under the leadership of Sheshbazzar (Ezra 1:5–11; cf. 1:1–4), or if they led another caravan of Hebrew returnees to Jerusalem sometime around 522 BC (Ezra 2:2, 64–65; 3:1–13). It seems likely that Ezra 2 presents a composite emigration record spanning the years from the edict of Cyrus to the completion of the Second Temple. If so, then Zerubbabel and Joshua probably led a mass emigration of Hebrews back to Judah, prompted by the ascension of Darius I to the Persian throne in 522 BC.[33] This may explain the enthusiasm and vigour of the restoration community for the temple construction project (Hag. 1:12–15), since those more recent emigrants would not have been jaded by the previous

---

33. See Hill (1998: 69).

two decades of failure to rebuild the temple.

The construction of the word *Satan* (lit. 'the satan') designates a functionary of the heavenly court whose role it is to accuse human beings of wrongdoing. The title *Satan* and the verb 'to accuse' are based on the same Hebrew verbal root. The 'right hand' is a position of authority in the biblical world, marking 'The Accuser, Satan' (NLT) as first officer in the heavenly court.[34] The identity of this unnamed figure, presumably a powerful angelic being who has access to God's heavenly courts, has generated much discussion. At this time in the historical development of Hebrew theology, the term *Satan* should probably be understood as a title or description of function, rather than a personal name. 'The Accuser' has a role similar to that of the *rabiṣu* official of Mesopotamia in the Old Babylonian court. This officer was the most important court personage after the judge, and was responsible for the preliminary examination of the accused at trials.[35] The word *Satan* simply means 'Adversary' (so NEB), and the function of the adversary may be performed either by human or divine beings (cf. 1 Sam. 29:4; 1 Chr. 21:1). The role of the adversary (or *satan*) is not always an evil one, as evidenced by Balaam's encounter with the angel of the Lord (Num. 22:22).

The context of Zechariah indicates that the function of the adversary is evil in its intent in that it seeks to discredit Joshua the high priest. The strong rebuke of *Satan* by the Lord supports this understanding. Satan or The Accuser appears to be a divine being or angel and a member of the Divine Council of YHWH, with the formal function of prosecuting attorney (cf. Job 1:6).[36] By the time of the NT, Satan is a personal name belonging to an evil angel who is prince of the demons (Mark 3:22). Satan is equated with the serpent (Rev. 12:9; 20:2; cf. Gen. 3:1) and the devil (Matt. 4:1), and he is identified as both the deceiver of humanity and the adversary

---

34. See the discussion of the Divine Council in Meyers and Meyers (1987: 183–187).

35. See van der Toorn (1999: 682–683).

36. See further the discussion of the Divine Council in Meyers and Meyers (1987: 183–187); and 'Satan', in van der Toorn (1999: 726–732).

of God and all that is good (2 Cor. 4:4; Eph. 6:11; Rev. 20:2).[37] On *the angel of the LORD* see the commentary on 1:11, p. 133.

2. The repetition of Satan's rebuke is emphatic, underscoring the divine election of Joshua and the people of Israel represented in the holy city of Jerusalem (cf. Zech. 1:17; 2:12). In prophecy, the word *rebuke* 'denotes divine invective against those who stand in the way of Yahweh's plan'.[38] The archangel Michael quotes this admonition in his dispute with the devil over the body of Moses (Jude 9). The vivid word-picture, *Is not this man a burning stick snatched from the fire?*, is a reference to the return of Joshua and the Hebrew people from the Babylonian exile 'by an act of divine grace'.[39]

3–4. Joshua's *filthy clothes* (v. 3) are symbols of the guilt and pollution of *sin* (v. 4) that prompted the divine judgment of exile. The word for *filthy* is found only here in the OT, but is closely related to two Hebrew nouns used for human excrement (cf. Deut. 23:13; Ezek. 4:12) and vomit (cf. 2 Kgs 18:27; Isa. 28:8).[40] Such defilement of the high priest makes his presence in the heavenly court an odious affront to God. The *angel* (v. 3) in charge of the scene in the heavenly court is probably *the angel of the LORD* introduced in verse 1. The direct address to remove the filthy clothes *to those who were standing before* Joshua in the prophet's vision (v. 4a) is a reference to other angelic beings present in the heavenly court serving as attendants (v. 4b; cf. NEB, 'in attendance on him' [i.e. Joshua]). The *rich garments* (NIV) or 'festal garments' (NAB) are the 'fine vestments' (NEB) or 'priestly robes' (JPSV) appropriate to the office of the high priest. The verb used to report that Joshua's sin had been *taken away* (NIV, NRSV) 'indicates divine forgiveness or the removal of guilt' (so NJPS).[41]

---

37. Cf. *ZIBBCOT* 5: 211–212; cf. Merrill (1994: 132–133) who recognizes the gradual development of a personal devil or accuser in OT revelation.

38. Meyers and Meyers (1987: 186).

39. Mason (1977: 50); cf. Baldwin (1972: 121), who links the reference to the firebrand to Amos 4:11: 'a proverbial saying to indicate privileged deliverance from God's providential chastisements'.

40. See further Boda (2004: 252).

41. McComiskey (1998: 1071).

5. The word for *turban* (NIV, NRSV) or 'miter' (NAB) is rare in the OT (only Job 29:14; Isa. 62:3; Zech. 3:5) and connotes an elaborate headdress associated with royalty (cf. NJPS, 'diadem').[42] The use of such an unusual term here may anticipate the later 'crowning' of Joshua (Zech. 6:9–15). The *turban* of the high priest was to be made of fine linen and set with a medallion of pure gold inscribed with the words *HOLY TO THE LORD* (Exod. 28:36, 39). Although Zechariah uses a different term for *turban*, he may allude to the turban which the high priest was to wear at all times so that the Lord will accept the people of Israel (cf. Exod. 28:38). The placement of the turban on Joshua's head is an act of ordination or dedication, and reinstates him in the priestly office and his role as mediator for the people. This placing of the priestly turban on Joshua's head, along with the new vestments, was emblematic of the restoration to a former position accomplished in the divine cleansing (i.e. Joshua to his service as high priest, and Israel as the people of God).[43]

6–7. The restoration to priestly service and access to the divine presence was conditional: *If you will walk in my ways and keep my requirements*, after the pattern of the Mosaic covenant (cf. Deut. 30:19–20). Joshua's privilege and position were contingent upon obedience to God. God will again sanction the priestly oversight of 'his temple and the courtyard surrounding it' (CEV). This priestly governance of the temple precincts would have included judicial duties and the collection and administration of revenues and offerings.[44]

Joshua is granted conditional access to the Divine Council of God's heavenly court (*and I will give you a place among these standing here*), an invitation to stand with the other angelic beings in YHWH's presence. This 'priestly access to the Divine Council is innovative', since usually God's prophets were granted this privilege (cf. 1 Kgs 22:19; Isa. 6:1–5).[45] Although the advantages to this access to the

---

42. See Meyers and Meyers (1987: 191–192); cf. Petersen (1984: 198).
43. See Boda (2004: 253) on the ordination of the high priest and the Day of Atonement as the backdrop for the clothing imagery in this vision.
44. Meyers and Meyers (1987: 196).
45. Ibid., p. 197.

Divine Council for the high priest are unclear, given the absence of
a monarch in Judah, the appointment may signify the expanding
role and authority of the office of high priest in the leadership of
post-exilic Judah.[46]

8. The imperative verb *Listen* is a call-to-attention formula in
hortatory discourse, emphasizing the gravity of the message that
follows. The *associates* mentioned may refer to the rest of the
Levitical priesthood ('other priests', CEV; 'colleagues', NRSV) or to a
small group or council of 'fellow priests' (so JPSV) who form some
sort of hierarchy in the Levitical priesthood.[47] This group of priests
addressed in the prophet's vision is *symbolic of things to come* (NIV;
'omen', NAB, NEB, NRSV) or types of greater realities in the future.
The word 'sign' or 'omen' 'connotes a phenomenon that is an act of
God Himself designed to communicate some mysterious truth'.[48]
That mysterious truth has to do with the relationship of the office
of the high priest to the Davidic covenant and the Branch who
symbolizes Davidic kingship (see further the commentary on 6:9–
15, p. 174ff.).

Joshua himself is not identified as the *Branch*; rather, he and the
other priests are symbols or prophetic signs pointing to a greater
priestly servant of God yet to come. Later, Joshua the high priest
is given the name *Branch* in the oracle that follows Zechariah's last
night vision (see the commentary on 6:9–15, p. 174ff.). Both the
terms *servant* and *Branch* are titles for the Messiah. Although Rose
understands the term 'Branch' as a personal name, he notes that
Zechariah does not use it in association with Zerubbabel's name
in Zechariah 3:3 or 6:12 (as in Zech. 4:6–10). This leads him to
conclude that Zechariah's oracles about the Branch are messianic
– but not royalist: that is, they are not announcing or encouraging
a restoration of the Davidic monarchy. As *servant*, the Messiah
obeys the will of God, even to the point of becoming a sin-offering
so that many may be counted righteous (Isa. 53:11; cf. Acts 3:13;
4:27). The Branch is also a metaphor for kingship: first because the

---

46. Cf. Petersen (1984: 208).
47. Cf. Meyers and Meyers (1987: 198).
48. Merrill (1994: 140–141).

symbolic name identifies the Messiah as a descendant of David, and hearkens back to the Davidic covenant and the divine promise of kingship granted to the dynasty of David (Isa. 11:1; cf. 2 Sam. 7:4–17); second, the prophet Jeremiah equates the 'Branch' with a Davidic king who will rule with wisdom and righteousness (Jer. 23:5; 33:15–17; Ezek. 34:23; 37:24).[49]

9. The abrupt shift from the symbol of the *Branch* (v. 8) to a *stone* is puzzling ('Look at the stone I have placed before Joshua, one stone with seven facets', NAB). The *stone* may anticipate the final stone in the temple laid by Zerubbabel (Zech. 4:7), or it may even refer to the foundation stone of Isaiah's prophecy (Isa. 28:16).[50] The *stone* may allude to the ephod of the high priest decorated with precious stones (Exod. 25:7; 35:9), or the rosette of pure gold attached to the turban of the high priest (Exod. 28:36–38). The cryptic reference to the engraving of an inscription on the stone recalls the engraved golden rosette set in the priest's turban and the engraved onyx stones fastened to the shoulder pieces of the high-priestly ephod (Exod. 28:9, 36–39). The mysterious inscription might be the phrase 'Holy to YHWH', since these words could be written in eight Hebrew letters. Given the context of Joshua's investiture, 'it makes most sense to try to understand the stone as something he would receive during such a ceremony'.[51] The number *seven* is sometimes used as the number of perfection and completeness in Hebrew tradition. The *seven* facets of the stone may be related to the seven lamps of the golden lampstand (Zech. 4:2). The 'facets' (lit. 'eyes', so ESV) of the stone probably symbolize knowledge and wisdom, and may allude to the *seven spirits* of God (cf. Rev. 1:4). In any case, the *stone* signifies authority and represents another messianic metaphor or symbol typified in the person and

---

49. See Rose (2000: 132; cf. p. 120 where Rose states that the 'Branch' imagery in Jer. 23:5 'suggests that only a divine intervention can safeguard the future of the Davidic dynasty'). See Boda (2004: 257) on the foreshadowing in the linking of David's line with priestly service in the temple.

50. *ZIBBCOT* 5: 213.

51. Redditt (1995: 65).

office of Zerubbabel, the governor of post-exilic Judah.

The removal of the sin of Israel in *a single day* alludes to the Day of Atonement (Lev. 16). Practically speaking, once the high priest is cleansed as Israel's mediator, the system of ritual sacrifice can be re-implemented and the nation can be cleansed in *a single day*. Understood prophetically, the phrase may be a veiled reference to the day of the crucifixion of Jesus Christ as the Lamb of God who takes away the sin of the world (John 1:29).

10. The phrase *In that day* is shorthand in the OT prophets for *the Day of the LORD* (cf. 2:11; Isa. 2:11: Joel 2:1; Zeph. 1:14). This eschatological Day of divine intervention in history brings both judgment of the wicked and deliverance of the righteous (cf. Zech. 12:8; 14:3). The *Day of the LORD* is an indefinite period of time of divine activity, but always impending, indicated by the frequent use of the participle form of the verb with a word of interjection (e.g. 3:8, 'Soon I am going to bring ...', NLT). The image of the Israelites sitting peacefully beneath the *vine and fig-tree* is a picture of security and prosperity under messianic rule in the OT prophets (e.g. Mic. 4:4), and reminiscent of the ideals achieved during the reign of King Solomon (1 Kgs 4:25).

Meaning

In Zechariah's vision, Joshua stands before the Lord as the representative of Israel, especially those of the exile. The twelve stones of the high priest's ephod and the two inscribed stones on the shoulder piece were perpetual reminders that the representation of Israel before the Lord was a function of the high priest (Exod. 28:9–12). Like a *burning stick snatched from the fire* (v. 2), Joshua and the Hebrew exiles were plucked by God from near destruction in Babylonia. Singed and soot-covered, they now stood before the Lord in the person of Joshua, facing the charges of The Accuser, *Satan* (vv. 1–2). Joshua's *filthy clothes* (v. 3) are symbols of the guilt and pollution of sin that prompted the divine judgment of exile. No doubt The Accuser contends that any priest clad in such a fashion is unfit for temple service (thus implying that the Hebrews are unfit to be the chosen people of God).

As the vision unfolds, the angel of the Lord orders other angels to remove the filthy clothes – a symbol of the removal of the sins

and guilt of Joshua (and the Hebrew people, vv. 3–4). The placing
of the priestly turban on Joshua's head, along with the new
vestments, are emblematic gestures of the restoration to a former
position accomplished in the divine cleansing (Joshua to his service
as high priest, and Israel as the people of God, v. 5). This restoration
to priestly service and access to the divine presence, however, are
conditional after the pattern of the Mosaic covenant (cf. Deut.
30:19–20). Joshua's privilege and position are contingent upon
obedience to God (vv. 6–7). Zechariah also learns that Joshua and
his priestly associates are a 'sign' (NJPS), an 'omen' (NAB, NRSV) or
'symbols' (NLT) of things to come – namely a future servant of God,
titled *the Branch* (vv. 8–10).

F. A gold lampstand and two olive trees (4:1–14)

Context

The images in Zechariah's fifth vision represent both unseen
spiritual realities and tangible earthly offices and persons. The solid
gold lampstand probably functions as a symbol for God, his purity
and holiness, and the light of his revelation (v. 2). The two olive
trees may represent the offices of priest and king in Israel, and the
two branches of the olive trees are emblems for Joshua and
Zerubbabel (vv. 3, 12). The golden oil may be a symbol of God's
Holy Spirit (v. 12). The focus of the vision is the issue of leadership
in post-exilic Jerusalem.

Comment

4:1. 'Then the angel who had been talking with me returned and
woke me, as though I had been asleep' (NLT). The series of visions
come to Zechariah in a single night. The return of the interpreting
angel to awaken the prophet suggests he had briefly lapsed into
sleep before the fifth vision appeared to him.

2–3. The interpreting angel who accompanies Zechariah through
the experience of the night visions takes a more active role as guide,
and calls the prophet to attention to view yet another image ('*What
do you see?*', v. 2a). The pacing of the sequence of night visions has
become such that Zechariah must be alerted to the new set of
images coming up 'on screen' so to speak. The first image Zechariah

reports is *a solid gold lampstand with a bowl at the top and seven lights on it, with seven channels to the lights* (v. 2b). The solid gold *lampstand* (Heb. *měnôrâ*) is a reference to the golden menorah of the Mosaic tabernacle replicated as the lamp for the Second Temple, in contrast to the ten lampstands of Solomon's temple (Exod. 25:31; 1 Kgs 7:49; cf. 1 Macc. 1:21). The *bowl* at the top is the fuel reservoir for the *lampstand*, and it has seven 'pipes' (NEB) or 'tubes' (NAB), each running to one of the 'seven lamps' (NAB, NEB). The 'seven pipes' or 'tubes' funnelling the oil to the 'lamps' are variously understood as 'lips' ('with seven lips on each of the lamps', NRSV) or 'spouts' ('Around the bowl are seven lamps, each having seven spouts with wicks', NLT).[52] The image of *two olive trees* flanking the lampstand bowl on either side complete the scene displayed in the vision. The *olive tree* was (and still is) a common and valued tree in Palestine, used symbolically in the Psalms to represent the righteous (Ps. 52:8) and children (Ps. 128:3). The two olive trees may symbolize an unending supply of oil for the lamp Zechariah sees in his vision, although Baldwin finds this interpretation untenable, since it implies divine dependence upon human sources.[53]

4–5. Many biblical commentators understand verses 4–10a (or vv. 6–10a) as an intrusive oracle interrupting the explanation of the vision (which resumes in v. 10; note the transposition of 3:1–10 to follow 4:14 in NEB; the transposition of 4:4–14 to follow 3:10 in NAB; and the transposition of 4:6b–10a to follow 4:14 in NJB).[54] Yet visionary literature reverses ordinary reality, and instead of expecting a smooth flow of narrative, the reader should 'be prepared for a disjointed series of diverse, self-contained units'.[55] The insertion of the oracle promising success to Zerubbabel in the rebuilding of the Jerusalem temple is an emphatic device intended to place the focus

---

52. See Meyers and Meyers (1987: illustrations 12, 13, 14); and *ZIBBCOT* 5: 214.

53. Baldwin (1972: 131); cf. Petersen (1984: 237).

54. Cf. Meyers and Meyers (1987: 242) who suggest the so-called insertion (Zech. 4:6b–10a) may not be a misplaced and intrusive pericope, but may have been original to the vision.

55. Ryken (1984: 170).

of attention where it belongs – not on Zerubbabel as God's agent, but on the God who empowers Zerubbabel.

As in the previous night visions, Zechariah asks the interpreting angel for an explanation of the images depicted in the vision. The angel seems a bit surprised that the prophet needs an explanation of the symbols portrayed in the vision, as if their meaning is obvious or transparent.

6–10. The thrust of the oracular interlude to Zerubbabel in Zechariah's fifth night vision is that God will enable both Zerubbabel and Joshua the high priest to rebuild his holy temple (v. 9).

6. This variation of the prophetic word formula, *This is the word of the LORD*, introduces a prophetic revelation comprised of two oracles (vv. 6–7 and vv. 8–10a). The formula serves both to legitimate the recipient of the divine revelation (here Zerubbabel) and to lend authority to the prophet's message as the revealed 'word of God' (this variation of the prophetic word formula is repeated in v. 8).

Joshua the high priest and Zerubbabel the Persian-appointed governor of post-exilic Judah were the leaders of the restoration community and the recipients of Haggai's message (Hag. 1:1). *Zerubbabel* (whose name means 'seed, shoot of Babylon') was the governor of post-exilic Judah, and Joshua was the successor to the office of high priest. The expression *governor of Judah* is applied to Zerubbabel only by the prophet Haggai (1:1, 14; 2:2, 21). The term *governor* is an Assyrian loan word and is a rather vague title describing a governmental official during both the pre-exilic and post-exilic periods of Hebrew history (cf. 2 Kgs 18:24; Esth. 8:9; Jer. 51:23; Ezek. 23:6). What is clear is that Zerubbabel was appointed governor by the Persian king, and Judah is a rather insignificant provincial territory firmly under the jurisdiction of the Persian Empire. Zerubbabel is mentioned in Haggai's second message (2:2, 4), and he is the subject of the prophet's fourth sermon, linking the governor to the line of David and hinting at the restoration of Davidic kingship in the reference to Zerubbabel as the Lord's *signet ring* (Hag. 2:20–23).

Zerubbabel is identified as the son of Shealtiel, the eldest son of the exiled King Jehoiachin (Ezra 3:2, 8; cf. 2 Kgs 24:12–17), and thus traced his lineage to the family of David as Jehoiachin's grandson.

The Chronicler, however, lists Zerubbabel as the descendant of Jehoiachin's third son, Pedaiah (1 Chr. 3:19). Commentators speculate as to whether Shealtiel adopted his eldest nephew, or if he was born to Shealtiel's widow by levirate marriage.[56] Zerubbabel is also mentioned in Zechariah (4:6, 7, 9, 10), and then he mysteriously disappears from the biblical record. Significantly in Haggai, each leader is introduced with a brief genealogical record designed to recall the Babylonian exile and God's faithfulness in preserving and bringing back a remnant of his people to the land of covenant promise.

Although Zerubbabel lacked the royal authority and resources of King David or King Solomon, God will enable him successfully to lead the post-exilic community in the rebuilding of YHWH's temple by the power of the *Spirit* (v. 6). Four months earlier, Haggai had assured Zerubbabel, Joshua and the people of Judah that God's *Spirit* remained among them (Hag. 2:4). In contrast to human *might* (a term denoting human prowess and military strength), God's *Spirit* (Heb. *rûaḥ*) will be the enabling force in bringing the Second Temple to completion. Since this is the same *Spirit* who worked with God at creation (Gen. 1:1), and it was this *rûaḥ* of God that divided the Reed Sea for the Hebrews in their exodus from Egypt and then folded the waters back on the Egyptian pursuers (Exod. 15:8, 10), a happy outcome is certain!

7. The reference to the *mighty mountain* may refer literally to the work of the masons in quarrying and shaping stones taken from the surrounding hillsides for the building of the Second Temple.[57] More likely, the expression is a figure of speech assuring Zerubbabel 'that no obstacle could prevent the completion of the Temple'.[58]

---

56. E.g. Baldwin (1972: 41); cf. Meyers and Meyers (1987: 10–11) who conclude that the confusion over Shealtiel's lineage cannot be satisfactorily resolved, yet they recognize Zerubbabel as his legitimate heir.

57. Cf. Ollenburger (1996: 770) who suggests that 'the great mountain is simply the rubble of the destroyed temple'.

58. Redditt (1995: 69); cf. McComiskey (1998: 1088). See the discussion of the cosmic mountain and temple motif in the ANE in Meyers and Meyers (1987: 244–245).

R. L. Smith understands the 'great mountain' (NAB) to have been an obstacle in the form of opposition to the rebuilding of the temple, perhaps the enemies of Judah and Benjamin mentioned in Ezra 4:1.[59]

The word *capstone* (a unique phrase in the OT; lit. 'the top stone', NRSV) is variously interpreted as a foundation stone, cornerstone ('keystone', NJB), head stone ('final stone', NLT), or boundary stone.[60] Associations with elaborate temple building rituals notwithstanding, the context of the passage (i.e. the reference to a completed temple, v. 9) suggest that the *capstone* (NAB, NIV) or 'final stone' (NLT) is when 'the laying of the last stone would be met with shouts of Grace, grace to it! [NRSV]'.[61]

The repeated word *bless* is variously rendered in the EVV ('Beautiful! Beautiful!', NJPS; 'Hail, Hail to it!', NAB; 'Hurrah! Hurrah!', NJB; 'Grace, grace to it!', NRSV). The translation *God bless it!* (NIV, NLT) takes the interjection as a prayer seeking God's favour upon this new temple. The repetition of a single word in Hebrew may be an emphatic device, 'intensifying the expression to the highest degree', or an idiomatic method 'to express entirety'.[62] Here both understandings of the idiom are appropriate, laying emphasis on the totality of God's favour in the Second Temple reconstruction project from beginning to end ('God has been very

---

59. R. L. Smith (1984: 206). Cf. Baldwin (1972: 129) who notes that the interrogative pronoun 'who' (Heb. *mî*) in the question 'Who are you?' (ESV) indicates that 'either Zerubbabel had personified the obstacles or the principal difficulties revolved around human obstructionists'.

60. See discussions of the term and the foundation rituals associated with such stones in Meyers and Meyers (1987: 246); Redditt (1995: 69–70); and *ZIBBCOT* 5: 214–215.

61. Redditt (1995: 69–70); cf. Baldwin (1972: 129–130): 'The strongest argument in favour of a completion stone is the demand of the sense of the passage. The foundation has been laid (v. 9) and the promise is that the building will be finished. Whether or not it was customary, in this case there will be a ceremony of rejoicing when the last stone has been laid, for this is no ordinary building.'

62. So Meyers and Meyers (1987: 249).

kind', CEV) and the sheer beauty of the structure.[63]

8–9. Zechariah's second oracle assures Zerubbabel and the people of post-exilic Judah that the Second Temple will be completed (with the reinforcement of a prophetic word formula, see v. 6 above). The completion of the Second Temple will validate Zechariah's prophetic ministry: *Then you will know that the LORD Almighty has sent me to you* (v. 9). The foundation for the Second Temple was laid sometime in 538 or 537 BC, probably under the leadership of Sheshbazzar, a prince of Judah and the first governor of the restoration community (Ezra 1:5–11). The meagre project was soon abandoned, and the construction site lay neglected for nearly two decades. Not until the preaching of Haggai in 520 BC did the initiative to rebuild the Jerusalem temple resume (Hag. 1:14). The Second Temple was completed in March of 515 BC, under the auspices of the Persian king, Darius I (cf. Ezra 6:14–15 which reports that the temple was completed by *the elders of the Jews* under the preaching of Haggai and Zechariah).

10. The rhetorical question, *Who despises the day of small things?*, may also be understood as an admonition: 'Do not despise these small beginnings' (NLT). Apparently there were those 'who were scornful on that day of small beginnings' (NAB; cf. Ezra 3:12; Hag. 2:3). Baldwin comments: 'Zechariah, like Haggai, implies that the "realists" were pessimistic about the building project (Hag. 2:3) … They wanted to see it succeed and were glad when it did, but their faith was too small. They would be surprised into rejoicing.'[64]

The meaning of the Hebrew phrase rendered 'plummet' is uncertain (e.g. 'stone of distinction', NJPS; 'select stone', NAB; 'chosen stone', NJB; The 'plummet' (NRSV) or *plumb-line* (NIV, ['capstone', NIV 2011], NLT) is based on the LXX (lit. 'stone of tin'). The NEB, 'the stone called Separation', is based on the Syriac version. According to Mason (1977: 56), the stone marks the completion of the Second Temple and symbolically shows the

---

63. Baldwin (1972: 130) comments that the repetition of the word *grace* 'draws attention both to the attractiveness of the building and to the grace God has shown and will show in the future'.

64. Ibid., p. 130.

people of Israel to be separated for service unto God (cf. Lev. 20:26).

The *plumb-line*, a cord with a tin or lead weight attached to one end, was used to determine true verticality in construction. Meyers and Meyers (1987: 253) translate 'tin-stone', perhaps a ceremonial stone used to commemorate the completion of a building project similar to the 'final stone' mentioned above (v. 7). Petersen (1984: 243) suggests 'tin-tablet', a building deposit of some sort acknowledging the completion of the temple (perhaps including a ceremony in which a stone from the ruins of the old temple was transferred to the new temple).[65] In any case, the stone in question signifies the completion of the Second Temple.

10b. The transition from the divine oracles (vv. 6–10a) back to the interpretation of the night vision is abrupt. The citation of the *seven eyes* is probably a reference back to the *seven lamps* mentioned in verse 2. The *seven eyes* of God 'is a metaphoric expression … for God's omniscience and omnipresence'.[66] No doubt the expression has connections with the *seven eyes on that one stone* in the previous night vision, lending continuity of imagery and theme to the fourth and fifth visions (cf. 3:9). The verb 'range over' may be translated 'scour',[67] indicating God's careful scrutiny of his creation, 'either to bring discipline or blessing'.[68]

11–14. The interview with the interpreting angel now resumes after the oracular interlude. The prophet's attention is directed to the *two olive trees on the right and the left of the lampstand* (v. 11) with such intensity that his question for an interpretation of the images is repeated (v. 12). The second iteration of the prophet's question specifies the *branches* of the olive trees, probably referring to 'the fruit-laden ends of the olive branches' ('tops of the olive trees', NJPS; 'sprays of olive', NEB; 'olive tufts', NJB).[69] Two new features peculiar to the imagery of the vision are referenced: *two gold pipes*

---

65. Cf. Redditt (1995: 69).
66. Meyers and Meyers (1987: 254).
67. Ibid.
68. Boda (2004: 273).
69. R. L. Smith (1984: 205).

and *golden oil* (v. 12). The word *pipe* is found only here in the OT. Given the previous description of the pipes that funnelled oil into the lamps (v. 2), these are probably similar 'tubes' (NJPS), 'channels' (NAB) or 'openings' (NJB) for supplying oil to the lamps.[70] The *golden oil* interprets the (lit.) 'gold' ('that feed their gold', NJPS) that symbolically represents the olive oil produced by the trees fuelling the lamps. The profusion of oil flowing from the spouts 'underscores the abundant supply of God's Spirit for the task at hand'.[71] Again, the interpreting angel expresses surprise or perhaps disappointment at the prophet's lack of understanding (v. 13).

Typically, the *two* trees or *anointed* ones (v. 14) are identified as Joshua the high priest and Zerubbabel the Persian-appointed governor, who are the leaders of post-exilic Judah at the time of Zechariah's ministry.[72] The verb *anointed* (lit. 'sons of oil') indicates that these two figures are 'consecrated with oil' (NEB). This expression differs from the more common term for anointing or anointed one (Heb. *mšḥ, māšîaḥ*), downplaying the messianic implications of the vision, while signalling the divine appointment of these post-exilic leaders. As high priest, Joshua would have been anointed with oil as part of his investiture to the office (cf. Exod. 30:30; Ps. 133:2). It is unlikely that Zerubbabel would have been anointed with oil for his installation as the Persian-appointed governor of Judah (although this remains uncertain). The fact that Zerubbabel may not have been an anointed official makes the identification of the two trees with Joshua and Zerubbabel problematic for some interpreters.[73] Alternately, Boda understands the two trees as the prophetic figures of Haggai and Zechariah, given their roles in the rebuilding of the Second Temple.[74] The lampstand signifies the temple as the location of God's presence and is fuelled by oil supplied by the prophets. Petersen understands the fifth night vision more conceptually,

---

70. Perhaps terracotta tubes according to Baldwin (1972: 131).

71. McComiskey (1998: 1092).

72. So Baldwin (1972: 132); Mason (1977: 48).

73. E.g. Rudolph (1976: 107–108); see the discussion in Petersen (1984: 231–232).

74. Boda (2004: 275).

recognizing the two trees as representative of two human functionaries installed in civic and religious offices of leadership (presumably the offices of the Persian governor of Judah and the high priest).[75] For Petersen, the vision carries several important messages, including: the Hebrew community will feature diarchic, not monarchic, rule; the leadership positions will be equal in status; and the two offices of leadership are not isolated from YHWH, constituting a divine-human symbiosis.[76] In light of later Judaism and the NT, the messianic implications of the fourth and fifth night visions are numerous and complex, since the plural 'sons of oil' implies two anointed ones or messiah figures (see commentary on 6:9–15, p. 174ff.).[77] The repetition of the word *earth* (vv. 10b, 14) emphasizes God's sovereignty over the created order.

Meaning
The crux of the vision of the lampstand and the two olive trees is that God will enable Zerubbabel (and Joshua) to rebuild his holy temple, an important message of encouragement to post-exilic Judah (v. 9). Theologically, the fifth vision reinforces three basic spiritual truths: first, with God everything is possible (cf. Matt. 19:26); second, God accomplishes his purposes in the world through human servants empowered by the Holy Spirit (v. 6; cf. Hag. 2:5; Zech. 7:12; John 16:5–15); and third, God delights in 'small beginnings' (v. 10; cf. Ezra 3:12; Hag. 2:3).

G. A flying scroll (5:1–4)

Context
This is the sixth of eight successive visions that Zechariah experienced in the same night. The prophet sees a billboard-size scroll flying through the air (v. 1). Presumably, the scroll is a Torah scroll, since it contains a reference to the curse and admonitions against theft and perjury (v. 3), all of which are itemized in the Mosaic covenant code

---

75. Petersen (1984: 234).
76. Ibid.
77. See Baldwin (1972: 132).

(cf. Exod. 20:7, 15, 16; Deut. 29:19–21). This vision hearkens back to the charge to the high priest Joshua to follow God's ways and serve him carefully by obeying the priestly prescriptions of the Torah (3:7). It also looks forward to the removal of sin from the community, portrayed in the seventh vision (5:5–11), and to Zechariah's sermons calling for social justice (7:9–10; 8:16–17).[78]

Comment

1. The image of a *flying scroll* suggests that the scroll was unrolled, waving in the wind like an unfurled flag or a banner for all to see. The word *scroll* is the usual term for a rolled piece of papyrus or parchment (i.e. leather made from animal skin; cf. Jer. 36:2; Ezek. 2:9). Oddly, the LXX translates 'flying sickle' (see NETS), perhaps confusing the word *scroll* (Heb. *měgillâ*) with the (rare) Hebrew term for 'sickle' (*maggāl*; cf. Joel 3:13 [MT 4:13]).

2. Zechariah responds to the question of the interpreting angel who still accompanies the prophet through the series of night visions. The detailed description of the size of the *flying scroll* may simply underscore the fact that the scroll was easily seen and read by all. Some commentators, however, interpret the details about the size of the scroll as an integral part of the message of the vision. For example, Meyers and Meyers (1987: 280) note that the dimensions of the scroll coincide with the dimensions of the *portico* (NIV) or 'vestibule' (NRSV) or 'porch' (CEV) of Solomon's temple (1 Kgs 6:3).[79] This was probably the place of administration of justice during the Hebrew monarchic period and may 'represent the revival of the priestly role in the administration of justice' in post-exilic Judah.[80] Either way, the excessive size and obvious meaning of the message embedded in the vision were intended to prompt repentance.

---

78. Webb (2003: 97) notes that 'the issue is *un*repentance – the continued presence in the community of people who persist in conduct offensive to God. His response to this problem … is eradication (Vision 6) and removal (Vision 7).'

79. Cf. Sweeney (2000: 616–617).

80. Boda (2004: 292); see further his discussion of the alternate interpretations of the dimensions of the flying scroll (292–293).

3. Zechariah receives a disturbing answer from the interpreting angel: *'This is the curse that is going out over the whole land.'* The term *curse* may be understood as an 'oath' (e.g. Deut. 29:12) or a 'curse' (Deut. 29:19). The close relationship between the two meanings of the word stems from the fact that the act of oath-taking in a covenant ceremony binds the parties to the attendant curses threatened for any violation of the agreement. Here the word alludes to the curses invoked against those who violate the stipulations of the Mosaic covenant (Deut. 29:20; cf. 28:15, 20). By means of the literary device of personification, 'the curse' is set loose like a law officer to do God's bidding in the punishment of covenant violations (v. 4; cf. Ps. 147:15; Isa. 55:11).

One side of the scroll says, *every thief will be banished.* Theft or stealing is prohibited in the Decalogue of the Mosaic covenant (Exod. 20:15). The verb *banished* (so NIV, NJB, NLT; 'cut off', NRSV; 'swept away', NAB, NEB) poses translation difficulties. This form of the verb is better rendered 'has gone unpunished' (so NJPS) or 'has been acquitted'.[81] The idea here is that the curse (v. 4) is going out against the evildoers, because the administration of justice in the land has lapsed and 'the guilty are going unpunished' (cf. 7:8–10; 8:15–16).[82]

The other side of the flying scroll says, *everyone who swears falsely will be banished.* To *swear falsely* (with the modifier *falsely* understood from v. 4) is to swear or take an oath to a lie, an act of 'perjury' (so NAB, NJB). The Decalogue forbids giving false testimony (Exod. 20:16; cf. Lev. 19:11–12; Deut. 5:19 which may be the source for Zechariah's message).

4. God will 'release' the curse against those in violation of the stipulations of the Mosaic covenant, especially with respect to the infractions of theft and 'perjury' (NJB). The personification of the curse of the Mosaic law recalls the personification of death climbing in through the windows at the time of the Babylonian exile (Jer. 9:21). The threat of divine judgment against the perjurer is addressed in more detail, as *swearing falsely by my* [i.e. YHWH's] *name*

---

81. Cf. Meyers and Meyers (1987: 286).

82. Boda (2004: 294).

(NIV, NRSV). Commentators agree that the covenant violations of theft and perjury may be related acts perpetrated by the same individual. In this case, the third command of the Decalogue (Exod. 20:7; Deut. 5:11) is also pertinent, since the misuse of God's name may have been involved in the defendant's oath of acquittal. As Meyers and Meyers observe, '[I]n certain cases an individual charged with a crime for which there are no witnesses is permitted to swear his way out of jeopardy … The point of the third commandment [of the Decalogue] is that Yahweh will not acquit a perjurer even if the miscreant swears himself innocent and is allowed to go free since there is no one to testify otherwise. The Decalogue warns against those who use this technique to avoid punishment when they are guilty.'[83]

God's curse is dogged in its determination to *remain* and root out ('to settle deep within his house', NJB) and 'demolish' (NEB) or 'consume' (NJPS, NJB, NRSV) the *house* of the evildoer. 'The efficacy of this curse is seen in the four verbs in this verse: "send out," "enter," "remain," "destroy." '[84] The word pair *timbers* and *stones* represents the two primary building materials in the biblical world and, as such, is a merism for a literal house or dwelling place. Beyond this, it seems likely that the expression is also a metaphor for one's material possessions, family and very life.[85]

Meaning
Zechariah's vision of the flying scroll is a reminder to the leaders and the people of post-exilic Judah that they are still obligated to obey the commandments of the Mosaic covenant. Beyond this, the Hebrew community need to understand that the conditional curses of the Sinai treaty are still operative. Those who violate the covenant stipulation are threatened with banishment (v. 3) and destruction (v. 4).

---

83. Meyers and Meyers (1987: 284).
84. Boda (2004: 295).
85. Cf. Merrill (1994: 170).

H. A woman in a basket (5:5–11)

Context
There is general agreement that the seventh vision continues the
theme of cleansing begun in the fourth vision with the investiture
of the newly clad high priest Joshua (3:1–10). Most commentators
also acknowledge that the symbolism of the evil woman in the
basket represents a seductive and dangerous force that is difficult to
contain (to the point of being pushed back into the basket which is
closed with a heavy lid [v. 8: 'And he rammed her back into the barrel
and jammed its mouth shut with the mass of lead', NJB]). In fact,
this evil is so potent and so aggressive that it cannot be confined, but
instead must be shipped back to its source (the land of Babylonia)
by divine decree. Beyond this broad understanding, however,
interpreters tend to part company when it comes to identifying the
evil woman named *wickedness* sitting in the *ephah* basket (and hence
the specific sin or sins being removed from post-exilic Jerusalem).

Comment
5. The interpreting angel who accompanies Zechariah through
the experience of the night visions calls the prophet to attention to
view yet another image. The rapid-fire sequence of dreamscapes
has so overwhelmed God's prophet that he must be prompted to
abandon his contemplation of the flying scroll and concentrate on
this new and somewhat bizarre scene.

6. The *measuring basket* ('basket', NIV 2011; Heb. *'êpâ*) was a
standardized unit of dry measure equivalent to approximately one-
half bushel. Typically, the baskets of OT times were woven of
willow or palm branches, reeds or cane. The word is variously
rendered in the EVV as 'barrel' (NJB, v. 7), 'tub' (NJPS) and 'bushel
container' (NAB). The condemnation of an unjust *ephah* or measure
by the OT prophets makes the association between the *ephah* basket
and evil a logical one (cf. Ezek. 45:10; Mic. 6:10).

Most EVV follow the LXX and Syr. (emending the MT to *'āwônām*)
in reading 'their guilt' (NAB, NEB, NJB) or 'their iniquity' (NRSV) for the
difficult MT 'their eyes' (Heb. *'ênām*). A few commentators prefer
'their eyes' (MT), and translate 'their appearance' or 'its shining, its
appearance' as a symbolic reference to the covenant-breakers of

Judah,[86] or more generally to the *ephah* or measuring basket.[87] The *land* refers to the territory of post-exilic Judah, especially Jerusalem and its environs, echoing the flight of the unrolled scroll over the land (5:3).

7. The opening interjection ('And behold', NJPS; 'At this', NJB) is often omitted or simply rendered adverbially (*Then*, so NIV, NLT, NRSV). The exclamation is important because it calls attention to the contents of the measuring basket (vv. 7–8), once the measuring basket or *ephah* itself has been introduced (vv. 5–6). The heavy metal lid is not a natural *cover* for the measuring basket (or perhaps clay barrel in the form of an *ephah* basket; cf. NJB, 'barrel'). The *lead cover* (Heb. *kikkar*, a talent [or sixty+ pounds] of *lead*) emphasizes 'the fact that an extraordinary device is being used to enclose forcefully and unalterably the Ephah's strange contents' (Meyers and Meyers 1987: 295–296). The heavy 'disc of lead' (NJB) is momentarily lifted from the measuring basket so that the prophet can glimpse the contents – a woman sitting inside the basket! Commentators have been troubled by the literal details of the imagery, since an *ephah*-size measuring basket would not be large enough to contain a seated human figure. This is visionary literature, however, where the fantastic becomes ordinary. Even as the flying scroll (5:1–4) takes on huge dimensions, the same may be the case for the measuring basket. Or it is possible that the image of the woman is a less-than-life-size statue or idol of a deity in the form of a female figure.[88]

8. The interpreting angel identifies the female figure in the measuring basket for Zechariah: *This is wickedness*. She is evil personified, an appropriate designation in the sense that the word for *wickedness* here is a feminine noun.[89] The term *wickedness* refers to evil generally, whether moral, civil or ceremonial (i.e. religious or cultic), and is sometimes used in word pairs as the polar opposite of *righteousness* (e.g. Prov. 13:6; Ezek. 33:12).

---

86. McComiskey (1998: 1100–1101).

87. So Meyers and Meyers (1987: 295–296).

88. Meyers and Meyers (1987: 295–296) for this discussion.

89. See Redditt (1995: 73–74) who notes that this need not be understood as an example of anti-feminine bias on the part of Zechariah.

The movement of the woman required a response by the interpreting angel: 'And he rammed her back into the barrel and jammed its mouth shut with the mass of lead' (NJB). It is unclear whether the woman in the measuring basket stood up or even tried to escape her *ephah* prison. The repeated verb rendered 'rammed' and 'jammed' indicates that forceful action was necessary to keep the woman named *wickedness* in her container ('threw ... slammed', CEV; 'thrust ... rammed', NEB; 'thrust ... pressed', NJPS, NRSV; *pushed ... pushed*, NIV). Clearer still is the threat that this malignant figure poses for the Hebrew people – so much so that the basket must be shipped back to its source (the land of Babylonia, v. 11).

Several explanations have been put forward in an attempt to identity more specifically the evils associated with the woman in the basket named *wickedness* (vv. 7–8). Most often, the woman is generally understood to represent a system of evil: the moral and socials ills, the ceremonial impurities and religious apostasy, and the injustices of the political and legal institutions of Israel regularly condemned by the Hebrew prophets. For some, the woman in the basket symbolizes the 'foreign women' brought into the Hebrew community through wrongful intermarriage (an issue for the prophet Malachi in Mal. 2:10–16, and one of the reform initiatives of Ezra and Nehemiah [cf. Ezra 9 – 10]). Finally, the woman may be a figure of 'spiritual adultery' or idolatry, since the evil of ritual prostitution is often linked with idol worship in the OT (especially the worship of Asherah and the Queen of Heaven; cf. e.g. 1 Kgs 15:13; 18:19; Jer. 7:18; 23:10; Ezek. 16:15; Hos. 2:2).[90] Whatever the case, God himself will both contain and remove the *wickedness* from his people and the land of Israel. Although 'cleansing' from sin is the gracious work of God (Ps. 51:2, 7), those guilty of sin and rebellion against God must turn to God and seek his cleansing for the forgiveness of sins and a restored relationship with him (cf. Ezek. 24:13).

9. The depiction of the two-winged creatures as *women* is unusual

---

90. See further the discussion in Harrington (2002: 495–496), who notes that the word 'wickedness' (Heb. *riš'â*) forms an anagram of the name Asherah, a Canaanite fertility goddess.

in the OT. Typically such divine or angelic beings are male figures. It is unclear whether these female divine beings are attendants of YHWH or the wicked woman enclosed in the *ephah* basket. If they are attendants of YHWH, then they represent a unique class of angelic beings in the heavenly realm. If they are the angelic retainers of the figure of *wickedness* (representing a foreign goddess), then their submission to the command of God demonstrates his power over false gods.[91] Either way, the role of these female attendants who carry off *wickedness* is significant in contrast to the evil woman confined in the measuring basket. The word *wind* (Heb. *rûaḥ*) may suggest a double entendre, since it means 'wind' or 'spirit' (even God's Spirit, cf. Zech. 4:6; i.e. 'gliding on the Spirit'). The wind is also an instrument of God at times (Ps. 104:3–4; Jon. 1:4).

The *stork* (Heb. *ḥăsîdâ*) is a migratory bird of the Mediterranean basin. Baldwin (1972: 137) has suggested wordplay with *stork* and 'faithful one' (Heb. *ḥāsîd*): 'The removal of Wickedness, like the removal of Joshua's filthy garments (3:4), was an act of free grace on the part of the covenant-keeping (*ḥāsîd*) God.'

The heavenly trajectory of the departing measuring basket is significant (*and they lifted up the basket between heaven and earth*). The symbolic removal of *wickedness* from the land of Judah was visible to those earthbound observers. If the evil represented by the female figure in the measuring basket is the sin of idolatry, the visible covering and removal of that sin indicates that God's judgment and forgiveness of Israel are complete and the work of restoration can move forward.

10–11. The destination for the departing measuring basket is *Babylonia* (lit. 'the land of Shinar', NJPS, NEB). More specifically, Shinar is a reference to the city of Babylon (v. 10). The prophets condemned Babylon as a place of idolatry and wickedness (Isa. 46, 47; Jer. 50, 51). Babylon is a metaphor for the evil of Rome and the Roman Empire in the NT (Rev. 17:5; 18:2; cf. 1 Pet. 5:13). The interpreting angel indicates that a building will be erected to house the woman in the measuring basket. This *house* is a 'temple' (NAB, NJB, NLT) or 'shrine' (NJPS), where the *ephah* basket will rest on a

---

91. See further the discussion in Meyers and Meyers (1987: 305–306).

'stand' (NJPS) or 'pedestal' (NJB, NLT). The reference to a 'temple' for the woman in the *ephah* basket and the placement of the basket upon a 'base' or 'pedestal' of some sort suggests that this woman named *wickedness* is a goddess of the Babylonian Pantheon.[92]

Meaning

The divine judgment of the Assyrian and Babylonian exiles purged the Hebrews of idolatry – one sin that the post-exilic prophets do not mention in their indictments of the restoration community. The land of Israel, however, was still contaminated by the spirit of idolatry. In the context of covenant relationship, the land is personified, so it too was defiled by Israel's idolatry. Hence, Zechariah's vision shows God removing the residue of pollution from idolatry from the Promised Land (Lev. 18:24–25). The symbolism of the vision would suggest that this spirit of idolatry has been confined, but still threatens the restoration community. For this reason God sends it back to Babylonia. The destination of the woman in the basket may be a piece of dramatic irony, since the Hebrew people had just returned from exile there (cf. Mic. 4:10). It may also be a metaphor for the removal of sin as far as the east is from the west so that it is remembered no more, as in the Psalms (Ps.103:12; cf. Isa. 43:25). It may even be that the *wickedness* in the basket is simply returning to its source to do its destructive work there, since the earlier visions of Zechariah make it clear that God intends to punish those nations who scattered and humbled Judah (Zech. 1:21).

I. Four chariots (6:1–8)

Context

Zechariah's first (1:7–18) and last (6:1–8) visions share the imagery of horses and the idea of rest. The messages of the two visions are essentially the same, although the details vary. The horses and riders of the first vision (1:7–18) patrol the earth as a divinely

---

92. See the discussion on temple ideology connected with the *ephah* basket in Meyers and Meyers (1987: 296–297); cf. *ZIBBCOT* 5: 216.

commissioned scouting party. The addition of the chariots (6:1) in the final vision (6:1–8) suggests that God is sending off these angelic agents on a military campaign.

Comment

6:1. The prophet's final vision begins with the same formula as that found in 5:1 (cf. the vision formulas in 1:18; 2:1 and see commentary on 1:18, p. 138).

The reference to *four chariots* pulled by teams of horses in Zechariah's last vision stands in contrast to the riders on horses in the first vision (1:7–18). Chariots were the 'storm troops' of the ancient world. They symbolize both the swiftness and the decisive power of God in his intervention in human affairs.[93]

Numerous explanations have been offered for the significance of the *two bronze mountains* of Zechariah's vision. Less likely are the suggestions that the bronze colour simply represents the rising sun tinting the mountains with early morning amber light or that the prophet has borrowed the imagery of Babylonian mythology depicting the sun-god rising between two mountains.[94] If the locale of Jerusalem is the geographical context of the vision, then the two mountains may be Mount Zion and the Mount of Olives flanking the Kidron Valley. More likely, given the themes of temple and divine presence in Zechariah, are the ideas that the two bronze mountains are enhanced images of the two bronze pillars that once flanked the entrance to Solomon's temple (1 Kgs 7:13–22), with bronze symbolizing the impregnable strength of God's abode.[95]

---

93. Baldwin (1972: 139).

94. E.g. Petersen (1984: 267–268); Redditt (1995: 75); and Boda (2004: 319). According to Mesopotamian mythology, Shamash the sun god rose between the twin peaks of the sacred mountain Mashu (cf. 'The Epic of Gilgamesh', in *ANET*: 88–89; and the iconographic portrayals in *ANEP*: 683, 684, 685). On the motif of the cosmic mountain in Canaan and cosmic mountain symbolism in the Solomonic temple, see Clifford (1972: esp. 79–80, 177–181).

95. See the discussions in Mason (1977: 59); Baldwin (1972: 139); and Webb (2003: 103).

2–3. The four chariots are pulled by horses of *red, black, white* and *dappled* colours. The first vision included horses of red, brown and white colours (1:8). The specific colours of the horses are the subject of some debate, as we learn from visionary literature elsewhere in the Bible that the colours of horses sometimes convey symbolic meaning (cf. Rev. 6:1–18). The colours, however, are insignificant to the meaning of this vision.

4. Following the pattern of the earlier visions, the prophet requests an explanation from the interpreting angel.

5. The four chariots are identified as the *four spirits* (so NIV, NLT) or 'winds of heaven' (so NJPS, NAB, NEB, NJB, NRSV; Heb. *rûaḥ*) by the interpreting angel. The *four spirits* or 'winds' of heaven are generally understood to represent the four primary compass points (see commentary on 2:6, pp. 143–144). Here the *four spirits of heaven* represented by the teams of chariot horses are personified as members of the Divine Council who report their reconnaissance missions to God. This suggests that each of the teams of chariot horses may transport an angelic being of some sort, just as the horses carried angelic riders in Zechariah's first vision (1:7–18). The fact that the teams of chariot horses have the capacity to serve as agents of God's judgment lends support to this idea (v. 8). The number *four* signifies 'God's worldwide dominion'.[96]

The verb *standing* may indicate taking a position or a stationing at a post ('presenting themselves', NJPS, NRSV; 'after being reviewed', NAB; 'attending', NEB). The language suggests that the *four spirits* or 'winds' are angelic beings who have presented themselves before God in the Divine Council, where they have received their orders and are now being dispatched to discharge those duties.[97] Boda reminds that 'God is "the Lord of the whole world," a title reinforced by his command over the four winds of heaven.'[98]

6–7. The horse-drawn chariots are sent out according to the points of the compass, with the black horses headed to the north

---

96. Mason (1977: 60).
97. Cf. Petersen (1984: 269–270).
98. Boda (2004: 321).

and the white horses to the west (lit. 'following them', NJB).[99] NJPS, NIV and NRSV adopt the slight, but conjectural, emendation of the MT, and understand the white horses to be headed towards the west,[100] and the dappled horses towards the south. The red horses are not mentioned (but it is presumed 'the roan [headed] to the land of the east', NEB). Given the location of Palestine, 'the significant horses were going north and south'.[101] Twice the horses are described as *powerful* (vv. 3, 7), and they are depicted as *straining to go throughout the earth* (or better, 'eager', NAB; 'impatient', NRSV). The prophet witnesses their dispatch, as the *four spirits* are commanded to *'Go throughout the earth!'* in verse 7.

8. It is unclear whether the interpreting angel continues to speak in verses 7–8,[102] or if the Lord himself enters the discourse (so NLT).[103] In bypassing the interpreting angel at the end of the sequence of night visions, God emphasizes the sure and effective implementation of his word to Israel through the prophet.

Mason (1977: 61) comments, 'Now there is peace, not the peace of helpless suffering, but peace because of God's universal sway. Babylon has been judged and the [Hebrew] exiles liberated.'[104] O'Brien's (2004: 202) observations regarding the reports of *rest* found in the first (1:11) and the last night visions (6:8) are helpful. She notes the progressive fulfilment or actualization of God's promises for restoration, prosperity and comfort for Israel attached to the first night vision (1:7–17) in the succeeding visions from two through to seven (1:18 – 5:11). In the first night vision, *the world is at rest and in peace* (1:11), evoking the prophet's protest in 1:12 because the restoration promised after the Babylonian exile is as yet

---

99. See the discussion in Petersen (1984: 263–263, n. b.).

100. See the full discussion in Meyers and Meyers (1987: 325–326).

101. Redditt (1995: 76).

102. So Petersen (1984: 271).

103. Cf. Meyers and Meyers (1987: 329) who identify the speaker in vv. 7–8 as YHWH on the basis of the possessive pronoun (*my Spirit*).

104. See further the discussion in Boda (2004: 323–324) on the wind of God as an expression of God's wrath spent against the Babylonians, on the basis of the parallels to the judgment of Elam in Jer. 49:36–37.

unfulfilled. In the final night vision, God's Spirit is at rest, since 'the intervening visions have "actualized" God's fulfillment of the promises made in 1:7–17'.[105]

Meaning

The basic message of Zechariah's first and last visions is summarized in the statement: *the Lord of the whole world* (6:5). God's control of the *four spirits of heaven* (v. 5) stresses his universal sovereignty over the nations. The fact that this message frames the night-vision section of Zechariah like a pair of bookends tells us that this truth claim was vital to the prophet's message of comfort and encouragement to post-exilic Judah.

The departure of the teams of chariot horses on a worldwide mission of military intervention establishes part of the core meaning for all the visions. God's revelation to Zechariah indicated that, beyond the rebuilt temple and a rejuvenated government, Israel could be assured that God would follow through on his promise to *shake the heavens and the earth … and overturn royal thrones* and establish his kingdom in the world (Hag. 2:21–22). 'Only when foreign nations were overthrown could the chosen people be truly free once again.'[106]

Zechariah's final vision highlights two enduring theological truths that are repeated themes in Zechariah and in the Bible as a whole. First, God is indeed Lord of human history (Isa. 46:9–10; Jude 25; Rev. 15:3). Secondly, God's word is absolutely sure and true (Matt. 5:17–20; John 10:34–35). These two messages are always relevant during troubled times, when the people of God need anchors or moorings for lives adrift – whether ancient or modern.

J. The crowning of high priest Joshua (6:9–15)

Context

Like the accompanying oracle (2:6–13) of the third vision (2:1–5), the eighth and last vision of Zechariah (6:1–8) includes an

---

105. O'Brien (2004: 202).
106. Craigie (1985: 186).

accompanying oracle (6:9–15). Some biblical commentators regard the oracle as a later addition to the night-vision section of the book, since the visions aptly conclude with the Spirit of God *at rest* (6:8).[107] Yet the symbolic-action message depicting the coronation of Joshua as both king and priest brings closure to the topic of leadership presented in the fourth (ch. 3) and fifth visions (ch. 4). In that sequence of visions, both Joshua the high priest and Zerubbabel the governor are singled out as divinely appointed leaders for post-exilic Judah. Zerubbabel, however, is conspicuously absent from this concluding vision addressing leadership in post-exilic Judah. This has raised numerous questions for interpreters of Zechariah's final vision.[108] In addition, the sermon attached to the last vision assures the Hebrews still living in the diaspora that they too have a stake in this Second Temple and the restoration God has planned for Jerusalem and the land of Israel (6:15a).

Comment

9. *The word of the LORD came to me.* (See commentary on 1:1 above on the prophetic word formula.)

10. The gifts for the tabernacle and Solomon's temple included large amounts of *silver and gold,* the offerings of choice for gods and kings in the ancient world (Exod. 25:3; 1 Chr. 29:2). The NIV inserts *silver and gold* as the object of the verbal action on the basis of the offering mentioned in verse 11, as the verb *take* is used elliptically (cf. NAB, 'Take from the returned captives …'). *The exiles Heldai, Tobijah and Jedaiah, who have arrived from Babylon* are unknown apart from the references in Zechariah 6:10, 14. They were recent returnees to Jerusalem from exile in Babylonia and apparently were the couriers designated by Jews still in Babylonia to deliver the donations to the Second Temple building fund. The name changes for two of the four individuals mentioned by the prophet (*Helem* instead of *Heldai,* and *Hen* instead of *Josiah,* v. 14) may be due to their desire to have their formal names entered in the official temple records.[109]

---

107. E.g. Mason (1977: 63); cf. Redditt (1995: 76–77).

108. See the summary in Webb (2003: 108).

109. Cf. Baldwin (1972: 146).

The construction of the verse is awkward, but it is assumed that Josiah is also a recent returnee from exile (in an earlier wave of Jewish emigrants from Mesopotamia; cf. NAB, 'Take from the returned captives Heldai, Tobijah, Jedaiah ... Josiah ... [these had come from Babylon]'). Some commentators speculate that Josiah son of Zephaniah had priestly ties as the son of the second ranked priest taken into Babylonian exile (2 Kgs 25:18), but this identification is uncertain.[110]

11. Presumably the prophet takes at least a portion of the offering of *silver and gold* brought for the Second Temple reconstruction by the three named couriers from Babylonia (v. 9).[111]

Redditt understands that Josiah is the craftsman who fashions the *crown*.[112] It seems more likely that the prophet crafts the tiara, since he is the recipient of the divine word (v. 9; perhaps using the tools of Josiah who may indeed have been a metal smith and whose house served as a smith shop as well).[113] The word (Heb. *ʿăṭārâ*) describes a crown or a wreath and is plural in the MT. The term is one of three words used for a royal crown or tiara in the OT (along with *keter* and *neẓer*), but was not limited to royalty, since in Isaiah 28:3 and Esther 8:15 it is worn by persons other than a king.[114] More difficult is the plural form of the noun 'crowns' (so NJPS); and though the ancient versions read 'crown' (e.g. LXX, Syr., Targ.), 'the principle of *lectio difficilior* [the more difficult reading] requires that the MT reading be preserved'.[115] The number of crowns in question may be one, two or even four (see. v. 14 below), depending

---

110. E.g. Petersen (1984: 274); Boda (2004: 336); cf. Meyers and Meyers (1987: 344–345) on the hypothetical, but plausible, identification; and Merrill (1994: 195) who cautions, 'there is no way of knowing if Josiah was his descendant'.

111. Note that Meyers and Meyers (1987: 348) suggest that the word order, *silver and gold*, may indicate that, as a medium of exchange, silver was more valuable than gold.

112. Redditt (1995: 77); also Webb (2003: 107).

113. So Boda (2004: 337).

114. See Redditt (1995: 77).

115. Petersen (1984: 275); cf. Meyers and Meyers (1987: 349–350).

upon the source consulted. The type or style of crown is also uncertain. The plural form of the noun is probably intended to describe a 'double crown' or a single crown comprised of two circles or bands of metal (one gold and one silver). Baldwin describes these eastern crowns as 'circlets, which could be worn singly or fitted together to make a composite crown'.[116] It is unclear whether the bands of gold and silver were intertwined or layered in Zechariah's account, but each band represented one of the offices to which Joshua was appointed (that of king and priest). The three (or four, see v. 10 above) Jewish envoys from Babylonia were both witnesses to, and honorees of, Zechariah's symbolic-action oracle.

12–13. The high priest Joshua is presented as *the Branch* (v. 12) who will complete the Second Temple. (On the messianic title *Branch*, see the commentary on 3:8, p. 151.) The symbolic-action oracle concluding the night-vision sequence (6:9–15) explains this typological relationship between Joshua and the Branch referenced earlier in the fourth night vision (3:1–10).

The literal meaning of this expression, *and he will branch out from his place,* may be rendered 'from under him someone will sprout up' (cf. NJB, 'where he is, there will be a branching out').[117] The one who will *build the temple of the LORD* (v. 13a) is the one who sprouts out of Joshua – *the Branch* previously identified in the fourth vision (3:8). The NIV and NLT understand the *priest* (Heb. *kōhēn*) to be the object of the verb (*and he will be a priest*), while other EVV view the word *priest* as the subject of the verb ('and a priest will be on the throne', cf. NJPS, NRSV). Some EVV agree with the LXX, 'And the priest shall be on his right' (NETS; cf. NAB, NEB, NJB). If the figure named *the Branch* also sits on the throne as priest, then he will wear two crowns (or one double crown), the symbols of kingship and priesthood, and thus unify the two offices.

It should be noted that the logical referent to *the two* (lit. 'the two of them') are the two thrones of the immediate context of verse 13 (the royal throne and the priestly throne). That is, *the Branch* will fill

---

116. Baldwin (1972: 141).
117. Meyers and Meyers (1987: 355).

the two roles of king and priest in perfect *harmony*. If a priest other than the Branch sits on the throne, 'then between the two of them [i.e. the king and the high priest] there shall be friendly understanding' (NAB). Zechariah makes a startling declaration: the Branch 'will rule as king from his throne. He will also serve as priest from his throne' (NLT). However, this should not completely surprise us, because such a development was anticipated in the Psalms, with the introduction of the king-priest who would rule after the manner of both David and Melchizedek (Ps. 110:2, 4). Rose considers the two portraits of the Branch (Zech. 3:8; 6:12–13) as primarily a reference to an unidentified future Davidic figure. Although the title *Branch* is ascribed to Joshua the high priest, the background for the term is Jeremiah 23:5–8, and the declaration that YHWH will bring him forth suggests this is a messianic oracle.[118] The NT identifies Jesus Christ as this Branch who is both king and priest after the order of Melchizedek (Heb. 7:1, 15). It would seem that the temple this Branch ultimately builds is the true place of worship – the sacred tent of the heavenly realm built upon the death, burial and resurrection of Jesus as the Messiah (Heb. 8:2; cf. John 2:19).

14. The construction is awkward, lacking an active verb (lit. 'The crowns will be for Helem … for a memorial'). The crown(s) remain in the Second Temple; they are not *given* to the four representatives of Jewish expatriates in Babylonia (so NIV), or placed in 'the care of' the men (so NRSV; cf. NJB, 'The crown will serve … as a memorial'; NLT, 'The crown will be a memorial in the Temple of the LORD to honor those …'). Redditt understands that four crowns were made, one for each of the men named.[119] This is unlikely, given the symbolic value of the crown(s) for the office of the high priest (since the language of v. 11 indicates that a single or '[one] crown' [NJPS] was placed on Joshua's head). The word *memorial* denotes an object that serves as a sign of remembrance, evoking memories of special events or persons. The symbolic crown(s) marking the investiture of Joshua in the

---

118. See Rose (2000: 140–141).
119. Cf. Redditt (1995: 77–78).

office of high priest was (or were) placed as a memorial in the Second Temple to the donors of the gold and silver. Thus 'the crown did not remain on the head of the high priest, nor did it become his possession. He, after all, was not the Branch.'[120] If the second of two crowns, a silver crown, is set on the high priest's head, the act is innovative for the priests, indicating 'Joshua's expanded role in the newly defined office of high priesthood' (yet falling short of full monarchic power).[121] If a single crown with double ringlets, one silver and one gold, is placed on the head of the high priest, not only is the role of the high priest expanded, the office of high priest and king are symbolically combined (at least temporarily) in the high priest Joshua. This suggests that Zechariah looks forward to a time when the Branch (of David) will be both priest and king. 'The symbolic coronation and the enigmatic term "Branch" referred to a future leader, who would fulfil to perfection the offices of priest and king ... In this way the priestly and royal offices will be unified.'[122] In either case, it served as a permanent reminder of Joshua's divinely ordained coronation as a type of 'priest-king', and as a visual aid for the priests in their teaching of this new development in the tradition of the Levitical priesthood.[123]

15. The remote regions Zechariah had in mind are unspecified (*those who are far away will come*). The purpose of the reference seems to be to recognize the contribution of diaspora Jews in rebuilding

---

120. McComiskey (1998: 1118).

121. Meyers and Meyers (1987: 50–51); see especially their discussion of the terms for crowns in the OT and their conclusion that the application of royal terms to the high priest in Zech. 3:5 and 6:11 'must be intentional and fully within the prophet's overall purpose'. R. L. Smith (1984: 218) notes that if both Zerubbabel and Joshua are enthroned, 'that would suggest a diarchy in Judah in post-exilic times'. Boda (2004: 341) connects the two thrones (v. 13) to Joshua, the priestly figure, and Zerubbabel, the royal figure (whose arrival from Babylon is imminent?).

122. Baldwin (1972: 145); cf. Hill (2008: 558).

123. See Baldwin (1972: 145).

the Second Temple, so that 'all Israel' might identify with the structure.

Each of the two accompanying oracles in the vision section of the book (2:6–13; 6:9–15) include a variation of the validation formula (*and you will know that the LORD Almighty has sent me to you*; cf. 2:9; 6:15). The prophets Haggai, Zechariah and Malachi faced a crisis in the credibility of the prophetic word during their early post-exilic period ministries. This was due to the fact that in the minds of the people the word of God had seemingly failed, since the promises of Jeremiah and Ezekiel for a new covenant and a Davidic ruler were unfulfilled (cf. Jer. 31:30; Ezek. 34:23). The validation formulas, however, were intended to do more than bolster flagging confidence in prophetic preaching. They are tied to specific acts of God in history, whether for judgment (2:9) or restoration (6:15), and served as an indirect reminder to the people to look about them and see God's handiwork in current events (even as Malachi bid post-exilic Judah to consider the fate of Edom, Mal. 1:4–5).

The conditional nature of the fulfilment of these divine revelations to Zechariah (*This will happen if you diligently obey*) connects the vision section of the book to the prologue. God will see that his plans for the restoration of Jerusalem and Judah are implemented, but the people must also participate in the work of God by obeying his word. The prophet's challenge to *diligently obey the LORD your God* (6:15b) brings his message back full circle to the call to repentance in the prologue (1:1–6). The promise of God's word would surely be fulfilled. The only question was whether the realization of Zechariah's visions would eventuate in the perpetuation of the grim reality of their current circumstances or in the joyful reversal of divine restoration. The answer rested upon the decision of the people to heed the call to *return to the LORD* (1:3).

Meaning

Joshua the high priest is identified as the *Branch*, and the one who will *build the temple of the LORD* (vv. 12–13a). He (and the priestly office) is invested with royal authority, as he will rule on his throne (v. 13b). Joshua and the Levitical priesthood, at least for a time, will

unify the offices of priest and king, a striking new development in
the leadership of Israel (v. 13c).[124]

---

124. Cf. Stuhlmueller (1988: 98) who notes that for an indeterminate time
period, 'the future of Israel lies with the temple and its priesthood'.

3. ZECHARIAH'S MESSAGES (7 – 8)

Context

Chapters 7 and 8 represent excerpts from messages or sermons preached by Zechariah, and as such they convey a 'patchwork quilt' of his thought and theology.[1] The first sermon condenses two messages: questions concerning fasting (7:1–7), and the prophet's reflection upon Israel's failure to practise social justice in the pre-exilic period of Hebrew history (7:8–14). The sermons have loose connections with the preceding symbolic-action oracle (6:9–15). In each case, the sections begin with the reception of delegations (from Babylonia and Bethel respectively), both units offer assurance that the Second Temple will be rebuilt (6:12; 8:3, 9), and both emphasize the importance of obedience to God's word (6:15; 7:8–14; 8:16).[2]

---

1. Craigie (1985: 189); cf. Stuhlmueller (1988: 106; citing Mason [1984]) on Zechariah's response to the question about fasting as a 'model sermon'.

2. R. L. Smith (1984: 220).

Comment

A. Zechariah receives a delegation from Bethel (7:1–7)

i. The delegation raises a question about fasting (vv. 1–3)

7:1. The third and final date formula of the book, *the fourth year of King Darius*, places the event on 7 December 518 BC. Nearly two years have elapsed since the series of night visions experienced by the prophet (cf. 1:7). It is possible that the date formula refers primarily to the timing of the delegation seeking answers to questions on fasting (vv. 2–7), rather than to the synopses of the prophet's messages. In either case, the date is near the mid-point between the refounding ceremony (Hag. 2:10–23) and the completion (Ezra 6:14), in terms of the temple rebuilding project.[3] (On *King Darius* see the commentary on 1:1, p. 124.)

2. *Bethel* was a town of Benjamin, some twelve miles north of Jerusalem. The site had a long history as a worship centre, notably as the place where Jacob had his ladder dream (Gen. 28:19), and as one of two temple cities during the era of the Hebrew divided monarchies (cf. 1 Kgs 12:29; Amos 4:4; 7:13). *Bethel* was resettled by Jews returning from the Babylonian exile (Ezra 2:28; Neh. 7:32). Nothing is known of these citizens of Bethel, *Sharezer and Regem-Melech, together with their men*, who served as envoys, although their names are of Babylonian extraction.[4] The MT is awkward, prompting some to read *Bethel* with *Sharezer* as a compound name, 'Bethel-Sharezer' (e.g. NAB, 'Bethelsarezer sent Regemmelech'). This reading then raises the question as to the point of origin of the delegation, perhaps journeying from Babylonia.[5]

The verb *entreat* translates a Hebrew idiom (lit. 'to soften the face') and refers to a ritual act that entailed asking God to grant a petition or make a ruling on a question, and probably included some kind of sacrifice or offering.[6] Given the context, the expression connotes

---

3. See Boda (2004: 353).
4. Meyers and Meyers (1987: 383).
5. Cf. Baldwin (1972: 150); Redditt (1995: 80–81); and Blenkinsopp (1998: 32).
6. See the discussion in Meyers and Meyers (1987: 384).

both a request to learn God's will and an initiative to gain his favourable response.[7]

3. The two prominent sources of divine revelation for Israel, *priest* and *prophet*, are still centred in the temple precincts, now under construction (cf. Mic. 3:11).[8] 'The priests were commissioned to offer interpretations or rulings for specific situations based on the law and to provide direct access to direct revelation through the use of Urim and Thummim' (cf. the priestly rulings on holiness laws in Hag. 2:10–14).[9] Zechariah, and perhaps Haggai, are among the group of prophets mentioned who provided 'direct revelation in oracular form' (cf. Ezra 5:1).[10]

The delegation to Jerusalem poses the question on behalf of *the people of Bethel* (cf. v. 2a, NIV, NLT), implied in the verb *to entreat* (v. 2b).[11] The question about the necessity of continuing the long-observed ritual fasting, lamenting the destruction of Solomon's temple in the *fifth month*, may have been prompted by the near completion of the Second Temple. Zechariah's formal answer to the question is delayed (cf. 8:18–19). Boda's (2004: 356) comment is insightful, suggesting that the delegation addressed the priests first, expecting an answer from them given the binary character of the question (i.e. it can be answered by yes or no): 'Instead, the delegation receives a far more complicated answer that deepens the view of their role [i.e. the priests] in inaugurating the new era of restoration (repentance) and expands their view of the eventual goal of this new era (nations).' More literally, the query addresses 'weeping' and the practice of 'abstaining' or restricting oneself (cf. 'weep and abstain', ESV; 'lament and abstain', NEB). This terminology reflects the vocabulary of the laity making the request (contra the more technical liturgical terminology used in

---

7. McComiskey (1998: 1124).

8. Cf. Mason (1977: 66), who comments that the priests and prophets function alongside one another as in the pre-exilic period (although he dates the visit of the delegation from Bethel to after the Second Temple is completed).

9. Boda (2004: 356).

10. Ibid.

11. See Redditt (1995: 81).

the response in v. 5 below).[12] The liturgical practice in question is the ritual fasting commemorating the fall of Jerusalem and the destruction of the temple by the Babylonians in 587 BC (as evidenced in the prophet's response in v. 5).

ii. The prophet's initial response (vv. 4–7)

4. Zechariah's response (vv. 4–7) is generally understood as a rebuke to the delegation from Bethel and a criticism of hypocritical liturgical practice on the part of the people. *Ask all the people of the land*: the prophet responds to a wider audience than the delegation from Bethel, including all *the people of the land* of Judah *and the priests*. Meyers and Meyers (1987: 387) identify *the priests* as simply part of the wider audience, 'since they are not conveyers of this kind of oracular response', unlike O'Brien (2004: 210), who sees the literary unit of 7:1–7 as 'Zechariah's polemic against worship practices at Bethel' (and by extension to Judah more broadly, given the reference to the people of the land?).

5. The terms *fasted* and *mourned* are technical liturgical terms for ritual abstinence from food, and ritual lamentation (NEB, 'fasted and lamented').[13] The series of ritual fasts commemorated events associated with the fall of Jerusalem to the Babylonians, including the destruction of the city and the temple in the *fifth month*, and the assassination of the Babylonian-appointed governor Gedaliah (seven years later) in the *seventh month* (see further commentary on 8:19, p. 199).[14] The reference to *seventy years* was the projected duration of the Babylonian exile by Jeremiah (cf. Jer. 25:9–11; 29:10).

The rhetorical question, *was it really for me that you fasted?*, anticipates the answer, 'No, certainly not!' As Petersen observes, 'The presumed answer is no … yet no reason is offered.'[15] The

---

12. Ibid.
13. Boda (2004: 358) notes that the prophet's use of the more technical language for fasting reveals 'the communicative nature of the fasting liturgy. It was designed to gain the ear of God and to express the repentance of the people.'
14. See the chronological chart in Boda (2004: 357).
15. Petersen (1984: 286).

prophet's response questions the motive of the people's participation in the ritual fasting, typically understood as an indictment
for their lack of sincerity and dutiful formalism in observing the
fast days.

6. R. L. Smith (1984: 224) suggests that the fasts of Zechariah's
time permitted some consumption of food and drink. This is
unlikely, as the expression 'eating and drinking' tends to refer to
daily nourishment,[16] although the immediate context may connect
the eating and drinking to the feast days of the Hebrew liturgical
calendar.[17] The ambiguity may be intentional, since in either case
the people are accused of failing to recognize God as the provider
of their daily nourishment.[18]

7. Zechariah's appeal to the *earlier prophets* is a theme in the first
half of the book, connecting his message to the prologue (1:4), and
demonstrating continuity with the preaching of the pre-exilic
prophets in the call for humility and sincerity in their worship of
YHWH. Meyers and Meyers (1987: 396) summarize:

> The theme of recalling traditional prophetic pronouncements and the
> people's response – or lack of response – is the central theme of this
> third part of Zechariah. Zechariah reviews past oracles delivered by the
> prophets, relates the results, considers the present situation, and looks
> toward the future. Each step of the way, prophetic utterance is invoked:
> earlier prophets (here and in 7:12), present prophets (8:9), and the
> prophet Zechariah's own oracular conclusion (8:18ff.).

Here the prophet's rhetorical questions assume the answer, 'Yes,
precisely so!' The specific period of the pre-exilic era Zechariah has
in mind, *when Jerusalem and its surrounding towns were at rest and
prosperous*, is unspecified. The point is the contrast with the former
days and the present reality of the Persian period. The territorial
size (and most likely the population) of post-exilic Judah and its
economic prosperity have been greatly reduced. Two overarching

---

16. Boda (2004: 359).
17. See Redditt (1995: 82).
18. McComiskey (1998: 1127).

purposes in the oracles of chapters 7 – 8 are identified. First, the sermons accentuate the folly of the former generation in squandering peace and prosperity by their refusal to repent (7:11–14). And second, they hint at the conditions the Persian period community might expect if they obey the message of Zechariah (8:1–19).[19]

Some commentators begin a new paragraph with verse 7, since it is assumed that verses 9–10 are a more appropriate summary of the message of *the earlier prophets* (v. 7) than verses 5–6.[20] Others begin the new paragraph with verse 8, since the prophetic word formula (*the word of the LORD came*) typically begins new literary units (so NEB, NJPS, NIV, NRSV).[21] In either case (even if two sermons have been combined), the two messages (vv. 4–14) belong together (so NJB), 'since the one aim is to bring home the purpose of fasting'.[22]

Meaning

The priests ministering in the Jerusalem temple received a delegation from Bethel, seeking a ruling on the continuation of the ritual fasting recalling the destruction of the temple by the Babylonians (vv. 2–3). Zechariah's initial response charged the people with hypocrisy, intimating that their ritual practices were self-serving (v. 6).

B. The call to covenant justice (7:8–14)

Context

In his follow-up to the delegation, Zechariah situates the questions related to fasting in a much wider context. Israel's failure to practise social justice as prescribed by the Mosaic covenant led to the Assyrian and Babylonian exiles (v. 14). Zechariah's call to repentance (1:3) is all the more urgent, given the history of Israel's stubbornness and rejection of the words of earlier prophets (vv. 11–12).

---

19. Boda (2004: 360).
20. E.g. R. L. Smith (1984: 225); Redditt (1995: 82); Boda (2004: 359); and McComiskey (1998: 1130).
21. Cf. Petersen (1984: 289); and Merrill (1994: 212).
22. Baldwin (1972: 154).

Comment

i. The admonition for social justice rejected by the Hebrew ancestors (vv. 8–12)

7:8. The prophetic word formula, *And the word of the LORD came again to Zechariah*, is considered by many commentators to be intrusive and mistakenly introduced by an editor who assumed that the messenger formula (*This is what the LORD Almighty says*, v. 9) began a new oracle.[23] Yet this formula indicates 'that the word of God entered Zechariah's consciousness as he found it in the writings of his prophetic predecessors, particularly the prophecy of Jeremiah'.[24] (On the messenger formula see further commentary on 1:1, pp. 124–125.)

9–10. Zechariah identifies four precepts or authoritative instructions for behaviour that ought to characterize the social life of Israel as a community bound to YHWH in covenant. The verb *administer* (v. 9; 'render', NAB, NRSV; cf. NLT, 'judge fairly') signifies the practice of executing justice in a formal judicial setting ('apply the law fairly', NJB). The term is also 'used in the wider meaning of restoring harmony and peace where there has been conflict and injustice'.[25]

The second positive injunction, to *show mercy and compassion*, clarifies and expands the understanding of *true justice*. The term *justice* is used to introduce the commandments of the Sinai covenant that regulate Israel's relationship with God and one another in covenant community (Exod. 21:1). To *administer true justice* is 'to do it with the spirit of faithful loyalty and tender compassion'.[26] *True justice* demonstrates concern for the individual and mitigating circumstances, and goes beyond simply executing justice according to the letter of the law ('deal loyally and compassionately with one another', NJPS).[27] Showing *mercy* and

23. E.g. Baldwin (1972: 155); and Meyers and Meyers (1987: 398).
24. McComiskey (1998: 1130).
25. Baldwin (1972: 155).
26. Boda (2004: 361).
27. Cf. Redditt (1995: 83), who comments that 'rendering true judgments included hearing cases on their merits, rather than submitting to bribes'.

compassion is God's basic self-proclaimed identity (Exod. 34:6–7).

The two precepts (v. 9) provide the groundwork for the admonitions that follow. In contexts emphasizing social justice, the word *oppress* means to mistreat or exploit economically those people on the margins of society (*Do not oppress the widow or the fatherless, the alien* ['foreigner', NIV 2011] *or the poor* [v. 10a]), who often did not have access to the same legal protection afforded the average citizen (cf. Exod. 22:22, 24; Deut. 10:18; 14:29; 16:11, 14; 24:14, 17–18; 26:12–13). The verbal construction of the clause conveys the sense of 'Stop oppressing ...', calling for an end to ongoing fraudulent practices (cf. NJPS, 'Do not defraud ...'). The issues of fasting (v. 6) and social justice are linked in Isaiah's call for true fasting (Isa. 58:6). The verb *think* (*evil of each other*, NIV [v. 10b]) is better rendered in a more active (and sinister) sense ('do not plot evil against one another', NJPS; 'do not secretly plan evil against one another', NJB). The second negative command parallels 8:17 (*do not plot evil against your neighbour*, NIV), where the prohibition is linked to swearing falsely ('do not love perjury', NJPS, NJB). The repetition of *one another* in verses 9–10 emphasizes the mutuality implicit in the Israelite covenant community.[28]

11. The word *refused* means essentially to ignore orders, whether verbal or written (as in YHWH's covenant stipulations, cf. Jer. 11:10). The Hebrew idiom, 'to set a defiant shoulder', signifies a haughtiness that belies an unabashed recalcitrance ('They presented a balky back', NJPS; 'they turned a rebellious shoulder', NJB; cf. Neh. 9:26, 29).[29] *But they ... and stopped up their ears.* The verb *stopped up* means to 'make dull' or 'be insensitive', and places full responsibility upon the people for their obstinacy ('and turned a deaf ear', NJPS; cf. Isa. 6:10). The same expression is used of Pharaoh when he 'hardened his heart' against God and refused to release the Hebrews (Exod. 8:32). Sadly, the history of Israel's relationship with YHWH was characterized by obstinacy (cf. Mal. 3:7).

---

28. On the mutuality of the Hebrew community, see Ollenburger (1996: 770); cf. O'Brien (2004: 213–214) on the resonances between Zech. 7:8–12 and other OT prophetic passages; and Petersen (1984: 289–290) on the parallels of Zech. 7:8–14 to Jeremiah.

29. Cf. Meyers and Meyers (1987: 402).

12. To make one's heart as *hard as flint* is to steel one's own will against the will of God. The word *flint* is rare in the OT and may be a word for diamond, the hardest substance known (cf. Jer. 17:1; Ezek. 3:9). The first and third words in the series of four terms used to describe Israel's intransigence refer to hearing, the second to the body, and the fourth to the heart or will.[30] The four expressions taken together (vv. 11–12a) portray pre-exilic Israel and Judah as incorrigibly rebellious. The pattern of four statements characterizing the Hebrew defiance of God and his covenant have their literary parallel in the four precepts characterizing God's ethical standards for Israelite social life (vv. 9–10).

The verb *listen* connotes 'obedience': the people 'refused to obey' (CEV) or 'they refused to pay heed' (NJPS). The noun *law* (Heb. *tôrâ*) is better rendered 'instruction' (NJPS, NLT) or 'teaching' (NAB, NJB), no doubt based on the law of Moses.

This is the third time Zechariah intimates his continuity with *the earlier prophets* (cf. 1:4; 7:7, 12). Nehemiah also recognized the agency and empowerment of God's Spirit in the prophets (Neh. 9:30), a reality they themselves were aware of at the time (cf. Mic. 3:8). Israel's stubbornness and hardheartedness provoked God's 'fury' (NJB), his 'terrible wrath' (NJPS), leading to the scattering of the people in the Assyrian and especially the Babylonian exiles (v. 14).

ii. God's punishment: exile (vv. 13–14)

13. The patience and longsuffering of YHWH notwithstanding (Exod. 34:6–7), he will respond in kind to his people – whether turning to them as they turn to him in repentance (1:3; cf. Mal. 3:7), or turning away from them as they turn their backs on him (v. 11; cf. Jer. 11:11; Ezek. 8:18).[31]

14. This form of the verb *scattered* occurs only here in the OT. The verb conveys the image of a raging storm and is typical of prophetic speech (cf. Isa. 40:24; 41:16; 54:11).[32] The expression calls

---

30. Meyers and Meyers (1987: 402).

31. Petersen (1984: 293–294) rightly places this passage in the context of covenant language.

32. Cf. Meyers and Meyers (1987: 404); and Boda (2004: 362–363).

to mind the word-picture from Hosea of the Israelites being scattered like chaff in the *whirlwind* (of exile, Hos. 13:3). The scattering of the Hebrews among the nations was one of the curses associated with the violation of the Mosaic covenant (cf. Deut. 28:36–37, 64).

The report that *the land was left so desolate … that no-one could come or go* is either a statement of hyperbole, emphasizing the extent of the destruction from the foreign invasions resulting in the (Assyrian and) Babylonian exiles; or the absence of travellers, given the grim reality of lawlessness and violence in the land after the destruction of the Judean monarchy.[33]

The *pleasant land* is the land of God's covenant promise (Ps. 106:24; Jer. 3:19). The responsibility for this reversal of fortune lay with Israel ('they turned a land of delights into a desert', NJB): divine judgment for covenant unfaithfulness in the form of idolatry (cf. Jer. 12:10).

Meaning

God's judgment, resulting in the destruction of Jerusalem, the desolation of the *pleasant land* and the scattering of the Hebrew people, was justified (vv. 13–14). This was due to Israel's disobedience, especially their failure to *administer justice and show mercy* (vv. 8–11). The recitation of the failure of their Hebrew ancestors to heed similar prophetic calls to social justice served as a veiled threat to Zechariah's audience – history, even the catastrophe of the Babylonian exile, was repeatable (vv. 11–12).

C. God's promise of restoration for Jerusalem (8:1–8)

Context

Like the previous chapter, this literary unit of Zechariah is an anthology of sayings from the prophet's sermons and messages. The highlights or 'sermon nuggets' in these collected works are joined by a series of five messenger formulas in each of the two larger literary units (*this is what the LORD Almighty says*: vv. 2, 3, 4, 6, 7 in 8:1–8; and vv. 9, 14, 19, 20, 23 in 8:9–23). This chapter is

---

33. See Redditt (1995: 84); and Meyers and Meyers (1987: 405).

connected to the previous one by the topic of fasting (questions posed in 7:2–7 and answered in 8:18–19) and the ethical demands of covenant relationship with YHWH (7:8–10; 8:16–17). The overall tone and message of the chapter, however, shifts from admonition and judgment to exhortation and restoration. The stylized sermons of chapters 7 and 8 set up the interplay of those two themes, judgment and restoration, in the two closing oracles of Zechariah (9 – 11, 12 – 14).

The collection of Zechariah's sayings or mini-oracles is arranged in a series progressing from the immediate to the more distant future. The messages are unified by the promises of restoration for God's city and his people, and are designed to instil hope in the post-exilic Jewish community. The first section (vv. 2–8) consists of five sayings (vv. 2, 3, 4–5, 6, 7–8), focusing on God's programme of 'urban renewal' for Jerusalem.

Comment

i. God's zeal for Zion (vv. 1–2)

8:1. (On the messenger formula introducing the collection of sayings and sermons, see further the commentary on 1:1 and 7:1 above.)

2. The verb 'to be jealous' echoes YHWH's zeal for Mount Zion and Jerusalem voiced earlier in 1:14 (see commentary, p. 135). The repetition of the word indicates the depth of God's passion for his city and his people ('intensely jealous', NAB). The semantic range of the root word ranges across the emotions of zeal and jealousy, and YHWH's zeal for his people is expressed 'in a passionate demand for exclusivity in relationship (Exod. 20:5; Josh. 24:19) and a passionate protection of his people (Isa. 42:13; Ezek. 36:5–6)'.[34]

The word *burning* can refer to God's wrath ('I am jealous for her with great wrath', NRSV). Here Zechariah follows Ezekiel's use of the combination of *burning* and *jealousy* 'to speak of Israel's deliverance' (Ezek. 36:6).[35] God's passion is a basic element of OT theology and

---

34. Boda (2004: 380).
35. Ibid.

marks him as a personal deity, not an abstract natural force. God is 'fiercely jealous' (NJPS) for Zion, and Zechariah's audience can be assured that God's 'furious jealousy' (NJB) will motivate him to act on their behalf.

ii. God's return to Zion (v. 3)

3. Zechariah's declaration that YHWH *will return to Zion and dwell in Jerusalem* reinforces the idea of the manifest presence of God in his creation. This is one of the great themes of the Bible, beginning with the intimate fellowship with God experienced by that first human pair (cf. Gen. 3:8–9) and ending with paradise regained when God himself will live with his people (Rev. 21:3). This divine presence was both represented and symbolized for Israel in the Mosaic tabernacle (Exod. 25:8) and later Solomon's temple (2 Chr. 7:2). The ark of the covenant was the tangible point of interface between God and the Hebrew people during OT times, because it was there where God met with his people (Exod. 25:22; cf. 1 Chr. 28:2).

The word *truth* (*City of Truth*) may be rendered 'faithful' (so NAB, NIV [2011], NJPS, NRSV). The prophet Isaiah likened the demise of Jerusalem to a faithful woman turned into a prostitute (Isa. 1:21). Zechariah shares Isaiah's vision for the reversal of Jerusalem's status to a 'Faithful City' (NJB) once again (Isa. 1:26). The word *truth* (or 'faithful') appears only in the messages of Zechariah (7:9; 8:3; 8, 16 [twice], 19), and the repetition of the term 'conveys the importance of the holy city for the process of establishing justice in society'.[36]

The reference to *the mountain of the LORD Almighty* may be an allusion to other prophetic teachings, emphasizing the inviolability of Zion as God's *Holy Mountain* or dwelling place by unclean and godless people (Isa. 52:1; cf. Joel 3:17).

iii. God restores peace and safety to Jerusalem (vv. 4–5)

4–5. Fittingly, 'the prophet uses two images that represent life at its two extremes (childhood and aged), the periods of greatest

---

36. Meyers and Meyers (1987: 413).

vulnerability'.[37] The images of the elderly 'in the squares of Jerusalem' (NJB) and 'boys and girls playing in the streets' (NEB) signal the re-population and resumption of normal family life in the once-decimated city of Jerusalem. The return of God's presence to his rebuilt temple will also bring the return of peace and safety for the inhabitants of the city (as envisioned by Jeremiah, cf. Jer. 30:18–22).

iv. God will bring his people back from exile and repopulate Jerusalem (vv. 6–8)

6–8. The Bible portrays the Lord as the God of the impossible or the miraculous ('Even though it seems impossible ...', NRSV, v. 6a; Job 42:2; Matt. 19:26). Whether giving Abraham and Sarah a child in their old age (Gen. 18:14) or delivering his own holy city to the Babylonians for destruction (Jer. 32:27), nothing is too difficult for the God who made the heavens and the earth (Jer. 32:17). The word *impossible* means to be *marvellous* (NIV) in the sense of a 'miracle' (NJB). Baldwin (1972: 160) comments, 'The fourth saying warns against allowing human reason to decide what God is likely to do' (cf. Gen. 18:14; Jer. 32:25). The verb *save* (v. 7a) is understood in the sense of 'rescue' (so NJPS, NAB, NJB, NLT) or 'deliver'.[38]

The phrase *from the countries of the east and the west* (v. 7b) is an idiom for all the regions where the Hebrew people have been dispersed (lit. 'from the land of the rising and the land of the setting of the sun', cf. Isa. 43:5–6). Even as God scattered Israel among the nations in his wrath, he will bring them back to repopulate Jerusalem in his mercy.

The covenant formula, *they will be my people ... I will be ... their God* (v. 8), signifies restored relationship between God and his people (perhaps an allusion to Jer. 31:33).

Meaning
The first section of Zechariah's second sermon (vv. 1–8) has parallels to the prophet's opening visions, and reminds the audience

---

37. Boda (2004: 380).

38. Meyers and Meyers (1987: 417–418).

that God is faithful to his covenant promises (v. 8) and still works miracles for his people (v. 6). This will be seen in the Lord's return and residence in Jerusalem (vv. 2–3; cf. 1:16–17), the restoration and security of the city of Jerusalem (vv. 4–5; cf. 2:2–5), and the regathering of the scattered former Hebrew exiles in Jerusalem (vv. 7–8; cf. 2:6–9).

D. God's promises to deliver and restore the remnant of Israel (8:9–23)

Context

The collection of Zechariah's sayings or mini-oracles is arranged in a series progressing from the immediate to the more distant future. The messages are unified by the promises of restoration for God's city and his people, and designed to instil hope in the post-exilic Jewish community. The second section (vv. 9–23) consists of four sayings (vv. 9–13, 14–17, 18–19, 20–23).

The first unit (vv. 9–13) is a sermon exhorting the people to support the reconstruction of the Second Temple and promising economic and agricultural blessings. A second exhortation to persevere in the temple rebuilding project includes an admonition underscoring the ethical demands of YHWH's covenant relationship (vv. 14–17). Next, a sermon on fasting addresses questions posed earlier on the topic by envoys from Bethel (or Babylonia? vv. 18–19).

The final section is a prophetic sermon about the nations seeking revelation from YHWH and the Jews, a distinctive feature of Jerusalem's future glory (vv. 20–23). The re-establishment of the divine presence in the midst of the Hebrew faithful was the great hope of the post-exilic restoration community: the Lord returning and living among his people again (*and I will return to Zion and dwell in Jerusalem*, 8:3). The theme of the return of God's presence to his temple connects the visions and messages of Zechariah (Zech. 1:16–17; 8:3; 14:3–5, 16–21; cf. Hag. 2:4–5). All this is in fulfilment of the promise of Ezekiel's temple vision, renaming the city of Jerusalem THE LORD IS THERE (Ezek. 48:35) – and reversing the divine abandonment witnessed earlier by the prophet (Ezek. 10:18–19).

Comment

i. The prophet's exhortation to rebuild the temple (vv. 9–13)

8:9. Zechariah references the foundation ceremony for rebuilding the Second Temple (v. 9a), and the prophets who were 'present' (NEB) at the event earlier in 520–519 BC, namely he and Haggai (cf. Hag. 1:1; Zech. 1:1; Ezra 5:1–2). Presumably, *these words spoken by the prophets* (or the 'promises uttered by the prophets', NJB) were the exhortations of Haggai, Zechariah and other unnamed contemporaries (cf. Hag. 1:6–11; 2:15–19). The expression *let your hands be strong* (v. 9b) is an idiom of exhortation, whether a call to battle (e.g. Judg. 7:11; 2 Sam. 2:7) or any challenging task that demands courage and perseverance.[39] In this case, the exhortation is focused on the effort required to build the Second Temple.

10. The phrase *before that time* recalls the period prior to the foundation ceremony for the rebuilding of the Second Temple in 520–519 BC. The NIV, *there were no wages for man or beast*, is vague. The expression indicates that 'there was no hiring of man or beast' (NEB; or 'there were no wages for men or hire for beasts', NAB; or 'men were not paid their wages and nothing was paid for the animals either', NJB). The aftermath of the Babylonian invasion of Judah brought severe economic suffering to the Jewish survivors, with consequent impact on the animals necessary for agricultural production (cf. Jer. 7:20; Ezek. 14:13). Earlier, Haggai had observed that the people of Judah were depositing what meagre wages they had in bags or purses filled with holes (Hag. 1:6)

Safe travel in Judah was compromised *because of the enemy*. Externally, the enemy included the Samaritans (cf. Ezra 4:1–5), and perhaps Ammonites, Arabs and other surrounding people groups who later opposed the rebuilding of the city walls of Jerusalem (cf. Neh. 4:7–9). The latter clause, 'since I had set each one against everyone else' (NJB), is more difficult to interpret (more lit., *I had turned every man against his neighbour*, NIV). The expression indicates that internal strife, as well as suspicion, fear and hostility, plagued the remnant of Hebrews inhabiting Judah. 'By representing Yahweh as the immediate

---

39. Cf. McComiskey (1998: 1144).

cause of the strife, the writer reveals an important prophetic concept that underscores the immanence of God in history.'[40]

11. The era of divine judgment is over; a reversal of fortunes will now begin, as an era of divine restoration accompanies the rebuilding of the Jerusalem temple and the return of God's people to right worship and the practice of social justice in a renewed covenant relationship with him.

12. The phrase *the seed will grow well* (lit. 'the seedtime of peace', NAB; 'a sowing of peace', NRSV) is unique to Zechariah in the OT. The word *peace* (Heb. *šālôm*) occurs four times in chapter 8 and is an important sub-theme of the prophet's message (vv. 10, 12, 16, 19). Zechariah establishes a relationship in the agricultural cycle between the opportunity for the Hebrews once again to sow their crops in peaceful times and reap abundant harvests – reversing the drought and blight described by Haggai (Hag. 1:10).

The language of agricultural bounty, *the ground will produce its crops, and the heavens will drop their dew*, has connections to the blessings associated with covenant obedience (cf. Lev. 26:3–10; Deut. 28:11–12).

The designation *remnant* is applied to the small community of Hebrews who returned to Judah from the Babylonian exile (cf. Hag. 1:12, 14). Theologically, the *remnant* signifies a small number of people who escape destruction as a result of the saving action of God. They are the link that bridges the threat of divine punishment with the promise of divine restoration as a testimony to God's faithfulness.[41]

13. God will *save*, in that his overturning of the *curse* of his judgment to the *blessing* of his favour will 'vindicate' (NJPS) the Hebrews as YHWH's elect nation. The reference to both *Judah* and *Israel* is significant in keeping with earlier prophetic promises of God's restoration of the Hebrews as one people in covenant relationship with their God (cf. Ezek. 37:15–23). The language is interesting in that restored Judah *will be a blessing*, either to themselves or to the nations referenced earlier (v. 13a). The reversal of fortunes

---

40. Ibid., p. 1145.
41. Cf. *NIDOTTE* 4: 17.

for post-exilic Judah not only makes them 'the symbol of blessing' to the nations (NEB), but also reinstates Israel as God's blessing to the nations, in keeping with covenant promises to Abraham (Gen. 12:1–3).

The repetition of the exhortation found earlier in verse 9, *let your hands be strong*, forms an inclusion or envelope for the section, highlighting the reversal of Jerusalem's fortunes (vv. 9–13).

ii. God's plans for Jerusalem (vv. 14–17)

14–15. The use of the verb *determined* in verses 14 and 15 ('resolved', NJB; 'purposed', NRSV) accentuates God's sovereignty, a mark of true deity (cf. Isa. 41:23).[42] As covenant maker and keeper, it is the prerogative of YHWH to implement the curses and blessings of the Mosaic covenant as he wills, in response to the behaviour of his people. The *good* that God intends to do has already been outlined in verses 12–13.

The repeated exhortation, *don't be afraid*, connects the oracle of verses 9–13 (cf. v. 13) with the oracle of verses 14–17. This formulaic expression of divine assurance brings closure to the salvation oracle.[43] The comforting expression echoes God's encouragement to the leaders and people of Israel at other decisive moments in Hebrew history (e.g. Josh. 10:8; 1 Chr. 28:20; Jer. 1:8) and reminds them that God will accomplish what he has set out to do.

16–17. These precepts 'sum up the character of those who are in relation with the Lord of hosts'.[44] The two admonitions (v. 16) and the two prohibitions (v. 17) are set in the context of the legal system of post-exilic Judah (*in your courts*, v. 16; lit. 'at your gates', NAB).[45] Boda calls attention to the priority of relationships in the covenant community, evidenced in the repeated phrase 'one another' (NRSV) in the first admonition (v. 16a) and the first prohibition (v. 17a).[46]

---

42. See Boda (2004: 394) on Zechariah's use of the term to signal a new era of redemptive history.

43. Cf. Westermann (1991: 42–43, 54–56, 121).

44. Baldwin (1972: 164).

45. Cf. *ZIBBCOT* 2: 260 on the role of the city gates in the biblical world.

46. Boda (2004: 395).

The repetition of the word *true* indicates the standard for justice in the courts is 'adherence to the "truth"'.[47] Speaking the truth and administering fair judgment is 'conducive to peace' (NJB).

The two prohibitions (v. 17) focus on the intents of the heart and thus address the spirit as well as the letter of the law. The first prohibition, *do not plot evil against your neighbour*, repeats the earlier command of Zechariah 7:10. The prophet warns against 'contriving evil' (NEB) against others, whether out of malice or for fraudulent purposes (see further the discussion in the commentary on 7:10, pp. 188–189).[48] The injunction 'do not love perjury' (NJB) repeats the prophet's indictment of those who *swear falsely* in 5:3. Falsifying evidence by lying under oath is a violation of the Decalogue (Exod. 20:16; Deut. 5:20; cf. Exod. 23:7), and it leads 'to a breakdown of mutual trust' within Israel's covenant community.[49] Zechariah's audience is guilty of the same sins that brought about the Babylonian exile, and this behaviour puts God's plans for the restoration of the post-exilic Hebrew community at risk (v. 16; cf. 7:8–10). Such behaviour is morally wrong and arouses God's anger, '"for all these things I hate," says the LORD' (v. 17c, NRSV). God's hatred of evil deeds and the people who persist in them (Ps. 5:5; Prov. 6:16) stems from his absolute holiness (Pss 5:4; 15:1; 24:3).

iii. Joyful fasting (vv. 18–19)

19. The fast in the early summer (the *fourth* month, Tammuz) lamented the breaching of the walls of Jerusalem by the Babylonian armies (2 Kgs 25:3–4; Jer. 52:6–7). The fast in midsummer (the *fifth* month, Ab) lamented the burning of Solomon's temple (2 Kgs 25:8–10; Jer. 52:12–14). The fast in autumn (the *seventh* month, Tishri) marked the anniversary of the assassination of Gedaliah, the governor of Jerusalem (2 Kgs 25:22–25; Jer. 41:1–3). The fast in the winter (the *tenth* month, Tebeth) lamented the beginning of the siege

---

47. Ibid.
48. Cf. Redditt (1995: 87) who suggests this plotting against one another may have been aimed at taking property from a neighbour.
49. Baldwin (1972: 164).

of Jerusalem by King Nebuchadnezzar of Babylonia (2 Kgs 25:1; Jer. 52:4).

Zechariah's oracle continues the theme of a reversal of fortunes for post-exilic Judah. Boda (2004: 397) notes that the word pair, *joyful* and *glad*, are used of the future restoration of Israel elsewhere by the Hebrew prophets (cf. Isa. 35:10; 51:3; Jer. 31:33; 33:10–11). The prophet calls the people to love what God himself loves, *truth and peace* (cf. Pss 29:11; 31:5). The repetition of the word *truth* makes this ethical ideal a sub-theme in chapter 8 (vv. 3, 8, 16, 19), thus tying God's promise of restoration conditionally to the covenant obedience of the people. Paul's citation of Zechariah 8:16 indicates that God's expectations have not changed (Eph. 4:25).

iv. The nations will seek the Lord in Jerusalem (vv. 20–23)

The final section is a prophetic sermon about the nations seeking revelation from YHWH and the Jews, a distinctive feature of Jerusalem's future glory (vv. 20–23). If the messenger formula (*This is what the LORD Almighty says*) signals individual sermon summaries, then verse 23 is a distinct message, establishing a parallel pattern of five messages in each of the literary units of chapter 8. Since the topics of verses 20–22 and verse 23 are similar, they are treated as a single unit here.

20–22. Zechariah's prediction that one day *many peoples* (v. 20) *and powerful nations* (v. 22a) will come to Jerusalem and worship the Lord with the Hebrews brings the covenant promise made to Abraham full circle in Israelite history – 'all the families of the earth will be blessed through you' (cf. Gen. 12:3). This segment of Zechariah's message is the nearest thing 'to an active missionary concept of the mission of the Jews that occurs in the Old Testament, outside the book of Jonah'.[50] Yet the difference between Jonah and Zechariah is striking, in that Jonah was commissioned to proclaim judgment for repentance to the Assyrians (Jon. 1:2). Here it appears that the reality of God's transforming presence among his people prompts the nations (to almost beg!) to join Israel in the worship of the Lord

---

50. Mason (1977: 73).

(v. 23).[51] The verbs *entreat* and *seek* are repeated in reverse order in the passage (vv. 21, 22). The phrase 'entreat the favor' (NAB) translates a Hebrew idiom (lit. 'to soften the face') and refers to ritual acts of prayer and petition (see commentary on 7:2, pp. 183–184). The verb *seek* also indicates activities associated with prayer in ritual contexts.

23. The number *ten* is understood symbolically as a large or complete number. The expression *from all languages and nations* (NJB; lit. 'tongues of the nations') is unique to Zechariah 8:23 in the OT. The eschatology of verses 18–23 incorporates an ever-expanding circle of people into God's redemptive plan, including those in Jerusalem and Judah (or Yehud), the neighbouring people groups and the more remote foreign nations.[52]

The repetition of the verb *take hold* ('ten men ... will take hold – they will take hold of every Jew', NJPS) indicates the forcefulness and urgency of the action (NLT, 'will clutch at the sleeve of one Jew'). The term *Jew* is rather rare in the OT (cf. Esth. 2:5; Jer. 34:9; 52:28, 30). Petersen deems it important, 'because it confers individual identity on those who venerate Yahweh', thus enabling them to attract the nations to worship in Jerusalem. The gesture of seizing the *hem* of the garment is an act of submission or loyalty, or a plea for help or mercy, depending upon the context (cf. 1 Sam. 15:27, where Saul clutches Samuel's robe in a last plea for mercy).

The nations are drawn to come with the Jews to Jerusalem on account of the report that God is once again resident among his people (*because we have heard that God is with you*), a sign of restored covenant relationship with YHWH and a fulfilment of prophetic oracles promising a return of his presence to his temple (see 8:3 above; cf. Ezek. 48:35; Zech. 1:16; Mal. 3:1).

Meaning
God's reversal of the plight of the remnant Hebrews from *an object of cursing* (vv. 12–13a) to a *blessing* (v. 13b) was as sure as his previous

---

51. Cf. Kaiser (2000: 73–74); and Routledge (2008: 326–327) who describes this aspect of the witness of Israel to the nations as 'centripetal universalism'.

52. Cf. Meyers and Meyers (1987: 441).

punishment of their sin (v. 14). God had *determined to do good again to Jerusalem and Judah* (v. 15). But such a dramatic restoration of the people of God was not automatic. The demands of covenant relationship with YHWH meant Israel was under obligation to live out the demands of the Mosaic charter (vv. 16–17; cf. 7:8–10).

Obedience to the revealed word of God is never optional (Deut. 4:1–2; cf. Col. 2:6).

4. ZECHARIAH'S ORACLES (9 – 14)

A. First oracle (9 – 11)

Context

The second part of the book of Zechariah is composed of two distinct literary units, chapters 9 – 11 and 12 – 14. The second half of Zechariah differs from the first in several ways. The literary genre of Zechariah 9 – 14 is more distinctively apocalyptic in character, combining cryptic historical allusions with futuristic visions. The tone of the prophet's message shifts from one of exhortation and encouragement to one of admonition and warning. This connects the closing oracles (chs. 9 – 11 and 12 – 14) broadly to the prologue to the book (Zech. 1:1–6) and the call to repentance which serves as the touchstone for the prophet's message. This portion of the book contains no direct references to the prophet, and the messages are assumed to date to a later period of Zechariah's ministry. The two closing oracles are composite in nature, in that they represent an anthology of the prophet's later sermons. They serve as a fitting conclusion to the book of Zechariah because, as

204 HAGGAI, ZECHARIAH AND MALACHI

Craigie has noted, the prophet's 'intimations of a future world are here taken up and elaborated in greater detail, and there is a similar concern which incorporates the Gentiles, along with the Jews'.[1]

Comment

i. Judgment against Israel's enemies (9:1–8)

The opening portion of Zechariah's first oracle (9:1–8) provides an appropriate introduction to the second portion of the book. The message of judgment against Israel's enemies combines the dual emphases of (third-person) threats (vv. 1–6a) and (first-person) promises (vv. 6b–8). The abrupt shift from the prophet's reporting of YHWH's words to direct speech by God himself is a shared literary feature of the two concluding oracles (chs. 9 – 11, 12 – 14). The alternating emphasis between the threat of judgment against the nations and the promise of deliverance for Israel is also characteristic throughout the second part of the book.

The first message (chs. 9 – 11) opens with a series of pronouncements of divine judgment against the traditional enemies of Israel (9:1–8). The geographical arrangement of the cities and nations is set in the order of a military campaign from north to south through Syria-Palestine. The threat of God's retribution was realized with the march of Alexander the Great through the region in 334–332 BC.

Three themes emerge in the first message (9:1–8) of the first oracle (chs. 9 – 11) that are repeated in the subsequent messages of the two closing oracles, including: God's judgment of the nations (vv. 1–6), the joining of the nations to Israel as people and worshippers of YHWH (v. 7), and divine protection for the nation of Israel (v. 8).

9:1. Like the book of Malachi, each of these last two speeches is prefaced by the compound title: *an oracle, the word of the LORD* (9:1; 12:1; cf. Mal. 1:1). The word *oracle* ('prophecy', NIV 2011; 'proclamation', NJB; 'pronouncement', NJPS; Heb. *maśśā'*) is a technical term for a prophetic pronouncement often understood as a 'burden', due to the

---

1. Craigie (1985: 199).

emphasis on divine judgment in this type of oracular speech.[2] The phrase *The word of the LORD* is known as the prophetic word formula, and typically introduces a report of prophetic revelation and invests that report with divine authority.

Hadrach was a city-state on the northern boundary of Syria. It was probably the ancient city of Hatarikka cited in Assyrian texts and is associated with the site of Tell Afis, south-west of Aleppo. *Damascus* was the capital city of the Aramean state that flourished in Syria during the tenth to eighth centuries BC. The rival Aramean kingdom was sometimes an ally and at other times an enemy to the divided kingdoms of Israel and Judah. The city lay adjacent to the Abana River and was located on the caravan route connecting Mesopotamia to the Mediterranean coast. The border of Damascus was regarded as the northern boundary of the ideal Hebrew state (Ezek. 47:16–18).

'For the eyes of all of humanity [mankind, ESV], including all the tribes of Israel, are on the LORD' (NLT). The second half of verse 1 is difficult, and the phrase 'the eyes of all humanity' may involve a textual error (reading 'Aram' for 'Adam': 'For to the LORD belongs the capital of Aram', NRSV; and perhaps 'city' or 'cities' for 'eye' [cf. RSV, 'cities of Aram']. *BHQ* omits the conjectural emendation).

2. *Hamath* was a fortress city near Damascus on the Orontes River, located on one of the southern trade routes from Asia Minor (modern-day Hama in Syria). Hamath was considered the northern boundary of Israel according to Numbers 13:21 and Joshua 13:5.

The twin Phoenician port cities of *Tyre* and *Sidon* were independent kingdoms located on the Mediterranean coast north of Israel (in modern-day Lebanon) and are often paired in biblical texts (e.g. Jer. 25:22; Joel 3:4). The cities were legendary for their wealth as a result of maritime trade. The OT prophets, however, condemned the pride and oppressive policies of the two cities and predicted their ultimate destruction (cf. Isa. 23; Ezek. 26:3–14; Amos 1:9–10). Their vaunted wisdom ('though they are very wise', NJPS) will be of no avail.

3–4. The word *stronghold* (Heb. *māṣôr*, v. 3a) is a pun on the name

---

2. See the discussion of the term in Baldwin (1972: 171).

for the city of *Tyre* (Heb. *ṣōr*). The verse makes reference to the famed island fortress of ancient Tyre (Isa. 23:3; Ezek. 26:5), captured and destroyed by Alexander the Great in 332 BC.

The paired phrase *silver like dust ... gold like the dirt* (v. 3b) is perhaps a fragment of a proverb about the famed wealth of *Tyre* (cf. Isa. 23:2–3; Ezek. 28:4–5); yet according to Isaiah, Tyre's wealth was set apart for the Lord (Isa. 23:18). The destruction forecast for Tyre (v. 4) echoes the judgment oracle of Ezekiel (cf. Ezek. 26:12–14).

5–6. The Philistine cities of *Ashkelon ... Gaza ... Ekron ... Ashdod* were located on the coastal plain of Israel, south of the port city of Joppa. The city of Gath was also numbered among the five principal cities of the Philistines (cf. 1 Sam. 6:17), who were perennial enemies of Israel (cf. 1 Sam. 4 – 5). They were defeated and subdued by David for a time (2 Sam. 5:17–25), but later regained some measure of autonomy. The prophets Amos and Zephaniah pronounce similar judgments against the same four Philistine cities (Amos 1:6–8; Zeph. 2:4–7). Zechariah's pronouncement may anticipate the report of Alexander's swift conquest of the Levant that will strike fear among the cities of Philistia, melting their pride as they in turn await their certain destruction and desolation. The reference to the *foreigners* ('mongrel people', NAB, NIV 2011, NRSV; 'half-breeds, NEB, NJB) who will occupy *Ashdod* is clearly pejorative (cf. KJV, 'bastard') and may anticipate the ethnically mixed marriages found among the Hebrews in the post-exilic era (cf. Neh. 13:23–24; Mal. 2:11).

7. The reference to *blood* and *forbidden food* is presumed to relate to ritual defilement in violation of Hebrew dietary regulations (not draining the blood from slaughtered meat or eating blood, cf. Lev. 17:10–14; Deut. 12:16; or eating ritually unclean foods, cf. Lev. 11; Deut. 14). The practices 'stood as a representation of their [i.e. the Philistines'] sinful lifestyle'.[3] God will remove evil from his people, and from all peoples in the coming age.

The gist of the two lines, 'But his remnant too will belong to our God, becoming like a clan in Judah' (NJB), is that the surviving peoples and the territory of Philistia will be subsumed under the

---

3. Redditt (1995: 113).

rule of God and the governance of a restored Judah. Redditt (1995: 113) comments that 'the thought is remarkable that traditional enemies within the land would be accepted on a par with ethnic Israelites'.

The city of *Ekron will be like the Jebusites*. The *Jebusites* were the Canaanite inhabitants of Jerusalem, conquered by David and absorbed into the tribe of Judah (2 Sam. 5:6–10).

8. The clause, *But I will defend my house*, is ambiguous ('And I will post a garrison for my house', NEB; 'I will encamp at my house as a guard', NRSV), but the intent is clear. Whether directly or indirectly, God will protect Jerusalem by 'encamping' in his temple (lit. 'house'), thus preventing the military destruction of his city and people by outsiders.[4] The Aramaic Targum connects Zechariah 9:8 with 2:5, and the promise of God's presence serving as a wall of fire around Jerusalem.[5] While Alexander the Great apparently spared Jerusalem, the city was later ruled by the Seleucid Greeks, and its temple profaned by Antiochus Ephiphanes IV (168 BC). Later still, the Romans would sack the city of Jerusalem and destroy YHWH's temple (AD 70). So the exact nature and extent of Zechariah's understanding of God's defence of Jerusalem and his temple are unclear.

Meaning

The numerous historical allusions in this section of Zechariah's message prove difficult to locate chronologically with any precision. The destruction of Damascus and Hamath (vv. 1–2) may be a reference to an earlier military campaign of the Assyrian King Sargon II (722–705 BC) who conquered both cities. The Phoenician port cities of Tyre and Sidon (vv. 3–4) were captured by the Persians, but they were not sacked and made desolate until Alexander the Great destroyed the cities on his campaign into Egypt (332 BC). The threat levied against the Philistine cities of Ashkelon, Gaza, Ekron and Ashdod (vv. 5–6) may have been realized when King Nebuchadnezzar of Babylonia defeated the Philistines in the 600s

---

4. Cf. Petersen (1995: 53).
5. Mason (1977: 87).

BC, or anticipated in Alexander's march across the Mediterranean world. The writer may be taking no particular historical viewpoint, but simply utilizing past events in the manner characteristic of apocalyptic literature to typify the ultimate victory of YHWH.[6] It is even possible that Zechariah's ambiguous recital of earlier history is a veiled allusion to Daniel's vision of the successive nations that would rule the Mediterranean world prior to the intervention of God's kingdom in the world (cf. Dan. 2). As such, the message of Zechariah becomes one of encouragement and hope for his audience – because God's plan for establishing his righteous kingdom was still intact and on course.

ii. Zion's coming king (9:9–13)

Context
The second message (9:9–13) of Zechariah's first oracle (chs. 9 – 11) confronts his audience with the coincidence of opposites. The first of the polar word pairs is the portrayal of Judah's coming deliverer as a king who is both victorious in battle, yet righteous and humble (v. 9). This king will bring peace to the nations and enjoy a universal reign (v. 10). The second of the polar word pairs is the dual reality of warfare and peace that has defined the course of human history.

Comment
9:9. The prophet depicts the reaction of Israel to a king's triumphant entry into *Jerusalem*. The celebratory language of joyful shouts echoes the prophet's earlier call for jubilation at the return of God to his temple (2:10). The poetic word pair, *Daughter of Zion*, *Daughter of Jerusalem*, is a personification of the city and connotes the tender character of YHWH's relationship with his people.

---

6. Cf. Baldwin (1972: 170). Amos does something similar in his panoramic series of judgment oracles against the nations neighbouring Israel, drawing on events across a range of historical periods. If Zechariah was familiar with Amos (which seems the case), he could be tapping an established prophetic technique.

The possessive pronoun *your* identifies the *king* as Jerusalem's (and Israel's) king. The pronouncement, *See, your king comes to you*, stands in stark contrast to the reality of Persian rule over Judah, which permitted no Hebrew kingship. Zechariah's reference to this coming *king* may be an allusion to the future Davidic king promised by Jeremiah (Jer. 33:15) and Ezekiel (Ezek. 34:23–24; 37:24).[7]

The coming king of Israel will be *righteous*: that is, he will rule with justice and fairness (cf. Jer. 23:5; 33:15; note some EVV render the term *righteous* with a military sense of 'triumphant', NRSV, or 'victorious', NJPS). The passive participle rendered *having salvation* in the NIV is awkward, and is variously rendered ('victory gained', NEB; 'victorious', NLT, NRSV). Following Meyers and Meyers (1993: 127), the expression indicates the king is saved or delivered by God: that is, 'the king's status is dependent upon divine action'.[8]

The word *gentle* refers to the virtue of humility ('humble', NLT, NRSV; 'meek', NAB), especially in relationship to God.[9] Donkeys are mentioned as mounts for the princes and kings of Israel (cf. Judg. 5:10; 10:4; 2 Sam. 16:2). The statement may be an allusion to Genesis 49:11, Jacob's blessing of Judah, which includes a reference to a donkey and his colt in the context of kingship, but the significance is unclear.[10] The expression 'donkey's colt' is attested at Mari, signifying a 'purebred' animal – one 'qualified to be a royal mount'.[11] 'The contrast offered by the specification of his mount is that this king is not coming in a military context (which would have featured a horse, mule, or chariot), but is coming in peace and humility.'[12]

---

7. Cf. Stuhlmueller (1988: 123–125) on the messianic implications of the passage (Zech. 9:9–10).

8. Cf. Boda (2004: 416). Commentators seeking a historical referent only for the coming king suggest figures like Darius I or Alexander the Great (although context suggests the king is a Hebrew); see the discussion in Sweeney (2000: 663–664).

9. Meyers and Meyers (1993: 127–128).

10. Cf. Fishbane (1985: 501–502).

11. Baldwin (1972: 179).

12. *ZIBBCOT* 5: 221; cf. Meyers and Meyers (1993: 31), who note that the three animal terms used in the verse 'represent the condition of royalty

The NT quotes the verse as a messianic reference in connection with the triumphal entry of Jesus, the Son of David, into Jerusalem at the beginning of his Passion Week (Matt. 21:4–5; John 12:15). Baldwin (1972: 179) notes that, 'only one animal is intended, despite Matthew 21:7'. Although the NT writers understood the triumphal entry of Jesus of Nazareth as a messianic fulfilment of Zechariah's prophecy about the coming king, they appropriately quoted only portions of Zechariah 9:9 consonant with the first advent of Jesus the Messiah.[13]

10. The kingdoms of Assyria, Babylonia, Persia, and even the Israelite kingdom of David, were established by military conquest. By contrast, God will dismantle the machinery of war and eradicate arsenals of stockpiled weapons (note the first-person voice indicating direct divine speech: *I will take away the chariots ... war-horses ... and the battle-bow will be broken*). Other OT prophets predicted a similar era of disarmament (cf. Isa. 2:4; 9:5; Joel 3:10; Mic. 5:10–11). The name *Ephraim* ('the chariots of Ephraim', v 10a) was a designation for the northern Hebrew tribes. The pairing of Ephraim and Jerusalem (v. 10b) and Judah and Ephraim (v. 13) signified a reunited Israel and the land of covenant promise regained.

The shift back to the third-person voice returns the focus to Israel's king (*He will proclaim peace to the nations*). The shift between third- and first-person voice in chapter 9 need not indicate multiple hands in the composition of the literary unit.[14] Rather, context certainly allows for God to be the speaker and, as Redditt (1995: 114) notes, the first-person speech is consistent with the message of 9:1–8: 'True, the king would rule but over a kingdom subjugated by God.'[15] The verb *proclaim* may be understood as a promise that will certainly be realized, a royal mandate imposing the king's

---

minus military power that characterizes the portrayal of the monarchic figure of Zech. 9:9–10'. See also the discussion of the symbolism associated with the donkey and the mule in the biblical world in Boda (2004: 416–417, esp. n. 30).

13. See further Merrill (1994: 256).

14. E.g. Lacocque (1981: 138–139); cf. Redditt (1995: 109).

15. Cf. Meyers and Meyers (1993: 132).

peaceful sovereignty upon the nations (cf. NRSV, 'he shall command peace').[16] The term *peace* (Heb. *šālôm*) refers primarily to the end of warfare (cf. NJPS, 'He shall call on the nations to surrender').

The universal extent of the king's *rule* is emphasized in the citation of Psalm 72:8, a royal psalm seeking God's blessing upon the Davidic king. The phrase *from sea to sea* is a type of merism for the universality of the king's rule. It may also echo the promise of YHWH at Mount Sinai regarding the borders of Israel (Exod. 23:31). The term *River*, usually understood as the Euphrates River (e.g. CEV), may also be an allusion to the primordial river of Ancient Near Eastern mythology from which the four rivers of paradise emerge. Taken together, the two expressions have cosmic implications and should be considered 'as part of the vocabulary representing the global extent of the king's rule'.[17] The phrase *the ends of the earth* is a poetic expression for the outer boundaries of the world as understood by the ancients (cf. Deut. 33:17; 1 Sam. 2:10; Isa. 45:22; Jer. 16:19). The passage (v. 10b) continues the global emphasis established in Zechariah's third vision (2:10–11) and his second sermon (8:20–23).

11. The section (vv. 11–13) highlights the transformation of Hebrew captives into God's warriors. Covenants were sealed with animal sacrifices in the biblical world (cf. Gen. 15:9–10). The phrase *blood of my covenant* has similarities to the blood of the covenant ceremony sealing the covenant between YHWH and Israel at Mount Sinai (Exod. 24:8). God's work of restoring Israel in Zechariah's day was rooted in his covenant faithfulness to his people, extending back to their post-exodus covenant experience brokered by Moses at the Sinai theophany.

The clause, *I will free your prisoners*, is better translated, 'I have released your prisoners' (NJB), since the verb tense indicates that groups of former Hebrew exiles have already returned to Judah from Mesopotamia – 'the act of liberation has truly begun'.[18] The *prisoners* were those Hebrews taken captive and enslaved in

---

16. Cf. Meyers and Meyers (1993: 134).

17. Meyers and Meyers (1993: 137–138).

18. Meyers and Meyers (1993:140).

Babylonia after the fall of Jerusalem (cf. Lam. 3:34), although at the time of Zechariah's writing the term refers to the second and even third generation of those original captives. The *waterless pit* suggests a dry well or cistern serving as a prison or 'dungeon' (NAB, NLT), and is a metaphor for the Babylonian captivity of the Hebrews. The image of the *waterless pit* calls to mind the story of Joseph who was thrown into a dry cistern by his brothers (Gen. 37:24).

12. The command to *Return to your fortress* is a call to those Hebrews still languishing in the Mesopotamian diaspora. The word *fortress* ('stronghold', NRSV) occurs only here in the OT and describes a place of protection and safety.[19] The *prisoners* figuratively confined in a dry well (v. 11) are also *prisoners of hope* ('waiting prisoners', NAB), bound to God and his covenant promises of blessing and restoration.[20]

Zechariah envisions a day when God *will restore twice as much* to Israel. The first-born son received a double inheritance according to the custom of the biblical world and codified in the Mosaic law (cf. Deut. 21:17). The prophet Isaiah forecasted a day when Israel, as God's firstborn, would receive a double portion (whether in joy and spiritual renewal, material gain or increased population is unclear) in recompense for the shame, suffering and devastation they had endured as an oppressed people (Isa. 61:7). The 'twofold reparation' (NEB) creates another intertextual link with the Joseph story and Jacob's blessing of Joseph with a double inheritance among the tribes of Israel (Gen. 48:5; 49:22–26).[21]

---

19. See further the discussion in Meyers and Meyers (1993: 142), who note that the term 'stronghold' fits the historical context, given the string of fortresses built by the Persians in the western provinces to stem Greek expansion. Petersen (1984: 55, n. f.) equates the word *fortress* with Zion (v. 9), given the alliterative play on the noun *ṣiyyôn* with the word *biṣṣārôn* ('fortress').

20. Cf. Ollenburger (1996: 810) on a restored Jerusalem (vv. 9–10) and a united Israel (v. 13) as the object of hope in Zech. 9 – 10.

21. See Boda (2004: 420); cf. Petersen (1995: 54, 61) and R. L. Smith (1984: 258), who understand the verb *return* (Heb. *šûb*) not as reparation, but as YHWH's return to Zion (rendering the call-to-repentance formula in Zech. 1:3 in a literal sense).

13. God declares himself a warrior who brandishes 'Judah as a bow' and 'Ephraim as his arrow' (so NEB). The phrase 'sons of Zion' indicates that the reference is to a unified Hebrew people, symbolized in the names *Judah* and *Ephraim*. After banishing the weapons of war (v. 10), YHWH forges his people into a *warrior's sword*, with a call to battle implied in the verb *rouse* (or 'arouse', NAB, NRSV; cf. 1 Chr. 5:26; Isa. 13:17; Dan. 11:2). This abrupt reversal may be explained, in part, by recognizing that, in his zeal for Jerusalem and Zion, the Lord Almighty will bring judgment against all the nations that plunder Israel – the apple of his eye (Zech. 1:15; 2:8–9).

The object of God's warfare is *Greece* or 'Javan' (NJPS), the name by which the Greeks were known to the Hebrews (e.g. Gen. 10:2, 4; Isa. 66:19; Ezek. 27:13; Dan. 8:21). The reference to *Greece* (Heb. *yāwān*) is more precisely the region of Ionia, a Greek area of south-west Asia Minor. The citation has proven puzzling for commentators, and many assume Zechariah alludes to the invasion of Alexander the Great and the later rule of the Seleucid Greeks over Syria-Palestine.[22] Yet other commentators have demonstrated that the reference to Greece 'reflects the military clashes between Greece and Persia in the early fifth century B.C.E.'.[23] More likely, Zechariah's reference to Greece echoes the indictment of Joel against the Greeks for their role in the slave traffic involving the people of Judah (Joel 3:6 [MT 4:6]). Rather than 'a war of liberation against an occupying Greek army ... Zech. 9:11–15 envisions a war to bring prisoners from Javan/Greece home to Zion, which has been secured already (9:1–10)'.[24]

Meaning

Zechariah heralds a *king* (v. 9) who will bring *peace to the nations* and enjoy a universal reign (v. 10). This coming deliverer of Judah is both righteous and humble (v. 9). Although he does not use the term

---

22. E.g. Barker (2008: 800); the reference to Greece is often taken as a gloss (e.g. NEB; cf. Mason [1977: 93]).

23. O'Brien (2004: 241).

24. Ollenburger (1996: 810).

'messiah', Zechariah stands in the tradition of the OT prophets who announced a restored Davidic kingship (cf. Isa. 9:6–7; 11:1; Amos 9:11). The NT writers recognized Zechariah's numerous predictions about the Messiah as fulfilled in the life and ministry of Jesus of Nazareth.[25]

iii. The Lord will appear and deliver his people (9:14–17)

Context

The chapter concludes with a theophany (v. 14): God appearing in his fierce glory to lead his people to victory over their enemies. The military imagery persists, but the language reverts back to third-person reporting of divine deliverance that is projected to some future time period – *that day* of biblical eschatology (v. 16).

Comment

14. *The* LORD himself *will appear* over Israel. The name LORD (Heb. *YHWH*) is the covenant name for the God of the Hebrews, and elicits the events surrounding the exodus from Egypt and the sojourn at Mount Sinai (Exod. 12 – 19). Three other names for God are used in the passage, including *Sovereign* LORD (v. 14c), LORD *Almighty* (v. 15) and *God* (v. 16). In combination, these divine names and titles underscore God's majesty, power and absolute rule. Isaiah had a similar vision of God's glory appearing over Israel (Isa. 60:2), and the language of theophany continues the theme of God's presence returning to Jerusalem in Zechariah's message (cf. 1:16; 2:5, 10–11; 8:3; 9:8; 14:4). It is possible that Zechariah has in mind the idea that YHWH will go before Israel like some kind of military banner or battle standard guaranteeing victory for his people.[26] It seems more likely that the prophet envisions a theophany of YHWH over Israel, much like the image of the winged sun disk that hovered over and protected the Persian king.[27]

The Sovereign LORD *will sound the trumpet*: perhaps an allusion to the

---

25. See further the discussion in Hill (2008: 574–575).

26. Cf. Merrill (1994: 261).

27. See further Hill (1998: 350, 362 and Fig. 13); and *ZIBBCOT* 5: 241.

blowing of a ram's horn (Heb. *šôpār*) by an angelic being (cf. Exod. 19:19; 20:18; Isa. 27:13), or a metaphor for thunder (cf. Isa. 29:6; Jer. 25:30; Joel 3:16). Zechariah's references to *lightning* and the *trumpet* call to mind Israel's covenant experience at Mount Sinai (cf. Exod. 19:16).

The verb *march* ('advance', NJB) has connotations of a military campaign. The 'whirlwinds' or *storms of the south* (NAB, NIV) as a military image depict God's devastating power and unpredictable swiftness as a Divine Warrior (Ps. 77:18; Isa. 66:15).[28] The whirlwind symbolizing God's military might advances from the *south* (lit. 'Teman', a town and region south-east of Jerusalem in northern Edom; cf. Jer. 49:20; Ezek. 25:13). Zechariah echoes an old tradition connecting YHWH coming out of the region of Seir and Edom in a theophanic thunderstorm (Judg. 5:4). Here the theophany takes the form of a desert sandstorm, a common feature of the weather in the general locale.

15. The verb *shield* is found infrequently in the OT, but in each of its eight occurrences the context is God declaring his intent to *defend* Jerusalem. Zechariah's use of the word may allude to God's shielding of Jerusalem during the Assyrian invasion of Judah led by King Sennacherib (cf. 2 Kgs 19:34; 20:6; Isa. 37:35; 38:6). The shield is defensive armament in warfare and is used as a title for God in the Psalms (e.g. Pss 28:7; 84:11). The image calls to mind the protection God promises to Jerusalem, as he *will be a wall of fire around it* (Zech. 2:5). The object of God's shield of protection is *them*, presumably the armies of Israel that God will muster both to *destroy* their enemies and *save* or deliver the Hebrew prisoners (v. 16; cf. v. 11). The armies of Israel may be in mind in the metaphorical reference to God's *arrow flashing like lightning* (v. 14b), since the sons of *Ephraim* are the arrow of God's bow (v. 13).

The line, 'they will devour, will trample on the sling-stones' (NJB), is difficult, as the translations in the EVV attest ('[His] slingstones shall devour and conquer', NJPS; *They will destroy and overcome with slingstones*, NIV; 'and they will defeat their enemies by hurling great stones', NLT). The verb 'devour' signifies military victory ('prevail',

---

28. See Boda (2004: 421) on Zechariah's use of divine warrior language.

NEB; *destroy*, NIV). The pelting of enemy slingstones will have no effect on the Israelite army, since God is their shield. The 'trampling' over the slingstones is another word-picture indicating triumph, and is used to describe the subduing of enemies (Num. 32:22, 29; Josh. 18:1). Israel will be emboldened in battle and jubilant in their celebration of victory, as those drunk with wine ('They will shout in battle as though drunk with wine', NLT).[29] They will drink and be rowdy. The *bowl* ('libation bowls', NAB; 'dashing bowl', NJPS) is a reference to the ceremonial sprinkling bowls filled with animal blood that were used in the rituals associated with animal sacrifice (cf. Exod. 24:6; 27:3; Lev. 1:5; 16:18; Num. 4:7).

The *corners of the altar* are the horns of the bronze altar of the tabernacle (Exod. 27:2; 38:2) upon which the blood of the animal sacrifices was to be sprinkled from the ritual bowls by the attending priests (Lev. 4:7, 18; 8:15; 9:9). The word-picture probably indicates Israel's victory is full or complete, like the sacrificial bowls brimming with blood.[30] Boda summarizes that verse 15cd 'describes the victory in battle through images drawn from drinking and sacrifice'.[31]

16–17. Israel's deliverance is credited to the covenant God of Israel. The phrase *flock of his people* calls to mind the Davidic shepherd who will lead, rescue, nurture and protect Israel as the flock of God (Ezek. 34; cf. Pss 77:20; 78:52; 80:1). The phrase *that day* (v. 16) is prophetic shorthand for the Day of the Lord, the eschatological day of an unspecified duration in which God judges the wicked, delivers the righteous and restores all of creation. Petersen notes that emphasis shifts from YHWH the shepherd to the splendour of the people 'viewed as numerous jewels on a crown, jewels that bedeck the landscape'.[32]

Grain and *new wine* (v. 17) are symbols of divine blessing and agricultural prosperity (cf. Deut. 28:11; Joel 2:23–24). The promise

29. Cf. Meyers and Meyers (1993: 154–155).

30. So Meyers and Meyers (1993: 155); and McComiskey (1998: 1172); cf. J. M. P. Smith (1912: 280–281).

31. Boda (2004: 422).

32. Petersen (1995: 66).

of a flourishing population of young men and women reverses the fortunes of the Hebrew exile (cf. Lam. 1:18; 2:21), and Israel's future hope rests on this new generation (cf. Zech. 8:5).

Meaning

The abrupt shifts in tone and theme in Zechariah 9, from a king who brings universal peace (vv. 9–10) to a God who brandishes a sword against the nations and attacks like the whirlwind (vv. 13–14), are a stark reminder that the dual reality of war and peace persists into the eschaton. It may be that Zechariah melds together separate sermons on the themes of war and peace for the purpose of accenting the Sovereign God as the Divine Warrior whose victories would ultimately establish permanent and worldwide peace.[33]

The more immediate takeaway for Zechariah's audience was the word of encouragement and hope, one of the messages embedded in apocalyptic literature for those discouraged and oppressed. The LORD *will appear* (v. 14) and *save* his people (v. 16), destroying their enemies in the process (v. 15). Israel will once again *sparkle like jewels* in *his land* of covenant promise (vv. 16–17).

iv. The Lord will restore his people (10:1 – 11:3)

Zechariah revisits the themes of Israel's regathering and return to their ancestral homeland of Palestine, the land of covenant promise (cf. Zech. 9:11–17). The third message of Zechariah's first oracle (chs. 9 – 11) consists of three sermons: a rebuke of faulty leaders (10:1–5); a promise that will strengthen, restore and redeem his people (10:6–12); and a taunt song of divine judgment against the regions of Lebanon and Bashan and their rulers (11:1–3). The key idea of the section is found in the repeated phrases declaring that God will strengthen his people by his power and restore them because of his compassion (vv. 6, 12). The passage anticipates the allegory about the good and evil shepherds that follows (11:4–17).

---

33. Cf. Craigie (1985: 200).

a. The Lord will care for his flock (10:1–5)

Context

This section of the oracle is variously divided. The transition in topics and voice in 10:1–5 is abrupt and has raised questions regarding the structure of the section. Yet the passage is recognized as one 'that creatively stitches the two chapters [i.e. chs. 9 and 10] together'.[34] Commentators question whether the unit should be divided at verse 2[35] or verse 3a, recognizing verses 3b–5 as an insertion of the narrator in the middle of the Yahweh-speech.[36] R. L. Smith rightly observes that verses 3–5 belong together.[37] The repetition of the refrain *I will strengthen* (vv. 6, 12) marks a logical literary unit. The passage contrasts the rebuke of false shepherds (10:1–5) with God's care as shepherd of his people (10:6–12). The focus on Judah in verses 3–5 provides a segue to a more detailed description of YHWH's restoration of all Israel.

Comment

10:1. The rainy season in Israel begins in the autumn (October) with the 'early rain', and ends in the spring with the 'latter rain' (March–May, cf. Deut. 11:14). The *rain in the springtime* fostered new growth, and the latter rain brought the crops to maturity. The OT prophets viewed rain as a sign of divine blessing (cf. Joel 2:23).

The reference to *the LORD who makes the storm clouds* may be an allusion to the contest to secure drought-ending rain between Elijah and the prophets of Baal (1 Kgs 18). Thus the passage 'probably contains a veiled polemic against Baal and Baalism', as a reminder that the people of Israel and Judah ended up scattered in distant lands (v. 9) as a result of Baal worship (cf. 2 Kgs 17:16–20; Jer. 19:5–9).[38]

---

34. Boda (2004: 437); cf. Redditt (1995: 118).

35. E.g. McComiskey (1998: 1175–1179); Webb (2003: 138–140).

36. E.g. Butterworth (1992: 187); cf. Redditt (1995: 118–119); and Boda (2004: 437).

37. R. L. Smith (1984: 263–263); note also the paragraph break at 10:3 in the EVV (e.g. NIV, NJB, NJPS, NRSV).

38. Barker (2008: 800).

2. The word *idols* ('household gods', NEB, NLT) may refer to cultic idols of some sort or even ancestor statues used in necromancy rituals, since consultation with the dead was a widespread practice in the biblical world. The association of the household gods with fortune-tellers and interpreters of dreams in the immediate context might suggest that Zechariah has 'ancestor figures' in mind, rather than idols.[39] Necromancy or consulting the dead for advice was forbidden for the Hebrews according to the Mosaic law (Deut. 18:10–11).

The term *diviner* ('augur', NJPS; 'fortune-teller', NLT) refers in general to those who practise forms of divination or soothsaying. The means of fortune-telling are not specified (whether mechanical manipulation such as mixing oil and water, or observation of natural events and signs), but according to Mosaic law all such practices were forbidden to the Hebrews (cf. Lev. 20:27; Deut. 18:10–11).

Dreams and visions were considered a source of revelation concerning future events in the biblical world (cf. Jer. 23:25–29). The true servants of YHWH recognized that the realm of forecasting the future through dreams and the interpretation of dreams was exclusively his domain (cf. Gen. 40:8; Dan. 2:27–28). Zechariah assesses the value of this kind of prophetic advice with a cluster of four synonymous terms: *deceit* ('worthless advice', NLT; 'utter nonsense', NRSV), 'lies' (NLT, NRSV), 'false dreams' (NRSV; 'illusions', NAB; 'falsehoods', NLT), and as a result of this kind of leadership, *the people wander like sheep oppressed for lack of a shepherd* (v. 4c).[40]

3. God's response is one of 'wrath' (NAB) against these faulty shepherds. The expression *my anger burns* (NIV, NLT; 'my anger is hot', NRSV) is an idiom that signifies unparalleled intensity, and most often this divine anger is directed against Israel.[41] Such is the case here; the

---

39. See the discussion in Meyers and Meyers (1993: 185–187).

40. The striking similarities in vocabulary between Zech. 10:1–2 and Jer. 14:1 – 15:4 are cited in Boda (2004: 439), n. 11; with reference to Mason (2003: 63–69); and Nurmela (1996: 114–119). See Meyers and Meyers (1993: 189) on the connection with divination and necromancy in the story of King Saul and the medium of Endor (1 Sam. 28).

41. Meyers and Meyers (1993: 194).

shepherds that God intends to *punish* are the *leaders* of Judah. The equation of the *shepherds* with the *leaders* of Judah should be understood in a broad sense to refer to both religious and civil officials, and especially to false prophets.[42] The repetition of the verb 'visit' (v. 3b, NAB) provides the foil for God's action in response to the faulty leadership misguiding his people. God intends to visit, that is, *punish* (NIV, NRSV) those misleading the people; by contrast, he intends to 'visit' (NAB, NEB), that is, to *care for* (NIV, NRSV) or 'look after' (NLT) his people. The twin themes of God's punishment of false shepherds and his restoration of the flock of Israel are developed in more detail (and in inverted order) in the sections to follow (Israel's restoration in 10:6–12; God's judgment of false shepherds in 11:4–17).[43]

4. The references to *the house of Judah* (v. 3b) and the simile comparing Judah to *a proud horse in battle* provide the segue to verses 4–5. The transition is terse, with the subject *Judah* implied from verse 3b ('From it', NJB; 'Out of them, NRSV; lit. 'from him'), and the verb 'shall come' (NAB, NRSV) usually moved forward to govern all four nouns from its position before the final noun in the series.[44] The image of a *cornerstone* (lit. 'corner' [of a building, street]) is applied to leadership in the OT (e.g. Judg. 20:2; 1 Sam. 14:38; Isa. 22:23; cf. NAB, 'From him shall come leader …').[45] The *peg* or *tent peg* continues

---

42. See discussion in Meyers and Meyers (1993: 195–196); Petersen (1995: 72–73) and Boda (2004: 440) are among those who suggest these leaders are not to be identified with Joshua and Zerubbabel.

43. See Achtemeier (1986: 155); and Webb (2003: 140).

44. See Meyers and Meyers (1993: 199), who note that the placement of the verb (*will come*) near the end of v. 4 in the MT may 'emphasize the rather dramatic shift in meaning that characterizes each of the four terms in this verse'. The singular suffix in the prepositional phrase *From Judah* (lit. 'from him', KJV) is usually understood in a collective sense with respect to *the house of Judah* mentioned in v. 3. Cf. Meyers and Meyers (1993: 199); Boda (2004: 441); although Kaiser (1995: 218, n. 4) understands the phrase 'from him' to refer to YHWH.

45. Cf. Boda (2004: 441) who cites Mason (2003: 79–80) on the *cornerstone* as an allusion to kingship on the basis of Ps. 118:22.

the application of building-related vocabulary to leadership (cf. NAB, 'chief'). The word conjures up numerous OT associations, since *tent pegs* were necessary for erecting the tabernacle (Exod. 27:19; 35:18), Jael delivers Israel with a *tent peg* (Judg. 4:21, 22), and Delilah braided Samson's hair with a *tent peg* (Judg. 16:14). The tribe of Judah was described previously as God's 'battle bow' (9:13). The 'warrior's bow' (NAB) was a symbol of royal power and military skill and prowess in the biblical world.[46] The final word in the series *ruler* ('commander', NEB, NRSV; 'officer', NAB; Heb. *nōgēś*) is a broad-based term ('every type of leader', NJB), perhaps a summary category indicating all types of leadership.[47]

The Aramaic Targum interprets verse 4 in reference to the Messiah ('From them will be their king, from them their anointed One ...').[48] The heavy emphasis on Christological typology in the OT by the Protestant Reformers has led many later interpreters to see a reference to a messianic figure in Zechariah's litany of leadership symbols.[49] For example, Kaiser (1995: 218–220) understands the list of leadership categories that will emerge out of Judah and stabilize Israelite government as four distinct titles for the Messiah in the OT.[50] Conversely, Mason and Hanson are among those who view the passage not as a reference to a messianic figure, but to the whole community of Israel, assuming 'the qualities and role of former leaders' (cf. NEB, 'and from them shall come every commander').[51]

---

46. On the bow as a royal image in the Ancient Near East, see Mason (1977: 100); cf. Brosius (1998: 13) who notes the importance of the king's bow-bearer in relationship to the king in Persian royal reliefs.

47. Baldwin (1972: 187–188) appropriately notes that here the word 'ruler' (Heb. *nōgēś*) is used in a positive sense, implying 'a man of action, determined to achieve his goal' (contra the negative meaning of the term as an 'oppressor' in Zech. 9:8).

48. Cf. Cathcart and Gordon (1989: 209).

49. E.g. Luther (1973: 111); Calvin (1979: 286–287).

50. Cf. Cook (1995: 137–138) who sees a triple messianic designation in Zech. 10:4.

51. Mason (1977: 100); cf. Hanson (1979: 331).

5. The adverb *together*, although the concluding word of verse 4, is typically read as the opening word of verse 5 (so NJPS, NEB, NIV, NRSV; but cf. NJB). Meyers and Meyers support the integrity of the MT, noting that the Masoretes connected the word 'together' with the verb 'will come', thus indicating that the verb and the adverb refer to all four subjects working in unity.[52]

The plural word *mighty men* ('warriors', NAB, NRSV) indicates that the series of terms in verse 4 refers collectively to a group or cadre of leaders. The term is an epithet for YHWH himself (cf. Deut. 10:17; Isa. 10:21; Jer. 32:18).

Meaning

The focal point of the section (vv. 1–5) is the Lord, who visits or cares for his people (v. 3) and whose presence enables them in battle (v. 4). God's presence among his people Israel is a repeated theme in Zechariah (1:16; 2:5, 10–11; 8:3; 9:8, 14; 14:4). 'Israel does not gain victory because of superior military tactics or weaponry but because of God's overpowering presence.'[53] The enemy Judah *will fight and overthrow* in battle (v. 5b) is unnamed. It seems unlikely that the target of this divine warfare is the group of faulty leaders indicted in verses 2–3a, since God intends to punish them on his own accord. Ollenburger notes that, 'curiously, the enemy with the founded cavalry is not identified' and 'they neither trample nor fight anyone. With alien shepherds and leaders under Yahweh's care (v. 3a) and its own royal and military leadership restored, Judah's enemies are confounded and ephemeral.'[54] More likely, the verse anticipates the siege of Jerusalem and Israel's battle against the nations envisioned in the second oracle (chs. 12 – 14).

---

52. Meyers and Meyers (1993: 204) cite the construction as an example of reverse gapping (or intentional omission of a grammatical feature).
53. Boda (2004: 443).
54. Ollenburger (1996: 814–815).

b. *The Lord will restore Israel (10:6–12)*

Context

The repeated refrain, *I will strengthen* (vv. 6, 12), encloses the section in a type of envelope construction. That God is the subject of all the action verbs in this literary unit is most apt (*strengthen*, vv. 6, 12; *save*, v. 6; *restore*, v. 6; *answer*, v. 6; *redeem*, v. 8; *bring back*, v. 10; *gather*, v. 10).[55] God and his Spirit are the change agents in bringing about a reconstituted Israel as the people of God (cf. Zech. 4:6; 8:7, 13).

Comment

10:6. The word *save* (NEB, 'grant victory'; cf. NJB, NJPS) is applied to the Israelite exodus from Egypt, the salvation-event of the OT (cf. Exod. 14:13; 15:2). Salvation or victory belong to the Lord (Ps. 3:8); only the God of Israel is mighty to save (Isa. 63:1). God's salvation or deliverance of Israel is a theme in Zechariah's preaching (cf. 8:7, 13; 9:16; 10:6; 12:7; see also the commentary on 8:13, pp. 197–198).

The references to *the house of Judah* and *the house of Joseph* signify a reuniting of the former divided Hebrew kingdoms of Judah and Israel into a single nation once again. The unity of the tribes of Israel is a theme in Zechariah (cf. 8:13; 9:13, 16), and is anticipated in the collective use of *the house of Judah* (v. 3) for all Israel, confirming Ezekiel's symbolic act of rejoining the *sticks* of Judah and Ephraim (Ezek. 37:15–23).

The Lord will *save* and *restore* his people Israel because of his *compassion* (NJPS, 'pardoned'; NAB, 'mercy'; NJB, NEB, 'pity'). The word *compassion* embodies female attributes of caring and nurturing, of maternal concern for one's children.[56] Compassion is an attribute of God (Ps. 111:4), but it is also a divine prerogative, as he will show *compassion* to anyone he chooses (Exod. 33:19). God's compassion extends to all those who fear him (Ps. 103:13) and is bounded only by the greatness of his unfailing love (Lam. 3:32). God's restoration of Israel will be so comprehensive, that it will be as though he had never 'cast them off' (NAB, NEB, NJB). The phrase *for I am the LORD*

---

55. Cf. Webb (2003: 141).
56. Meyers and Meyers (1993: 209).

their God is a formula expressing covenant relationship (see the commentary on 8:8, p. 194).

7. The joy and gladness that Zechariah predicts for Israel in response to God's work of restoration in that future eschatological day agrees with the visions of rejoicing foretold by fellow OT prophets (cf. Isa. 25:9; 65:13; Joel 2:23; Zeph. 3:14). The foretaste of that future deposit was realized in the rejoicing that accompanied the building and completion of the Second Temple under the leadership of Zerubbabel (Zech. 4:10).

8. The verb *signal* also means 'whistle' (so NAB, NEB, NJB, NLT). Typically the word has a negative, even derisive, meaning in the OT.[57] Here the term is used in a positive sense as a sign that God's intentions to restore Israel are underway. The expression continues the pastoral imagery of the extended passage, because shepherds in biblical times herded their flocks by whistling or piping to them (cf. Judg. 5:16).

To *redeem* (Heb. *pādâ*) can also mean 'to ransom' as a legal act of redemption (e.g. buying slaves out of their servitude or indentured status, or the redemption of a firstborn through sacrificial ritual; cf. Exod. 21:8; Num. 3:46; 18:15). The term has associations with the Hebrew exodus when the Lord redeemed Israel from slavery in Egypt (Deut. 15:15; 24:18).

The statement that *they will be as numerous as before* is perhaps an allusion to the rapid population growth of the Hebrews during their sojourn as slaves in Egypt (Exod. 1:6–7, 20). The propagation of the Hebrew nation was one of the promises of God's covenant with Abraham (Gen. 12:1–3; cf. 22:17; 32:12). The prophet's allusions to the Hebrew exodus from Egypt remind the people of Israel that God remembers and keeps his covenant promises

9. Even as the Lord has remembered his covenant people, his people will *remember* him. The verb *remember* (Heb. *zākar*) may be a form of wordplay on the meaning of Zechariah's name ('YHWH remembers').[58] Remembering God and his work in history has the power to transform the people of God, because 'recalling God's

---

57. Meyers and Meyers (1993: 213).

58. Barker (2008: 805).

past saving work becomes a bridge from a grim present to a blessed future'.[59]

10. The repetition of the clause, *I will bring them*, indicates that the return of Israel to the land of covenant promise from their dispersion in exile 'would be God's work alone, a result of his grace' (cf. Isa. 35:10 which also mentions the 'redeemed of the LORD returning to Zion').[60] The mention of Egypt and Assyria is representative of the universal dispersion of the Hebrews during the several exiles throughout Israelite history (cf. Isa. 7:18; Mic. 7:12).[61] The place name *Gilead* designates the region east of the Jordan River that included territory north and south of the Jabbok River (cf. Deut. 3:12–13). The Hebrew tribes of Reuben and Gad were assigned to occupy southern Gilead, while the half-tribe of Manasseh was assigned to occupy northern Gilead (cf. Josh. 12:2–6; 13:8–28). *Lebanon* refers to the region north of Israel running from Lake Huleh to near Riblah. The area was known for its snow-capped mountains and was considered part of Israel's covenant land (cf. Deut. 1:7; 3:25; Josh. 1:4). The regions of Gilead and Lebanon represented 'Israelite territory to be populated under optimal conditions, i.e. the eschatological restoration of all Israel'.[62]

11. The line, *They will pass through the sea of trouble*, recalls the exodus from Egypt, when YHWH struck the waters of the Red Sea (lit. 'Sea of Reeds', NJPS) and opened a dry path to safety for Israel (Exod. 14:21–22; 15:6, 22; cf. Pss 77:16, 19; 78:13).

God's power to controvert the forces of nature in drying up mighty watercourses (*all the depths of the Nile will dry up*; cf. Isa.19:5–7) signifies his rule over the nations as well (cf. Isa. 17:12–14; 40:15–17). As a consequence, *Assyria* loses its *pride* (or sovereignty), and *Egypt* its *sceptre* (or royal authority: 'God acts as creator, imposing

---

59. *NIDOTTE* 1: 1102.

60. Redditt (1995: 121).

61. See Merrill (1994: 280); cf. Redditt (1995: 121) on possible allusions to exodus imagery taken from Hos. 8:13 and 11:5.

62. Meyers and Meyers (1993: 223); see also Meyers and Meyers (1994: 271). According to Zechariah, even these regions *will not be room enough* for restored Israel.

order on chaos, subduing enemies, and establishing Israel and its king (Pss 33:6–14; 89:9–27 [8–26]).[63]

12. The first-person speech of YHWH resumes as abruptly as it ended in verse 10. God will *strengthen* the people in his own name, *the LORD* – the name of Israel's covenant God (Exod. 3:14; 6:3; cf. Isa. 41:8–10). The statement, *and in his name they will walk*, has affinities to Micah 4:5, *we will walk in the name of the LORD our God*. The verb *walk* signifies a posture of covenant obedience on the part of Israel ('and they will follow me', CEV; 'and they will march in my name', NJB), and the reflexive form can be understood in the sense of habitually or continually (i.e. 'they will walk continually').[64]

Meaning

The key idea of the section is found in the repeated phrases that God *will strengthen* and restore his people (10:6, 12), to the degree that it will be as though they had never been *rejected* (v. 6). This divine enabling will result in Israel's obedience to YHWH's covenant (v. 12). The Lord will do this because of his *compassion* for his people (v. 6).

c. Lament over the destruction of Lebanon (11:1–3)

Context

Given the ambiguity of the shepherd motif in the second half of Zechariah, the lyric poem of 11:1–3 is an intentional Janus-type literary unit, a transitional piece bridging the shepherd imagery (10:1–3; 11:3, 4–17) and the twin themes of restoration and judgment in chapters 10 and 11 (10:5, 11; 11:1–3, 4–6, 15–17).[65]

The brief poem is difficult to interpret, drawing as it does from both arboreal and pastoral imagery with no direct links to any

---

63. Ollenburger (1996: 815).

64. Barker (2008: 806) (but alternately, 'by my authority they will go wherever they wish', NLT); cf. Boda (2004: 446), who notes that, given the context, the word probably refers to "the exercise of dominion over an area" … The restored community will regain control over their land.'

65. See Ollenburger (1996: 817); cf. O'Brien (2004: 249).

particular historical context. The arboreal imagery is taken directly from the jungle-like features of the areas of Bashan and Gilead adjoining the Jordan River.[66] Quite apart from how one understands the complex imagery, mixed metaphors and vague historical and political allusions, Baldwin and others correctly recognize that the poem stresses the downfall of the arrogant.[67]

Comment

11:1–2. The references to *Lebanon* and *Bashan* (an area of tableland north of Gilead and north-east of the Sea of Galilee) connect the poem to the geographical citations of the previous oracle (cf. 10:10). Both regions have experienced significant deforestation, or will soon do so, according to the prophet. The trees mourning figuratively over the deforestation of 'the jungle of the Jordan' (so NJPS, NAB) may be understood as a response to the necessary clearing of the *dense forest* (v. 2) and *lush thicket* (v. 3) of the region to accommodate the overflow population of restored Israel (cf. 10:10).[68]

3. Figurative language, *shepherds … lions*, describes the leaders of Lebanon and Bashan lamenting the destruction of the heavily timbered slopes – the pride and livelihood of each region (cf. Jer. 25:34, 38). Baldwin, Rudolph and Petersen are among those commentators who suggest that Zechariah has in mind the leaders of the nations, especially those who have been oppressors of Israel.[69] Hanson and Boda identify the *shepherds* and *lions* as local Jewish

---

66. Jeremiah refers generally to these areas teeming with vegetation and animal life as *Jordan's thickets* (Jer. 12:5; 49:19; 50:44). See further the discussions in Baldwin (1972: 192); and Meyers and Meyers (1993: 247–248).

67. Baldwin (1972: 192); cf. Ollenburger (1996: 818): 'Zech 11:1–3 constructs a paradigm of Yahweh's action against what is proud and lofty, especially in a political sense.'

68. Cf. Meyers and Meyers (1993: 224).

69. Cf. Baldwin (1972: 192); Rudolph (1976: 200); and Petersen (1995: 82) (see n. 81 on the form-critical recognition of the international idiom of the poem).

leaders contributing to Zerubbabel's demise.[70] Given the propensity for intentional ambiguity in many of the messages of the Hebrew prophets, a rigid distinction between the two groups of leaders is unwarranted.

The name *Bashan* means 'fruitful', and the region was well known for its mighty oak trees (v. 2; cf. Ezek. 27:6) and *rich pastures* (cf. Jer. 50:19; Mic. 7:14).[71]

Meaning
The cryptic poem probably rehearses the destruction of the forested areas of Lebanon and the regions of Bashan/Gilead by the Babylonians during the series of campaigns into Syria-Palestine, which eventually resulted in the destruction of Jerusalem and the exile of surviving Judahites to Babylonia (Jer. 25:8–14, 32–38; cf. Hab. 2:17).[72] Lebanon and Bashan are ciphers or representations of the nations (much like *Assyria* and *Egypt* in 10:10–11), who will also experience divine judgment in *that day* when God fully restores his people in the land of their covenant heritage (cf. Zech. 9:16).

v. The two shepherds (11:4–17)

Context
The passage is difficult to interpret due to the obscure nature of the language and the lack of an immediate historical context for the story (e.g. the reference to the ousting of three shepherds in one month, v. 8). Thus, it is unclear whether this is a reflection on the

---

70. Cf. Hanson (1979: 334–337); Boda (2004: 461).
71. The exact meaning of the phrase is uncertain: 'their glory is despoiled', NAB, NRSV; 'their majesty has been ravaged', NJB; cf. LXX, 'their greatness suffered misery!' (NETS).
72. The influence of Jer. 25:34–38 on Zech. 11:1–3 is widely recognized (e.g. Jer. 25:34 = Zech. 11:2); see Nurmela (1996: 133–136); and Ollenburger (1996: 818) on further borrowing from Jeremiah by Zechariah. It is possible that the references to Lebanon and Bashan are veiled allusions to Jeremiah's characterization of the two as treacherous allies of Judah during the Babylonian crisis (cf. Jer. 22:20, 22).

recent Babylonian exile or a warning about a future onslaught against the Hebrew people. In addition, Zechariah's role in the allegory is puzzling, because the prophet is first charged to care for God's flock as a good shepherd (vv. 4–14), and then to play the part of a worthless shepherd (vv. 15–17).

The metaphor of the shepherd for the leaders of the nations and the people of Israel provides the theme that links the last three messages (9:9–17; 10:1 – 11:3; and 11:4–17) of Zechariah's first oracle (chs. 9 – 11; cf. 9:16; 10:2–3; 11:3, 5, 7–9, 15–17). The final message of the first oracle (11:4–17) combines the genres of (shepherd) allegory with a report of symbolic action.[73] The text may be understood as 'an enacted prophecy, akin to those many cases in the Book of Ezekiel, where the prophet was instructed to perform certain actions which symbolized their own meaning'.[74] It is possible, however, that the report of symbolic action is simply a literary device designed to carry the gist of the prophet's message from God to the people of post-exilic Judah (v. 11).[75] Given the nature of prophetic ministry, the lines between allegory and literal sign-act may be difficult to distinguish. The passage is a first-person narrative, an autobiographical account of the prophet's response to God's directives. Unlike the previous messages in the oracle, the tone is entirely pessimistic, pronouncing divine judgment on shepherds and flock alike.[76] The passage may be outlined in three sections: Zechariah's commission (vv. 4–6); the prophet's fulfilment of the commission by means of two sign-acts (vv. 7–14); and a second divine commission to Zechariah (including the repetition of the first sign-act, vv. 15–17). As in the case with the taunt song of 11:1–3, Zechariah's sign-act reports have connections with the preaching of earlier exilic prophets, especially Jeremiah (Jer. 23) and Ezekiel (Ezek. 34; 37).

---

73. See the discussion of the various understandings of the literary form of the passage in Petersen (1995: 89) who identifies two sign-acts (cf. Boda [2004: 461] who identifies three sign-acts).

74. Craigie (1985: 208).

75. So Merrill (1994: 288).

76. Cf. Mason (1977: 105).

Comment

a. Zechariah's commission (vv. 4–6)

11:4. *This is what the* LORD *my God says.* The messenger formula appears for the first and only time in the first oracle (chs. 9 – 11) and marks a new section in the message. The prophet Zechariah is the recipient of the divine commission.

God's prophet is charged to 'be a shepherd' (NRSV) to a doomed flock of animals (*Pasture the flock marked for slaughter*). The *flock* that Zechariah is to tend is the people of Israel. The prophets acting as shepherds tending to God's people were to provide wise leadership, spiritual guidance and sound instruction, especially in the law of Moses. The goal of their teaching and example was to instil righteousness in the people – true knowledge of YHWH, obedience to his covenant, and worship appropriate to the Lord Almighty (cf. Jer. 23:1–5; Ezek. 34:1–6; Mal. 2:7–8). Like other prophets before him (cf. Isa. 6:9–13), Zechariah is commissioned to fail in one sense, because the people of Israel are destined for the *slaughter* of divine judgment.[77] Like sheep fattened for butchering, the people are treated like a mere commodity – disposable merchandise in a corrupt and oppressive economic system.

5. The *buyers* of the Hebrew people were probably military officials or merchants of the occupying foreign powers, foreign allies, or domestic slave-traders who purchased the people for slave labour. The word *slaughter* may indicate a literal 'killing' (NJB) of people, or it may be a metaphor for slavery – a dehumanizing of persons and a more indirect form of 'slaying' (NAB) people. In either case, the repetition of the verb in verses 4–5 calls attention to the gross injustice of the situation. The injustice of trafficking in slave-trade is further compounded by the fact that those engaged in the practice do so with 'impunity' (NAB).

Those who sell the people like sheep at the market include the

---

77. Meyers and Meyers (1993: 252–253) note that, since the rest of the passage indicates that some of the sheep are survivors, the lexical range of the verb 'slaughter' (Heb. *hārag*) can mean that the total flock is 'ruined', not butchered.

shepherds themselves, the leaders of the Hebrew people. The selling of the people by their own leaders may refer both to slave-trading and the sale of persons unable to pay their debts to creditors (cf. Amos 2:6; 8:6; see Deut. 15:1–11). The motivation for these merchants in human trade is wealth, evidenced in the testimony: '*I am rich!*' A twisted theology of YHWH's covenant blessing emerges, as what Petersen refers to as the 'mercantile bounty' of the merchants is considered a sign of divine favour.[78] Meyers and Meyers note that the expression is the structural equivalent of saying I 'will not be held guilty'.[79] The buyer incurs no guilt and the seller assumes no wrongdoing – yet those who seek ill-gotten gain ensnare themselves (Prov. 1:19), and God will judge those who garner wealth through injustice (Ezek. 22:13).

6. The moral corruption of the people and their leaders is such that God will *no longer have pity* ('spare', NAB) on the guilty parties. The phrase, *people of the land*, is somewhat ambiguous and may refer to the Hebrews in the land of Israel,[80] or the nations of the earth ('inhabitants of the earth', NAB, NEB, NRSV). The set of verbs that follows indicates the scope and certainty of God's resolve to judge the guilty, as he will *deliver* the people to leaders who *oppress*, with no intention to *rescue* them. Zechariah's harsh language echoes that of Jeremiah and Ezekiel, who announced that YHWH will withdraw his *pity* and bring the judgment of the Babylonian exile against Judah because of their idolatry (cf. Jer. 13:14; 21:7; Ezek. 5:11; 7:4; 9:5, 10). The verse foreshadows later NT teaching in which God eventually gives people over to their own sinful desires and behaviour (with attendant consequences; cf. Rom. 1:24–32).

b. The sign-act of the shepherds' staffs (vv. 7–14)
7. Zechariah obeyed God's commission and took up the duties of shepherding his flock, the Hebrew people of post-exilic Judah. The phrase *particularly the oppressed of the flock* (NIV) is awkward and ambiguous. The reading of the LXX ('merchants', which compresses

78. Petersen (1995: 92).
79. Meyers and Meyers (1993: 255).
80. Barker (2008: 809); cf. Baldwin (1972: 194).

two Heb. words into a single form) indicates that the prophet took up his task 'on behalf of the sheep merchants' (NRSV; cf. NAB, NEB). Alternately, the NJB, 'Then I pastured for slaughter the sheep belonging to the sheep-dealers', emphasizes the relationship of the flock to the leaders of Judah, not the role of the leaders of Judah as Zechariah's employers.

The *two staffs* allude to the tools of shepherding, the rod and the staff (cf. Ps. 23:4). The staff or crook was a symbol of leadership in the biblical world. In ancient Egypt, the ornamental shepherd's crook held by the Pharaoh represented his just rule of the people. Unlike the prophet Ezekiel who joined two sticks into one, symbolizing the reunification of the two Hebrew kingdoms (Ezek. 37:15–19), Zechariah dramatized the reversal of YHWH's covenant relationship and Israelite unity by breaking the two staffs (vv. 10, 14).

The symbolic use of names (*one called Favour and the other Union*) is often associated with the sign-acts of God's prophets (cf. Hos. 1:4–9). Here the word *Favour* ('Goodwill', NJB) suggests divine blessing, as in Psalm 90:17. This divine favour may refer generally to YHWH's covenants with Israel through Abraham (Gen. 12:1–3), Moses (Exod. 19 – 24) and David (2 Sam. 7:12–16). Later, the breaking of this staff symbolizes the fracture of God's covenant with the nations (cf. v. 10). The term *Union* ('Unity', NJPS, NRSV; 'Bonds', NAB) has legal connotations and indicates a formal tie between two parties.[81] The second staff symbolized the unity of the Hebrew tribes melded into a single nation during the reign of King David (cf. 2 Sam. 5:1–3). The association between the symbolic action of Zechariah employing two staffs and the account of Ezekiel's sign-act joining two sticks is widely recognized (Ezek. 37:16–17).[82]

8–9. In a relatively short period of time (*one month*, v. 8a), Zechariah 'did away' (NAB) with *three shepherds* or leaders of the post-exilic Hebrew community.[83] His actions were not well received by

81. Cf. Meyers and Meyers (1993: 264).

82. E.g. J. M. P. Smith (1912: 305); cf. Nurmela (1996: 136–138).

83. The enigmatic historical reference has prompted more than forty different identifications for the three shepherds, including the last three

the wider community, however, and the people *detested* ('were disgusted with', NJPS; 'hated', NLT) the prophet for the removal of these leaders (v. 8b). Zechariah *grew weary* ('became impatient', NLT, NRSV; 'lost patience', NJB) and resigned his commission as shepherd to Israel, declaring to the people (and to God?): *I will not be your shepherd* (v. 9a). The term *grew weary* is used elsewhere in the OT to refer to an inability to endure a trying situation.[84] So the prophet 'abandons the sheep to death, loss, and to self-destruction. In doing so, Zechariah opens the way for the disastrous situation Yahweh announces in v. 6.'[85] The final clause, 'And let those who remain devour each other' (NLT), may be understood metaphorically as various forms of injustice levied against the poor by the rich and against the people by their leaders (cf. Mic. 3:3).

10. The breaking of the *staff called Favour* ('snapped it in two', NEB) symbolized the *revoking of the covenant* ('annulling', NEB, NRSV) God had made *with all the nations* (NIV), although there is no explicit reference in the OT to a covenant between YHWH and the nations. The prophet may be referring to *a covenant of peace* by which God promised to protect Israel from the nations (cf. Ezek. 34:25, 28),[86] or 'all the peoples' (NJB) understood as the Jewish colonies scattered among the foreign powers.[87] The latter understanding is preferred, since 'the passage makes so much more sense if seen as concerned with the prophet's people'.[88] Meyers and Meyers boldly suggest that

---

kings of Judah, certain high priests from the intertestamental era, or various leaders from the offices of king, priest and prophet (see further the discussions in Baldwin (1972: 194–197); Redditt (1995: 98); cf. Meyers and Meyers (1993: 265), who observe that the number three is symbolic of completeness, and conclude that the passage is 'deliberately vague and, thereby, inclusive'. Ollenburger (1996: 821) rightly summarizes: 'It has proven futile to try to identity these three shepherds, or to determine why there are three.'

84. Boda (2004: 464).
85. Ollenburger (1996: 821).
86. Ibid., p. 822.
87. So Baldwin (1972: 198).
88. Redditt (1995: 126); cf. Webb (2003: 147–148).

Zechariah actually proclaimed the dissolution of the historical covenant binding Israel to YHWH as the people of God.[89] Quite apart from the precise understanding of the covenant Zechariah has in mind, as Ollenburger (1996: 822) observes, the predatory sheep-merchants 'are now freed to prey on the sheep'.

11. The prophet's symbolic breaking of the staff signalled the dissolution of the covenant of *Favour*. The dramatic sign-act (and presumably the interpretive sermon accompanying it) was immediately recognized by the audience as *the word of the LORD*. The question as to the composition of the prophet's audience remains unresolved, whether the righteous remnant among the oppressed Hebrews,[90] or the 'sheep merchants' (so NAB, NRSV; 'dealers', NEB).[91] The context of verse 12 suggests that the sheep-dealers are the intended audience, since the prophet requests his pay from them (v. 12).

12–13. The prophet requests his 'wages' for his work as a pastor-teacher of the people from the leaders or merchants (who apparently hired him for the task), with the proviso that they may keep his pay since he has broken his contract with them (v. 12). Once the transaction is complete (the prophet's severance pay in the allegory), the Lord commands Zechariah to perform another sign-act and *throw* his salary ('deposit', NJPS), paid in silver into the 'Temple of Yahweh' (NJB; v. 13). The repetition of the verb *throw* indicates the contemptuous nature of the symbolic action – accented by the sarcastic commentary: 'this princely sum at which they have valued me!' (NJB; 'a measly thirty pieces of silver', CEV; v. 13b).[92] McComskey (1998: 1200–1201) notes the 'immediacy to the divine presence' in the prophet's first-person speech (vv. 10–13),

---

89. Meyers and Meyers (1993: 270). This seems unlikely: 'Since it is impossible to find in Scripture a covenant agreement that Yahweh entered into with the nations, the covenant here must consist of unilateral strictures placed on them by God' (McComiksey [1998: 1197]).

90. Merrill (1994: 295–296).

91. See commentary on v. 7 above, pp. 231–232.

92. Cf. Petersen (1995: 97).

permitting easy movement from the words of the prophet to the words of YHWH.

The silver was to be given as a donation to 'the potter in the Temple of the LORD' (NLT, v. 13c). Baldwin (1972: 199) speculates that a guild of potters may have been minor temple officials, due to the ongoing need for sacred vessels in temple worship rituals (cf. Lev. 6:28). The word *potter* (Heb. *yôṣēr*) is similar in sound to the word for 'treasury' (Heb. *'ôṣār*; cf. Syr. 'treasury'), prompting the reading 'throw it into the treasury' (so NAB, NEB, NRSV).[93] It is noteworthy that the NT account of the betrayal money Judas threw onto the floor of the temple combines Zechariah 11:12–13 and Jeremiah 32:6–9, and makes reference to both the *treasury* (Matt. 27:6) and the *potter's field* (Matt. 27:10). The LXX translates, 'throw it into the furnace', suggesting that the silver was melted down by a smelter or founder and recast into a silver vessel of some type for use in the temple rituals (cf. NJB, 'Throw it to the smelter'). The price of a slave during a later period in the biblical world was *thirty pieces of silver* (cf. Exod. 21:32). During the earlier period of biblical history, the standard rate for slave trade was twenty shekels of silver (cf. Gen 37:28).[94]

14. The third sign-act of the passage, the breaking of the *second staff called Union*, symbolically annulled the unity of the Hebrew tribes as a nation achieved under King David (cf. 2 Sam. 5:1–3). The dissolution of 'the family ties between Judah and Israel' (NRSV) breaks the bond uniting Israel as the people of God established in the Sinai covenant (cf. Exod. 19:6) and overturns the sign-act of Ezekiel joining the sticks of Judah and Israel into one nation (Ezek. 37:18–19, 21). The pre-exilic era of a divided Hebrew nation, Israel and Judah, is now replayed in the post-exilic era of Hebrew history.

---

93. Cf. Sweeney (2000: 681) who renders the expression: 'throw the money to YHWH in the temple' (i.e. understanding the word *potter* in the sense of God as Creator or fashioner).

94. Thirty pieces of silver was a considerable amount of money in the ancient world (more than two years' wages for the average labourer, according to Baldwin [1972: 198]). Rather than sarcasm, the expression contributes to the overall theme of reversal in the allegory (so Meyers and Meyers, 1993: 279).

c. Zechariah commissioned a second time (vv. 15–17)

Zechariah's resignation from his post as shepherd to Israel in the
allegory of the shepherds is temporary, as God recalls him to a
second stint in that symbolic role. The relationship and meaning of
the two reports of Zechariah's commissioning as a shepherd
bringing a prophetic message to post-exilic Israel by means of
symbolic action are disputed. For example, the first report (vv. 4–14)
depicts the prophet as taking on 'the role of a shepherd who
abandons his post to symbolize Yahweh's breaking of the covenant
with the people'.[95] The second report expands on the first, as the
prophet takes on the role of a worthless shepherd, symbolizing the
kind of leadership the community will now experience since
YHWH's covenant has been annulled.[96] By contrast, Redditt (1995:
127) considers the second episode (vv. 15–17) as essentially a
repetition of the first (vv. 4–14). It seems more likely that the second
episode is a continuation, not a duplication of the first, in which
Zechariah describes the leadership crisis in post-exilic Judah through
the foil of portraying a divinely appointed shepherd faithful to his
calling (but rejected to the point of quitting), juxtaposed with the
portrayal of a worthless shepherd who shirks his duties.[97]

15. The directive to take the *equipment* ('gear', NAB, NJB;
'implements', NRSV) of a shepherd is probably a reference to the
rod and staff (see v. 7 above).[98] The prophet is charged to play the
role of a *foolish shepherd* ('good-for-nothing', NJB; 'worthless', NEB;
NLT). The descriptive adjective *foolish* connotes more than simple-
mindedness or incompetence. The shepherd is *foolish* 'because he
oppresses the people',[99] much like the shepherds portrayed by
Ezekiel as the enemies of God (Ezek. 34:7–10). These corrupt and
greedy leaders are motivated by self-interest, not like the shepherd
who rescues the scattered sheep, feeds them and tends to the

---

95. O'Brien (2004: 252).
96. Ibid.
97. So Boda (2004: 466).
98. On the clothing and gear of the shepherd in the biblical world see
    Meyers and Meyers (1993: 282).
99. *NIDOTTE* 1: 308.

injured and weak among the flock (cf. Ezek. 34:11–16).

16. Since YHWH 'has annulled the covenant with the people, he will allow an uncaring shepherd to rule them'.[100] The role of the shepherd is to tend the flock of sheep, *care for*, *seek*, *heal*, and *feed* the animals in his charge (cf. Ezek. 34:16). This shepherd's oversight runs contrary to the expected norm at every point.

The expression *tearing off their hoofs* is a cryptic Hebrew idiom for the wanton and ravenous search for the last morsel of edible meat on an animal carcass by a predator or scavenger (cf. CEV, 'He will just dine on the fattest sheep, leaving nothing but a few bones'). The prophet Micah used similar language to describe the leaders of Judah, whose unjust rule was akin to eating the flesh of the people (Mic. 3:3).

17. The word *woe* (Heb. *hôy*) is a technical interjection in prophetic literature, usually introducing an announcement of malediction in the form of a curse or judgment oracle (e.g. Ezek. 34:2; Amos 6:1; Mic. 2:1; Nah. 3:1; Zeph. 2:5).[101] 'If the *hôy* oracles of the prophets go back to the cry of lament for the dead, to cry *hôy* is tantamount to a prediction of death, a proclamation of the judgment of Yahweh.'[102] Unlike *the worthless shepherd who deserts the flock*, the faithful shepherd's task is an ongoing search-and-rescue mission (cf. Ezek. 34:11–12).

The woe-oracle against the worthless shepherd takes the form of a poetic curse invoked for desertion of the flock (*May the sword strike his arm and his right eye!*). The maiming of the arm and the blinding of the right eye are figures of speech that represent the physical and mental abilities of the shepherd. The loss of the *arm* and the *eye* render the worthless shepherd powerless, thus ending his selfish and opportunistic rule.[103]

Meaning

It is unclear whether the allegory of the shepherds is a reflection on the recent Babylonian exile or a warning about a future 'slaughter

100. O'Brien (2004: 252).

101. *TDOT* 3: 363–364.

102. Boda (2004: 467).

103. See further the discussion in Meyers and Meyers (1993: 291–292).

and scattering' of the Hebrew people. Zechariah's role in the allegory is also puzzling, since the prophet is first charged to care for God's people as a good shepherd (vv. 4–14), and then to play the part of a worthless shepherd (vv. 15–17). Quite apart from the ambiguity of the allegory, basic theological truths emerge from the story describing shepherds (leaders) and sheep (people). First, leaders are prone to abuse their authority and power, given the inclinations of fallen people in a fallen culture (vv. 5, 8). Second, shepherd-leaders must have compassion for the sheep or people under their care, unlike those shepherds who do not spare their own sheep (v. 5). And third, 'human perversity and ignorance are so profound that human beings will not even accept good leadership if God gives it to them' (vv. 7–8).[104]

B. Second oracle (12 – 14)

Zechariah's second oracle may be outlined in five sections: the future deliverance of Jerusalem (12:1–9); a spirit of grace poured out on the inhabitants of Jerusalem (12:10–14); a fountain for cleansing Israel's sin (13:1–6); the scattering of the sheep (13:7–9); and the Lord will rule the earth (14:1–21). The theme of the opposition of the nations against Jerusalem binds the four messages of the oracle together, as the nations are gathered against Jerusalem at the beginning (12:1–9) and the end of the prophet's last sermon (14:1–15). The apocalyptic tone of the oracle is set by the repetition of the phrase *on that day*, a prophetic shorthand for the eschatological Day of the Lord (12:3, 4, 6, 8, 11; 13:1, 2, 4; 14:4, 6, 8, 9, 13, 20, 21).

The second oracle offers a mixed picture of divine judgment and blessing, with portents of both destruction and deliverance determined for Jerusalem. The theological focal point of the second oracle is the purification of the people of Israel from their sin (13:1). The second oracle (and the book of Zechariah) culminates with the inauguration of the universal kingdom of the Lord Almighty (14:16–21).

---

104. Craigie (1985: 210).

i. Future deliverance of Jerusalem (12:1–14)

Context

The first chapter of Zechariah's final oracle has two sections: the assault of the nations against Jerusalem (vv. 1–9), and the repentance of Israel (vv. 10–14). The outward victory of Israel over the aggressor nations is complemented by the inward spiritual renewal of the penitent people – and both are accomplished by God.[105] The deliverance of Jerusalem (v. 9) bridges the opening section of the second oracle with the visions and earlier messages of Zechariah (especially 2:1–5 and ch. 8). The outpouring of the spirit of grace (v. 10) leading to repentance connects the unit with the prophet's call to repentance inveighed in the prelude (1:1–6). Zechariah's return to the theme of the spiritual renewal of God's people helps to join the two oracles (chs. 9 – 14) with the larger Hag-Zech-Mal corpus.

a. God defends Judah and Jerusalem (vv. 1–9)

Comment

12:1. *An oracle* (see commentary on 9:1, pp. 204–205). Like the first oracle (9:1), the messenger formula (*the word of the LORD*) introduces the second oracle and adds the imprint of divine authority to the message. The first oracle (9:1) is delivered against the nations neighbouring Israel, while the second oracle is a message *concerning Israel* (12:1). The opening verse contains a three-line hymn-like doxology praising God as Creator (v. 1).[106]

Three specific spheres of God's creative activity are itemized: 'the heavens', 'the earth' and 'the human spirit' (NRSV). The use of a participial form of the verb for each of these divine epithets emphasizes the ongoing or perpetual nature of God's creative activity. The first two domains of God's creative power have

---

105. Cf. Mason (1977: 118).
106. Cf. R. L. Smith (1984: 275); and Petersen (1995: 110–111) who considers the triad of participial and doxological clauses of v. 1 to be the prologue to the 'on that day' montage of Zech. 12:3 – 13:9.

parallels in Psalm 104 and the book of Isaiah, where we learn that God alone *stretches out the heavens like a tent* (Ps. 104:2; Isa. 42:5; 44:24) and that *he set the earth on its foundations* (Ps. 104:5; Isa. 51:13). The verse is an appropriate introduction to the prophet's final oracle, because it anticipates the consummation of all things in the universal worship of YHWH (Zech. 14:6–9).

The reference to God as the one who 'formed the human spirit within' (NRSV) is unique to Zechariah 12:1 in the OT. The prophet likely drew on the imagery of the Genesis account of the creation of humanity, which states that the Lord God formed the man's body from the dust of the ground and breathed the breath of life into his nostrils (Gen. 2:7). The statement has a close parallel in the psalmist's description of YHWH as the one who made human hearts, 'so that he understands everything they do' (Ps. 33:15, NLT). This explains the effectiveness of God's outpouring of *a spirit of grace* (v. 10) upon the people of Israel that will prompt repentance in that eschatological day – as our Maker he knows everything about us (cf. Ps. 139).

2. The city of *Jerusalem* is a key theme in chapter 12 (mentioned ten times). Thus, 'The constant repetition ... depicts the eschatological future of Jerusalem – representing Zion, Judah, and all Israel – in the context of the rest of the world, and the future of Jerusalem as the setting of the royal leadership that will be restored to power.'[107]

The *cup that sends all the surrounding peoples reeling* (cf. NAB, 'bowl to stupefy'; NLT, 'intoxicating drink'; or 'bowl of reeling', so NJPS; 'cup of reeling', NRSV) is a unique expression for Jerusalem in the OT. The cup of wine or strong drink is a common metaphor for God's judgment in the OT prophets (e.g. Isa. 51:17; Jer. 25:15; Hab. 2:16). 'Those who attack Jerusalem will be rendered incapacitated like a drunk.'[108] In the NT, Jesus understood the suffering of the cross as a *cup* of divine wrath (Matt. 26:39, 42), and the book of Revelation portrays God's judgment as *bowls of God's wrath* poured out upon the earth (Rev. 14:10; 16:1).

---

107. Meyers and Meyers (1993: 342–343).
108. Boda (2004: 483).

3. The phrase *On that day* is shorthand in the OT prophets for
the Day of the Lord. It is repeated in 12:4, 6, 8, 9, 11; 13:1, 4 in what
Petersen (1995: 111) calls an 'on that day' montage.

Like the first oracle, Zechariah's second oracle has global and
cosmic overtones, with references to *the nations* and the universal
rule of God.[109] Jerusalem had been assailed by the nations in the
past (e.g. Assyria, 2 Kgs 18; Babylonia, 2 Kgs 25), drinking the cup
of divine wrath to the dregs (cf. Isa. 51:17). The prophet envisions
a future day when the nations will once again be assembled against
Jerusalem, but now they will drink the cup of God's judgment, as
the Lord Almighty will intervene and defend his holy city (Zech.
2:8–9; 9:14–15; 14:3; cf. Jer. 25:15–26).

The reference to *an immovable rock* is another unique OT metaphor
for Jerusalem. The 'heavy stone' (NRSV; cf. 'weighty stone', NAB)
brings self-inflicted injury on those who would attempt to lift it. This
'burdensome stone' is a link between the two halves of the book,
noting that the prophet's previous references to stones use imagery
associated with the temple – 'the physical and spiritual core of
Jerusalem'.[110] Jerusalem will prove *an immovable rock* for those who
attempt to conquer and control her, because the city was founded
by YHWH, and he loves it more than any other city (Ps. 87:1–2). The
prophet must refer to an eschatological day beyond the fall of
Jerusalem to the Romans in AD 70 (cf. Joel 3:9–16; Rev. 16:16–21).

4. *Panic* (NAB, 'fright'), *madness* (NLT, 'lose his nerve') and *blindness*
are among the curses threatened against Israel for covenant disobedience (Deut. 28:28). The Day of the Lord will witness a reversal, as
these curses will be turned against Israel's enemies. The language
calls to mind the stories of the Aramean soldiers struck with blindness (2 Kgs 6:18), and the panic the Lord stirred in the camp of the
Aramean army assembled against Israel so that they fled in confusion into the night (2 Kgs 7:6–7).

I will keep a watchful eye. The open eyes of God are 'an indication of his provision for those who stand in desperate need',[111]

109. See Boda (2004: 482).
110. Meyers and Meyers (1993: 317).
111. *NIDOTTE* 3: 666.

as illustrated in the story of Hagar (Gen. 21:19).

5. The first saying of the section (vv. 1–3) mentions *Jerusalem* and *Judah*, with the focus on Jerusalem; whereas the second (vv. 4–5) and third (vv. 6–7) sayings reverse the order to *Judah* and *Jerusalem*, thus widening the geographic venue and establishing ethnic and religious ties between the capital and the outlying province.[112] The MT reading, *leaders of Judah* (NAB, 'princes'; NJB, 'rulers'), is preferred over the emended 'clans of Judah' (NEB, NLT, NRSV).[113] The recognition by the *leaders of Judah* that God intervenes on behalf of *the people of Jerusalem* is a first step in resolving the rift between rivals, as their confession suggests mutual encouragement and the siding of Judah with God and the city of Jerusalem.[114] The confession, *the LORD Almighty is their God*, is a variation of the formula signifying covenant relationship with YHWH (see the commentary on 8:8; 10:6, pp. 194–195, 223–224).

6. The 'firepot' signifies a *brazier* (so NJPS, NAB, NEB, NJB) or a 'firepan' holding a 'flame' (so NLT; cf. CEV, 'fire ball'). Bronze or gold firepans were used to carry hot coals to or from the sacrificial altars of both the tabernacle and the temple (Exod. 27:3; 1 Kgs 7:50). In the eschaton, YHWH will set Israel like a firepan burning with hot coals among the nations, both to destroy and purify with fire akin to that which consumed the ritual sacrifices of Hebrew worship. Although the terminology differs, the *flaming torch* may also allude to the 'smoking firepot' and *blazing torch* as symbols of the Abrahamic covenant (and God's election and protection of Israel, cf. Gen. 15:17).[115] Interestingly, Judah's position 'among the enemy is turned to advantage. As instantaneously as fire ignites dry tinder and ripe sheaves, so will Judah inflict devastation on the enemy while

---

112. Petersen (1995: 114–115).

113. Ibid., p. 108, n. e. R. L. Smith (1984: 275) and others call attention to the rivalry between the people of Judah and the inhabitants of Jerusalem in vv. 4–8; but Petersen (1995: 115) comments that the 'saying does not suggest tension between the capital and the hinterlands'.

114. See Mason (1977: 116); and Baldwin (1972: 204).

115. So Larkin, (1994: 157).

Jerusalem watches.'[116] The security envisioned for Jerusalem here at the beginning of the final oracle gives way to the capture and ransacking of the city before YHWH's intervention at the end of the oracle (14:2). In the OT, fire is a symbol of both God's judgment and divine presence, and 'both thoughts are prominent here. The victory is really God's.'[117]

7. The order of divine deliverance, *Judah* then *Jerusalem*, is highlighted and calls attention to the importance of the relationship of the two entities – and the recognition that 'each needs the other and neither is to lord it over the other'.[118] The phrase *house of David* refers to the dynasty or royal family of King David and occurs only in the oracles of Zechariah in the post-exilic prophets (Zech. 12:7, 8, 10, 12; 13:1). The immediate reference is probably to the governor Zerubbabel (although his abrupt exit from the accounts of the Hag-Zech-Mal corpus is a puzzle; see the commentary on 4:6, pp. 156–157). Zechariah may allude to the Davidic covenant (2 Sam. 7) and the restoration of Davidic kingship envisioned by Jeremiah (Jer. 23:6; 33:15, 17, 21, 22) and Ezekiel (Ezek. 34:23, 24; 37:24, 25).

8. On *the LORD will shield*, see commentary on 9:15 above.

The feeblest among them will be like David, Israel's warrior-king, who was celebrated in song as Israel's champion after killing the Philistine giant Goliath (1 Sam. 18:7).

The bold statement, *the house of David will be like God*, applied to the Davidic family as the leaders of Israel, has proven difficult for interpreters. The early versions struggled with the simile as well, as the Targum reads: 'and the house of David shall prosper like princes';[119] and the LXX translates: 'and the house of David will be like a divine house' (NETS, 819). As king, David was the adopted son of YHWH (cf. 2 Sam. 7:14; Ps. 2:7). Thus, Zechariah 'democratizes' the Davidic covenant by figuratively conferring this adoption status on the people and leaders of post-exilic Judah.[120] Given the role of

116. Baldwin (1972: 204).

117. Mason (1977: 116).

118. Baldwin (1972: 204).

119. Cathcart and Gordon (1989: 218).

120. Petersen (1995: 119–120).

Aaron as a stand-in for Moses as a complementary spokesman for God as background for Zechariah's comparison (cf. Exod. 4:16), the leaders of Judah will have a similar supportive or complementary role to the house of David under divine aegis.[121]

The second simile, *like the Angel of the LORD*, modifies, explains and perhaps softens the first. The title signifies a manifestation of YHWH himself as a Divine Warrior in this context and recalls the deliverance and protection he provided for Israel during their exodus from Egypt (Exod. 14:19; 15:3). The comparisons to *David* and *the Angel of the LORD* are figures of speech that serve only to magnify God's glorious deliverance of his people Israel. By means of divine enabling, the weak will become strong and the strong will become as powerful as God.[122] (See further the commentary on *the Angel of the LORD* in 1:11 and 3:1, pp. 133–134, 147–149.) The OT reports that 'Suppliants had addressed David saying he was "like the angel of God" (1 Sam. 29:9; 2 Sam. 14:17, 20; 19:27). This was an honorific, consciously exaggerated. The fulfilment in Jesus proved to be an understatement.'[123]

9. The final verse of the section both summarizes and interprets the figures of speech in the opening saying of the passage (vv. 2–3; cf. 2:9). 'The fact of a world conflict is assumed and final victory for Jerusalem, whether literal or figurative, is assured.'[124]

Meaning

God will deliver Jerusalem and destroy the nations who besiege the city in the eschatological Day of the Lord (v. 9). Jerusalem will be an

---

121. See Meyers and Meyers (1993: 331–332).

122. See Merrill (1994: 317); cf. Barker (2008: 816); and Mason (1977: 177) who extends this to the special relationship David had with God – 'a "democratizing" of the messianic role'.

123. Baldwin (1972: 204–205). Cf. Ps. 45:6 where the psalmist declares that the throne of the Davidic king is God's throne, or that the Davidic king himself is addressed as 'God', given the special relationship the king has with YHWH as a result of the adoption clause in the Davidic covenant (2 Sam. 7:14).

124. Ibid., p. 205.

immovable rock (v. 3), and the city will *remain intact* (v. 6). God himself will *shield* the inhabitants of Jerusalem, and he will enable the people for battle with prowess like the famed Israelite warrior *David* (v. 8).

b. A spirit of grace poured out, and mourning over the pierced one (vv. 10–14)

Context

In this section of the prophet's second oracle, 'We are approaching the most mysterious and profound part of Zechariah's message … the necessary place of suffering and weeping in the coming kingdom of God.'[125]

Comment

10. The verb *pour out* ('fill', NJPS) has affinities with the language of Joel's prophecy of the pouring out of God's Spirit in the Day of the Lord (Joel 2:28 [MT 3:1]; cf. Ezek. 39:29). Here the divine blessing is a spirit of *grace* ('pity', NEB; NJPS; 'compassion', NRSV) and *supplication* ('compassion', NEB; NJPS; 'petition', NAB; 'prayer', NJB; NLT). The word *grace* signifies a demonstration of favour or good will from one to another. Here the disposition of favour takes the form of pity and remorse, as the people of Judah come to grips with their criminal behaviour. The word *spirit* is best understood as a disposition or a 'persuasion or conviction from YHWH that prompts a course of action'.[126] It seems best not to make a rigid distinction between the disposition of the human spirit[127] and the Spirit of God enabling this disposition,[128] given Zechariah's understanding of the role of God's Spirit in the restoration community (Zech. 4:6; cf. 7:12). The word *supplication* is related to the same verbal root as *grace*. The term connotes an earnest plea for

---

125. Webb (2003: 159). The eschatological formula (*on that day*) at the start of v. 9 may begin a new saying (e.g. Petersen [1995: 120]; cf. NJB) or complete the previous saying, so that v. 10 introduces a new paragraph break (e.g. Baldwin [1972: 205]; cf. NIV, NLT, NRSV).

126. Merrill (1994: 318); cf. McComiskey (1998: 1214).

127. Ollenburger (1996: 828).

128. Cf. Barker (2008: 818).

divine mercy (cf. Ps. 28:2), in this context a prayer of contrition and repentance. The two terms 'highlight two aspects of the ministry of God's Spirit: granting his people favor with himself through renewed relationship and invigorating them to respond to him in penitence'.[129] The recipients of this divine outpouring are *the house of David and the inhabitants of Jerusalem*, marking continuity with the audience of the previous section of the oracle (cf. 12:7).

They will look on me, the one they have pierced. The enigmatic reference to a *pierced* one has proven to be one of several difficult passages to interpret in the latter chapters of Zechariah. First, there is the problem of establishing the proper reading of the passage, since many commentators emend the Hebrew text to read: 'They will look on *him* whom they have pierced.'[130] The more difficult (and preferred) reading is the MT: 'They will look on me whom they have pierced' (NLT, supported by the notable ancient versions).

A second question concerns the antecedent of the pronoun *me* in verse 10: that is, who will Israel 'look on'? In context, the speaker is God, and the subject and the object of the audience's attention is God himself. Thirdly, what does the prophet mean by the verb *pierced*, and how then has Israel *pierced* God? One possible understanding is that the Hebrews pierced God metaphorically by their rebellion and unbelief, leading to their exile (cf. the expansion of the LXX in Zech. 12:10, 'and they shall look upon me, because they have mocked me'; cf. NETS, 'and they shall look to me because they have danced triumphantly, and they shall mourn for him').[131] Or they may have pierced God symbolically in the rejection of his representatives, the priests and prophets. Some scholars have even attempted to correlate this symbolic piercing of God with the martyrdom of some historical figure commissioned by God to

---

129. Boda (2004: 485); cf. Meyers and Meyers (1993: 336) on the reversals of disposition 'instigated by Yahweh'.

130. See the discussions in Mason (1977: 118–119); and R. L. Smith (1984: 276, n. 10a); cf. NJPS, 'They shall lament to Me about those who are slain'; NAB, 'They shall look on him whom they have thrust through'; NRSV, 'They will look on the one whom they have pierced.'

131. Cf. Redditt (1995: 132–133).

speak to Israel (e.g. the 'shepherd' of Zech. 11:4–17 or Onias III, a later high-priest; cf. 2 Macc. 4:34).[132] Given the larger context of Zechariah's message, his audience probably understood the statement both figuratively as a reference to the rejection of YHWH's prophets by their ancestors (cf. Zech. 1:4; 7:11–12), and literally to one or more of God's servants (whether prophets, priests or royalty) recently murdered by the Davidic and priestly leadership of Judah.[133]

The Christian interpretation of Zechariah's second oracle considers the *pierced* one as a messianic reference, fulfilled in the wounding and death of Jesus of Nazareth.[134] The NT cites Zechariah 12:10 in connection with the piercing of Jesus' side by a Roman soldier while he hung on the cross (John 19:34, 37).[135] The vision of Jesus the Messiah in the book of Revelation also alludes to Zechariah 12:10, in a veiled reference to the Jews as the ones who pierced Jesus (Rev. 1:7). But Craigie is probably correct in his observation that the passion narrative of the NT Gospels does not fully exhaust the meaning of Zechariah's vision.[136] The crucifixion of Jesus is the centrepiece of the Christian gospel, and it accounts for his title as the 'Lamb that had been killed' (Rev. 5:6, NLT). It is also true that many Jews were filled with remorse and repented, and

---

132. Ibid.; and Sweeney (2000: 689); see further the discussion of the verb 'pierce' (Heb. *dāqar*) in Meyers and Meyers (1993: 337–340); and *NIDOTTE* 1: 983.

133. Cf. Baldwin (1972: 208).

134. The *b. (Talm.) Sukka* 52a understands the verse as referring to the slaying of the Messiah.

135. John's Gospel (19:37) quotes Zech. 12:10 in the third person ('they will look on *him* whom they pierced') rather than the first person (*me*) of the OT text. Baldwin (1972: 206) has commented that the Gospel writer was simply intending to give the general sense of the OT passage from the viewpoint of recent historical perspective (i.e. the Gospel account makes reference to the OT promise and the NT fulfilment of the events associated with Jesus' death in the immediate past tense; cf. John 19:35).

136. Craigie (1985: 214–215).

believed in the crucified and resurrected Jesus as a result of the apostolic preaching at the day of Pentecost (Acts 2:36–41). Yet Paul envisioned a time (after the complete number of Gentiles have come into the kingdom of Christ) when *all Israel will be saved* (Rom. 11:25–26).[137] It may be that Paul had in mind Zechariah's outpouring of a *spirit of grace* (12:10) that will turn the Hebrew people back to God in repentance at the second advent of Jesus the Messiah.

The repetition of the verb *mourn* ('lament', NJPS; lit. 'beat the breast')[138] in this section (vv. 10 [twice], 11 [twice], 12) indicates the pervasive extent of the remorse and repentance on the part of the people. The similes comparing the mourning to that for an *only child* or a *firstborn* son signify the intensity, depth and bitter character of their mourning.

11. What is meant by the reference to *the weeping of Hadad Rimmon* is unclear. The names *Hadad* and *Rimmon* are the Syrian equivalent for the Canaanite storm god Baal.[139] Some see an allusion to the ritual wailing for the pagan fertility gods whose death and descent to the underworld was commemorated by annual ceremonies.[140] Others identify Hadad Rimmon as an unknown place name, where King Josiah was killed by Pharaoh Neco in his ill-advised intervention against the Egyptians at Megiddo (2 Kgs 23:29–30; 2 Chr. 35:20–24), or still others posit a reference to a day of mourning commemorating the event of King Josiah's death established by the Hebrews (cf. 2 Chr. 35:25).[141] Whatever the exact meaning of the phrase *Hadad Rimmon*, this day will be one of unparalleled mourning for the Hebrews.

12–14. The *land* (v. 12) refers to the people of the land (NJB, 'And the country will mourn clan by clan'); the city of Jerusalem, its

---

137. See further the discussion of 'all Israel' in Moo (1998: 719–723).

138. Cf. *NIDOTTE* 3: 283–285.

139. See the discussion of Rimmon in Meyers and Meyers (1993: 343).

140. E.g. R. L. Smith (1984: 279), who sees the analogy that the Hebrews will wail as loudly and deeply as the pagans for their fertility gods; cf. Mason (1977: 120), who suggests that the Hebrews will see their former worship as little better than idolatry.

141. E.g. Meyers and Meyers (1993: 343–344).

environs and the region of Judah seem to be the focus of the passage.[142] The mourning of the Hebrews in isolation (NLT, 'alone'; NRSV, 'by themselves'), clan by clan, stresses 'the genuineness of the repentance [vv. 12–13]. None is merely being influenced by the tears of the others, nor acting hypocritically, as the professional mourners did.'[143] The repetition of the gender-segregated mourning further emphasizes the depth and the extent of the lamentation.[144] Four distinct *clans* or 'families' (NAB, NLT, NRSV) are mentioned for their culpability in the death of the pierced one. The *house of David*, the royal lineage of the ideal Hebrew king, has already been introduced in the oracle (v. 7). The reference to the *house of Nathan* (v. 12) is ambiguous. *Nathan* was the third son born to David in Jerusalem (2 Sam. 5:14; 1 Chr. 3:5; cf. Luke 3:31). His royal lineage brings further emphasis to the house of David and complements the two priestly lineages that follow in the list of mourners.[145] *Shimei*, the son of Gershon and the grandson of Levi (Num. 3:17–18, 21; 1 Chr. 6:16–17), represented another of the priestly families of the Levites. Taken together, the catalogue of mourning families represents the political and religious leadership of Israel.

Meaning

The Day of the Lord will bring about the repentance of Israel, which is the thesis of Zechariah's message (cf. 1:3). God will accomplish this by an outpouring of *a spirit of grace and supplication* on his people (v. 10). The lines between the present reality and the future hope blur in apocalyptic literature. For Zechariah, prediction is also invitation – small beginnings have an immediacy that must be recognized and seized (cf. 4:10).

---

142. So McComiskey (1998: 1216).

143. Baldwin (1972: 210).

144. Cf. Petersen (1995: 122).

145. See the discussion in Meyers and Meyers (1993: 346–347), who support the identification of the house of Nathan as a royal line.

ii. A fountain of cleansing (13:1–6)

Context

The second message (13:1–6) of the second oracle (chs. 12 – 14) has a single theme: cleansing from sin. This cleansing will be applied to the dynasty of David and the people of Jerusalem (v. 1), the target audience of the previous message (cf. 12:7, 10). Previously, Zechariah said that, in the coming eschatological day, these parties will be delivered from the nations (12:1–9) and will receive a spirit of grace and prayer for mourning (12:10–14). The fountain of cleansing (13:1) will result in the purification of Hebrew religion (vv. 2–6), with specific implications for idolatry, the prophets and the gift of prophecy. The third message (13:7–9) extends YHWH's cleansing to the people of the land (13:9). The purification of God's people will take place in three stages: a fountain of cleansing will be opened (v. 1); YHWH will banish idols and false prophets (vv. 2–6); YHWH's leader (shepherd) will be struck down, the people (sheep) scattered and judged, and a remnant will be refined (vv. 7–9).[146] The first verse of the message (13:1) is understood by some as the conclusion of the first message of the second oracle and is included with 12:10–14 as a complete literary unity.[147] Still others acknowledge that the phrase *on that day* (13:1) indicates a new literary unit that begins in chapter thirteen.[148]

Comment

13:1. The word *fountain* refers to a spring or flowing water source that is tapped or unleashed. The metaphor signifies an 'artesian well' that gushes forth pure water to provide cleansing and purification.[149] Later, Zechariah describes the continuous flow of this spring or fountain as *living water* (Zech. 14:8). In the NT, Jesus proclaimed himself to be the source of this living water (John 4:14), and John's vision of the new heaven and the new earth describes a river flowing

---

146. Cf. O'Brien (2004: 267).

147. E.g. Baldwin (1972: 207); cf. NRSV.

148. See the discussion in R. L. Smith (1984: 280); so NIV, NLT.

149. Cf. Merrill (1994: 328).

with the *water of life* coursing out of the throne of God and the Lamb (Rev. 22:1–2; cf. Ezek. 47:1–12). The verb *be opened* suggests that the *fountain* or spring is readily available; it only needs to be tapped. The participial form of the verb 'implies that the fountain is to be opened continuously'.[150]

The purpose of this fountain is *to cleanse them from sin and impurity*. This kind of thorough cleansing or purification was symbolized in the ritual washings and sacrifices of OT worship practices (cf. Exod. 30:17–21; Heb. 10:1–2). Such cleansing was a provision of the new covenant promised by Jeremiah (Jer. 31:34) and Ezekiel (Ezek. 36:25). The word *sin* is a general term for human misconduct in the form of disobedience to the laws of God (cf. Deut. 9:18). The term *to cleanse* is an infinitive verbal form, with the object implied (cf. NJPS, 'a fountain ... for purging'). The word *impurity* (Heb. *niddâ*) often describes sexual impurity and ritual impurity (cf. Lev. 15:19; Ezra 9:11; Ezek. 18:6; 36:17). This fountain of cleansing may foreshadow the forgiveness of sin in the new covenant era (cf. Jer. 31:34; Ezek. 36:25). The two terms are connected with water in the book of Numbers in contexts associated with the ritual purification of priests (Num. 8:7) and the cleansing of unclean persons contaminated by contact with polluting substances.[151] Zechariah has reworked familiar texts, replacing the 'waters' passages of Numbers 'with the "cosmic fountain opened by Yahweh" ... that enables this passage to achieve its effect of assuring that the past deeds of the restored rulers and bureaucrats have been duly admitted (12:10), mourned (12:10–14), and now washed away'.[152] Taken together, the two words indicate that the Hebrews will experience a complete moral and spiritual cleansing as a result of their sorrow and mourning over their sin (Zech. 12:10–14).

2. The *one pierced* will be 'cut off' (so NRSV), in the sense of 'erase' (NJPS, NEB, NLT) or 'destroy' (NAB). In the ancient world the expression 'to cut off the names' meant 'to cut off the idols themselves,

---

150. R. L. Smith (1984: 280).

151. See the discussions in Meyers and Meyers (1993: 365–367); and Boda (2004: 489–490).

152. Meyers and Meyers (1993: 367).

for a name symbolizes and represents the thing named'.[153]

The verb *remember* (v. 2b) may have a more specialized meaning in this context, signifying speaking the names of the idols ('they shall be mentioned no more', NAB; 'they shall not be uttered any more', NJPS).

To *remove* (v. 2c) in this verbal form 'frequently involves the disposal of some negative quality (e.g. Eccl. 11:10), as is certainly the case here'.[154] The *prophets* mentioned are false prophets, whether those who make false claims in YHWH's name or those who prophesy in the name of other gods. Since Zechariah anticipates a time when such prophecy will cease, this may be a reference to a very particular type of false prophecy, the details of which now escape us. The true prophets of YHWH were empowered to speak by the Spirit of YHWH himself (Isa. 48:16; Mic. 3:8). God will remove the false prophets and the *spirit of impurity* or 'unclean spirit' (JPSV, NRSV) that result from the apostasy of idolatry and pollute the land. The details concerning the idol worship condemned by Zechariah are unclear. The return to the worship of foreign idols by the Hebrews, given the experience of the Babylonian exile, is questionable. Redditt (1995: 134) speculates that some type of (mechanical?) oracular device was being consulted that the prophet associated with idolatry (cf. 10:2). Alternately, the reference may be metaphorical, suggesting that the temple worship then in practice was 'little better than idolatry'.[155]

3. The removal of the prophets is so complete that all prophesying is equated with lying.[156] The speech-act of prophecy is

---

153. Redditt (1995: 134). Redditt (1995: 135) links the false prophecy
      contextually to the crime of parents striking their sons who prophesy,
      incited by the message of these false prophets. Boda (2004: 492–493)
      relates the false prophecy more generally to clever deception and
      legitimization by appeal to ancient traditions, given Zechariah's allusion
      to earlier scriptural types of 'cover-ups'.
154. Meyers and Meyers (1993: 370).
155. Mason (1977: 121).
156. Boda (2004: 491) and Webb (2003: 164–165) restrict this to false
      prophecy.

such an affront that even parents will charge and execute their own children as false prophets, in keeping with Deuteronomic law (Deut. 13:1–5; cf. 18:15–22). The irony of the condemnation of prophecy in a prophetic text is heightened by the message of earlier prophets that rebuked those who prevented God's prophets from prophesying (cf. Jer. 11:19–22; Amos 2:2).[157] The passage may anticipate the new covenant of Jeremiah (Jer. 31:31–34), when there will no longer be a need for people to instruct one another in the way of the Lord.

4–6. The phrase *On that day* (v. 4) is shorthand for the eschatological Day of the Lord, and marks verses 4–6 as a new literary unit. The stigma attached to prophesying as a deceptive practice will prevent individuals from donning the 'prophet's clothes' (v. 4, NLT). The reference to the 'hairy mantle' (NAB, NRSV; 'hairy cloak', NJB) recalls the distinct clothing, a camel- or goat-hair cloak, of the prophets Elijah and Elisha (e.g. 1 Kgs 19:13, 19; 2 Kgs 2:8, 13, 14; cf. Matt. 3:4). The denial (v. 5) by those accused of being a prophet may allude to Amos, who testified that he was not a member of the prophetic guild, but was a shepherd and tender of sycamore figs, called by God to serve in such a manner (cf. Amos 7:14–15). The reference to *wounds* on the body (v. 6; 'scars', NEB; 'gashes', NJB) may allude to the self-inflicted injuries sometimes characteristic of ecstatic prophecy in the biblical world (cf. 1 Kgs 18:28).[158] The retort that the bruises were received at the *house of …* *friends* (v. 6) seeks to give the impression that the wounds were the result of some kind of domestic violence, perhaps to shield the abuse of parents who are to stab or pierce their own child who prophesies (v. 3). Petersen (1995: 128) summarizes that, by the end of the lengthy montage (Zech. 12:1 – 13:6), the emphasis has shifted from the city of Jerusalem to the people within Jerusalem and the environs of Judah; but there is still conflict, and leadership issues remain (whether among the Davidic rulers or the prophets).

---

157. Ollenburger (1996: 831).

158. See Meyers and Meyers (1993: 382–383) who speculate this may have been the case for Hebrew prophets as well (cf. 1 Kgs 20:35).

Meaning

Israel's history was a story of covenant relationship with YHWH constantly compromised by the worship of idols and the flawed teaching of false prophets. The cleansing of Israel from *sin and impurity* (v. 1) may refer to the implementation of the promise of the new covenant (Jer. 31:33–34).[159] Since God himself would again be present with his people, there would no longer be any need for prophetic figures who mediated his word to the people. Zechariah, then, anticipates Joel's vision of a time when everyone is a prophet because of the outpouring of God's Spirit (Joel 2:28–29; cf. Acts 2:16–21). This universal knowledge of God will bring about the cessation of the prophetic gift (Jer. 31:34; cf. 1 Cor. 13:9–10).

Naturally, in Christian interpretation of the OT, Zechariah's oracle describing the fountain of cleansing anticipates the Christ-event, the cross of Jesus the Messiah and the cleansing from sin that results (cf. 1 John 1:7).[160]

iii. The scattering of the sheep (13:7–9)

Context

The third message of the second oracle (chs. 12 – 14) describes a future day when a divinely appointed leader of Israel will be killed (v. 7). This will result in the dispersion of the people of Israel, with a portion of the nation being given over to divine judgment and destruction (v. 8). Another portion of the nation will experience spiritual renewal, as a result of the God-ordained testing and suffering that refine the faith and purify the character of the godly remnant (v. 9ab). The traumatic process of divine judgment and refinement brings about covenant renewal, the restoration of a right relationship between God and his people (v. 9bc), thus fulfilling Zechariah's vision of God once again living among his people and his glory resting in Jerusalem (cf. Zech. 1:16; 2:5, 10–11; 8:3, 23).

This subunit of Zechariah's second oracle (vv. 7–9) is a poem that resumes the shepherd theme of 9:16; 10:2–3 and 11:4–17 in the

---

159. Cf. Mason (1977: 121).

160. See further the discussion in Boda (2004: 494–510).

first oracle (chs. 9 – 12). The poem is 'a self-contained little gem' and is regarded as the climax of chapters 12 – 13.[161] The close association between Zechariah 13:7–9 and 11:17 prompts the NEB to insert the passage there as the conclusion to the series of shepherd sayings.[162] There is no compelling reason to rearrange the text, however, given the logical relationship of Zechariah 13:1–6 and 13:7–9 in association with instruction regarding false prophecy in Deuteronomy 13:1–5.[163]

Comment

7. The literary device of apostrophe (a form of personification), *Awake, O sword*, opens the poem. The weapon, a symbol of death and destruction, is called forth to strike God's *shepherd*, a *man who is close* to God himself (v. 7b; 'my partner', NLT; 'my associate', NRSV).

The verb *strike*, 'when used with "sword," … means to inflict mortal wounds'.[164] Previously, the *worthless shepherd* was the one to be struck down by the sword (11:17). Now the faithful *shepherd* who partners with God in leading his people will be struck down, and as a result *the sheep will be scattered* (v. 7c).

The scattering is an act of divine judgment, and the impact is felt by leaders, people and tragically even the *little ones* ('the young', NJB; 'shepherd boys', NJPS, NEB).[165]

The identity of the shepherd or leader who is struck down is a matter of scholarly debate. Some link the figure to the worthless shepherd who abandons the flock (11:17).[166] Others connect the slain leader with Zechariah the prophet, whose ministry had been rejected by the post-exilic Jewish community.[167]

8. The magnitude of this unspecified act of divine judgment is

---

161. Baldwin (1972: 212); cf. Frost (1952: 135).

162. Cf. J. M. P. Smith (1912: 316–317); and Rudolph (1976: 213).

163. See Redditt (1995: 136); Baldwin (1972: 212); cf. D. R. Jones (1962: 251).

164. Meyers and Meyers (1993: 387).

165. Cf. Ollenburger (1996: 833). Zechariah draws his image of the 'little ones of the flock' from Jer. 49:20; 50:45.

166. E.g. R. L. Smith (1984: 283); Ollenburger (1996: 833).

167. E.g. Mason (1977: 112).

catastrophic, but God will preserve a remnant of his people and he will forgive their sin (Jer. 50:20; cf. Isa. 65:9).[168] The fractional portions may be an allusion to Ezekiel's sign of the coming judgment of God in the dividing of his shaven hair into three equal parts (Ezek. 5:2, 12). Zechariah envisions an eschatological repetition of the Babylonian exile for Israel.[169] In John's apocalyptic vision, one-third of the people on the earth are killed in a series of three plagues that are part of God's judgment of sinful humanity at the end of the age (Rev. 9:15, 18).

9. The word *fire* is often used as a metaphor for divine judgment by the OT prophets (e.g. Isa. 66:15; Jer. 4:4; Ezek. 36:5; Amos 5:6). This divine judgment may take the form of a natural disaster, such as an earthquake, a pestilence or the outbreak of plague, or even the horrors of war. The purpose of God's fire may be the destruction of the wicked or the testing and purification of the righteous, as it is here.

Zechariah borrows the image of God purifying his people like *gold* and *silver* in the smelter's furnace from Isaiah (1:25), Jeremiah (6:29), and Ezekiel (22:22). Malachi, a later contemporary of Zechariah, equates the day of God's visitation with *a refiner's fire* (Mal. 3:2). God himself is portrayed as the divine metallurgist, crouching over the fire as he refines and purifies the Levites *like gold and silver* (Mal. 3:3).[170]

The expression *they will call on my name* is an idiom for prayer: in this case, a prayer of confession of sin and a plea for help in the form of divine intervention and deliverance.[171] *'They are my people'* ... *'The LORD is our God.'* The two expressions are sometimes understood as elements of the 'adoption formula' of covenant relationship, depicting the intimate bond between God and his people Israel (cf. Exod. 19:5; Jer. 30:22; 31:33). Zechariah's language is reminiscent of Hosea's prediction that one day God will plant Israel in the land:

168. Barker (2008: 821) connects the event to the First Jewish War (AD 66–73); cf. McComiskey (1998: 1223).

169. Cf. Merrill (1994: 338).

170. Cf. *ZIBBCOT* 5: 238–239.

171. Cf. *NIDOTTE* 3: 972.

he will say, *'You are my people'*, and the people will respond, *'You are our God'* (Hos. 2:23). The declarations of loyalty by God and Israel restore the covenant relationship symbolically portrayed in the breaking of two staffs in the earlier shepherd allegory (11:10, 14).

Meaning
The traumatic process of God's 'corrective affliction' of Israel in the striking of the shepherd and the scattering of his sheep (v. 7) will restore the covenant relationship with YHWH.[172] God will again identify Israel as *my people*, and the people will acknowledge that *the LORD is our God* (v. 9). Quite apart from the historical setting of the oracle, Jesus interpreted it eschatologically, identifying himself as the shepherd struck down by God (Matt. 26:31; Mark 14:27).[173]

iv. The Lord will rule the earth (14:1–21)
The final message of the second oracle (chs. 12 – 14) blends visions of both judgment and salvation for Israel and the nations.[174] Israel is to be besieged by the nations, and teeters on the verge of utter destruction when the Lord himself intervenes and delivers his people (vv. 3–4). As a result, the nations are punished by a ghastly plague, an awesome display of divine judgment (v. 12). The nation of Israel will be restored as the people of God, and Jerusalem will be exalted as the political and religious centre of the world (vv. 16–17). God's rule will be established over all the earth (v. 9), and a divinely ordained transformation of the created order will take place (vv. 6–8, 10). Fittingly, God's holiness will be the pervasive characteristic of his rule over all the earth (vv. 20–21).

There is general agreement on the apocalyptic nature of chapter 14, with its emphasis on God's judgment of the nations and the deliverance of Israel in the coming Day of the Lord.[175]

---

172. Cf. Scott (1971: 145–146).
173. Cf. R. L. Smith (1984: 283–284); and Boda (2004: 514–518).
174. See Mason (2003: 172–200); and O'Brien (2004: 280–281) for a list of examples of OT allusions in Zech. 14.
175. Hanson (1979: 391) suggests that Zech. 14 is 'cast in the form of the new hybrid salvation-judgment oracle, which levels salvation and

Understanding the literary structure of chapter 14 has proved to be problematic for interpreters. Numerous methodologies and strategies have been employed in attempts to explain the diverse elements of Zechariah's final message.[176] Boda (2004: 522) cogently summarizes several of the more prominent approaches to the structure of the chapter, including: Hanson's (1979: 372) tightly scripted outline comparing the passage to ancient conflict myth after the motif found in apocalyptic literature; and Petersen's (1995: 137–139) more loosely configured montage consisting of ten vignettes of a more literary style than the more oral character of the sayings of the montage in Zechariah 12:1 – 13:6.

Zechariah's final chapter (ch. 14) demonstrates an overall structure,[177] and the phrase *on that day* is an organizing principle within the passage.[178] The approach here adapts that of Petersen, Webb and Boda, among others, dividing the chapter into logical units on the basis of the eschatological formula (*on that day*), syntactical breaks and thematic unity.[179]

This last instalment of Zechariah's apocalyptic vision for Israel has parallels to his first message introducing his second oracle to post-exilic Judah (cf. Zech. 12:1–9). As Petersen (1995: 137–138) notes, chapter 14 is similar to Zechariah 12:1 – 13:6 in the repetition of the phrases *on that day* or *the day of the LORD*. Further, the two prophetic sermons share the themes of the nations waging war against Israel, with God defending his people and punishing

---

judgment words simultaneously against two different segments within a divided nation'.

176. Despite the diverse material comprising Zech. 14, Petersen (1995: 16) does identify a general plotline, moving from disruption to resolution, then to radical holiness. Ryken (1984: 170) reminds that one should be prepared for abrupt shifts in topics in a 'disjointed series of diverse, self-contained units' when reading OT visionary literature.

177. Boda (2004: 522).

178. Petersen (1995: 137–139); cf. Webb (2003: 177).

179. Petersen (1995: 139) identifies ten sayings; Webb (2003: 177) divides ch. 14 into seven sayings; this approach marks six sayings (vv. 1–3, 4–5, 6–11, 12–15, 16–19, 20–21).

the nations for their insurrection. The two passages exhibit notable differences as well, with God himself gathering the nations against Jerusalem (Zech. 14:2), and great cosmic upheaval accompanying the events of that eschatological day (Zech. 14:3–6, 10–11).

The overall message of Zechariah's two oracles (chs. 9 – 14) transmits three basic hopes of the Hebrew community in post-exilic Jerusalem: the reunification of the Davidic kingdom, the re-establishment of the Davidic monarchy, and the restoration of Jerusalem as the Davidic royal city.[180] The NT understands these hopes as fulfilled (at least partially) in the first advent and (eventually completely) in the second advent of Jesus the Messiah, who, as the Son of David (Matt. 21:9, 15), came preaching the kingdom of heaven (Matt. 4:23), refused earthly kingship to establish a greater kingdom (one *not of this world* [John 18:36]), and promised to return to Jerusalem to *sit upon his glorious throne* (Matt. 19:28; cf. Matt. 24:30; 25:31; Acts 1:11).

a. The Lord defends Jerusalem (vv. 1–3)

Context
The content of the entire chapter 'nests under' this heading, *A day of the LORD is coming*, casting an ominous shadow on the closing oracles of Zechariah's message and emphasizing the role of the Lord as the primary actor in the events to come.[181]

Comment
   1. This impending *day of the LORD* is one of both judgment and deliverance for Israel. The nations are affected by this eschatological day as well; Jerusalem will be that predicted cup of reeling for the nations (12:2). It is also a day of 'cosmic change' and 'end-time reversal'.[182] Amos cursed those Hebrews who longed for the day of YHWH, because they assumed it was a day of deliverance and

---

180. Redditt (1995: 144).

181. See Webb (2003: 177).

182. See Redditt (1995: 141).

blessing only (cf. Amos 5:18). The prophets Joel (1:15; 2:1) and Malachi (3:2; 4:1) envision a similar future day for Jerusalem.[183] The audience of the prophet's speech is Jerusalem. The cryptic statement, *Your plunder will be divided among you*, foreshadows the following verse: the city will be ransacked by the nations ('and the plunder taken from you shall be shared out while you stand by', NEB).

2. Zechariah's earlier vision of the nations assembled for war against Jerusalem omits the grim detail that YHWH's judgment against the nations comes at a heavy price for the city and its people (cf. 12:2–5). *The city will be captured, the houses ransacked, and the women raped* in the savage attack by the foreign armies. *Exile* or 'captivity' (NLT) is the fate for half of the city, while 'the rest will be left among the ruins of the city' (NLT; cf. 13:8–9).[184]

3. As in the earlier vision, the LORD himself *will go out and fight* ('make war', NJPS) against the nations (cf. 12:9). The reference to God fighting in the day of battle casts him in the role of Divine Warrior (e.g. Exod. 15:3; Deut. 1:30; Isa. 42:13), and recalls those past occasions when he has intervened on behalf of Israel ('as he has fought in times past', NLT; e.g. Exod. 14:14; 15:6; Deut. 2:24; 3:3).[185] Some look to find (even partial) fulfilment of Zechariah's eschatological day in the warfare against the Jews and Jerusalem by the Greeks or Romans. Others see the warfare language as a metaphor for the interplay of divine blessing and judgment of Judah and Jerusalem throughout history. Given the ambiguity of the phrase *in the day of battle* (lit. 'on a day of battle'), McComiskey (1998: 1227) cautions against 'searching for a specific

---

183. See Mason (2003: 174–175) on the parallels between Joel 3 [MT 4] and Zech. 14.

184. Redditt (1995: 139) cautions against pressing the numbers as a literal measure of the percentage of the decimation of Jerusalem's population as a result of this eschatological event (cf. Baldwin [1972: 216] who estimates that only one-sixth of the population of Jerusalem would remain).

185. On the role of YHWH as warrior see Miller (1973: 60–144, esp. 140–144); Lind (1980: 23–34); and Longman and Reid (1995: 69–71).

battle of Yahweh against his enemies'.[186]

Meaning
Israel has a champion: YHWH the warrior wages battle against the nations (v. 3).

b. The Lord comes to the Mount of Olives (vv. 4–5)

Context
Zechariah specifically identifies the Mount of Olives as the site of YHWH's theophany, accompanied by his angel armies. The theophany is the realization of the frequently cited epithet for YHWH in the post-exilic prophets: The LORD of Hosts or LORD of the Angel Armies.

Comment
4. The theophany of YHWH on the *Mount of Olives* brings about such geological upheaval that the topography of Jerusalem is reconfigured, creating two mountains separated by *a great valley*. The designation, *Mount of Olives*, is a hill east of Jerusalem. The name occurs in the OT only in Zechariah 14:4 and 2 Samuel 15:30. David crossed the mount in his flight from Absalom (2 Sam. 15:30, 32), and Solomon built a shrine to the Moabite god Chemosh there (1 Kgs 11:7). Zechariah's prophecy recalls Ezekiel's vision of YHWH's abandonment and return to Jerusalem by the same eastern route (cf. Ezek. 11:23; 43:1). This prompts Mason (1977: 125) to suggest that perhaps the place name was associated 'with the idea that Jerusalem's rightful ruler would come back to the city that way'. In the NT, Jesus taught his disciples about the signs of the end times from the slopes of the Mount of Olives (his so-called 'Olivet Discourse', Matt. 24). Forty days after his resurrection, Jesus ascended into heaven from the Mount of Olives, and the message of the attending angels to the disciples implied that he would return there in a similar fashion (Acts 1:11–12).

---

186. Cf. Barker (2008: 825) who states, 'The final, complete fulfilment, then, must lie in the future.'

5. Zechariah describes an *earthquake* that will crack open the mountain (*the Mount of Olives will be split in two*, v. 4) and create a valley running east and west through the fissure. In light of this event, the meaning of verse 5 is difficult to discern. Either this valley will become an escape route for the Hebrews fleeing Jerusalem in the face of the assault against the city by the nations (so NIV, NLT, NRSV; following the MT), or the valley will be filled and blocked like it was during the earthquake at the time of King Uzziah (so NAB, NEB, NJB; following the LXX; Targ.).[187] A different vowel pointing of the same Hebrew root word renders the two separate meanings, and 'either is equally possible'.[188] Baldwin's (1972: 218) mediation of the difficulty is helpful, noting: 'It is impossible to be sure how the text read originally, but the general meaning is clear. The earth movements which open a valley eastwards will also block up the Kidron valley, so providing a level escape route from Jerusalem.' Earthquakes are also part of the eschatological imagery associated with the Day of the Lord in Amos (cf. Amos 6:11; 8:8; 9:1–5).

The meaning of the term *Azel* ('Jasol', NJB; 'Asal', NEB; 'Azal', NRSV) is uncertain. Meyers and Meyers identify Azel as a district of Jerusalem on the north-east side of the city, inhabited by Benjaminites who were descendants of Azel.[189] The place name Beth-Azel establishes the validity of Azel as a toponym (cf. Mic. 1:11). Following the LXX, other EVV translate the word as a locative phrase, 'alongside' or 'the side of (it)' (cf. NAB, 'reaches its edge'). King Uzziah ruled Judah from 792 to 740 BC. The date of the earthquake mentioned is unknown, although Amos tied the beginning of his prophetic ministry two years before the devastating event (Amos 1:1) to it. According to Baly (1974: 24–25), major earthquakes occur in Israel about every fifty years, and lesser tremors more frequently.

---

187. See the discussion in Mason (1977: 125–126).
188. Mason (1977: 126). The repeated word in the Heb. text (*nstm*) may be alternately understood as a second-person active verb from the root *nws* ('you will flee', so the MT); or a third-person passive verb from the root *stm* ('it will be blocked up', so LXX and Targ.).
189. Meyers and Meyers (1993: 426).

The identity of *the holy ones* is uncertain, but the phrase is probably a reference to the angelic host that worships God and serves as his army (cf. Job 5:1; Ps. 89:5, 7).

Meaning

At a particular time in Israel's history, at a specific geographical location, the dreams, visions and oracles of God's prophets are fulfilled – the Lord will come! (v. 5).

c. The Lord's unique day (vv. 6–8)

Context

The cosmic cataclysms and seismic upheavals of the Day of the Lord impact on the natural order, another aspect of the reversal that characterizes that eschatological day.

Comment

6–7. The seismic upheaval of the earth in the coming Day of YHWH has its counterpart in the heavens, as *there will be no light, no cold or frost* (v. 6). Such cosmic cataclysms are another motif characteristic of apocalyptic literature in the Bible. The final two words of the verse are obscure and may mean "'the splendid ones (stars) congeal'', that is, lose their brightness'.[190] Many English versions follow the variant rendering of the ancient versions (i.e. LXX, Syr., Targ. and Vulg.) and read *cold or frost* (SO NEB, NIV, NRSV), indicating a transition to a temperate climate. There shall be 'one continuous day' (NAB). Isaiah has a similar vision of Jerusalem's future glory: the sun and moon will no longer be necessary for light because the presence of God will be the everlasting light of the new order (Isa. 60:19–22). It may be that the light of the sun and moon is simply washed out by the brilliant light of the glory of God. The NT portrays the new Jerusalem in a similar fashion, with continual daylight and no need for the sun or moon, because the glory of the Lamb illuminates the city (Rev. 21:22–25).

8. The phrase *living water* 'designates fresh water flowing from

---

190. Baldwin (1972: 218).

natural springs rather than ... stale water ... that has been collected
in cisterns' (cf. NJPS, 'fresh water').[191] Zechariah's oracle describing
'life-giving waters' (NLT) flowing out of Jerusalem recalls Ezekiel's
vision of a stream (that becomes an impassable river), flowing from
the temple of Jerusalem eastward to the Dead Sea (Ezek. 47:1, 6).
The prophet Joel had a similar vision of a fountain that bursts forth
from the Lord's temple to water the arid environs of Jerusalem (Joel
3:18). The waters of this stream bring life and healing, and
everything it touches becomes fresh and pure (even the Dead Sea,
cf. Ezek. 47:8–9). The waters are symbolic of the life-giving
presence of God living once again among his people. Zechariah's
vision expands Ezekiel's image of life-giving water in that this river
flows both east and west, suggesting that divine blessings would
extend worldwide.[192] Zechariah's vision of the river of life-giving
waters flowing from Jerusalem foreshadows *the river of the water of
life* that flows from the throne of God and the Lamb in the new
Jerusalem (Rev. 22:1). No doubt this is the OT passage Jesus alludes
to when he declares himself to be the *living water* (John 7:38).

Unlike the wadis of Palestine that flow with water only
sporadically as a result of the seasonal rains, the continual flow (*in
summer and in winter*) of the life-giving waters from Jerusalem are not
dependent upon the seasonal rainfall.[193] Historically, a weak point in
Jerusalem's defence was the city's dependence upon an external
water supply for part of the year.[194]

A river 'flowing continuously' (NLT) will provide the new
Jerusalem with an abundant and permanent water resource. The
climate, diurnal light, water supply and terrain are all part of the
eschatological transformation that will bring 'wonderful harvests'
(NLT) to the land of Israel (cf. Isa. 30:23–26).[195]

---

191. Meyers and Meyers (1993: 434).
192. See Redditt (1995: 141).
193. Cf. Baldwin (1972: 219).
194. Redditt (1995: 141).
195. Meyers and Meyers (1993: 442).

Meaning

The transformation of the created order in the Day of the Lord has links to the creation account of Genesis 1, and connects Zechariah's visions with the restoration envisaged in his sermons (cf. 8:3–5, 8, 12–13, 20–23).[196] Like Isaiah, Zechariah looked for God to *create new heavens and a new earth*, and a new *Jerusalem* (cf. Isa. 65:17–18).

d. The ghastly plague against people and animals (vv. 9–15)

Context

The Lord acts on his previous claim that he is *very jealous for Jerusalem and Zion* (1:14).

Comment

9. God's intervention as Divine Warrior for Israel culminates in his universal rule (*The LORD will be king over the whole earth*; cf. 2:10–13). Zechariah envisions the fulfilment of the enthronement Psalms that affirm: YHWH is king (Pss 93:1; 97:1); he subdues the nations (Ps. 47:3); Jerusalem will be elevated above the whole earth (Ps. 48:1–2); the idols and the kings of the nations will bow before YHWH in worship (Pss 97:7; 99:3); the mountains will be levelled (Ps. 97:5); and his righteousness and holiness will permeate the world (Pss 93:5; 98:9). All of these elements are present in Zechariah's message about the Lord who will rule the earth.[197] The declaration that *there will be one LORD* in that day is both a reaffirmation of the Hebrew credo that YHWH is one (Deut. 6:4), and a once-for-all renunciation of idolatry.

10–11. *Geba* was a village belonging to the tribe of Benjamin, some six miles north-north-east of Jerusalem (Josh. 18:24). It was resettled by the Hebrews after the Babylonian exile (Ezra 2:26). The location of *Rimmon* is uncertain. The accompanying expression *south of Jerusalem* provides the general direction of the site (and suggests the place may not have been well known in Zechariah's day). Taken together, the two place names describe the north-south extent of

---

196. Cf. Boda (2004: 525–526).

197. See further the discussion in Mason (1977: 128).

Jerusalem's outlying regions, an area that will become a 'plain' (NAB, NLT, NRSV; *like the Arabah*, NIV).

The eschatological *Jerusalem* will sit atop a vast plain as YHWH's 'cosmic mountain', and the city and the temple will be the central focus and conduit of 'Yahweh's involvement with humanity'.[198] The references to the city gates and other features that follow appear to reflect a pre-exilic configuration of Jerusalem, and Zechariah probably alludes to Jeremiah's prediction of a rebuilt Jerusalem (cf. Jer. 31:38–39). The exact location of the *Benjamin Gate* is unknown. It has been identified with the Sheep Gate (cf. Neh. 3:1, 32) and the Upper Gate.[199] Its general location on the east wall just north of the Temple Mount seems certain.[200] The *First Gate* ('Old Gate', NJPS, NLT), which has been situated by some scholars on the western wall of Jerusalem, has been identified with the Old City Gate (Neh. 3:6), also called the Mishneh Gate. Meyers and Meyers prefer to situate the gate on the eastern wall of the city.[201] The *Corner Gate* was located on the western wall of Jerusalem (cf. 2 Kgs 14:13; Jer. 31:38), probably in the vicinity of the Jaffa Gate in today's Old City of Jerusalem.[202] The *Tower of Hananel* is mentioned several times in the OT, but its location on the city wall of Jerusalem is unknown (cf. Neh. 3:1; Jer. 31:38). Meyers and Meyers place the tower near the Benjamin Gate.[203]

The *royal winepresses* are not mentioned elsewhere in the OT and their location is unknown. It is assumed they were located just south of the City of David, near the King's Pool (Neh. 2:14) and the King's Garden (Neh. 3:15).[204]

Zechariah's final oracle returns full cycle to his earlier vision of a densely populated and secure city of Jerusalem (*Jerusalem will be secure*, v. 11; cf. 2:4; Joel 3:20). The prophets Amos (Amos 9:15), Isaiah (Isa.

---

198. Meyers and Meyers (1993: 441, 444).
199. Cf. Bahat (1990: 30).
200. Meyers and Meyers (1993: 445).
201. Meyers and Meyers (1993: 446).
202. Cf. Bahat (1990: 30).
203. Cf. Meyers and Meyers (1993: 446–447).
204. Meyers and Meyers (1993: 447).

60:17–18), Jeremiah (Jer. 31:40) and Ezekiel (Ezek. 34:25–28) all forecast a day when Jerusalem will enjoy perpetual peace and security.

12. The same word *plague* is used to describe the divine judgments against the Egyptians at the Hebrew exodus (cf. Exod. 9:14). The term denotes torment or calamity generally, whether in the form of pestilence, disease, war or natural calamity (cf. Jer. 14:11–12). As divine judge, God strikes against those who rebel against him with sudden and deadly plagues – whether the nations or his own people Israel (cf. Num. 14:37; 2 Sam. 24:21). Previously, the prophet spoke of the Lord striking the horses of the besieging nations with *panic* and *blindness*, and their riders with *madness* (cf. 12:4). Here the plague also afflicts the armies and the animals (v. 15) of the nations attacking Jerusalem, but it takes on a different form. *Their flesh … eyes … and tongues will rot.* The plague that Zechariah portends is a lethal disease of an unspecified nature. The term for *rot* signifies decay, putrefaction or wasting away. Here the word describes an unnatural and accelerated festering of wounds, or perhaps a rampant cancerous growth of some sort ('their people will become like walking corpses', NLT). The prophet's horrific language portrays 'an agonizing death'.[205] Those interpreters given to a more literal (and sensational) approach to biblical prophecy equate the plague of rotting flesh with the effects of massive amounts of radiation on human flesh in the aftermath of nuclear war.

13. The word *panic* ('tumult', NAB; 'terror', NJB) signifies confusion, generally speaking. In this context it refers to a deadly panic ('frenzy', CEV) induced by YHWH himself among the enemies of Israel. The prophet Isaiah uses the same word in describing the Day of the Lord as a day of tumult and terror (Isa. 22:5; see further the commentary on 12:4, pp. 241–242). As in Zechariah 12:4, the agent of the panic and plague directed against the enemies of Israel is the Lord himself.

14. *Judah* will be an ally of Jerusalem against the attacking nations (cf. 12:6). The Day of the Lord is characterized by reversal, as God

---

205. Meyers and Meyers (1993: 452–453).

will turn the tables on the nations and do to them as they have done to Israel. The capture of the *wealth* of the nations overturns the looting of Jerusalem by the nations announced by the prophet earlier (14:1). Zechariah's reference to *great quantities of gold and silver* recalls Haggai's prediction that one day the treasures of all the nations will come to YHWH's temple (Hag. 2:7–8).

15. The divine plague unleashed against the nations will also strike *all the animals* in the military camps of the nations.

Meaning
God's intervention as Israel's Divine Warrior culminates in his universal rule (v. 9), and the restoration and permanent security of Jerusalem (v. 11). The declaration that there *will be one LORD, and his name the only name* (v. 9) 'stresses exclusive worship of Yahweh'.[206]

e. Celebration of the Feast of Tabernacles (vv. 16–19)

Context
The prophet returns to the subject of the nations addressed earlier in verses 2, 12. Ironically, and in further demonstration of the reversal characteristic of the Day of the Lord, the nations that formerly assembled and waged war against Jerusalem are now required to assemble and worship in Jerusalem with Israel annually in the pilgrimage Feast of Tabernacles (v. 16; cf. Isa. 56:3–8). Zechariah anticipates the realization of the covenant promise that Israel would be a blessing to the nations and a light to the Gentiles (Gen. 12:1–3: cf. Ps. 24:10; Isa. 49:6; 60:3).

Comment
16. Mosaic law stipulated three annual pilgrimage festivals for Israel: the Feast of Unleavened Bread (including Passover), the Feast of Harvest (Pentecost, the spring harvest) and the Feast of Ingathering (Tabernacles, the autumn harvest; Exod. 23:14–19; cf. Deut. 16:1–17).

The compound title for the God of Israel, *the King, the LORD*

---

206. Boda (2004: 526).

Almighty, accents his universal rule as Sovereign of all the peoples of the earth, and his incomparable power as Creator and Covenant Redeemer of his people Israel. The repetition of the compound title *the King, the LORD Almighty* (vv. 16, 17) and the epithet *LORD Almighty* (v. 21) in the last two sections of Zechariah's final oracle rightly showcase God as the one to whom all glory and homage is due.

The *Feast of Tabernacles* was an annual festival marking the beginning of the autumn harvest season and was one of the three Israelite pilgrimage festivals (cf. Exod. 23:14–19). Also known as the 'Feast of Shelters' (NJB, NLT), or 'Feast of Booths' (NJPS, NAB), the seven-day celebration commemorated the Hebrew wilderness experience after the exodus from Egypt. The festival falls in the biblical month of Tishri (September–October of the Julian calendar). Mosaic legislation calls for the Israelites to construct some type of temporary shelter (a booth, tent or lean-to), and presumably live in it for all or some portion of the week-long feast (cf. Lev. 23:33–43; Num. 29:12–40; Deut. 16:13–17). The feast recalled the temporary homes of Israel's wilderness wanderings, and afforded the worshipping community the opportunity to offer thanksgiving for God's provision – both then and now. The festival was also a time for instruction in social concern for the disadvantaged and reliance on God as a sojourner or pilgrim in this world. This pilgrimage festival was an appropriate one to retain in the restored order of the kingdom of God, because thanksgiving will characterize the worship of the messianic era (cf. Isa. 51:3; Jer. 33:11). The one pilgrimage feast uniting all the nations with Israel in the worship of YHWH is the Feast of Tabernacles, perhaps the oldest pilgrimage festival (cf. Judg. 21:19; 1 Sam. 1:3).[207] This festival is singled out because 'it was the great religious occasion of the year': a celebration of great joy and thanksgiving, emphasizing agricultural fertility and the gift of rainfall; remembering the exodus and deliverance from slavery in Egypt; open to the nations (giving the event an eschatological flavour); and with enthronement implications of honouring the

---

207. So Baldwin (1972: 222).

kingship of God – all themes important to Zechariah's final oracle.[208]

17–19. *Jerusalem*, and the temple of YHWH as the cosmic centre of God's universal kingdom, is a repeated motif in the eschatological visions of the OT prophets (cf. Isa. 56:6–7; 66:23; Hag. 2:7; cf. Isa. 2:2–4 = Mic. 4:1–3 where the nations come to Jerusalem to receive instruction). Zechariah's vision (v. 17) echoes his earlier predictions that the nations will travel to Jerusalem to seek the Lord (8:20–22), and anticipates the new Jerusalem of John's Apocalypse (Rev. 21:10–27).

The word *worship* (vv. 16, 17) means to bow down or even kneel in prostration ('bow low', NJPS). The act of bowing down reflects the language of the royal court and the heavenly court: 'an ancient and traditional sign of obeisance or paying homage. It acknowledges the superiority of the one to whom a person genuflects.'[209] Nations that refuse to join in the pilgrimage festival worship will be subject to a *plague* (v. 18): *they will have no rain* (v. 17; on *plague* see further commentary on v. 12, p. 267). The lack of rainfall was one of the curses God pronounced against Israel for covenant disobedience (cf. Deut. 28:22–24). Here that curse is extended to the nations by virtue of God's rule over all peoples. Egypt is singled out for mention, perhaps because it was the origin of the Hebrew exodus (of which the Feast of Tabernacles was to be a reminder, Lev. 23:43),[210] and in the past it was a nation that 'had suffered the most from the plagues at God's hands. If it did not participate in the future, it would suffer again.'[211]

Meaning

God's warfare against the nations will yield his annual worship by the nations, yet not without penalty if they refuse to celebrate the Hebrew pilgrimage festival of Tabernacles. The story of God entering, reclaiming and re-inhabiting his creation moves closer to

---

208. See Mason (1977: 132); and Webb (2003: 181).
209. Meyers and Meyers (1993: 466).
210. Cf. Ollenburger (1996: 839).
211. Redditt (1995: 143).

its grand finale – universal doxology when *everything that has breath will praise the LORD* (Ps. 150:6).

f. Holiness in Jerusalem (vv. 20–21)

Context

The last unit of the final oracle begins and ends with the eschatological phrase *on that day*; thus the expression bookends the entire second oracle (cf. 12:3). Webb (2003: 182) summarizes: 'The keynote of the seventh and last unit (20–21) is holiness, which is another name for God's supremacy and perfection.' Holiness is the signature characteristic of Zechariah's eschatological day, and it 'will pervade all aspects of life' and 'will be the ruling element in eternity'.[212]

Comment

20. *HOLY TO THE LORD.* This was the logo inscribed on the gold medallion attached as a front-piece to the turban of the high priest of Israel (Exod. 28:36). According to Zechariah, that destiny will be fulfilled in the messianic kingdom. The holiness characteristic of this eschatological day is anticipated in the cleansing of Joshua the high priest and his clothing in *rich garments* ('festal apparel', NRSV). Even as the Levitical priesthood was set apart as *holy to the LORD*, so the nation of Israel was set apart at Mount Sinai to serve Yahweh as a kingdom of priests and a holy nation (Exod. 19:6). According to Zechariah, that destiny will be fulfilled in the messianic kingdom. The anthem, *Holy, Holy, Holy is the Lord God Almighty*, forms the foundation of the angelic worship in heaven (Rev. 4:8; cf. Isa. 6:3). It also explains the mandate to Israel to be holy, even as God is holy (Lev. 11:44).[213]

The reference to the 'harness bells' (NLT), a term unique to Zechariah in the OT, illustrates that 'in this new Jerusalem that which was unclean will be made clean'.[214]

---

212. McComskey (1998: 1244).
213. See further the discussion in Meyers and Meyers (1993: 487).
214. Cf. Boda (2004: 528), who cites Merrill (1994: 365) on the horse as a ritually unclean animal according to Mosaic law (Lev. 11:1–8).

21. The bronze *pots* of the temple were used to carry away ashes from the burnt offerings, as well as the remnants of the sacrificial animal, and in some cases they served as cooking utensils for the meals prepared for the priestly families from those portions of the sacrifices designated as edible (cf. Exod. 27:3; 38:3; Lev. 7:6, 15). The holiness of YHWH's kingdom will transform even the mundane cooking utensils into *sacred bowls* (v. 20), like those used in the sacrificial ritual of the temple: that is, 'the distinction between the sacred and profane would be eliminated'.[215]

Many of the EVV interpret the MT 'Canaanite' as 'merchant' or 'trader', on the basis of the commercial activity associated with the Canaanite in Zephaniah 1:11 and Hosea 12:7 (e.g. ESV, NAB, NJB, NLT, NRSV). Boda (2004: 529) states that 'there will be no room for such merchants, who may have abused worshipers through exorbitant prices' for the proper utensils and offerings required for sacrifice.[216] The expression may be a euphemism for the idolater, or simply another way of saying that under the rule of God the traditional boundaries (e.g. ethnicity) will be dissolved.[217]

Meaning

The 'closing verses of the book show us the whole of Jerusalem and Judah as one vast sanctuary, in which everything is holy, from the explicitly religious vessels of the temple to the most common cooking pots ... Everything is sanctified by God's presence, and partakes of his perfection.'[218] The pervasive holiness of the

---

215. Redditt (1995: 144); what Petersen (1995: 160) describes as a 'radical sacrality'.

216. Cf. Ollenburger (1996: 839). The Jerusalem temple was a kind of central bank during the Persian period. Zechariah envisions a day when such commercial activity in the temple will end (and calls to mind Jesus' cleansing of the temple in the NT, Matt. 21:12–17).

217. Meyers and Meyers (1993: 489–491); cf. Mason (1977: 133) who understands the term 'Canaanite' as a symbol of apostasy and religious syncretism; and Webb (2003: 182) who regards the expression as a metaphor for the idolater.

218. Webb (2003: 182).

eschatological day eliminates the Levitical concerns for ritual purity
and the idea of '"graded holiness" that informed priestly understanding'.[219] The final verses of Zechariah offer commentary on
the OT prophetic theme of God one day being resident with his
people in Jerusalem, agreeing with Joel that *The LORD dwells in Zion!*
(Joel 3:21), and affirming Ezekiel's concluding coda, an epithet for
Jerusalem: *THE LORD IS THERE* (Ezek. 48:35). And Zechariah joins
the chorus of OT prophets who anticipated the revelation of the
new Jerusalem, when *God himself will be with them* (Rev. 21:3), as *the
throne of God and of the Lamb will be in the city* (Rev. 22:3).

---

219. Ollenburger (1996: 839); cf. McComiskey (1998: 1244) who notes that
    'nothing will belong to the sphere of the common or profane'.

MALACHI

INTRODUCTION

Malachi's sermons were directed to a tough audience. His congregation included the righteous, the disillusioned, the cynical, the callous, the dishonest, the apathetic, the doubting, the sceptical and the outright wicked. What does a preacher say to this type of crowd? As a sensitive pastor, Malachi offered the 'valentine' of God's love to a disheartened people.[1] As a lofty theologian, he instructed the people in a basic doctrinal catechism, emphasizing the nature of God as universal King, faithful Suzerain and righteous Judge. As YHWH's stern prophet, Malachi rebuked corrupt priests and warned of the coming day of God's judgment. As a spiritual mentor, he called his audience to a more sincere life of worship, and challenged the people to embrace the ethical standards of the Mosaic covenant. But above all, Malachi was YHWH's messenger, and his vital word to Israel was profoundly simple: *'I have always loved you,' says the* LORD (1:2).

1. See Klein (1986: 143–152).

1. Title and text

Malachi is the last book in the collection known as the Minor Prophets (or the Book of the Twelve in the HB). The book takes its title from the name of the prophet Malachi, identified in the superscription (1:1) as the bearer of God's message to post-exilic Judah. Alternately, some scholars consider Malachi to be a title or appellative for an anonymous person responsible for compiling the book. That approach assumes that the reference to *my messenger* (Heb. *mal'ākî*), who prepares the way for the coming of the Lord to his temple (3:1), was borrowed as the title for the book. This commentary assumes that the book takes its title from the prophet named Malachi.[2]

The Hebrew text (MT) of Malachi is in a very good state of preservation. Portions of the book are attested by fragments of the Dead Sea Scrolls or Qumran (Q) manuscripts, including Malachi 1:13–14 and parts of 2:10 – 4:6. Preliminary study of these fragments reveals that portions of these manuscripts (4QXIIa) agree with the Septuagint (or LXX) against the MT.[3] Two verses in the MT of Malachi are especially difficult to interpret (2:15, 16), due both to textual corruption and grammatical anomaly. It may be that the text at this point has 'suffered perhaps at the hands of scribes who took exception to its teaching'.[4]

Overall, the Greek OT (LXX) represents a faithful translation of the MT. The tendency for interpretive expansion and loose paraphrasing characteristic of the LXX in the prophetic books continues in Malachi as well (for examples of the former see 1:7; 2:2, 4; 3:2; and for examples of the latter see 1:3, 9; 2:10, 11). Hellenistic influence and certain theological motivations prompting midrashic exegetical practice are also discernible in the text of the LXX (e.g.

---

2. LXX has changed the first-person form (Malachi = *my messenger*) to a third-person form ('his messenger', NETS). The lack of supporting manuscript evidence for the alteration leads Baldwin to conclude that the change 'only serves to reinforce the originality of the MT' (Baldwin 1972: 226).

3. See further Fuller (1991: 47–57); and Ulrich (1997: 220–318).

4. Baldwin (1972: 261).

1:1; 1:12; 2:13). Some versions of the LXX reorder the last three verses of Malachi so that the book does not end with the threat of divine judgment (i.e. reading 4:6 after 4:4).

The versification of the MT differs from the versification of EVV at the close of the book of Malachi. The HB orders the last six verses of the book (Mal. 4:1–6) as a continuation of chapter 3 (MT = 3:19–24). The versification of the EVV is used throughout this commentary on Malachi.

2. The prophet Malachi

The Hebrew name Malachi means 'my messenger' or 'my angel', although context precludes the latter meaning. Based on the translation of Malachi 1:1 in the LXX ('by the hand of his messenger', NETS), some scholars have taken the name Malachi to be a title for an anonymous prophet, perhaps a play on words with 3:1, *my messenger* (Heb. *mal'āki*). (See further comments under 4. Author, p. 279.)

The Bible records no biographical information for Malachi, nor is he referenced elsewhere in the biblical documents (although Malachi is listed among the Twelve Prophets in 2 Esdras 1:40). According to Jewish tradition, the prophets Haggai, Zechariah and Malachi were among the founders of The Great Synagogue.[5] This body of Jewish leaders is alleged to have played a major role in post-exilic times in preserving Scripture and handing on the traditional precepts and lore. It is further believed by the rabbis that, after these three prophets died, the Holy Spirit departed from Israel.

Evidence from the Targums indicates that some of the Aramaic versions regarded Malachi as a name or title for Ezra the scribe.[6] Likewise, later Jewish tradition codified in the Talmud explained the name Malachi as a pseudonym for Ezra.[7] The Christian commentators Jerome and Calvin also espoused this viewpoint.[8] Given the

---

5. See *b.* (*Talm.*) *baba Batra* 15a.

6. See Cathcart and Gordon (1989: 229, n. 2).

7. Cf. *b.* (*Talm.*) *baba Megilla* 15a.

8. Cf. Cathcart and Gordon (1989: 229, n. 2).

lack of compelling evidence to the contrary, it is best to regard
Malachi as the proper name of a Hebrew prophet. Unfortunately,
from our vantage point today he remains a relatively obscure figure
ministering during the early Second Temple period of Judaism.

3. Historical background

Malachi addressed Jews in the recently formed province of
Judah (or Yehud) in the Persian satrapy of Eber-Nahara
('Trans-Euphrates' in some translations) during the reign of King
Darius I (522–486 BC). His audience included expatriates resettled
in Judah and the descendants of those Hebrews who survived
the Babylonian sack of Jerusalem but were not deported to
Mesopotamia.

Politically, Judah struggled for identity amid a sea of hostile
neighbouring satrapy provinces. The office of provincial governor
was still in its infancy, and the provincial bureaucracy was in an
embryonic stage of development. Any deference shown to Judah by
the Persian overlords, religious or otherwise, was largely a matter of
political pragmatism, since the Persian army needed a base of
operations for the conquest and control of Egypt.

Religiously, the Second Temple had been completed, but it paled
in comparison to its Solomonic predecessor. Temple worship was in
a sorry state, as worshippers cheated God in their sacrifices and
tithes. The priesthood was also in need of reform, as the ministry
of the apathetic priests was actually leading people into sin, not
out of it! The hopes raised by Haggai and Zechariah for a revival of
the Davidic dynasty rooted in the figure of Zerubbabel seem to
have disappeared by the time of Malachi. The priests and the Levites
are the 'power-brokers' when he preaches to Judah.

Socially, Malachi confronts a population given to religious
cynicism and political scepticism. The disillusionment of the post-
exilic Jewish community was prompted by several theological
misunderstandings, including: the expectations of wealth that
Haggai had promised once the Second Temple was rebuilt (Hag.
2:7, 18–19); the restoration of the Davidic covenant predicted by
Ezekiel (Ezek. 34:13, 23–24); and the implementation of Jeremiah's
new covenant (Jer. 31:23, 31–33). In the minds of many in Malachi's

audience, God had failed his people. (See further Haggai: Historical background, pp. 45–46.)

4. Author

The book is silent on the issue of authorship, although it is assumed that the prophetic word formula (*The word of the LORD ... through Malachi*, v. 1) signifies that Malachi penned his own oracles. (See further 2. The prophet Malachi, pp. 277–278 and the commentary on 1:1 [Superscription], pp. 288–290.)

5. Date and occasion of writing

The book of Malachi is variously dated between 500 and 400 BC. Those dating the book nearer to 500 BC appeal to the similarities between Malachi and Haggai and Zechariah in literary style and language. Those placing the book around 450–430 BC cite the overlap between Malachi and the reforms of Ezra and Nehemiah in addressing similar religious concerns and social ills.[9] This reading of Malachi prefers a date nearer 500 BC for the writing of the book. It is possible that the battle between the Persians and Greeks at Marathon (c. 490 BC) was the occasion that prompted Malachi's message. The prophet may have interpreted that titanic struggle between East and West as at least a partial fulfilment of Haggai's prediction that God was about to *shake the heavens and the earth* and *overturn royal thrones* (Hag. 2:21–22).

6. Audience

Malachi's first oracle (1:1–5) is addressed generally to the Hebrew community living in post-exilic Jerusalem and its environs. The prophet's second oracle (1:6 – 2:9) is aimed specifically at the priests and Levites serving in the Second Temple. The final four oracles (2:10–16; 2:17 – 3:5; 3:6–12; 3:13 – 4:3, including the call to repentance, 3:6–12) of Malachi's prophecy are once again directed broadly

---

9. See Hill (1998: 77–84).

to the inhabitants of post-exilic Judah, although the Levites are specifically mentioned again in the fourth oracle or disputation (cf. 3:3–4). The righteous Hebrews within the restoration community are singled out and contrasted with the wicked in the final oracle (cf. 3:16–18).

7. Literary style

Like Haggai and Zechariah, the speeches of Malachi are essentially third-person prose summaries of the prophet's sermons, and are formally classified as belonging to the genre of oracular prose. The messages are oracular in nature because they represent authoritative prophetic speech motivated or inspired by God himself. By prose, we mean that the literary texture of Malachi is a blend of prosaic and rhetorical features, approaching poetic discourse, but distinctive of prophetic style. This kind of prophetic speech is often characterized by formulaic language. Examples of these stylized expressions in Malachi include: the prophetic word formula (*the word of the LORD*, 1:1), the messenger formula (*says the LORD Almighty*, e.g. 1:8, 14; 2:4), the self-introduction formula (*I am the LORD*, 3:6), and the call-to-repentance formula (*return to me*, 3:7).

The discourse units in Malachi may be broadly categorized as judgment speeches, since they accuse, indict and pronounce judgment on the audience. More precisely, the literary form of Malachi's oracles may be linked to Westermann's 'legal-procedure' (or trial speech) and the 'disputation'.[10] The disputation speech pits the prophet of God against his audience in combative dialogue. Typically, in Malachi the disputation features the following elements:

- a truth claim declared by the prophet
- a hypothetical refutation on the part of the audience in the form of a question
- the prophet's answer to the audience rebuttal by restating his initial premise
- the presentation of additional supporting evidence

---

10. Westermann (1991: 169–176).

The desired outcome in both covenant lawsuit and disputation speeches 'is to leave the opponent devoid of further argumentation and resigned to the divine decision'.[11] The disputation developed as an alternative form of prophetic speech because the people were unresponsive to the more conventional prophetic speech. This rhetorical-question-and-disputation format gave rise to the dialogical method of exposition peculiar to the later rabbinic schools of Judaism (cf. the teaching method of Jesus in Matt. 5:21, 27: *You have heard that it was said ... but I tell you ...*).

8. Intertextuality

Like other OT authors, Malachi was familiar with earlier and contemporary biblical texts. Similarities in the use of words, phrases and wider literary, thematic and theological contexts suggest Malachi's interdependence with these portions of the HB/OT. Malachi alludes widely to other OT literature, especially the books of Exodus and Deuteronomy, and other prophetic books such as Isaiah, Jeremiah, Joel and Ezekiel.[12] Many of these intertextual relationships are noted in the commentary.

The NT contains several quotations and allusions to the book of Malachi:[13]

Mal. 1:2–3//Rom. 9:13
Mal. 1:6//Luke 6:46
Mal. 1:7, 12//1 Cor. 10:21
Mal. 1:11//2 Thess. 1:12; Rev. 15:4
Mal. 2:7–8//Matt. 23:3
Mal. 2:10//1 Cor. 8:6

---

11. Patterson (1993: 303).
12. For a list of intertextual citations in Malachi, see Hill (1998: 401–412).
13. Ibid., pp. 84–88 for a full discussion. It is worth noting that the early chapters of the Synoptic Gospels appeal to Malachi, while the passion narrative especially draws on Zechariah 9 – 14. This may be instructive as to how this prophetic collection was read by the NT writers and the early church.

Mal. 3:1//Matt. 11:10; Mark 1:2; Luke 7:27
Mal. 3:2//Rev. 6:17
Mal. 3:3//1 Pet. 1:7
Mal. 3:5//Jas 5:4
Mal. 3:7//Jas 4:8
Mal. 4:2//Luke 1:78
Mal. 4:5//Matt. 11:14; 17:10–12; Mark 9:11–13
Mal. 4:5–6//Luke 1:17

9. Message

The thrust of Malachi's preaching may be placed under the umbrella theme of 'covenant', specifically the covenant of Jacob (i.e. the patriarchs; cf. Mal. 1:2), the covenant of Levi (2:5), the covenant of marriage (2:14) and the covenant of Moses (4:4).[14] The basic idea of a covenant is essentially that of a treaty or pact that establishes a relationship between parties, with attendant obligations and responsibilities. It is not surprising, then, that three of the book's disputations deal with right relationships. We should also take note of the fact that God's messenger works on the premise that proper knowledge of God is essential to maintaining these right relationships (as seen in his first disputation).

First, the prophet calls the people back to a *right understanding* of who God is – Israel's Father, Suzerain and Covenant-maker (1:2–5). Next, he admonishes the priests and the people to return to the practice of *right worship* by participating in the temple sacrifices with honesty and integrity (1:6 – 2:9). The prophet addresses the issue of *right relationships* in marriage by decrying divorce and encouraging loyalty on the part of spouses (2:10–16). *Right relationships* must extend to the community at large, in attitudes and behaviour that promote honesty, because God is just (2:17 – 3:5). The honesty foundational to social justice must also motivate *right giving* to God, because he is gracious and generous in his response to those who are faithful (3:6–12). Finally, Malachi summons his audience to a *right relationship* with God, because he is faithful to his word and

---

14. Cf. McKenzie and Wallace (1983: 549–563).

desires genuine worship (3:13 – 4:3). Interestingly, a pervasive sub-theme in the book is honesty, as three of the six disputations urge the people of post-exilic Judah to embrace this virtue.

10. Theological concerns

The book of Malachi is primarily a theology of YHWH.[15] The prophet reminds his audience that YHWH is *father* of Israel (1:6), as well as *master* and *king* (1:6, 14). Wary of the extremes of familiarity and formality, Malachi is careful to present a balanced picture of the Lord Almighty. God is sovereign over both the nations (1:3–5, 11, 14) and Israel as his elect nation or *treasured possession* (1:2; 3:17). Yet his love for Israel (1:2) does not preclude divine testing, and even judgment for the sake of purifying his people (3:2–3).

The prophet recognizes God as both the maker and keeper of the covenant with Israel (1:2; 2:10), and he understands the status of Israel as an adopted child by virtue of that covenant relationship (1:6). The conditional nature of YHWH's covenant placed a premium upon Israel's obedience to the treaty stipulations and the necessity of repentance for a breach of the covenant relationship (3:7, 16–18). Finally, Malachi acknowledges that Israel's relationship with YHWH demands both vertical and horizontal responsibilities, in the form of proper worship and social justice (1:10–14; 3:5).

Malachi preaches a lofty doctrine of marriage as companionship with the spouse of one's youth (2:14), and parenting as a shared responsibility (2:15). He calls attention to the sacred nature of the husband-wife relationship, by placing the covenant of marriage (2:14, 'marriage vows', NLT) within the context of the covenant between God and Israel (2:10).[16] This explains his censure of easy divorce and the exhortation to remain loyal to one's marriage vows (2:16). In one way, Malachi's teaching anticipates the more rigid instruction of Jesus and Paul on divorce (cf. Matt. 19:9–11; 1 Cor. 7:1–16). In context, the prophet's prescriptive treatment of divorce

15. See VanGemeren (1990: 204–208); cf. *NIDOTTE* 4: 927–929; *NDBT*: 260–262.

16. Hugenberger (1998: 27–47).

may be a reaction against the exclusivist tendencies of post-exilic Judaism to re-establish the ethnic purity of Israel diluted by inter-marriage.

Malachi's eschatology conforms to the conventional prophetic paradigm of threat and promise. Like Zechariah, Malachi pictures divine judgment as both punishment for sin and a call to repentance (3:7). The goal of God's judgment is the purification and restoration of the faithful of Israel (3:3–4). The NT understands that the work of the 'messenger' or forerunner who prepares the way for the Lord's appearance at his temple was realized in the ministry of John the Baptist (3:1; 4:5–6; cf. Matt. 11:14). Malachi also makes an original contribution to Old Testament eschatology with his reference to the *scroll of remembrance* in which the names of the righteous are recorded (3:16; cf. Dan. 12:1; Rev. 20:12).

ANALYSIS

1. **FIRST DISPUTATION: YHWH'S LOVE FOR ISRAEL (1:1–5)**
   A. Superscription (1:1)
   B. YHWH's love for Israel (1:2–5)

2. **SECOND DISPUTATION: INDICTMENT OF FAITHLESS PRIESTS (1:6 – 2:9)**
   A. YHWH dishonoured by improper worship (1:6–14)
      i. Contemptible animal sacrifices condemned (vv. 6–10)
      ii. YHWH's name profaned (vv. 11–14)
   B. Insolent priests rebuked (2:1–9)
      i. Threat of curse for dishonouring YHWH (2:1–3)
      ii. YHWH's covenant defiled by faulty instruction (2:4–9)

3. **THIRD DISPUTATION: INDICTMENT OF FAITHLESS PEOPLE (2:10–16)**
   A. YHWH's covenant profaned by disobedience (2:10–12)
   B. Covenant of marriage profaned by divorce (2:13–16)

4. **FOURTH DISPUTATION: YHWH'S MESSENGER OF JUDGMENT (2:17 – 3:5)**
   A. YHWH's justice challenged (2:17)
   B. YHWH will come to his temple (3:1–4)
   C. YHWH's judgment (3:5)

5. **FIFTH DISPUTATION: THE CALL TO SERVE YHWH (3:6–12)**
   A. The call to repentance (3:6–7)
   B. The call to bring the whole tithe (3:8–12)

6. **SIXTH DISPUTATION: THE DAY OF YHWH (3:13 – 4:3 [MT 3:21])**
   A. Obedience to YHWH challenged (3:13–15)
   B. Obedience to YHWH vindicated (3:16–18)
   C. Day of YHWH – judgment and vindication (4:1–3 [MT 3:19–21])

7. **APPENDICES (4:4–6 [MT 3:22–24])**
   A. Charge to obey the law of Moses (4:4 [MT 3:22])
   B. Elijah and the Day of YHWH (4:5–6 [MT 3:23–24])

COMMENTARY

1. FIRST DISPUTATION: YHWH'S LOVE FOR ISRAEL (1:1–5)

Context

Malachi's first speech-act is directed to the post-exilic community of Judah at large and is intended to persuade the audience of YHWH's love for Israel (1:2–5). The instruction begins with the Lord's love for Israel (1:2), and this opening disputation serves as a thesis statement for the prophet's entire message. As a thesis oracle, the opening disputation sets the tone (both admonition and exhortation), introduces the format (disputation), and presents the theme (YHWH's covenant with Israel) of the entire book.

Such reassurance was necessary amid growing scepticism, due to what Malachi's audience interpreted as the (apparent) failure of the Zion visions of Isaiah, Haggai and Zechariah. Malachi's task was to correct wrong thinking about post-exilic Judah's covenant relationship with YHWH. As his vassal or servant, the restoration community was in no position to make demands on God as their suzerain or overlord. This thesis disputation challenges the people of Judah to consider the precedent of history, both in terms of God's previous faithfulness to Israel and his propensity to judge them for lapses of covenant obedience. The prophet's appeal to recent events in Edom only served to underscore the seriousness of the divine threat. Loving God was not a cause for blessing but a condition, for God himself remains the only cause.[1]

The literary form of the first oracle is that of prophetic disputation, related to the judicial or trial speech pattern of prophetic literature. The disputation speech pits the prophet against his audience in a type of charge versus counter-charge format (whether the prophet is engaged in real dialogue with his audience or the dispute is imagined as a literary device is unclear). As with all of Malachi's disputations, the three-part formula of declaration (by the prophet as protagonist, 1:2a), refutation (by the particular recipients of the oracle as antagonist, 1:2b), and the prophet's rebuttal (1:2c–5) is readily discernible.

Comment

A. Superscription (1:1)

1. The literary form of the opening verse is that of superscription. (See commentary on the superscription for Hag. 1:1, pp. 60–62.)

The superscription of Malachi identifies the form or genre of the prophetic speech, the preacher (and author) of the sermons, and the audience. The word *oracle* (Heb. *maśśā'*) is a technical term for a particular type of prophetic speech (e.g. Isa. 13:1; 15:1; Nah. 1:1; Hab. 1:1; Zech. 9:1; 12:1. See also commentary on Zech. 9:1, pp. 204–205). Older versions render the word as 'burden' (e.g. KJV), emphasizing the prophetic utterance as a message of threat and doom. More recent versions translate the term *oracle* (e.g. NIV ['prophecy', NIV 2011], NRSV) or 'message' (e.g. NJB, NLT) as a general designation of a prophetic pronouncement. The larger context of the prophet's sermons justifies the conflation of both threat of doom and divine utterance in the term. In either case, the use of the technical term impregnates Malachi's message with a certain primacy and immediacy.[2]

---

1. So Collins (1984: 214–215).
2. Cf. Baldwin (1972: 237); and Verhoef (1987: 188).

The phrase, *the word of the LORD,* is another technical expression in prophetic literature and signifies a prophetic word of revelation (the so-called prophetic word formula).[3] According to Tucker (1977: 68), 'the fundamental intention of the superscription is to identify the prophetic books as word of God'. This combination of the word *oracle* and the phrase *word of the LORD* serves to strengthen 'the force and validity of the prophetic words at a time when such speech was rare'.[4] Clearly then, the compound title identifying Malachi as both *oracle* and *word of the LORD* marks the book absolutely as divine revelation and the authoritative word of God to the Hebrew community.

The audience of Malachi's sermons is *Israel,* the name applied to the Hebrew people in 1:5, 2:11, 16 and 4:4 [3:22]. The proper noun 'Israel' was the name given to Jacob, the second son of Isaac, after his encounter with the angel of the Lord at the Wadi Jabbok (Gen. 32:28). The name 'Israel' was used to designate the whole remnant of the Hebrew nation during the Babylonian exile and upon their return to the province of Judah (or Yehud) under Persian supervision (cf. Ezek. 3:1; Ezra 2:2). The prophet's appeal to Israel recalls the OT prophecy concerning the rejoining of the divided Hebrew kingdoms of Israel and Judah as one nation now fulfilled (cf. Ezek. 37:15-22).

The preposition *through* is a translation of the Hebrew idiom ('by the hand of'), indicating that Malachi is the human agent of the prophetic speeches. Grammatically, the expression denotes instrumentality and can refer to the act of writing or speaking, a so-called genitive of authorship.[5] The phrase says something about the prophetic responsibility, stressing the prophet's role as God's spokesperson and watchman to Israel (cf. Ezek. 3:4-11, 16-21). We are reminded that 'through his call, the prophet finds himself immediately in the divine presence. The prophet never acquires the word; he merely reports what Yahweh has said in his hearing.'[6]

---

3. Cf. *TDOT* 3: 111.
4. Meyers and Meyers (1993: 91).
5. Cf. *IBHS* § 9.5.1c, p. 143.
6. Andersen and Freedman (1980: 151).

The superscription of Malachi differs slightly from those of Haggai 1:1 and Zechariah 1:1 (omitting the verb *came* [e.g. *the word of the LORD came*, Hag. 1:1]). The variation in Malachi's superscription shifts the emphasis from the messenger to the message, calling attention to the tone of the sermons (dialogical), the content (instruction and encouragement coupled with judgment), and the theological focus on the immanence of YHWH instead of his transcendence. The LXX adds the clause, 'Do place it upon your hearts' (NETS), to the end of the superscription, perhaps influenced by the phraseology of Malachi 2:2 (cf. 4:6). (On the name *Malachi*, see 4. Author, p. 279.)

Meaning
The superscription to Malachi legitimizes the prophet as a divine messenger and validates the authority of his message as the word of God to post-exilic Judah.

B. YHWH's love for Israel (1:2–5)

Context
Malachi's first sermon alludes to Jacob as the heir of the covenant God established with Abraham (1:2). This promissory covenant joined God and Abraham (and his descendants) in an exclusive relationship, foundational to all subsequent OT covenants (cf. Gen. 12:1–3). Malachi's assertive speech is intended to assure the post-exilic Hebrew community that God's unconditional covenant love for Israel is still operative (1:3), despite the recent experience of Babylonian exile. The goal of YHWH's covenant relationship with the Hebrews and the core of Malachi's message was reciprocity, in the sense that Israel's duty was 'to reciprocate God's love, not in the original sense of emotion, but in the form of genuine obedience and pure devotion'.[7]

Comment
 2. The prophet's opening declaration, 'I have always loved you'

---

7. *TDOT* 1: 115.

(NLT), reminds Israel of their privileged position as the people of God. The word *love* (Heb. *'āhab*) has covenant implications when describing the relationship between the Lord and the Hebrew people. God's covenant love 'is an act of election which makes Israel Yahweh's child'.[8]

The retort by Malachi's audience in the form of a rhetorical question challenges the statement of God's love for Israel ('Really? How have you loved us?' NLT), although no specific challenges or accusations are levied. Malachi preaches to a crowd harbouring doubts, even scepticism, about their relationship to God as his elect people. The perceived inability of God to prevent the Babylonian exile spawned a spirit of indifference that verged on practical atheism. The remainder of the oracle is designed to convince the audience that the original assertion of God's love for Israel is indeed true.

The foil of *Esau* and *Jacob* (vv. 2b–3a) frames the prophet's rebuttal to the audience's refutation of God's love for Israel. The names Esau and Jacob recall the patriarchal traditions concerning the rivalry of the twin brothers (Gen. 25:22–26). Esau and Jacob became the ancestors of the nations of Edom and Israel respectively. The rivalry between the twins, foreshadowed at birth, persisted into the exodus era, when the Edomites denied Israel passage to the east (cf. Num. 20:14–21; 21:4). Israel and Edom coexisted peacefully until the reign of King Saul. Later King David subjugated the Edomites (2 Sam. 8:13–14), and Judah controlled Edom as a satellite state, until the Edomites revolted and regained autonomy during the reign of King Jehoram (2 Kgs 8:20–22). The reiteration of God's love for Jacob identifies both Jacob and his descendants as the heirs of the Abrahamic covenant, and is a reinforcement of the divine testimony affirming the election of Israel as God's *treasured possession* (3:17).

3. The word *hate* (Heb. *śānē'*) is the antonym for the verb *love* noted above (v. 2a). The two terms are used as a polar word pair in OT legal and prophetic texts (e.g. Deut. 7:10; Amos 5:15). Even as God's love for Jacob indicates his election of Israel as his covenant people, God's animosity toward Esau signifies his rejection of Esau

---

8. Andersen and Freedman (1980: 576–577).

and his descendants. The expression describes 'the hostility of a broken covenant relationship'.[9] Such is the case here, as God rejected Esau (and consequently his descendants the Edomites) because Esau despised and rejected the tokens of covenant relationship with YHWH (cf. Gen. 25:34; 26:34–35).

Esau was the ancestor of the Edomite nation, and the *inheritance* or territory of Edom was located on the south-eastern rim of the Dead Sea. The region of Edom extended from the Brook Zered in the north to the Gulf of Aqaba in the south. God instructed the Hebrews not to provoke the Edomites to war when they passed through their territory on the journey to Canaan after the exodus from Egypt, because he had given the area, also called the hill country of Seir, to Esau (Deut. 2:2–6).

The MT, *to the desert jackals*, is difficult, as seen in the confusion in the ancient versions (e.g. LXX and Syr. interpret 'desert dwellings' [cf. NJB, 'dwellings in the wastelands'], and the Vulg. reads the equivalent of the Heb. 'dragons' or 'serpents of the desert' [cf. NJPS, 'beasts of the desert']). The jackal is both a wild and an unclean animal according to Levitical law (cf. Lev. 11:26–27), and functions as a symbol of the desolation and defilement of Edom in a fashion similar to that of Isaiah's invective against Edom (Isa. 34:13, 14; cf. 35:7).

4. Unlike the Israelites who returned from captivity in Babylonia to re-inhabit Judah and rebuild Jerusalem and the Lord's temple, Edom will experience no such restoration. The certainty of divine judgment against the nation of Edom is a consistent theme in the prophetic oracles of judgment against the nations (e.g. Isa. 34:5–17; Jer. 49:7–22; Ezek. 25:12–14; Joel 3:19; Amos 1:11–12; Obad.; cf. Lam. 4:21–22).

LORD Almighty. This compound name for God is prominent in OT prophetic literature and is variously translated 'LORD of Hosts' (NRSV) or 'LORD of Heaven's Armies' (NLT). The title occurs twenty times in Malachi (1:6, 8, 9, 10, 11, 13, 14; 2:2, 4, 8, 16; 3:1, 5, 7, 10, 11, 12, 17; 4:1, 3). (See commentary on Hag. 1:2, pp. 63–64.)

The story of Esau is one of selfishness and contempt for the

---

9. Andersen and Freedman (1980: 525).

tokens of YHWH's covenant (cf. Gen. 25:34). The nation of Edom was renowned for its wisdom (Jer. 49:7; Obad. 8), but came to personify the pride of a self-centred existence (cf. Jer. 49:16). The Edomites were allies of the Babylonians in the sack of Jerusalem. As a result, they became a people group perpetually under the wrath of God, a *Wicked Land*, because of their violent crimes against their Israelite brothers in league with the Babylonians in the invasion of Judah in 587 BC (Obad. 10, 12; cf. 2 Kgs 25; Ps. 137:7–9). Later they moved into the region of the Negev after the area was wrested from Judah by the Babylonians (cf. 2 Kgs 24:8–17). The Edomites occupied Judean villages well into the Persian period (cf. 1 Esdr. 4:50), and centuries later Judas Maccabeus subdued Edomites then living in Judah (1 Macc. 5:65). The exact date of Edom's collapse is unknown, and the specific circumstances surrounding its demise are uncertain. Edom apparently remained largely independent of Babylonian influence until around 550 BC or so (cf. Jer. 40:11). According to scholarly consensus, a coalition of Arab tribes gradually infiltrated, overpowered and displaced the Edomites sometime during the fifth century, making Petra their capital city. Surviving Edomites either moved to Idumea or were absorbed by the Nabateans.[10]

5. Much like the audience of Malachi's earlier contemporary Haggai, the people were still 'looking for much and finding little' – and blaming God for their plight (Hag. 1:6, 9). The prophet offered his audience three external proofs of God's enduring covenant love for Israel. The first is the word of divine revelation, YHWH's declaration that he still loves Israel (v. 2). The second piece of supporting evidence was more tangible, if the people would only observe the current events unfolding around them – God destroyed the nation of Edom! The event was actually an answer to the psalmist's prayer requesting that God judge the Edomites for their part in the destruction of Jerusalem (cf. Ps. 137:7). The psalmist reminds us that remembering God's work in history is still a potent antidote for

---

10. On the history and archaeology of ancient Edom, see further: *ABD* 2: 287–295; *ZIBBCOT* 5: 90–93, 235–236; Hoglund (1994: 335–347); Bartlett (1989); Bienkowski (2001: 198–213).

those in a crisis of faith (e.g. Ps. 73:2, 16–17). The third demonstration of God's covenant love for Israel stood in their midst: the Second Temple had been rebuilt (cf. v. 4).

The expression, *Great is the LORD*, is an epithet for YHWH stemming from the so-called Zion tradition of the first book of the Psalter (Pss 35:27; 40:16 [MT 17]; cf. Ps. 48:1). This 'greatness of God proclaimed on Zion includes in particular a universal kingship over the whole earth and over all gods'.[11]

The compound construction joining the Hebrew prepositions 'from' and 'upon' (yielding *beyond*) gives rise to two distinct interpretative traditions. One emphasizes YHWH's covenant relationship with Jacob (v. 2) and his suzerainty *over* Israel.[12] The second stresses the sovereignty of YHWH in the destruction of Edom and the tendencies toward *universalism* in Malachi's later disputations, and reads *beyond* the territory of Israel (e.g. NIV, NJB, NLT, NRSV). The immediate context of the first sermon (including the Zion tradition epithet) and the accent on God's universal rule in the later disputations (e.g. 1:11, 14) tilt the discussion in favour of God's rule *beyond* the region of Israel (cf. Vulg.; LXX; 'beyond the borders of Israel', NETS). The word *border* (Heb. *gĕbûl*) is better rendered 'land' (NAB) or 'territory', since the term may 'also be defined by a genitive that designates the "territory" as the possession of persons or groups'.[13]

Meaning

The prophet's first oracle (1:2–5) is intended to persuade his audience that YHWH still loves Israel and that his ancient covenant with them remains intact. The goal of YHWH's covenant relationship with the Hebrews, and the essence of Malachi's message, was reciprocity, in the sense that Israel's duty was to respond to God's love in genuine obedience. The prophet's rhetorical refutation of the claim that YHWH had not loved Jacob reveals the depth of crisis of faith in post-exilic Judah (v. 2). Mallone (1981: 28) has observed that faith in crisis often needs the support of external evidence.

---

11. *TDOT* 2: 407.

12. See Verhoef (1987: 206); cf. GKC §119c, pp. 377–378.

13. *TDOT* 2: 365.

Malachi offered his audience external 'proofs' of YHWH's enduring covenant love for Israel, and in so doing he reminds us that remembering God's work in history is still a potent antidote for those in a crisis of faith. In the NT, Paul appealed to Malachi's declaration of God's love for Israel as an illustration of divine prerogative: God's election of the faithful is not dependent upon human desire or effort, *but on God's mercy* (Rom. 9:16; cf. 9:13).

2. SECOND DISPUTATION: INDICTMENT OF FAITHLESS PRIESTS (1:6 – 2:9)

Context

Malachi's second disputation consists of two distinct speech-acts, with the Lord as the subject of the first (1:6–14) and the Levitical priesthood as the subject of the second (2:1–9). The prophet's first speech is designed to persuade his audience that YHWH is truly Lord. His second speech both warns and threatens the priests for their failure to honour YHWH as Lord.[1] Both oracles are addressed to the priests, with the vocative, *O priests*, marking the opening of each section of the two-part sermon (1:6; 2:1).

Fishbane (1985: 334) has demonstrated that Malachi's second disputation is a post-exilic example of aggadic exegesis of the Aaronic blessing (Num. 6:23–27). Typically Jewish (h)aggadic exegesis draws forth latent meanings from traditional texts, and in this case turns the priestly blessing into an 'anti-blessing' – a curse (1:14; 2:2).

---

1. Watts (1987: 376).

The context of the opening unit (1:6–10) of the first speech-act (1:6–14) is the temple liturgy of animal sacrifice. The people and the priests are complicit in improper worship: the former for bringing inferior animals for sacrifice, and the latter for offering such blemished sacrifices to God (1:8). Malachi attempts to shame his audience into honouring God with appropriate sacrifices, by contrasting the offerings given to the Persian governor with those presented to YHWH (1:9).

Like the other oracles of the book, Malachi's second sermon features pseudo-dialogue (1:6) and rhetorical question (1:13) as part of the dispute between the prophet and the Levitical priesthood. The three-part disputation formula of prophetic declaration (1:6ac), audience refutation (1:6d), and the prophet's lengthy rebuttal (1:7 – 2:9) is discernible. The inclusion of exclamatory words such as 'Behold!' (KJV; 'Lo', NAB; 2:3) and *now* (1:9; 2:1), and the use of the vocative, *O priests* (1:6; 2:1), accents the hortatory style of the two speech-acts. In addition, the foil created between YHWH and the priests by means of first-person and second-person pronouns intensifies the confrontational tone of the dispute (e.g. *you, O priests* and *my name*, 1:6).

A. YHWH dishonoured by improper worship (1:6–14)

i. Contemptible animal sacrifices condemned (1:6–10)

Comment

6. By analogy to the human conventions related to social role and status, YHWH deserves *honour* as a father, and respect ('reverence', NAB; 'awe', NJB) as a *master*. At issue in this unit of Malachi's second disputation (1:6–8) are the core cultural values of honour and shame found across the biblical world.[2] The prophet emphasizes YHWH's ascribed or inherent honour as both *father* and *master*. The idea of YHWH as *father* is tied to his role of Creator (2:10; cf. Deut. 32:6) and specifically to his election of Israel as his chosen people (1:2; 3:17). The notion that YHWH is *master* (or 'Lord', Heb. *'ādôn*) over

---

2. See Pilch and Malina (1998: 106–115).

his servant Israel is rooted in the Sinai covenant, establishing the
relationship of God as suzerain over his vassal Israel after he had
delivered or redeemed them from slavery in Egypt.[3]

Malachi uses the term *priest* (Heb. *kōhēn*) in an inclusive sense,
making no distinction between priest and Levite in rank or function (i.e. the dual roles of worship leader and teacher).[4] Like Haggai
and Zechariah, Malachi understood the priests collectively as the
'national leaders' of post-monarachic Judah and the logical complement to the citizens of the province.[5]

The participial form of the verb *show contempt* (NIV, NLT; 'despise',
NAB, NJB, NRSV) indicates that this is an ongoing, even habitual, state
of affairs, and the repetition of the word sets the tone and theme
for the oracle (1:6, 7, 12; 2:9). The term indicates a breach of
covenant and disloyalty in a 'sacral-legal' relationship, much as it
does in Ezekiel 16:59.[6] Given the earlier reference to Jacob and Esau
in the opening disputation (1:2–5), Malachi may be alluding to the
story of Esau who despised his birthright and sold it to Jacob for a
meal (Gen. 25:34). The priests of Judah have despised their
birthright (i.e. the covenant with Levi, 2:4), and their position of
privilege and ministry is at risk (2:3). Furthermore, they jeopardize
the standing of the entire community before God because of their
misteaching of the Torah (2:8).[7]

The tenor of the reported response of the priests (*How have we
shown contempt for your name?*) is difficult to assess, whether genuine
surprise, honest doubt, or cynicism bordering on insolence. The
prophet's harsh rebuke in 2:3 suggests the latter. The word *name* is
a key theme in the prophet's second disputation, occurring eight
times (1:6 [twice], 11 [3 times], 14; 2:2, 5). Malachi uses the term to
represent the essence of God's being, especially his sovereignty, love
and faithfulness to Israel as revealed in his covenant name YHWH.

7. The prophet, speaking directly for God, provides a specific

3. Verhoef (1987: 212).

4. O'Brien (1990: 146–147).

5. Meyers and Meyers (1987: 387).

6. Cf. *TDOT* 2: 62–63.

7. Cf. Baker (2006: 227).

answer to the reported question posed by the priests (1:6). The verse introduces 'the scandalous conditions in which the priests offer sacrifice'.[8] The priests have persisted in offering YHWH improper worship by bringing defiled sacrifices to the temple altar. The term *defiled* signifies ritual pollution or contamination that disqualifies or renders unfit in religious terms an object (or person) for service in the worship of YHWH. This ritual pollution or contamination is the result of some violation of the holiness code specified in the law of Moses (in this case the laws concerning acceptable animal sacrifices, cf. Lev. 22:17–25; Deut. 15:21). The participial form of the verb describing the actions of the priests ('putting', NJB; 'offering', NRSV) indicates that this is a repeated behaviour pattern. The word *food* (lit. 'bread') probably represents any foodstuffs offered as 'sacrifices' (NLT) to God. The context indicates that this *food* consists primarily of animal sacrifices (1:8). The *altar* probably refers to the bronze altar of burnt sacrifice located in the east courtyard anterior to the temple (cf. Exod. 35:16; 38:30; 1 Kgs 8:64; Ezra 3:2–3).

8. Mosaic law forbids offering lame, blind and flawed animals as a sacrifice to God (Deut. 15:21). The purpose of the worshipper in so doing is obvious, as defective animals could be culled from herds and flocks, and offering these inferior animals lessened the economic impact of the sacrificial ritual on family finances. The priests were responsible for judging the merits of the kinds of sacrifices the people were bringing to the temple for offerings to the Lord (cf. Lev. 27:11–12, 14). Malachi upbraids the priests for declaring acceptable and offering to YHWH sacrifices that were in direct violation of the Mosaic law. The laxity of the priesthood in their responsibility for the oversight of appropriate temple worship was hardly a recent problem in Israel, as attested by the pre-monarchic story of Eli's corrupt sons (1 Sam. 2:12), the pre-exilic report in Ezekiel (22:26) and the later post-exilic reports of Ezra (9:1; 10:5) and Nehemiah (13:4–9, 22, 29–30).

The repeated statement (*Is that not wrong?* NIV, NRSV; lit. 'it is no evil') is usually construed as an interrogative construction ('Is it not

---

8. Glazier-McDonald (1987: 50).

evil?' NAB; 'Is this not wrong?' NJB). Alternately, and more likely, the
expression may be understood as a sarcastic declaration by the
prophet: 'There is no evil!' (cf. NJPS, 'it doesn't matter!'; NEB, 'there
is nothing wrong'). The prophet further shames the Levitical
priesthood by pressing home the honour due to YHWH stressed
previously (1:6) in the analogy to gifts offered to the *governor*. The
obvious answer to the rhetorical question is an emphatic 'No!' The
governor is probably a reference to the Persian-appointed governor of
the province of Judah.

9. The imperative verb *implore* (NAB, NIV, NRSV) translates an
idiomatic construction (lit. 'to soften the face'), in the sense of 'to
entreat the favour of, appease, pacify' ('plead', NJB; 'beg', NLT;
'placate', NEB).[9] Theologically, the idiom conveys the important idea
that 'an official human entreaty can persuade God to respond to
the petitioner in some way'.[10]

The plea, *be gracious*, is the expected response of God to the
priestly petition. Yet the actions of the priests in offering defiled
sacrifices (*with such offerings*, NIV) have nullified YHWH's mercy ('The
fault is yours. Will he show favour to any of you?' NRSV). The reference to the graciousness of God is an allusion to the Aaronic bene-
diction (Num. 6:24–26), since the priestly intercession for Israel was
supposed to result in divine blessing for Israel.[11] The term is also a
reminder that grace and favour are fundamental attributes of
YHWH (Exod. 34:6–7). The indictment of the corrupt priesthood
for offering impure worship to YHWH in the rhetorical questions
that follow indicates that the prophet's message is not so much a
call to repentance as a sarcastic jibe at their intercessory function
(cf. NLT).[12] The shift to the first-person plural pronoun (*us*) both
personalizes the prophet's message (as Malachi includes himself in
the community) and recognizes the implications of the priestly
disobedience for the entire community – priests and people are
guilty before the Lord.

---

9. See Taylor and Clendenen (2004: 270).
10. Meyers and Meyers (1987: 384).
11. See Fishbane (1985: 332–334).
12. Cf. Glazier-McDonald (1987: 51); Taylor and Clendenen (2004: 270–271).

10. Malachi's strong words need little explication. 'It would be better to close the temple complex than to continue worship that insults God.'[13] The prophet's shocking statement is the first true directive in the book, and a 'tragic irony'.[14] The irony runs thick at two levels, since leading worship for the people of Israel is the Levitical commission: the priesthood would be unemployed, and God would be denied the one thing he seeks from all of his creation – worship. The reference to the *temple doors* pertains either to the double doors of the temple entrance from the course of the priests,[15] or to the entrance to the court of the priests where the tables for sacrifice were located.[16] The closing of the temple doors at the wrong time 'denotes the interruption of sacrificial worship',[17] and YHWH's response is radical because the command halts the 'calendrical … system of sacrifices'.[18]

The priestly duties included arranging the wood and the prescribed pieces of the sacrificial animal, and kindling the fire on the altar of burnt offering, so that offering made by fire might please the Lord (Lev. 1:7–9). The defiled sacrifices offered by the priests were 'pointless' (NJB), 'to no purpose' (NJPS), 'in vain' (NRSV) for two reasons: first, they were unacceptable as offerings to YHWH; and second, they yielded no benefit or blessing to the worshipper.

God takes 'no pleasure' (NAB, NRSV) in the priests or their ministry, because he 'desires' (NEB) or 'delights' (NRSV) in obedience more than sacrifice (1 Sam. 15:22). For this reason, the offerings they bring are unacceptable. Such irreverence on the part of the priests must be rejected by God and repudiated by his prophet. The real issue is not so much the blemished sacrifices, as the malpractice of the Levitical priesthood.

---

13. Stuart (1998: 1305).
14. Taylor and Clendenen (2004: 271).
15. Mason (1977: 144).
16. Cf. Baldwin (1972: 246).
17. *TDOT* 3: 232.
18. Petersen (1995: 183). Malachi may allude to the opening of the sanctuary doors by Samuel after his vision from the Lord as a foil to his call to close the temple doors (cf. 1 Sam. 3:15).

Meaning

Malachi's opening discourse is addressed to the priests and Levites and is designed to convince them that YHWH is truly Lord (1:6). As both Father and Lord, he deserves honour and respect, not contempt and irreverence. The gist of the first portion (1:6–10) of the second oracle is the rebuke of the priesthood for overseeing improper worship of YHWH at the Jerusalem temple (1:7–8). Better to halt the sacrificial ritual and close the temple than to bring useless and unacceptable offerings to the Lord Almighty (v. 10).

ii. YHWH's name profaned (vv. 11–14)

Context

God chose Jacob (1:2) and established a covenant relationship with Israel to make his name great among the nations (1:11, 14; cf. Gen. 12:1–3; Isa. 49:6). The theme of the worship of YHWH by the nations is central to the second disputation, and reflects the pattern of the universal worship of YHWH projected in the Hag-Zech-Mal corpus (cf. Hag. 2:7; Zech. 14:16–17). The prophet correctly understood that Israel's proper worship of YHWH had global implications. Beyond the worship of post-exilic Judah at the Second Temple and that of the diaspora Jews, Malachi seems to have in mind the eschatological future when the rule of God will be established over all the earth, and the nations will worship him as the true Sovereign.

Comment

11. The threefold repetition of the word *name* (see the discussion in 1:6 above) unifies the verse and reminds the priests (and the people) of something they have forgotten or chosen to ignore – YHWH is truly great! The triad of declarations that 'YHWH is great' (vv. 5, 11, 14) are climactically structured, culminating in the proclamation that YHWH is a *great king*. The epithet may constitute a type of liturgical refrain (cf. Ps. 76:2; Jer. 10:6).[19] Mason (1977: 145) observed that 1:14 completes the lesson of 1:11, each containing similar charges raised against the priests and climaxing in

---

19. Cf. Glazier-McDonald (1987: 64); and Petersen (1995: 187).

the universal worship of YHWH. Moreover, the universal worship of YHWH (v. 11) anticipated by Malachi is the central theme of the second disputation.[20]

This verse is at once both difficult to interpret,[21] and perhaps Malachi's most original contribution to the development of OT prophecy.[22] Achtemeier is probably correct in her assessment that verses 11 and 14 do not refer to the worship of the heathen, or to diaspora Jews or Jewish proselytes, but to 'the future establishment of the kingship of God over all the earth ... the purpose that underlies every prophetic book'.[23]

The phrase, *from the rising to the setting of the sun*, is a merism, a figure of speech in which two constituent parts represent the whole. In this case, the merism indicates the territorial extent of the nations paying homage to YHWH, every place from the east to the west (NEB, 'from furthest east to furthest west').

According to one ancient tradition, YHWH expected worship from Israel in *every place* he caused his name to be remembered (through theophany, Exod. 20:24).[24] Since YHWH is Creator, it is only natural that all creation should extol his universal glory (cf. Ps. 148:5, 11–12).

Burning *incense* (lit. 'to send up in smoke') on the altar of incense was one of the daily duties of the priests (Exod. 30:1–10). The burning of incense was a symbol of prayer, mediated by the priesthood as intercessors for Israel (Ps. 141:2; cf. Rev. 5:8; 8:3–4). The burning of incense was common to the religious ritual of the biblical world, and this coupled with the reference to cultic offerings

---

20. Verhoef (1987: 222).
21. See Merrill (1994: 339–401, 403); see also the succinct summary of the interpretive options in R. L. Smith (1984: 313); cf. Gordon (1994: 56).
22. So G. A. Smith (1943: 647).
23. Achtemeier (1986: 177); cf. Tate (1987: 399) who agrees that contextually this imminent future understanding of the passage fits the eschatological emphasis of the book of Malachi as a whole. See also the full discussions in Baldwin (1972: 246–250) and Glazier-McDonald (1987: 55–61).
24. See Durham (1987: 320).

in general (see the discussion below) is appropriate to Malachi's assertion that the nations will worship YHWH.

The adjective *pure* refers to ritual purity (or being ceremonially acceptable), as understood and required by the holiness laws of the Mosaic covenant. The Levitical priests of Malachi's day were guilty of the same cultic violations censured by Ezekiel: the failure to discern between the spheres of the holy and the profane, the clean and the unclean (Ezek. 22:23–31). The basic meaning of the word *offering* is 'gift', and in religious contexts it is a generic term for offerings and sacrifices of various types.[25] The *pure offerings* envisioned by the prophet anticipate the rejuvenation of the priesthood and the restoration of proper temple worship in post-exilic Judah – in the present situation.[26]

12. The disjunctive connective, *but*, introduces a shift in participants (the nations vs the priests) and a contrast in action (a pure offering vs a polluted offering). Thematically, the section (1:12–14) continues the indictment of the priests for liturgical malpractice. The participial form of the verb *profane* emphasizes the ongoing state of affairs (lit. 'but you are desecrating it').[27] Ironically, the guardians of Israel's covenant relationship with YHWH were habitually profaning his temple with impure sacrifices.

The clause, *and of its food, 'It is contemptible'*, is problematic, attested by the divergences in the ancient versions and modern EVV (lit. 'its fruit is despised, [even] its food [in reference to the Lord's table or altar]'). The noun 'fruit' is rare, and is found elsewhere in the OT only in Isaiah 57:19 ('the fruit of the lips', ESV). The NAB, NIV and NRSV regard the word as a variant repetition of *food* and delete it as secondary. The better approach is to understand the second noun (*food*) as an explanation of the rarer first noun ('fruit'; cf. 'and its fruit, that is, its food may be despised', ESV; 'and the meat, the food can be treated with scorn', NJPS).[28]

---

25. Cf. *NIDOTTE* 2: 980.

26. Cf. Mason (1977: 144); see further the discussion in Hill (1998: 188–189).

27. Cf. *IBHS* § 37.6b, p. 624.

28. See Hill (1998: 190–191); cf. Baker (2006: 231).

13. The word *burden* is a rare OT term (found elsewhere only in Exod. 18:8; Num. 20:14 and Lam. 3:5). It refers to the effects of exhaustion and weariness ('O what a bother!', NJPS; 'How irksome!', NEB; 'How tiresome it all is!', NJB; 'What a weariness this is,' NRSV).[29] As a result of the tedium and boredom associated with their repetitive 'chores', the disgusted priests 'scorn to fill their office'.[30] Petersen (1995: 185) suggests that the priests found both their vocational duties and the prophet's relentless criticism to be a nuisance.

The verb *sniff at* means 'to blow, gasp', and in this form, 'to snort'. The modern EVV agree that the expression signifies a gesture of insolence and derision (NAB, 'you scorn it'; NJB, 'you sniff disdainfully at me'; NLT, 'you turn up your noses'; NRSV, 'you sniff at me'). The repetition of the corrupt practices related to the animal sacrifice rituals (1:13b) only serves to underscore the indictment levied against the priests for sacrilege in discharging the duties of their office (cf. 1:8). The spirit of King David, who would not offer to God burnt offerings that cost him nothing (2 Sam. 24:24), was sadly lacking in the priests of Malachi's day.[31]

The list of inferior animals brought for sacrifice has changed slightly from the previous catalogue of unacceptable offerings (1:8). Here 'stolen' animals ('what has been taken by violence', NRSV; 'you bring in what you seize', NAB) replaces *blind* animals at the head of the list. The prophet may refer to the unlawful snatching of animals (i.e. trespassing and poaching of animals for use as sacrificial offerings). The NEB ('mutilated') and NIV (*injured*) interpret the term to refer to animals that had been attacked and torn or mauled by wild animals, since such meat was not to be eaten and presumably was unfit for sacrificial offerings (cf. Lev. 7:24; 17:5).[32]

14. The word *curse* is a harsh one, and to bind a curse upon another was a grave speech-act in the ancient world. The curse formula 'is the most powerful "decree" expressed by an authority,

---

29. Levine (1993: 491).

30. Glazier-McDonald (1987: 62).

31. Cf. Merrill (1994: 397).

32. Cf. Glazier-McDonald (1987: 63) who notes that 'a priest would be unable to recognize a pilfered animal'.

and by means of it a man or a group that has committed a serious transgression against the community or against a legitimate authority (God, parents) is delivered over to misfortune'.[33] Malachi is the only prophet among the Twelve Minor Prophets who resorts to the curse, and does so after the pattern of Deuteronomy (27:15–26; cf. Jer. 48:10). The curse is related to the violation of a vow (specifically the substitution of a blemished sacrificial animal for a healthy one). The 'covenant-based curse [thus affects] not only the one who pledged the animal but also the ritual officiant – decision maker'.[34]

The phrase *great king* may be an allusion to the hymnic affirmation that YHWH is *the great King over all the earth* (Ps. 47:2) or *the great King above all gods* (Ps. 95:3). Berlin's insight that 'when the Lord is recognized as king, pridefulness and disobedience are gone, applies to the circumstances addressed by Malachi'.[35] If the Levitical priesthood had properly acknowledged YHWH's sovereignty, then they would not have been under prophetic indictment for malpractice in the offering of temple sacrifices.

The participial form of the verb *fear*, when used in combination with the word *great*, refers to the numinous nature of God – 'terrible … identical with his holiness'.[36] This 'terribleness' is an attribute of both YHWH (e.g. Exod. 15:11) and his name (e.g. Deut. 28:58; Ps. 99:3). The complementary relationship between the rhetorical questions of 1:6 and the pronouncements of 1:11 and 1:14 is significant. The first question (*Where is the honour due to me?*) has its reply in the declaration that *my name will be great among the nations* (v. 11b). The second question (*Where is the respect due to me?*) finds its rejoinder in the testimony that YHWH *is a great king* and his *name is to be feared among the nations* (v. 14d). The arrangement neatly connects verse 6 with verses 11 and 14, creating a well-crafted and thematically unified literary panel within the second sermon.[37] (See further the discussion of 1:11, pp. 302–304.)

---

33. *TDOT* 1: 411.

34. Petersen (1995: 187).

35. Berlin (1994: 143).

36. *TDOT* 6: 300.

37. Petersen (1995: 185).

Meaning

The second unit (1:11–14) of the first speech-act (1:6–14) continues the indictment of the priesthood for profaning temple worship (v. 12). Their irreverence for God in discharging their priestly duties compromised Israel's role as a model for the universal worship of YHWH (v. 11) and sullied his reputation among the nations as a great king (1:14).

B. Insolent priests rebuked (2:1–9)

i. Threat of curse for dishonouring YHWH (2:1–3)

Context

The second speech-act (2:1–9) of Malachi's second disputation (1:6 – 2:9) is a warning directed specifically to the Levitical priesthood (2:1) and an elaboration of the curse invoked at the end of the first speech-act (1:14). The two units of the second speech-act (2:1–3 and 2:4–9) are connected by a pair of key words, *honour* (2:2) and *reverence* (or 'fear', NAB; 2:5). Thus, the first unit (2:1–3) of the second speech-act is structured as a response to the rhetorical questions posed in the first speech-act: *Where is the honour due to me? Where is the respect due me?* (1:6).

Comment

2:1. The Levitical priesthood is the prophet's target audience for the entire second disputation (see 1:6 above). The referent intended in the phrase *this admonition* (Heb. *miṣwâ*, 'commandment'; so NAB, NJB) is ambiguous. Petersen (1995: 187) understands the phrase as a summary of the stipulations of the Mosaic covenant (Deut. 7:11 and is 'something that is readily doable (Deut. 30:11)'. Glazier-McDonald (1987: 64–65) considers the word as a synonym for judgment (Heb. *mišpāṭ*) and assumes that Malachi's speech-act itself (2:1–9) is the *admonition* (so NIV; or 'decree', NEB). It seems better to identify *this commandment* with the contents and maintenance of the covenant of Levi mentioned in 2:4.[38] The prophet's 'charge'

---

38. Cf. Verhoef (1987: 237–238); cf. Jones (1962: 189); Petersen (1995: 187).

(NJPS) is not a separate verdict of judgment, but rather a reference to the command of the priestly office as a divinely ordained
sacral institution. The core of *this commandment* is summarized in
observing the word of YHWH, keeping his covenant, teaching
Jacob God's law, and offering sacrifices upon YHWH's altar (Deut.
33:9–10). It is this standard by which Malachi indicts and judges
the priests.

   2. The verb *listen* means 'to listen' or 'hear' in the sense of 'obey'
(NJPS, cf. Deut. 28:15). The idiom *to set the heart* occurs six times in
the Hag-Zech-Mal corpus (Hag. 1:5, 7; 2:15, 18 [twice]; Mal. 2:2
[twice]). The expression indicates that this is a matter of the will,
not the emotions ('make up your minds', NLT; 'sincerely resolve',
NJB; 'resolve', NIV 2011). The form of the verb *listen* indicates the
conditional clause, suggesting the potential for fulfilment (pending
repentance on the part of the priests, cf. 3:7).

   The word *curse* is a rather rare OT term (occurring only in Deut.
28:20; Prov. 3:33; 28:27; and Mal. 2:2; 3:9). Used in combination with
the verb *send*, the construction suggests that Malachi has the curses
of Deuteronomy 28 in mind. The priestly *blessings* under the threat of
God's curse include both their prayers of blessing for the congregation of Israel (cf. Num. 6:24–27)[39] and the blessings they receive in
the form of material benefits received as compensation for their
service in the temple.[40]

   The clausal adverb *Yes* ('Indeed', NRSV) has an emphatic force,
and several of the EVV insert the adverb *already* in an effort to convey
the sense of recent past action (e.g. NAB, NIV, NRSV). Petersen (1995:
189) considers Malachi's statement as 'a radically innovative claim',
in that he has combined the conditionality of the Sinai treaty with
the covenant of grant (i.e. the covenant of Levi, 2:4) in order to
explore the covenant relationship between YHWH and the Levitical
priesthood.

   3. The exclamatory interjection 'Behold!' (ESV; 'Now', NJB) is
omitted in the NIV. In combination with the participial form of the
verb *rebuke* (Heb. *gā'ar*), the construction describes immediate

---

39. Cf. Keil (1975: 442–443).
40. See Rudolph (1976: 265).

circumstances ('I am rebuking'),[41] or imminent future action ('I am going to ...', so NJB). The word *rebuke* is sometimes emended to Hebrew *gāra'* ('separate, take away'), on the basis of the LXX ('Behold, I separate the shoulder at you', NETS; 'Lo, I will deprive you of the shoulder', NAB; 'I will cut off your arm', NEB; 'Now, I am going to break your arm', NJB).[42] In keeping with the provisions of the Mosaic covenant, the punishment for covenant violations extends from the parents to subsequent generations (Exod. 20:5–6). A double entendre with the lit. 'seed' (NJPS, 'I will put your seed under a ban') is possible, given the crop failure in post-exilic Judah (cf. Syr., 'Behold I will rebuke the seed of the ground').[43]

The word *offal* (NEB, NJB; 'dung', NAB, NIV 2011, NRSV; 'manure', NLT) is a technical term for the entrails or waste parts of the butchered sacrificial animal (especially the undigested contents of the stomachs).[44] According to Levitical law (Lev. 4:11–12; 8:17; 16:27), the *offal* (Heb. *pereš*), along with the animal's head, legs and entrails, are to be disposed of by burning on the ash heap outside the camp. The Targum dispensed with the metaphor and translated, 'I will make visible on your faces the shame of your crimes.'[45]

The final clause of the MT is problematic, given the abrupt shift to the third person in the verb *carried off* (lit. 'and he will lift you up to it'). The third-person form is probably a reference to YHWH, who will dispose of the priests even as they dispose of the waste materials of the animal sacrifices (cf. LXX, 'And I will take you to the same place', NETS). The implied place of disposal, figuratively applied, is the ash heap ('and you will be carried out to its [heap]', NJPS). Petersen (1995: 189) summarizes: 'Here, in the final element of the sentence, the priests now have the status of dung, something that must be removed from the ritual complex. What was holy has now become impure. Ritual logic requires its destruction. No more radical condemnation of the Aaronid line can be imagined.'

---

41. E.g. R. L. Smith (1984: 309).
42. See Hill (1998: 200).
43. Cf. Baldwin (1972: 253); Glazier-McDonald (1987: 67–68).
44. Levine (1993: 462).
45. Baldwin (1972: 253); cf. Cathcart and Gordon (1989: 232).

Meaning
The priests are threatened with a curse, indeed are already under a curse according to the prophet (v. 2), for their failing to honour God as their top priority. The dishonour and shame they have brought upon YHWH by their liturgical malpractice will fall to them.

ii. YHWH's covenant defiled by faulty instruction (2:4–9)

Context
The priests were responsible for the spiritual and moral condition of the people of Israel (cf. Deut. 33:8–11). The Levitical priesthood was charged to model covenant keeping for the rest of Israel in teaching the Mosaic law and service of leadership in temple worship. Right behaviour and proper worship on the part of the people were dependent upon sound priestly instruction of the Torah and virtuous priestly example in the ministry of worship (cf. Hos. 4:4–9). The covenant of Levi was thus meant to be a covenant of life and peace for priests and people (v. 5).

Comment
4. There is no reference to the establishment of a covenant between YHWH and Levi, the ancestor of the Levitical priesthood (although Neh. 13:29 also mentions *the covenant of the priesthood and of the Levites*). The OT preserves allusions to such a covenant, including: Exodus 32:26–29 (in response to the purge by the sons of Levi after the golden calf episode at Sinai);[46] Numbers 25:11–13 (in response to the heroic deed of Phinehas in staying the plague at Baal Peor);[47] Deuteronomy 33:8–11 (Moses' poetic blessing of the tribe of Levi);[48] and Jeremiah 33:20–21 (a reflection on a covenant with the Levites [i.e. the Mosaic covenant?]).[49] Although not formally identified as a covenant, the language of Malachi has

---

46. See Baldwin (1972: 254).
47. Cf. Glazier-McDonald (1987: 79–80).
48. So Verhoef (1987: 245).
49. Cf. *ABD* 4: 294–295.

affinities with the blessing of Moses on the tribe of Levi (Deut. 33:8–11).[50]

The phrase *this admonition* ('this warning', NIV 2011; 'this commandment', NJB) is to be distinguished from the perpetual *covenant with Levi* as both the condition by which the priests serve YHWH and the means by which they are led to repentance (2:1–3).[51] The prophet 'expresses hope that the covenant between Yahweh and Levi may be salvaged'.[52]

5. The benefits of covenant relationship with YHWH for Levi (and the Levitical priesthood) included *life* and *peace*. The words *life* (Heb. *ḥayyîm*) and *peace* (Heb. *šālôm*) combine to express wholeness, well-being, health, long life, prosperity, safety and protection as the benefits of covenant relationship with YHWH.[53] God's blessing of *life and peace* was extended to Israel through the priestly ministry of mediation and intercession, solemnly summarized in the Aaronic blessing (Num. 6:24–26). Fishbane (1983: 115–121, as cited in Schuller, 1996: 861) notes that much of Malachi's second sermon is to be read against the backdrop of this priestly blessing, as the prophet systematically negates the benefits of the prayer for the disobedient priests. The implied mutuality of commitments for obedience on the part of the Levitical priesthood and blessing from YHWH suggests the intersection of the promissory covenant tradition (the covenant of grant with Levi) and the obligatory covenant tradition (the suzerain-vassal treaty with Israel).[54]

The benefits of life and peace were granted to Levi to fill him with awe, thus prompting willing and obedient service to God.[55] This covenant is life-giving for the Levites and the people of Israel, since the priests were guardians and instructors of the knowledge of God from one generation to the next.

---

50. See the discussion in Stuart (1998: 1305).
51. See Baldwin (1972: 254).
52. Petersen (1995: 190).
53. Cf. *TDOT* 4: 333–335.
54. See further the discussions in Glazier-McDonald (1987: 70); Hill (1998: 205–206;) and Stuart (1998: 1316–1317).
55. Cf. Baldwin (1972: 255); Merrill (1994: 404).

The semantic range of the word 'fear' includes *reverence* (NIV), 'respect' (NJB), 'fear' (NAB). The verb *stood in awe* (or 'lived in awe', NEB) can also mean 'to be filled with terror' (cf. KJV, 'and was afraid before my name').[56] In either case, on occasion the Levitical priesthood 'honored their obligation and ... acted according to the content and purport of God's covenant with them'.[57] The priests of Malachi's day have fallen far short of the exemplary model of the classical or ideal priesthood.

6. The section (2:6–8) is a three-verse poem expanding on the historic duties of the Levitical priesthood begun in 2:5.[58] The word *instruction* (Heb. *tôrâ*) refers to the legal and pedagogical functions of the Levitical priesthood rooted in the Mosaic law (Deut. 33:9–10; cf. Jer. 18:18; Ezek. 7:26). This covenant-based teaching was probably derived from both oral and written traditions and included instruction on ceremonial requirements, as well as rules of moral conduct – 'guidance into the right way of life'.[59] The *true instruction* of Levi stands as a foil for the teaching of Malachi's Levitical contemporaries that caused many to stumble (into sin, 2:8).

The expression *walked with me* is used theologically in the sense of covenant obedience, 'setting God as the center of human life'.[60] The juxtaposition of the phrases *my covenant was with him* (2:5) and *he walked with me* (v. 6) admirably portrays the ideal of mutuality in covenant relationship with YHWH.[61] *Peace* (Heb. *šālôm*) refers to 'full harmony with the will of God', and *uprightness* ('justice', NJB) refers to 'the moral integrity of their [i.e. the priests'] behavior and conduct'.[62] The NJPS version understands the two words, *peace* and *uprightness*, as a hendiadys for 'complete loyalty' on the part of the Levitical priesthood.

---

56. Cf. Verhoef (1987: 247); and see the comments on the Eng. trans. in Stuart (1998: 1320).
57. Verhoef (1987: 247).
58. Stuart (1998: 1320).
59. Glazier-McDonald (1987: 70).
60. *TDOT* 3: 395.
61. Glazier-McDonald (1987: 71)
62. See Verhoef (1987: 249); cf. CEV, 'because he obeyed me and lived right'.

The word *turned* (Heb. *šûb*) signifies repentance (see the discussion of 3:7 below). Priestly instruction rooted in the Mosaic law of an earlier era led people to desist from doing evil ('held many back from iniquity', NJPS) and *turned* (or 'converted', NJB) them back to God.[63]

7. The reference to the *lips* is a type of metonymy in which the physical organ represents the function of speech. The verb *preserve* means to 'guard' (NRSV) or 'safeguard' (NJB) God's word in the sense of maintaining and perpetuating the tradition and eagerly teaching it (cf. CEV), because people rely or 'hang on the words of the priests' (NEB). The priests 'were to mediate God's instructions concerning ethics and morals and ritual when persons came to them for Torah, teaching out of a knowledge of God gained in intimate prophetic-like communion with him'.[64] The *knowledge* the priests preserve and teach is 'the knowledge of God in the torah for which the priest is responsible'.[65]

The priests were supposed to be mediators of God's word and will, a *messenger* (Heb. *mal'āk*) like other agents of divine revelation, angels and prophets.[66]

8. The disjunctive adverb *but* introduces the sad reality that the priests of Malachi's day stand in stark contrast to the Levitical ideal. The use of the emphatic second-person pronoun *you* (left untranslated in most EVV) along with the verb (*turned*) heightens the contrast ('But you yourselves have turned aside …', NJB). The verb *turned* (NIV) means to 'turn aside' (NRSV), fall away ('But you have turned your backs on me', CEV) or desert ('But you priests have left God's paths', NLT). Right behaviour on the part of the people of Israel in covenant relationship with YHWH was dependent upon sound priestly instruction of the Torah and the virtuous example of the

---

63. See Verhoef (1987: 249.)
64. Achtemeier (1986: 178); cf. Dentan and Sperry (1956: 1132–1133): 'This verse contains both the noblest statement of the function of the priesthood to be found in the Old Testament and the highest estimate of its dignity.'
65. Andersen and Freedman (1980: 352).
66. Cf. Stuart (1998: 1321). On the possible wordplay with the prophet's name, see Hill (1998: 213).

priests as covenant-keepers themselves. Malachi rebukes the priests
for failure on both counts. The *way* refers to 'that course' (NJPS) or
'God's path' (NLT), outlined in the preceding review of the Levitical
ideal (2:5–7).

The people of Judah did not *stumble* over the instruction of the
priests. Rather, they stumbled over or violated the covenant law of
YHWH because of the misinterpretation of that law by the priests
('Your teachings have led others to do sinful things', CEV; 'Your
instructions have caused many to stumble into sin', NLT).

The verb *violated* in this form means to 'spoil, ruin, corrupt' (so
NJPS, NRSV), in the sense that the priests have 'broken the agreement' (CEV) that God established with Levi. The prophet uses
strong language ('you have destroyed the covenant of Levi', NJB) to
underscore the gravity of the situation. The priests have defiled
themselves and broken covenant with God, but not irreparably so.
God will punish and shame the priests for their malpractice, but
they may be purified through repentance and restored to office (cf.
3:3–4). The covenant with Levi may be understood in a collective
sense as the covenant with the *Levites* (so NJPS, NEB) with reference
to their distinctive office and commission to serve YHWH and his
people.

9. Instead of the blessing of *life and peace* (2:5), God has punished
the priests for their breach of covenant by bringing 'contempt' and
'shame' upon them (making them 'despicable and mean', NEB;
'contemptible and vile', NJB; 'despised and abased', NRSV). Divine
retribution is meted out on the principle of measure for measure, in
that the priests had despised God's name (1:6), so now YHWH
makes the priests a despised group.

The charges of corruption against the priests remain unspecified, apart from their misinterpretation and misteaching of
YHWH's covenant law ('being partial in applying the law', NJB;
'show partiality in your rulings', NJPS). The clause reads (lit.), 'and
you are not lifting up faces [of the people] in Torah'. The priests
have not only failed to obey God's law, but they have also been
derelict in 'raising faces' in the Torah: that is, they have neglected to
demonstrate the grace of kindness and fairness in their administration of the rules of Torah. The construction may form a type of
envelope for the second disputation with the rhetorical question

posed in 1:8: 'Will he [i.e. God] lift up your face?' The prophet concludes his second sermon by answering that very question, as the priests are not lifting up the faces of the people in Torah. How ridiculous to suppose that the priesthood might expect God to grant them favour when they could not reciprocate in kind to the very people they were commissioned to serve![67] What hope is there for sheep without a shepherd (cf. Jer. 50:6)?

Meaning
Sadly, the priests of Malachi's day provided neither sound instruction in God's Torah nor virtuous example in the worship of YHWH. Instead, they turned away from the Mosaic law and led the people astray (v. 8). The prophet's remedy for the corrupt priesthood was correct instruction in the knowledge of God (v. 7). Such teaching would promote proper worship and restore righteous living (vv. 5–6). Until such time as that spiritual renewal took place, the principle of sowing and reaping remained in effect: the priests were despised and humiliated, even as they despised their official role and the God who commissioned them (v. 9; cf. 1:13).

---

67. See the discussion in Schuller (1996: 861).

3. THIRD DISPUTATION: INDICTMENT OF FAITHLESS PEOPLE (2:10–16)

Context

The shift in style from an adversarial second-person accusation (2:8–9) in the second disputation to an inclusive first-person plea (*Have we ...? Why do we ...?*; 2:10) in the third disputation is striking, serving to enhance the intensity and urgency of the plea for unity.[1] Malachi the prophet now speaks to his audience as Malachi the pastor, and even as the fellow citizen. Clearly, the disjunction in form indicates that the topic of marriage and divorce is crucial to Malachi's overall message. In fact, this discussion of faithlessness in marriage is a prelude to the treatment of faithlessness to the economically oppressed and socially disadvantaged in the fourth oracle, and faithlessness to God in the fifth oracle.

Malachi's third disputation is a combination of dialogical and expressive speech-acts intended to persuade the audience (summarized in the question, 'Why, then, do we break faith with one

---

1. Ogden and Deutsch (1987: 94).

another?' NJB; 2:10–12), and an assertive speech-act intended to instruct and exhort the audience (summarized in the admonition, *So guard yourself in your spirit, and do not break faith*, NIV; 2:16).[2] The first speech-act (vv. 10–12) addresses the subject of improper marriages and prefaces the initial declaration (*Judah has broken faith*, v. 11) with a series of three rhetorical questions (v. 10). The declaration is underscored by an oath formula threatening a curse ('May the LORD banish ... [NEB], v. 12). The second speech-act addresses the subject of divorce and includes the people's refutation (v. 14a) of the prophet's declaration (vv. 10–13) and rebuttal (vv. 14b–16). Malachi's third sermon is the only disputation that ends with a prohibition, after the form of the commands in the Decalogue – *Do not break faith*.

Biblical scholars are unanimous in their assessment of Malachi 2:10–16 as a notoriously difficult passage to interpret.[3] Both textual corruption and grammatical anomaly combine to make this disputation the most problematic of Malachi's oracles (especially v. 15, one of the most obscure verses in the entire HB).[4] The orality attributed to the disputational format of Malachi's sermons and the troublesome topic of divorce only compound the complexities faced by the interpreter.

The third disputation is aimed at the community at large, leaders, priests and people making up the *one* people of YHWH (v. 10). The basic message of the oracle is twofold: God detests (religious) intermarriage and divorce (vv. 11, 16). Both are despicable crimes before YHWH, and an affront to the essence of covenant relationship socially and religiously – faithfulness and loyalty. These covenant transgressions have defiled the people of Judah and polluted their worship of God, thereby desecrating his temple (2:11). The emphasis on *one* in the disputation (vv. 10, 15) indicates that the entire community stood under the prophet's condemnation and the threat of judgment – a threat announced in the fourth disputation.

---

2. Cf. Watts (1987: 376).

3. Baldwin (1972: 260).

4. So Mason (1990: 245).

Comment

A. YHWH's covenant profaned by disobedience (2:10–12)

10. The two opening rhetorical questions mark the third speech as distinctive among the prophet's disputations; all the others begin with a declarative statement. The rhetorical questions anticipate an affirmative answer and 'aim not to gain information but to give information with passion'.[5] The parallelism of the two interrogative clauses indicates that Malachi is equating *Father* with *God*.[6] The image of God as Father is rather rare in the OT. Malachi earlier appealed metaphorically to God as 'father' in the second oracle, when he addressed the issue of unworthy animal sacrifices (1:6). The Song of Moses also identifies God as the Father who created and established Israel (Deut. 32:6). The point of the figure of speech is that 'Yahweh cares for the people and is responsible for their existence.'[7] The repetition of the number *one* is a reminder that Israel owes its existence to a single source, YHWH and his covenant.[8]

The word 'faithless' means to 'break faith' (NAB, NJB, NRSV), 'deal treacherously with' (HCSB), and conveys the sense of 'betrayal' (NLT). The idea of 'faithlessness' is the central thesis of the third disputation (note the repetition of the Heb. word *bāgad* ['act faithlessly'] in vv. 10, 11, 14, 15, 16).

To *profane the covenant* (NIV, NJB, NRSV) means to fail to acknowledge as holy, and as such is a 'violation' (NAB, NLT) of God's covenant. Malachi's audience has profaned or violated the Mosaic covenant in their transgression of the stipulations related to divorce (cf. Deut. 7:3–4; 24:1–4). There is a sense in which the community has committed sacrilege with respect to YHWH's name as well, since he seals his covenant with his own word and name (Isa. 45:23).[9] Like the word 'faithless', the term *profaning* is a harsh verb,

---

5. *IBHS* § 18.2g, p. 322.

6. Mason (1977: 49); cf. Baker (2006: 251–252).

7. *TDOT* 1: 17.

8. Glazier-McDonald (1987: 83).

9. Cf. *TDOT* 4: 410–412.

rendered 'profane' (NAB, NJB, NRSV), *desecrate* (NIV) or 'violate' (NEB), and is used again in verse 11.

The reference to 'the covenant of our ancestors' (lit. *fathers*, KJV, NIV) is ambiguous and is variously understood as the Abrahamic covenant,[10] the Mosaic covenant of Sinai,[11] or, in context, the covenant of Levi (cf. 2:4).[12] Given the echo of Deuteronomic language in the third disputation and the explicit obligations of the Mosaic law, the covenant of the ancestors is probably an allusion to Israel's covenant experience at Mount Sinai.[13]

11. The prophet's response is terse and direct. The people of Judah were betraying marriage partners who expected and deserved fidelity. Israel has acted with treachery in violating the covenant of marriage (v. 14) and consequently her covenant relationship with YHWH. Mason (1977: 149) comments that here the message of Malachi 'shows an acute awareness that the terms of the covenant bound them in loyalty to each other as well as to God'.

The word *detestable* (NIV, NJB, NLT) denotes something 'abominable' (so NEB, NRSV) or 'abhorrent' (NJPS) to God and prohibited to the Hebrews. The term is applied to idol worship (Deut. 7:25–26), perverse sexual practices (Lev. 18:27, 29, 30), participation in the occult arts and human sacrifice (Deut. 18:9–13) of the Canaanites and surrounding nations.

The clause, 'the sanctuary of the LORD, which he loves' (NRSV, lit. 'holiness of YHWH'; cf. Lev. 19:8), is often understood as a reference to the Second Temple in post-exilic Jerusalem (e.g. Syr., ESV, NAB, NJB, NIV). Alternately, the phrase may denote the very character of God: 'holiness' as the supreme essence of his being ('Judah has violated the holiness of the LORD', NEB). Given that Judah had *broken faith* on two levels, it is possible that the ambiguity here is intentional. The Jerusalem temple was built for the name of YHWH, the God of Israel (1 Kgs 8:20). The same *love* that motivates God's election of Israel (1:2) animates his *love* or zeal

10. E.g. Baldwin (1972: 258).

11. E.g. Redditt (1995: 170).

12. So Mason (1977: 149).

13. See Glazier-McDonald (1987: 87–88); cf. Verhoef (1987: 267).

for the temple – and his own name.[14]

The phrase *daughter of a foreign god* (NEB, NIV, NRSV) is probably a reference to foreign or non-Hebrew women.[15] Others understand the phrase as a metaphor for a foreign goddess (cf. NLT, 'by marrying women who worship idols'; NAB, 'Judah ... has married an idolatrous woman').[16] However, the phrase *daughter of a foreign god* as constructed is best understood as a metaphor for foreign women. The expression is used in a collective sense of foreign women who have married into the Hebrew clans of post-exilic Judah (presumably as a result of divorce just addressed by the prophet).

The Mosaic law prohibited Hebrew intermarriage with foreigners in a variety of contexts (Exod. 34:16; Lev. 21:14; Num. 36:6; Deut. 7:3–4; 13:6–9). Malachi's condemnation of exogamy, however, is not based on the grounds of race or ethnicity, as there are examples of Hebrew intermarriage with foreigners (e.g. Joseph and Asenath, Gen. 41:45; Moses and Zipporah, Exod. 2:21; Boaz and Ruth, Ruth 4:13). Rather, the prophet's invective against such marriages targets sedition, the betrayal of legitimate and lifelong marital relationships with insidious social and religious consequences. Malachi's figure of speech in protest of the practice of intermarriage with non-Hebrews also echoes Mosaic law and serves as both reminder and warning that 'foreign cults penetrate into Israel through the daughters of foreign nations' (cf. Deut. 7:3–4).[17]

12. Malachi's response to those who violate the marriage stipula-

---

14. Petersen (1995: 194); and O'Brien (1990: 67–69; idem. [2004: 300]) are among those reviving the 'cultic' interpretation of Mal. 2:10–16 by conjectural emendation of the MT of v. 11 to read: 'Judah has profaned the very holiness of Yahweh. He loves Asherah.' This approach lacks any supporting textual evidence, and there is little indication historically that idolatry was a widespread issue among the Hebrews during the early Persian period (see the discussion in Hill [1998: 231]).

15. Cf. Glazier-McDonald (1987: 92–93); Hill (1998: 232–233); Redditt (1995: 171).

16. E.g. Petersen (1995: 199–200); and O'Brien (2004: 300).

17. *TDOT* 2: 337; cf. Glazier-McDonald (1987: 92–93); Hill, (1998: 232–233).

tions of YHWH's covenant is harsh, taking the form of a malediction or curse. The verb *cut off* has been variously understood to mean
blotting out or destroying the evildoer and his descendants (cf.
NJPS, 'leave to him … no descendants'),[18] or as some form of
excommunication from the Hebrew community (cf. NEB, 'banish';
NIV 2011, 'remove').[19] Although the exact form of punishment the
prophet prescribes is unclear, the intent of the idiom is evident, as
'such technical, cultic language … is used … for the removal of
persons or elements that are disruptive of the covenant between
Yahweh and Israel'.[20]

The clause, 'any to witness or answer' (NRSV), is difficult, as
observed in the various renderings of the verse in English. The MT
(lit. 'he who awakes and he who answers') may be understood
idiomatically as 'everyone' (*the man who does this*, NIV; 'every last man
who has done this', NLT). The NRSV emends the Hebrew *'ēr* [ru]
('arouser, answerer') to *'ēd* [du] ('witness'; cf. NAB and NJB, 'witness
and advocate'). The gist of the passage seems to extend the
prophet's curse beyond those who have wrongly divorced their
wives to include any who aid and abet those in Judah practising
intermarriage with non-Hebrews.[21] Beyond this, even attempts to
appease God by offering ritual sacrifice will be to no avail. The
prophet effectively censures anyone who is party to such improper
marriages.[22]

Meaning

Malachi declares that the *one God* holds claim over Israel as Creator
and Father (v. 10). The practice of intermarriage with foreign
women has violated the marriage stipulations of the Mosaic
covenant, and this breaking of faith with God and one another has

---

18. E.g. Calvin (1979: 548); J. M. P. Smith (1912: 50).
19. Achtemeier (1986: 182).
20. Cf. Meyers and Meyers (1993: 367); cf. *TDOT* 7: 345.
21. See the discussion in Hill (1998: 234–235); cf. Sweeney (2000: 36) who
    connects the Heb. expression *'ēr wĕ'ōneh* (lit. 'the one who wakes and
    answers') with Er and Onan (see Gen. 38:1–4).
22. See J. M. P. Smith (1912: 51).

jeopardized the organic unity of the Hebrew people as YHWH's elect nation (v. 11). Such treachery prompts the threat of a curse – some form of divine judgment, whether expulsion from the community or worse (v. 12). The prophet's admonition is a call to loyalty: loyalty to God and his covenant, and loyalty to one another as a covenant community.

B. Covenant of marriage profaned by divorce (2:13–16)

Context
The social ills confronted by Malachi were partially the result of the sheer pragmatism of the Jewish restoration community in response to the depressed local economy. Drought and blight had earlier affected agricultural production (cf. Hag. 1:11). Intermarriage with resident foreigners (2:11), the neglect of the socially disadvantaged (3:5), and reneging on the tithe (3:9) were symptoms of the severe economic pressures faced by post-exilic Judah. The problems of intermarriage and divorce around the time of Malachi are known from the records of Ezra (Ezra 9, 10) and Nehemiah (Neh. 13). Malachi's speech censuring divorce was likely prompted by the actions of men divorcing their wives and marrying foreign women in order to gain access to local commerce by marrying into the trade guilds and business cartels.

Comment
13. The people of Judah profaned YHWH's covenant by inter-marrying with foreign women, and they compounded their sacri-lege (*Another thing you do*) by *flooding* (or 'drowning', NEB) the Lord's altar with hypocritical laments. The particular combination of terms for *weeping* and *wailing* ('groaning', NAB, NRSV; 'moaning', NEB, NJPS) is unique to Malachi 2:13 in the OT. Although the basis for the people's recognition of a severed relationship with YHWH is unspecified, they clearly sense God has rejected their worship – *because he no longer pays attention to* [their] *offerings or accepts them.*

14. The reported audience response is brief, perhaps because the prophet has already supplied one answer in explanation of God's rejection of the worship offered by the people of post-exilic Judah, that of intermarriage with non-Hebrews (vv. 10–12). Their response seems to be one of genuine disbelief that their acts of piety have laid no claim on God,[23] rather than one of defiance.[24]

The phrase *acting as the witness* has covenantal connotations, and adds to the judicial tone of the disputation. According to Stuart, the job of the covenant witness was that of an enforcer or guarantor, not simply a court witness who gives testimony at a trial: 'A covenant witness was the third party who could and did make sure that the direct parties to the covenant kept its terms.'[25] Later the prophet warns that YHWH will be a 'ready witness' (NJB) at the trial of the evildoers in the community (3:5).

The prophet uses the verb *break faith* for the third time in disputation (see vv. 10, 11), as he states explicitly a second reason behind YHWH's rejection of the worship offered by his people (v. 13). Malachi had already given one answer in explanation of YHWH's refusal to accept the people's worship: that of intermarriage with non-Hebrews (vv. 10–12).

The word *partner* (NJPS, NIV, NJB; cf. NAB, NRSV) is found only here in the OT. The verbal root is used in architectural contexts to signify a 'seam' or 'joint' in building and construction (e.g. Exod. 26:6, 9, 11).[26] The word thus connotes a 'permanent bonding'. The expression suggests that the wife is not property to be discarded at will, but an 'equal ... as a covenant partner'.[27] The phrase *wife of your marriage covenant* (NIV, supplying the word *marriage*) is also unique to Malachi in the OT ('your wife by covenant', NJB, NRSV; 'betrothed wife', NAB; 'covenanted spouse', NJPS; 'your wife by solemn covenant', NEB).

Biblical commentators are divided on the question of identifying the *covenant*, whether Malachi is referring to the 'covenant of the ancestors' (v. 10) or to marriage itself as a covenant. Hugenberger (1998: 124–167) makes a strong case that the prophet construes the Hebrew marriage contract as a solemn covenant to which YHWH

23. Cf. Verhoef (1987: 73–74).
24. Cf. Ogden and Deutsch (1987: 96).
25. Stuart (1998: 1337).
26. Cf. *TDOT* 4: 95–96.
27. Garland (1987: 420).

is witness (cf. Gen. 31:50; Prov. 2:17).[28] Malachi uses these two unique OT expressions in a type of hendiadys construction to explain the earlier phrase, *wife of your youth* (14b). This threefold description of the wife (as *wife of your youth*, *partner* and *wife of your marriage covenant*) 'serves to emphasize the closeness, the intimateness of the relationship between the marriage partners and to make the treacherous behavior of the spouse even more odious'.[29]

15. As mentioned above, this verse 'is hopelessly obscure',[30] and 'it is impossible to make sense of the Hebrew as it stands ... each translation, including the early versions, contains an element of interpretation'.[31]

The construction of the first clause is terse and ambiguous. Quite literally, either: 'Has not one made?' or 'Has not he made one?' In the first instance, the number 'one' is the subject of the verb ('to do, make') and is understood in context as a reference to God ('Did not the One make [all]?', NJPS; 'Did not one God make her?', NRSV). The object of the verb must be supplied. In the second instance, the number 'one' is understood as the object of the third-person verb form ('he made'), with the implied subject *the LORD* from verse 14, or *one God* from verse 10 (*Has not [the LORD] made them one?* NIV ['Has not the one God made you?', NIV 2011]; 'Did he not make one being?' NAB; 'Did he not create a single being?', NJB). The prophet may be using a figure of speech or an idiom known and understood by the audience, but lost to us due to the ellipsis. In either case, Malachi grounds the argument for faithfulness in marriage, and the denunciation of divorce in God and his creation of humanity.[32]

The next phrase is equally cryptic, rendered literally: 'Even a residue of spirit belongs to him' (cf. KJV, 'Yet had he the residue of the spirit'). The word for 'residue' or 'remnant' in the MT (Heb.

---

28. Cf. Hill (1998: 243); Stuart (1998: 1337); Baker (2006: 255–256).
29. Glazier-McDonald (1987: 101); cf. Achtemeier (1986: 182), who summarizes that this is 'one of the most sublime understandings of the marital relation' in the OT.
30. J. M. P. Smith (1912: 54).
31. Baldwin (1972: 261).
32. Hill (1998: 243–245).

šĕ'ār) is sometimes emended to *šĕ'ēr*, *flesh* or 'body', making the word pair 'body and spirit' (cf. NAB, 'Did he not make one being, with flesh and spirit'; NIV, *In flesh and spirit they are his*; NLT, 'In body and spirit you are his'; NRSV, 'Both flesh and spirit are his'). The word *spirit* (Heb. *rûaḥ*) in this context refers to the 'life force' or 'life principle' animating all living things (cf. NJPS, 'So that all remaining life-breath is his'). The gist of the first portion of verse 15 seems to be that God created man and woman to be one being (assuming the marital relationship of Gen. 2:24?), and that all life belongs to God (implying that the union of man and woman is fixed in the creation principle and is not to be violated or severed?).[33]

The cardinal number *one* is definite, thus assuming a previously mentioned subject (presumably *the LORD*, v. 14), suggesting Malachi refers to the 'one God' (NEB, NRSV). The emphasis on *one* in verse 15 heightens the oneness embodied in the marriage relationship (cf. Gen. 2:24), and provides a solid rationale for the prophet's stance on divorce. The participial form of the verb 'desire' conveys the sense of God continually 'seeking' (NJPS, NJB), 'desiring' (NRSV), or even 'requiring' (NAB, NEB) a godly progeny, 'Godly offspring' (NRSV). The core issue is not human procreation or Hebrew ethnic purity, but the religious and social implications that the treachery and betrayal of intermarriage and divorce have for Israel's covenant relationship with YHWH. God is seeking faithful children: that is, descendants of Abraham, Isaac and Jacob who love him, obey him and hold fast to him (Deut. 30:19–20), and those who love justice, hate wrongdoing and act faithfully (Isa. 61:8–9).[34]

The sense of the verb *guard* is to 'keep watch on your spirit' (NEB), in such a way as to protect one's self from influences and situations that would compromise the marriage relationship.

The clause repeats the verb *break faith* for the fourth time in the disputation (cf. vv. 10, 11, 14). The command is repeated at the end of verse 16 (with some variation) and forms the central thesis of the prophet's third sermon. The repetition of the phrase *wife of your youth* at the beginning of verse 14 and the end of verse 15 encases a

33. Ibid., pp. 245–246; and Baker (2006: 256–257) for further discussions.
34. Cf. Hill (1998: 247–248).

literary subunit in the passage and calls attention to the victim of the treacherous behaviour. The construction of the admonition has the force and urgency of calling a halt to activity already in progress ('Stop being faithless!').[35] The warning against breaking faith with one's marriage partner sets the stage for the stern words about divorce that follow.

16. The verb *hate* (NJPS, 'detest') is a jarring word. The third-person form of the verb proves awkward ('For he hates ...'; cf. NIV 2011, 'the man who hates and divorces his wife') and is usually emended to a first-person form (as in 1:3). The MT, *he hates*, makes good sense if one presumes the subject ('the One') of the verb has been intentionally omitted from verse 15 ('For [the One] hates divorce'). The verb rendered *divorce* means to 'send away' (cf. KJV, 'For the LORD ... he hateth putting away'). The occurrence of the verbs to 'hate' and 'send away' in Deuteronomy 24:3 suggests that Malachi is alluding to the divorce statutes of the Mosaic law (Deut. 24:1–4), and it is likely that he is addressing abuses from the misapplication of the Mosaic divorce laws in post-exilic Judah. The LXX understands the construction as a conditional clause ('But if, since you hate her, you should send her away ...' [NETS]).

The clause, 'To divorce your wife is to overwhelm her with cruelty' (NLT; cf. NEB), is terse and difficult to interpret (lit. 'and he covers violence on his garment'; cf. NRSV, 'and covering one's garment with violence'), as both the internal structure of the clause and its relationship to the preceding clause are subject to differing understandings. The word *violence* is a harsh word and is used of 'brutal, deplorable acts that violate God's order'.[36] One option is to interpret the clause quite literally as conveying the idea of 'getting blood on a garment when making a violent attack on someone else'.[37] A second approach understands the clause more figuratively, as one might don clothing ('covering oneself with lawlessness as with a garment', NJPS), or as a figure of speech for one's inward

---

35. See R. L. Smith (1984: 320).

36. Baker (2006: 260).

37. Clark and Hatton, (2002: 423); cf. Stuart (1998: 1343); and Baker (2006: 259–260).

character (*and I hate a man's covering himself with violence as well as with his garment*, NIV). It seems best to understand the idiomatic expression of covering one's garment with violence more literally as a reference to a man behaving unjustly towards his wife by divorcing her ('The LORD ... hates anyone who is cruel enough to divorce his wife', CEV).[38] The prophet deemed divorce a social crime and an act of violence or injustice, because it fractured the 'social glue' of the divinely ordained marriage covenant and deprived the divorced woman of the dignity and protection due to her according to the spousal agreement.[39]

The repetition of the admonition (to the husband) to *not break faith* (with his wife) in verses 15 and 16 forms a subunit within the section discussing divorce (vv. 13–16). The message of the book of Malachi pivots on the theme of faithfulness versus faithlessness as mirrored in the marriage and divorce customs of post-exilic Judah. The NJB, 'Have respect for your own life then, and do not break faith', adduces both the personal and corporate implications of the prophets, because 'It is in the best interests of the individual as well as the community that families should not be broken by divorce.'[40] Tragically, Malachi's message apparently had little impact on the marital customs of his audience, since the reforms of Ezra and Nehemiah address these same abuses a generation or two later (cf. Neh. 13:23–27).

Meaning

Malachi espoused a lofty view of marriage, equating it with a covenant relationship. He passionately preached a message of faithfulness and loyalty to one's marriage partner (v. 14), and warned his audience not to break faith in marriage (vv. 15, 16), because God has made marriage partners one (v. 15). Since divorce is an act of violence against a marriage partner, God hates divorce and the damage created by fractured marital relationships (v. 16). The prophet recognized that loyalty to the marriage covenant both

---

38. Clark and Hatton, (2002: 425–426); cf. Glazier-McDonald (1987: 111).
39. Cf. Hill (1998: 252).
40. Baldwin (1972: 262).

fulfilled God's creation mandate for the man-woman relationship and contributed to the stabilization of society. Later, Jesus affirms the Genesis ideal for marriage (cf. Gen. 2:24) and offers a strict interpretation of the Mosaic laws regarding divorce (Matt. 19:1–12; cf. Deut. 24:1–4).

4. FOURTH DISPUTATION: YHWH'S MESSENGER OF JUDGMENT (2:17 – 3:5)

Context

Malachi's fourth sermon consists of two speech-acts: the first is an assertive speech in the form of a disputation intended to assure the audience that God is just (2:17 – 3:1); the second is an expressive speech posed in the form of a threat that the people will soon experience God's justice (3:2–5). According to VanGemeren (1990: 204), the message of the third oracle (faithlessness in marriage, 2:10–16) and the message of the fifth oracle (faithlessness to God, 3:6–12) turn upon the hinge of divine judgment threatened in the fourth disputation (2:17 – 3:5).

Adapting Achtemeier's (1986: 172) approach to Malachi as a courtroom drama, the fourth disputation constitutes the formal indictment (2:17 – 3:5), the fifth disputation represents the judge's verdict (3:6–12), and the final disputation is the sentencing of the defendant (3:13 – 4:3). The fourth disputation is addressed to the 'righteous sceptics' in post-exilic Jerusalem at large, including the priests (3:3). This is deduced from the emphasis placed on the order of purification (of the righteous, vv. 3–4) before judgment (of the wicked, v. 5). The prophet confronts all those who have interpreted God's apparent non-involvement in the current crisis of faith within the community as the failure of divine love (1:2–5) and divine justice (2:17).

Malachi's fourth sermon is a more complex disputation, including: the prophet's declaration (2:17a)), the audience's refutation (2:17b), the prophet's second declaration (2:17cd), followed by the prophet's rebuttal (3:1), and concluding with the threat of divine judgment (3:2–5).

Comment

A. YHWH's justice challenged (2:17)

2:17. God's people have *wearied* him with insincere prayer and hypocritical worship (cf. NIV, NJB, NLT, NRSV). The particular form of this verb *wearied* occurs only in Isaiah 43:23, 24 and Malachi 2:17. In Isaiah, the word is used in combination with the term *burden* which also means *wearied*. In this indictment, the prophet rebukes his audience for impugning God's character as a righteous judge (v. 17). Calvin's (1979: 563) translation ('saddened his spirit') aptly conveys the effect that, more than fatigue, the people have 'saddened God's spirit' by their faulty and insincere religious words and ritual acts devoid of any conviction, loyalty or devotion.

Malachi's audience protests against the prophet's charge of any wrongdoing by repudiating the notion that somehow they had wearied God with their talk (*How have we wearied him?*, 2:17b). Their response anticipates the later remonstrance of innocence at the prophet's call to repentance in 3:7. The people contend they have dutifully served God (3:14).

The specific content of the hypocritical speech that has wearied God is revealed in Malachi's second declaration (2:17cd). The (self-?) righteous sceptics of Malachi's audience challenged God on two accounts: first, they accused him of injustice in responding to sin within the community ('Any evil-doer is good as far as Yahweh is concerned', NJB). And second, they questioned his presence and participation in the affairs of the community (*Where is the God of justice?*). The gravity of these allegations is attested by the inclusive nature of the prophet's response, addressing not just the pious sceptics, but the entire restoration community.

Malachi's audience accused God of 'taking delight' (NJB, NRSV), or *being pleased* (NAB, NIV, NLT) with evildoers. This reported speech of the audience contradicts the prophet's message in the second disputation, where the Lord Almighty 'takes no delight' in those who offer improper sacrifices at the temple (1:10). Such misperception and distortion of divine truth are common among those confronted with a historical reality that overturns their preconceived (and sometimes faulty) theological paradigm (cf. 3:14).[1]

The epithet *God of justice* is also found in Isaiah 30:18. The context of Isaiah's declaration serves as the answer to the question posed by Malachi's audience: YHWH waits to be gracious to Israel, and blessed are those who wait for him. Most EVV render the Hebrew word *mišpāṭ* with the abstraction *justice* (so NIV, NLT, NRSV; cf. NAB, 'Where is the just God?'). Note the same word also occurs at the beginning of 3:5, forming a type of partial envelope construction framing the fourth disputation. There the same word is translated *judgment* (NAB, NIV), as the context indicates that God will *testify against* the evildoers (so NAB, NIV, NRSV; cf. 'I will put you on trial', NJB, NLT). The question posed in 2:17 seems to imply both ideas as a form of wordplay, since justice is a character trait of God and the act of judgment belongs to him, given his role as righteous judge (cf. NJB, 'Where is the God of fair judgment now?'). Malachi's audience asks, *Where is the God of justice?* (2:17). The God of justice replies, *So I will come near to you for judgment!* (3:5).

Meaning
The substance of the fourth disputation is that of disparity (real or perceived) between divine justice and human justice, between the ideal and the reality of the retribution principles as they are played out in covenant relationship with YHWH. Verhoef (1987: 287) attributes the unrest in post-exilic Judah to the perception that the law of retribution was inoperative. Baker (2006: 268) equates the attitude of the restoration community with 'religious relativism'.

---

1. Cf. *TDOT* 5: 103–104.

Neither understanding is entirely correct. Rather, the righteous in Malachi's audience resented the fact that they still languished under the corporate curse of the law of Moses due to the disobedience of other (even previous?) community members. It appears that the pious sceptics clamoured for the 'new covenant' paradigm of Jeremiah (Jer. 31:29–30) and Ezekiel (Ezek. 18:3–4), divine justice executed upon an individual rather than a corporate (or generational) basis.

B. YHWH will come to his temple (3:1–4)

Context
The fourth oracle forecasts a time when covenant loyalty will be a defining trait of post-exilic Judah. God will accomplish this by visiting his people with divine judgment, a refiner's fire that purifies and restores righteousness (3:2–4). Malachi's audience struggled with the problem of theodicy (God's justice in relation to the problem of evil, 2:17). This led to false conclusions about God (2:17; cf. 3:14–15) and prompted them to clamour for the Day of the Lord, the eschatological day of God's visitation (3:1). Theirs was not a theological crisis of belief, as much as an issue of lifestyle. It was a matter of Israel's moral and spiritual purity as YHWH's vassal, more than God's justice meted in the retribution principle of covenant relationship with him. Malachi's audience learned that divine justice comes to those who seek it, but not necessarily applied in ways they had anticipated.

Comment
3:1. The combination of the interjection *See* and the participle *send*, with the first-person independent pronoun (*I*), is an exclamation of immediacy ('I am sending', NRSV). The construction connotes an ominous imminency. The expression *my messenger* (Heb. *mal'ākî*) plays on the prophet's name *Malachi*. The word *messenger* may indicate either an angel or a human being functioning as a divine courier, although Malachi's audience would not have made careful distinctions between angel and messenger, since in Bible times angels were God's messengers.[2]

The adjoining clause (*who will prepare the way*) is indefinite ('clear a

way', so NEB, NJB). The background for the imagery is the highway
construction language of Isaiah, which alludes to the practice of
removing obstacles, straightening out curves, and grading roadways
to achieve a smooth surface for royal processionals in the ancient
world (Isa. 40:3; 57:14; 62:10).[3] The task of YHWH's messenger is
to clear the way before the Lord's epiphany by removing the obstacles of self-interest, spiritual lethargy and unrighteous behaviour
characteristic of the people of post-exilic Judah.

The adverb *suddenly* (NAB, NJB, NRSV) calls attention to the
surprising and unexpected visitation of the Lord to his temple.
Sceptics within the restoration community have assumed God's
disinterest and non-involvement in the spiritual climate of post-
exilic Jerusalem. They are mistaken. Discerning observers of God's
ways throughout Hebrew history have recognized a pattern of
divine pronouncement followed by YHWH's sudden activity (cf.
Isa. 48:3). Malachi's audience will experience a similar scenario.

The term *Lord* is a title of respect for YHWH's messenger. The
word is an epithet for YHWH himself in Zechariah 4:14; 6:5, and
with the definite article (as is the case here) the Lord is always paired
with YHWH, suggesting that this is whom Malachi has in mind as
well. The construction may constitute wordplay, with the use of
Lord posed in the rhetorical question of the second disputation ('If
I am Lord [*master*, NIV], where is my respect?', 1:6), for there will be
no question that YHWH is Lord when he comes!

The participial form of the verb (*desire*) indicates the ongoing
nature of the people's craving for divine intervention into their situation. Previously the prophet used the same participle to indicate
that God was *seeking* a righteous offspring (2:15). The two passages
create a foil yielding an irony, in that YHWH seeks a righteous or
godly offspring, and in their *seeking* of the Day of the Lord (3:1),

---

2. See Stuart (1998: 1350); cf. Baker (2006: 270).

3. See McKenzie (1968: 16); cf. Westermann (1969: 38–39), who reads the
language of Isaiah against the backdrop of the great processional
highway of Babylon used for cultic parades and enthronement festivals;
and Glazier-McDonald (1987: 138–139), who assumes this for Mal. 3:1
as well. See also *ZIBBCOT* 5: 238–239.

the people hasten the very judgment that will purge the sin preventing them from becoming the 'godly seed' of YHWH. The despairing righteous Jews seek divine judgment on evildoers, as indicated by their distorted dogma that YHWH has considered evildoers good (2:17). Like the audience of the prophet Amos, the people of Judah fail to realize fully the impact of their request. Their seeking of the Day of the Lord will hasten its coming, and 'They will get what they asked for, but it will not be what they wanted.'[4]

The restored Jerusalem temple is a touchstone for each of the post-exilic prophets. Haggai rallied the people to rebuild the sanctuary destroyed by the Babylonians (Hag. 1:8). Zechariah envisioned the divine cleansing of priest and people and the restoration of godly priestly leadership and service in temple worship (Zech. 3 and 4). Sadly, the prophet Malachi rebuked both priest and people for their corrupt and hypocritical worship, to the extreme of advocating shutting down the temple ministry (Mal. 1:10). The possessive, *his temple*, underscores God's supremacy as owner and occupant of the sanctuary (cf. *my altar*, 1:7, 10; *my house*, 3:10). It is fitting that the Lord's epiphany will be centred in the Jerusalem temple, since the sanctuary was the abode of God's glory and the symbol of his presence and rule over Israel and the nations (1 Kgs 8; 2 Chr. 7:1–3; Ps. 11:4; Hab. 2:20; cf. Exod. 25:8).[5]

Malachi's audience probably would have understood the *messenger of the covenant* as a divine being (like an angel) on the basis of the parallel with the angel of YHWH in Exodus 23:20–23.[6] Malachi appears to mention three distinct figures in his eschatological projection to the time of God's visitation: *my messenger, the Lord* and *the messenger of the covenant* (3:1). In the context of formal temple entrance in the ancient world, it is possible Malachi envisions YHWH in a processional flanked by two angelic retainers. The question

---

4. Andersen and Freedman (1989: 521).

5. In the NT, Jesus equated the Jerusalem temple with his own body and his impending death, burial and resurrection (cf. John 2:19–22); see the discussion in Beale (2004: 192–200).

6. See the discussion in Stuart (1998: 1350) on the similarities between Mal. 3:1 and Exod. 23:20.

remains as to whether these two 'messengers' are distinct divine beings or some sort of dual representation of 'the Angel of Yahweh'.[7]

Traditional Christian interpretation has identified the initial *messenger* figure as John the Baptist, on the basis of NT fulfilment as interpreted by Jesus himself (cf. Matt. 11:3, 10, 14). The *messenger* [or angel] *of the covenant* has been understood Christologically since patristic times as a reference to Jesus Christ, and hence equated with *the Lord* who comes to his temple (cf. Luke 2:21–40; John 2:12–22).[8] This has fixed a two-character understanding of Malachi 3:1 in Christian biblical interpretation – John the Baptist as the *messenger*, and Jesus the Messiah equated with *the Lord* who is *the messenger of the covenant* (i.e. the new covenant predicted by Jeremiah and fulfilled in the Christ-event; Jer. 31:31–34 ; Luke 22:20–23).[9]

The people *desire* a divine visitation ('whom you look for so eagerly', NLT) – yet another ironic verbal echo of the opening disputation of the fourth sermon. Malachi's audience *desires* the epiphany of the Lord, assuming that theophany will bring about the justice they are looking for and assume they deserve. Earlier the people had accused God of 'desiring' (being *pleased with*) the evildoers (2:17). This suggests that 'the prophet seems almost to be taking his audience to task for inexact exegesis, not fully understanding either the meaning of the term *desire* or the nature of God'.[10]

The verse concludes with another exclamation of immediacy (an interjection combined with a participle ['to come']: 'indeed, he is coming', NRSV). The storm clouds gather, and what (at least some of) the people *seek* and *desire* will soon arrive – the coming of YHWH as Divine Judge. There will indeed be a sudden and unexpected epiphany at the temple of YHWH, but the consequences of this event, eagerly awaited by the post-exilic religious community, will yield a startling reversal of human calculations. The zeal for the appearance of YHWH at his temple ought to have been tempered

---

7. See the discussion in Hill (1998: 289).
8. See Ferreiro (2003: 299–301).
9. Cf. Stuart (1998: 1350–1352).
10. Baker (2006: 270).

with the understanding that divine judgment will begin with them, not the evildoers, not their enemies – as Malachi is not loathe to observe. As is often the case, popular expectation for the outcome of the Day of the Lord is tragically mismatched with the reality of the event (cf. Amos 5:18: 'Woe to those who crave the day of Yahweh').[11]

2. The two rhetorical questions introducing the prophet's expressive speech-act (*Who can endure ...? Who can stand ...?*) emphasize the fact that it is no small thing to desire the Day of the Lord. The two graphic metaphors that follow provide the rationale for the inability of anyone to stand before YHWH when he appears: *he will be like a refiner's fire or a launderer's soap* (NIV). The *refiner's fire* (NIV, NJB, NRSV) or 'smelter's fire' (NJPS) was the means by which precious metals were separated from unwanted metals and other impurities.[12] Malachi borrows the imagery of God refining his people by smelting away the dross of their wickedness from the prophets Isaiah (1:25), Jeremiah (6:29; 9:7) and Ezekiel (22:17–22), and there may be some interdependence between Malachi 3:2–3 and Zechariah 13:9.[13] The launderer's or fuller's soap was a strong detergent for 'bleaching clothes' (NLT; cf. 'fuller's alkali', NJB; 'fuller's lye', NAB). The word *soap* is rare in the OT, occurring only in Jeremiah 2:22 and Malachi 3:2, and it describes an alkaline salt or soda powder produced from a plant. The word for *soap* (Heb. *bōrît*) is a form of wordplay with the term for *covenant* (Heb. *běrît*), a key theme in Malachi. It is unclear whether the washing process refers to the laundering of clothes or to the second stage of the smelting process, which utilizes lye or potash as a reagent in separating the dross from the precious metal.[14] Whether the prophet appeals to the imagery of two common trades (smelter and launderer or fuller) or to a two-stage process of metallurgy, the idea of divine testing and cleansing for the purpose of purification is unmistakable (cf. Ps. 66:10; Dan. 11:35; 12:10).

---

11. Andersen and Freedman (1989: 520–522).

12. Cf. *ZIBBCOT* 5: 238–239.

13. See Hill (1998: 276–277).

14. Cf. *ZIBBCOT* 5: 239.

3–4. Malachi had previously rebuked the priests in the second disputation for failing in their duties as ministers of the temple rituals and teachers of the Mosaic law (1:8, 10, 13; 2:6–8). The priests are singled out as the target of God's refining process, 'because they were the mediators between God and his people, and were therefore also responsible for the religious decline of the people. Thus purification of the people has to start with them.'[15] Once purified, 'they shall be fit to bring offerings to the LORD' (NEB; cf. NLT, 'so that they may once again offer acceptable sacrifices to the LORD').

The prophet may have had the post-exodus Mosaic period in mind as the *days gone by* or the ideal era of Hebrew covenant relationship with YHWH (cf. the reference to Phinehas in 2:5).[16] Taken together, the two expressions probably allude more generally to those times in Israelite history when the Hebrew priests and people faithfully served YHWH. In either case, the reference serves as an important reminder to the priests and the people of post-exilic Judah that they have a legacy they can aspire to emulate.

Meaning

Malachi's fourth sermon forecasts the impending day of God's visitation (vv. 1–4) to judge evildoers (v. 5). The prophet seems to mention three distinct figures in his reference to the coming Day of YHWH: *my messenger, the Lord* and *the messenger of the covenant* (3:1). The ambiguities surrounding the precise number and identity of these eschatological figures who have roles in this theophany continue to invite scholarly discussion. Beyond specific identifications, it is important to recognize that the divine messengers carry out a thorough purification of God's people. The eschaton will witness the transformation of God's people into a holy community, by a spirit of burning, washing and cleansing (3:2–3; cf. Isa. 4:3–4; Zeph. 3:11–13, 17). The desired outcome of this difficult and painful process of 'refining' is genuine worship offered to YHWH by his faithful people – now spiritually renewed. Malachi reminds us not to be overzealous in a selfish desire to hasten the Day of the

---

15. Verhoef (1987: 291); cf. Baker (2006: 272).

16. See Baldwin (1972: 266).

Lord, because when the time comes for judgment 'it must begin
with God's household' (1 Pet. 4:17, NLT).

C. YHWH's judgment (3:5)

Context
Ironically, God will come and administer justice to the poor, the
widow, the orphan and the foreigner – the very people who have
been trampled and defrauded by those selfishly desiring the divine
visitation! He will serve as witness, judge and executioner against
the evildoers, and stand as advocate for the oppressed. The failure
of the priests and people to fear the Lord Almighty links the first
dispute (1:6) with the fourth disputation (3:5).

Comment
   5. The people's plea for justice (2:17) does not go unheard. God
will first purify the priests and the believing remnant within the
restoration community (3:1–4), and then he will judge the evildoers
(3:5). God's *justice* (2:17) and *judgment* (3:5), embedded in the Hebrew
term *mišpāṭ*, frames the sermon. The two concepts are inseparable
as character traits of a righteous God, and together they serve to
correct the faulty theology about God and his response to evildoers
(2:17). In this regard, Malachi has affinities with earlier prophets
who proclaimed justice for the righteous and judgment for the
wicked (cf. Zeph. 2:8–10; Joel 3:16–21 [MT 4:16–21]).
   The word 'witness' suggests a legal proceeding ('I will appear
before you in court, prompt to testify', NEB; 'I am coming to put
you on trial and I shall be a ready witness', NJB; 'At that time I will
put you on trial. I am eager to witness against all', NLT). God takes
on multiple roles in Malachi's courtroom setting: that of expert
witness, prosecuting attorney and judge – how could the people not
fear YHWH?
   God's testimony against his people includes five specific indictments for covenant violations, related to both moral and social
justice issues. *[A]gainst sorcerers* denotes those who practise witch-
craft and black magic, occult activities prohibited by Mosaic law
(cf. Deut. 18:10). The custom to which Malachi refers is probably
some form of fortune-telling, predicting the future for personal

gain.[17] [*A*]*dulterers* refers to anyone who has sexual intercourse with the wife or the betrothed of another man, behaviour forbidden in the Decalogue of the Mosaic covenant (Exod. 20:14; Deut. 5:18). [*P*]*erjurers* ('liars', NLT) are literally 'those who swear falsely' (NJPS, NRSV), and presumably inferring those who lie under oath (i.e. commit perjury). The seriousness of these crimes is evidenced by the fact that adultery was a capital offence (Lev. 20:10; Deut. 5:20; 22:22), and in certain cases both sorcery (cf. Lev. 20:6, 27; Deut. 18:10) and perjury (Deut. 19:18–19) were punishable by death.

Mosaic law prohibited the withholding of wages from the labourer ('those who oppress the wage-earner', NJB; 'those who cheat employees of their wages', NLT; cf. Lev. 19:13; Deut. 24:14). Mosaic law also guaranteed protection of the widow and orphan from mistreatment (Exod. 22:21–22; Deut. 10:18; 24:17; 27:19) and offered them certain privileges in the form of a type of social security (Deut. 14:29; 16:11, 14; 24:19–21; 26:12–13). The term *alien* (NIV, NRSV; Heb. *gēr*) is rendered variously as 'foreigner' (NJB, NLT), 'stranger' (NAB, NJPS), 'sojourner' (ESV). The word describes a person who has separated him- or herself from clan and homeland for any number of reasons. The Hebrew term *gēr* or 'sojourner' occupies an intermediate position between a native of the land (Heb. *'ezraḥ*) and a foreigner (Heb. *nokrî*), and has the status of a legal immigrant.[18] The clause is terse, and the verb 'thrust aside' is usually understood to mean the sojourner was denied justice in some manner (*deprive aliens of justice*, NIV; 'rob the foreigner of his rights', NJB). The Hebrews were charged to love those who are foreigners or resident aliens among them, because God defends their cause and they too were of the same social standing during their Egyptian sojourn (Deut. 10:18–19).

The final clause of the prophet's fourth sermon links *doing evil* with *not fearing* YHWH. The list of behaviours attributed to the evil-doers can be categorized on the basis of a single common denominator: the failure to 'respect' (NJB) and revere God. The word *fear* is a rich and complex OT word and, when used in covenant

---

17. Cf. *ZIBBCOT* 5: 239–240.
18. Cf. *TDOT* 2: 443.

contexts, invariably it is intended to motivate obedience to God's commands (Deut. 5:29; 6:2, 24; 8:6).[19] The Hag-Zech-Mal corpus begins with the people responding to Haggai's message by *fearing the LORD* (Hag. 1:12), but by the time of Malachi many in post-exilic Judah *do not fear the LORD* (v. 5; cf. 3:16).

Meaning
Divine justice is always linked to God's ethical demands in the realm of human justice. Malachi recognized that spiritual decline may be reversed by a renewal movement that includes moral reform. Hence, implicit in his threat of divine judgment (v. 5) is the call for the practice of social justice.

---

19. Cf. *TDOT* 6: 290–314, esp. pp. 313–314 on 'Fear of God as Devotion to Torah'.

5. FIFTH DISPUTATION: THE CALL TO SERVE YHWH (3:6–12)

Context

Malachi's fifth oracle contains two disputations: one concerning the tithe (3:8–10), embedded within another, the call to repentance (3:6–7). Analysed as a series of speech-acts, this penultimate disputation consists of three elements: a divine assertion (*I ... do not change*, v. 6), intended to assure the audience of God's constancy; a divine summons to repentance (*Return to me*, v. 7), meant to persuade the audience to shift their loyalty back to YHWH; and a divine challenge (*Test me in this*, v. 10), aimed at convincing the audience of YHWH's commitment to restore his people.[1] The fifth oracle also resumes the thought of the first (1:2–5), God's covenant love for Israel.

Adapting Achtemeier's (1986: 172) approach to Malachi as a courtroom drama, the fourth disputation constitutes the formal indictment (2:17 – 3:5), the fifth disputation represents the judge's

---

1. Watts (1987: 376–377).

verdict (3:6–12), and the final disputation is the sentencing of the defendant (3:13 – 4:3). The apparent non-effect of the summons to repentance in the fifth disputation is all the more remarkable, in that the prophet's call to renew loyalty to YHWH is sandwiched between two sermons emphasizing the themes of judgment and purification.

God's declaration, *I the LORD do not change*, was a reminder to post-exilic Judah of the constancy of his divine character that continually manifests itself in unimpeachable faithfulness to this covenant word (cf. Num. 23:19). Israel had failed to recognize that her destiny and God's affirmation of constancy were entwined. The ancient covenant YHWH had established with Israel's ancestors was still valid, due to his steadfast character (Exod. 34:6–7) and his unswerving loyalty to his promissory oath (Ps. 111:5; cf. Ps. 89:34 [MT 35]). The very fact that repentance and restoration remained an option for Israel was testimony to God's enduring love for his people (cf. 1:2, *I have always loved you*).

Like Malachi's fourth sermon, the fifth sermon is a more complex disputation, including the prophet's declaration (3:6–7b), the audience's refutation (3:7c), the prophet's rebuttal (3:8a), a second refutation by the audience (3:8b), and the prophet's final rebuttal (3:8c–12).

Comment

A. The call to repentance (3:6–7)

6. The emphatic adverb, *surely*, sets the tone and focus for the fifth disputation, since it modifies the clause in itself, calling attention to God and his constancy.[2] The verse consists of two balanced clauses contrasting God and Israel. The opening phrase of the first couplet may be understood as a verbless clause, 'I am the LORD' (so NJPS); or as the appositional subject of the verb, 'I do not change' (i.e. *I the LORD do not change*; so NIV; NRSV). The use of the covenant name YHWH invoking the exodus experience of the Hebrews

---

2. Cf. *IBHS* § 39.3.4e, pp. 665–667.

makes the former more likely.[3] The form of the verb *change* conveys both the sense of the indefinite perfective ('I have not changed', HCSB), and the instantaneous perfective (*I do not change*, NIV, NLT, NRSV).[4] Malachi's affirmation that YHWH has not changed should not be construed primarily as a metaphysical statement, a theological commentary on the nature of God's being. Rather, the declaration attests the faithfulness of YHWH to his covenant agreement with Israel. God has not changed with respect to his unwavering commitment to his covenant, nor has he changed the terms of the pact. This divine constancy is rooted in God's basic character revealed in his autobiographical testimony to Moses in Exodus 34:6–7.[5]

The second clause of the couplet is ambiguous, perhaps intentionally so, given the penchant for double entendre in OT prophetic literature. A cue for this understanding may be found in the phrase *descendants of Jacob*. The expression designates the national entity or collective community of Israelites living in post-exilic Judah. The use of the name *Jacob* (Heb. *ya'ǎqōb*) could be a pun ('the cheat'; Heb. *'āqab*), since the prophet will later indict the people for cheating God (v. 8).[6] The vocative, *O descendants of Jacob* (NIV), is in order despite the lack of a preceding imperative verb, and is in keeping with the emphatic purpose of the antithetical pronouns *I* and *you* and the hortatory nature of the disputation. The plural noun 'sons' (KJV) can indicate individuals of both sexes, hence the rendering 'children' (NRSV) or *descendants* (NIV, NLT).

Apart from God's mercy and compassion (cf. Exod. 34:6–7), Israel would have 'perished' (NRSV; 'be consumed', KJV; cf. Isa. 1:28; Jer. 5:3; Ezek. 5:13; Hos. 11:6; Zech. 5:4). It may also mean 'cease' or 'come to an end', permitting the alternative reading: 'nor do you cease to be sons of Jacob' (so NAB; cf. NEB, NJB). The idea here is

---

3. Baker (2006: 288).

4. Cf. *IBHS* § 30.5.1b, d, pp. 486–488.

5. Baker (2006: 288); see further the discussion of the 'Immutability of the Everlasting God' in Taylor and Clendenen (2004: 404–408).

6. See Mason (1977: 155); cf. R. L. Smith (1984: 331, n. 8a) on the LXX translation 'cheat' (Gk *pternizei*) for the MT 'rob' (Heb. *qāba'*).

that the descendants of Jacob continued to imitate their father (cf.
Gen. 27:36). The people of Israel 'remain constant in evil ... the
people have always been "cheaters"'.[7] As in the case of the verb
change (6a), the verb *destroy* (or 'cease', depending upon the translation) may be rendered as an instantaneous perfective (*you are not
destroyed*, NIV) or an indefinite perfective ('you have not been
destroyed', HCSB). Rendering the verb *destroy* (rather than 'cease')
seems the better option, because 'the translation ... stresses the fact
of God's unchangeableness as the reason for Israel's continued existence'.[8] Quite apart from either translation (i.e. an explicit understanding of Israel as a perpetual covenant violator deserving God's
judgment or an implicit reference to Israel as unceasing cheats): 'The
fact is that neither God nor Israel had changed' (Baldwin 1972: 267–
268). But, unlike Edom mentioned previously in the first disputation, Israel had not been destroyed (cf. 1:2–5).

7. The reference to the decrees of God in the following clause
suggests that the prophet is alluding to the aftermath of Israel's
exodus from Egypt. That first generation of Hebrews liberated
from Egyptian bondage failed to trust God, rebelled and were
denied entry into 'God's rest' – the land of covenant promise (Deut.
1:26, 32, 34–35; cf. Ps. 95:11; Heb. 3:16–19).[9]

To *turn away* (cf. NJB, 'evaded'; NLT, 'scorned') connotes rebellion
and mutiny, wilful rejection of divine instruction, when used in the
context of covenant language (cf. Jer. 6:28; Hos. 7:14).[10] The people
have not *kept* ('failed to obey', NLT) God's *decrees* (NIV, NJPS;
'statutes', NRSV), an umbrella term for the entirety of the law of
Moses.[11] There is no more serious admonition in the OT, as the
charge to obey the statues of YHWH pervades the book of
Deuteronomy (more than fifty times; cf. Jer. 16:11; 35:18; Ezek.
11:20; 18:9, 19, 21). The prophet Ezekiel envisioned a time when
the Davidic Servant would instil obedience to the statutes of

---

7. Mason (1977: 155).

8. Verhoef (1987: 300); cf. Glazier-McDonald (1987: 176–177).

9. See Glazier-McDonald (1987: 181–182).

10. See the discussion in Andersen and Freedman (1980: 475–476).

11. Cf. *TDOT* 5: 145.

YHWH in restored Israel (Ezek. 37:24). The conjunction joining the two perfective verb forms serves as a hendiadys, representing two aspects of a complex situation: 'rejecting and disobeying' God's laws.

Return to me, and I will return to you. In contexts expressing covenant relationship, the word *return* (Heb. *šûb*) expresses a change of loyalty on the part of Israel or God. Typically, the term is understood as 'repentance', a complete change of direction back to God, or a total reorientation towards YHWH. The imperative verb and the inversion of the independent pronouns ('you' [the people] implied and 'I' [YWHW]) convey a sense of urgency, demanding an immediate response from the audience. Malachi repeats the phraseology of the earlier call to repentance by Zechariah (Zech. 1:3; cf. Hag. 1:12–14), a key theme in the Hag-Zech-Mal corpus. Regrettably, the repetition indicates that little has changed in the intervening years.[12]

Malachi's audience are not genuinely seeking new information upon which to base their repentance and restoration to right relationship with God. Rather, the response (almost a quip?) is a self-serving protestation of their assumed innocence. The attitude expressed in their self-righteous denial is reflected in the interpretive translation: 'But you ask, "How can we return when we have never gone away?"' (NLT). The restoration community claimed no knowledge of sin or conceded any need for repentance. The people seem to assume that the fault in the broken relationship with God lay with YHWH, since they had returned to the land but the tangible benefits of covenant relationship had not yet materialized (cf. Mal. 3:14–15).

Meaning

Malachi's fifth disputation is primarily a summons to repentance (v. 7). Covenant relationship with YHWH can only be renewed as the people of post-exilic Judah reorient their loyalty away from sin and self and towards God. Only then will their worship be purified and made acceptable to God, and as a result the social ills decried by the prophet will begin to be rectified.

---

12. See Hill (1998: 302, 322–323).

B. The call to bring the whole tithe (3:8–12)

Context
The self-interest rebuked by Haggai (Hag. 1:4–6) persisted in post-exilic Judah into Malachi's day, attested by the offering of inferior animals for ritual sacrifice at the temple (Mal. 1:7–8). The failure of the people to obey the Mosaic laws regarding the tithe were presumably the result of both spiritual lethargy (even unbelief), and stinginess due to the variety of socio-economic pressures faced by the Hebrew community seeking to rebuild after the Babylonian exile.

Comment
8. Malachi's use of the generic 'man' (so ESV) or 'anyone' is instructive, since it suggests that he is speaking of humanity in general.[13] The prophet is appalled at the behaviour of his fellow Hebrews, implying that even the pagan Gentiles would not engage in such a misdeed.

The fourfold repetition of the verb *rob* (NIV, NRSV; Heb. *qābaʿ*; 'cheat', NLT; 'defraud', NJPS) in verses 8–9 underscores the gravity of the offence in denying God the tithes and offerings due to him. The word is somewhat rare in the OT (used elsewhere only in Prov. 22:23), but it is well established in later Talmudic literature to mean 'to take forcibly'.[14] The use of the participial verbal form in verse 8a indicates that this cheating of God is an ongoing practice. The LXX translates 'deceive, defraud' (Gk *pternízō*; lit. 'go behind the back') in verses 8–9, reinforcing the wordplay with the name Jacob (Heb. *ʿāqab*; '[T]he people have always been "cheaters".').[15]

As in the previous disputations, the prophet anticipates the response of his (somewhat incredulous?) audience. As in the case of the earlier refutation of Malachi's call to repentance (3:7c), the people question the accusation that they have been cheating God. The impudence prompting both responses betrays their pride in religious formalism (cf. 3:14) and their spiritual blindness to the

---

13. Cf. *TDOT* 1: 83–84.
14. Baldwin (1972: 268).
15. Mason (1977: 155).

circumstances surrounding them (i.e. the curse they are living under with drought, pestilence, famine, poverty; cf. v. 9).

The *tithe* or 'tenth part' refers to the general tithe of the produce of the land prescribed by Mosaic law (cf. Deut. 12:6, 11, 17). The *offering* may be a gift or 'contribution' (so NEB, NJB) made to YHWH or his sanctuary, and may include gifts of produce from the land, along with material goods (e.g. construction materials and garments) or personal valuables (e.g. gold, silver and precious stones). The pairing of the two terms (*tithes and offerings*) suggests that the prophet calls for payment of both the tithe and the tithe tax, thus appealing for a comprehensive renewal of the ritual giving practices of the post-exilic community. The tithe tax was the 'tithe of the tithe' prescribed in Numbers 18:26 for the general provision of the central sanctuary.[16]

9. The verb *curse* means 'to bind with a curse' (NIV, *You are under a curse*). The syntactical symmetry of the sentence signals the reality of the community's plight. The nightmare of divine judgment is being played out even *now* in post-exilic Judah ('you are *now* being afflicted with a curse').[17] The word *curse* is definite ('with *the curse* you are being cursed'; cf. NEB, 'There is a curse, a curse on all of you'), suggesting that the prophet is equating the experience of post-exilic Judah with 'the curse' of the Mosaic covenant (cf. Deut. 28:20, 27). This would explain the sense of urgency attached to Malachi's call to repentance and covenant renewal with YHWH.

The cause of the divine curse was directly related to the robbery or cheating of God in the failure to pay the tithe and the tithe tax. The people were naively or willingly oblivious to the obvious cause and effect of their behaviour in view of covenant stipulations and attendant blessings and curses. The explicit declaration of such by the prophet Haggai to the previous generation was apparently lost on Malachi's audience as well (Hag. 2:17).

The phrase *the whole nation* (lit. 'the nation – all of it') is both inclusive, as all the people of Judah are guilty of robbing God in their tithes and offerings, and somewhat pejorative, in that the prophet

---

16. See Petersen (1995: 216).

17. Ibid., p. 212; cf. Hill (1998: 305–306).

uses the word *nation* (Heb. *gôy*), perhaps equating Israel with the surrounding pagan nations.

10. The command to *bring the whole tithe* bridges the other two mandates in the disputation (*return*, v. 7 and *test me*, v. 10). The prophet's call to deliver the tithes and offerings to the temple storehouse is a more pointed answer to the earlier question posed by the audience as to how they were robbing God (v. 8).

The nature of God's request (*Test me in this*) is extraordinary,[18] and a rare but not unique divine challenge in the OT.[19] The prophet's command is not in violation of the prohibition against 'testing God' (Deut. 6:16). The word for testing in that context (Heb. *nāśā'*) means to 'try' or 'prove' (or even 'tempt') from a posture of arrogance and cynical unbelief. The term employed here (Heb. *bāḥan*) signifies testing from a posture of honest doubt, with the intent to encourage and approve faith in God. The divine invitation to 'put God to the test' (NLT) offers the restoration community an opportunity to prove the faithfulness of YHWH to his covenant promises by the experience of their obedience.

The expression *floodgates of heaven* is a figure of speech for rainfall and abundant agricultural produce as tangible signs of God's covenant blessing (and what the people of Judah have been looking for; cf. Hag. 1:6, 10–11; 2:16, 17, 19). The prophet's use of words such as *open*, *storehouse* and *heavens* suggests he has in mind the blessing of abundant rainfall of the Deuteronomic blessing (Deut. 28:12).[20]

The unique expression, *you will not have room enough for it* (cf. Ps. 72:7), quantifies God's blessing, and is variously rendered: 'without measure' (NAB), 'in abundance' (NJB), 'an overflowing blessing' (NRSV). The point is clear: God's response to the obedience of his people will be a floodtide of divine blessing in the form of agricultural good fortune.

11. Crop failure due to pestilence, blight and disease is one of the curses threatened against Israel for disobedience to the stipulations of the Mosaic covenant (Deut. 28:22; cf. Hag. 1:6, 10–11; 2:17).

---

18. See Petersen (1995: 217).
19. Cf. Redditt (1995: 180).
20. Baker (2006: 286).

Earlier, Malachi had rebuked the offspring of the corrupt priests (2:3). Now God will *prevent* (NIV; or 'rebuke the locust', NRSV) pests from devouring the 'offspring' or produce of the land. In addition to the blessing of ample rains yielding abundant agricultural produce, God will 'forbid' (NAB, NJB) pestilence and blight from ravaging the crops, in response to the obedience of the people in honouring God with the whole tithe.

12. Malachi's message is strategically tied to the knowledge and worship of God among the nations (1:11, 14; 3:12). The mission of YHWH's covenant people was connected to the nations from the very beginning, as God's covenant with Abraham included a clause of blessing for the nations (Gen. 12:1–3). The phrase *call you blessed* (so NAB, NIV, NJB; 'count you happy', NEB, NRSV) renders the verb (Heb. *'āšar)* meaning 'consider fortunate, call happy'. While the praising of Israel by the nations is 'in harmony with election theology',[21] the source of this favour and blessing is also acknowledged in their acclaim – Yahweh himself as the God of the nations. The nations that once formerly taunted and subjugated the people of Israel will be obliged to acknowledge its 'favoured nation' status, and Israel will more effectively fulfil its commission as the ensign of Yahweh's light and glory to the nations (Isa. 42:6; 60:3; 61:9, 11; 66:19).

The expression *delightful land* (NAB, NIV), 'favoured land' (NEB) or 'most desired of lands' (NJPS) is unique to Malachi in the OT. The verse reminds that the fate of the Hebrew people and the land of Yahweh's covenant promise are really one. The territory of Judah as a *desirable land* stands in stark contrast to Edom as the *Wicked Land* or 'territory of evil' in the first disputation (1:4). The new epithet for God's inheritance also overturns the stigma and shame of the Babylonian exile, when the land of Israel was scorned and but a byword among the nations (Jer. 18:16; Lam. 2:15; cf. Deut. 28:37).

The fourfold repetition of the messenger formula, *says the LORD Almighty*, in the fifth disputation (vv. 7, 10, 11, 12) underscores the urgency of the prophet's call to repentance and the certainty of the promise of restoration as 'the word of God'.

---

21. *TDOT* 1: 447.

Meaning

At the core of the prophet's dispute with his audience over repentance is *reversal*. As the people reverse their attitude and behaviour with respect to YHWH's covenant, so YHWH will reverse the experience of the people living in the land of covenant promise. The call to bring the whole tithe to the temple (v. 10a) was more than simply the reinstitution of legalistic giving to fulfil the formal obligations of the Mosaic law. The challenge to test God (v. 10b) by responding in obedience and bringing the required tithe was not a cause-and-effect formula for material blessing. Malachi recognized that this robbery of God was merely a symptom of a more serious cancer. The stinginess of post-exilic Judah was rooted in unbelief. Only by returning to a posture of faith and reverence could the people experience the wisdom of the sage: 'It is possible to give freely and become more wealthy, but those who are stingy will lose everything' (Prov. 11:24, NLT). Malachi understood that turning to God in spiritual renewal must begin somewhere, and he deemed the practical act of obedience to the Mosaic laws regulating the tithe to be an important first step in reasserting the community's fidelity in covenant relationship with YHWH. Clearly, 'Good harvests alone ... would not make a country *a land of delight* ... there were spiritual counterparts to the fruits of the soil.'[22]

---

22. Baldwin (1972: 269).

6. SIXTH DISPUTATION: THE DAY OF YHWH (3:13 – 4:3 [MT 3:21])

Context

Like Malachi's fifth sermon, the prophet's last disputation offers a more complex series of charges and countercharges, including the prophet's opening declaration (3:13a), the audience's rebuttal (3:13b), the prophet's second declaration (3:14–15), a narrative interlude (3:16), and the prophet's final rebuttal (3:18 – 4:3 [MT 3:21]).

The final sermon is a blend of several speech-acts, including assertive speech intended to persuade (vv. 13–15), narrative report designed to elicit a response (v. 16), assertive speech of assurance (vv. 17–18), and an assertive speech of warning (4:1–3 [MT 3:19–21]. The closing disputation exhibits the hortatory style (terse and direct first-person speech) and the same self-referential congruence of the prophet's earlier sermons. Unlike the earlier speeches, the prophet does not resort to the use of the rhetorical question as a response to the pseudo-dialogue with his audience. Rather, he concludes with an exclamatory utterance (3:18 – 4:3 [MT 3:21]). The final oracle, similar to the fifth oracle, is directed to the restoration community at large, leaders, priests and people. The LXX and Vulg. begin a new chapter at 3:19 [= 4:1], adopted by the modern versions.

The final disputation repeats the message of God's desire for covenant faithfulness on the part of his people. The key issues in the prophet's last oracle are the seeming triumph of wickedness over righteousness and God's apparent laxity in judging the sin within the community. Malachi's response to the problem of theodicy is fixed in the coming day of YHWH, when the wicked will be separated from the righteous by the fire of God's judgment, and the righteous will experience the vindication of divine justice.

A. Obedience to YHWH challenged (3:13–15)

Comment

13. The prophet accuses the people of speaking 'strong' or 'hard' (NJPS, NEB) words against the Lord. The construction conveys the sense of *overruling*,[1] as if Malachi's audience not only spoke ('terrible things', NLT) against God, but also sought to enforce their words (or theology?) upon him ('You have defied me in word', NAB).[2]

The final sermon follows the script of the previous speeches, as the reported response of the people is one of denial, even (feigned?) surprise. Baldwin understands that the community has spoken against YHWH 'unwittingly'.[3] Others charge that this question was not posed in good faith, implying a denial of Malachi's indictment and challenging him to forward supporting evidence.[4] The report of the council of the righteous (v. 16) suggests that the motive of the community lies somewhere between these two positions.

14. To *serve God* describes the service of proper worship of YHWH, and obedience in keeping the stipulations of his covenant. This terse saying has the ring of a proverb, perhaps spoken often in

1. Stuart (1998: 1374).
2. Andersen and Freedman (1980: 472).
3. Baldwin (1972: 271); cf. Stuart (1998: 1375).
4. See J. M. P. Smith (1912: 76) who notes the people were busy with 'malicious gossip' directed against the Lord; cf. Verhoef (1987: 315).

Judah during Malachi's day.[5] The mercenary doubters in the prophet's audience complained that their personal acts of right-eousness were 'useless' (NEB, NJB), 'vain' (NAB, NRSV), 'foolish' (CEV), since they did not produce the intended or promised results.[6] Such conduct towards God is deemed useless for two reasons: first, the righteous go unrewarded (v. 14b); and second, the wicked go unpun-ished (v. 15).

The noun *gain* implies 'increase, profit, profit-making' (cf. NAB, 'what do we profit ...?'). The form is related to a technical term associated with carpet making (i.e. cutting off a completed piece of woven material, hence 'taking one's cut, profit').[7] The issue was not one of illegal economic gain or profit. Rather, it was related to the interpretation of the blessings and curses theology of the Mosaic covenant (Deut. 28). The righteous within post-exilic Judah assumed that their acts of piety and obedience to the covenant stipulations and worship rituals gave them claim to the goodness and blessing of God. Such misconceptions concerning the corporate nature of the blessings and curses of the Mosaic covenant are understandable if the people presumed that the theology of individual responsibility preached by Jeremiah (31:27–30) and Ezekiel (18:3) as part of YHWH's new covenant with Israel was now operative.[8]

The clause, *going about like mourners*, complements the previous clause ('obeying his commands', NLT). This pair of activities suggests a cause-and-effect relationship that never materialized (cf. NAB, 'going about in penitential dress in awe of the Lord of hosts'?).[9]

15. The audience refutation reveals the motivation for their sarcastic taunt of 2:17 (*Where is the God of justice?*). The justice of

---

5. Cf. Stuart (1998: 1378).
6. Cf. Baker (2006: 293).
7. Cf. *TDOT* 2: 207.
8. See Hill (1998: 333).
9. See Jones (1962: 203) who suggests that the suppliants were not 'disinterested' in the outcome of their rites of mourning and penitence.

God (as experienced in the retribution principle of covenant blessings and curses) has been inverted in the minds of the people. The
arrogant ('proud', NAB) are *blessed* ('the happy ones', NJB), the *evildoers
prosper* ('are successful', NEB), and those who *challenge God* ('tempt
God with impunity', NAB; 'dare God to punish them', NLT) *escape*
('suffer no harm', NLT). Previously, the prophet Ezekiel had stated
that covenant breakers cannot escape the judgment of God (Ezek.
17:15). Malachi's audience contests instead that such escape by evildoers was commonplace.

Meaning

The mercenary doubters of post-exilic Judah have complained that
the practice of religious requirements yielded no tangible advantage
(v. 14). In fact, their experience of suffering and poverty in the real
world showed that evildoers were actually the ones who had gained
the upper hand (v. 15). Malachi devotes the rest of his final sermon
to responding to the charges of YHWH's alleged mistreatment of
the righteous in the restoration community.

B. Obedience to YHWH vindicated (3:16–18)

Context

The prophet returns to the identity crisis among the people of God
diagnosed in the opening disputation (*How have you loved us?*, 1:2).
Pastor Malachi assures his audience, especially *those who feared the
LORD* taking counsel with one another (v. 16), of two essential
truths: Israel is still God's *treasured possession* (v. 17a), and *compassion*
is still the defining characteristic of YHWH (v. 17b; cf. Exod.
34:6–7).

Comment

16. Those who *feared the LORD* revere, honour and show faith in
God with respect to his covenant (cf. CEV, 'All those who truly
respected the LORD').[10] They are to be contrasted with the *evildoers*
in verse 15 (cf. LXX, 'Those who fear the LORD spoke against these

---

10. Cf. *TDOT* 6: 296.

things [i.e. the wrong conclusions about God's justice', NETS]).

The combination of the verbs to *listen* and to *hear* indicates YHWH's deep interest in the Hebrew faithful and his ready willingness to notice and respond to the words of the righteous (cf. NJB, NRSV, 'the LORD took note and listened'). The reflexive use of the verb *talked*, in combination with the phrase *with each other*, conveying reciprocity, denotes the sincerity and purposeful intent of the dialogue among the YHWH fearers (cf. CEV, 'started discussing these things').

The concept of heavenly scrolls or books recording the deeds and destinies of human beings is known elsewhere in the OT (see Exod. 32:32; Pss 56:8–9; 69:28; 139:16; Dan. 7:10; cf. Isa. 4:3; 65:6) and the ancient world.[11] Malachi's *scroll of remembrance* has a parallel in the scroll of records mentioned in Esther 6:1. Such documents were catalogues of names and a record of events. YHWH's *scroll of remembrance* contained the names, words and deeds of those who feared and honoured him, and it will serve as the basis for God's winnowing of the righteous from the wicked in the coming day of judgment (v. 18).

To *honour his name* means to 'value' or 'esteem' (ESV, NJPS) the name of YHWH by 'keeping his name in mind' (NEB, NJB) as a prompt for covenant obedience. The entire clause serves as a foil to the earlier reference to the despisers of YHWH's name (1:6).

17. Malachi has abbreviated the covenant relationship formula (*I will be their God, and they will be my people*) found in the prophetic books (e.g. Jer. 31:33; Ezek. 36:28; Zech. 8:8). The expression is God's assurance that his covenant promises to Israel remain intact and will be fully realized in some future time.

God *will spare* the righteous (NEB, NIV, NJB, NLT, NRSV; but NJPS, 'be tender'; NAB 'have compassion') because they are his treasured possession.[12] The phrase *treasured possession* is also a covenant term that describes the privileged status of Israel as the people of God, his 'prized possession' (NJB), so to speak. The righteous will not just

---

11. See the discussion in Glazier-McDonald (1987: 220–221); cf. *ZIBBCOT* 5: 241.

12. Cf. *TDOT* 3: 378.

escape God's wrath in the coming day of judgment; they will be delivered or preserved as beloved children.[13] Compassion and showing mercy are among YHWH's defining attributes in his auto-biographical declaration to Moses (Exod. 34:6–7). Malachi echoes Joel 2:18, which relates the restoration of Israel's fortunes in the Day of YHWH as a result of his compassionate reorientation to his people. The righteous are compared to the son or daughter who *serves* his or her parents, in the sense of responding as an obedient child (CEV, NLT).

18. Previously, the people had complained that God no longer made any *distinction* (NIV) between the righteous and the wicked (v. 15). The use of the verb to *see* conveys the sense of perceiving or knowing as a result of experience (NJPS, 'you will come to the see the difference'). Malachi's allusion to an earlier example of God's differentiation between the *righteous* and the *wicked* is ambiguous, and is perhaps a reference back to the judgment of Edom (1:4). The terms *righteous* and *wicked* represent classes or categories of people, those who are just in conduct and upright in character versus those who are guilty in a general legal sense of covenant transgression.[14]

As with the children who obey their parents (v. 17), the word *serve* here also conveys the sense of obedience to God ('those who obey me by doing right and those who reject me by doing wrong', CEV).

Meaning

Despite appearances, the paradigm for divine justice has not been inverted. God will convincingly demonstrate the distinction between the righteous and the wicked on the day he acts (v. 18).

C. The Day of YHWH – judgment and vindication (4:1–3 [MT 3:19–21])

Context

The Babylonian exile had raised anew the inscrutable question of human suffering, especially the suffering of the righteous. Malachi's

---

13. See Stuart (1998: 1384).
14. See the discussion in Hill (1998: 344).

audience were probing the issue of theodicy, with their question: *Where is the God of justice?* (2:17). Malachi's solution was simple: place one's fate in the hands of YHWH and consider the end of the matter from the beginning. God's justice will prevail in the vindication and restoration of the righteous and the ultimate judgment and destruction of the wicked.[15] The Day of YHWH will bring about clarification of values: not prosperity versus privation with respect to material things, but guilty versus not guilty (or righteous) in relation to spiritual things.[16]

Comment

4:1. The coming *day* that Malachi announces is the Day of YHWH, the eschatological day of God's visitation that brings both 'disaster and deliverance' for Israel and the nations.[17] This Day of the Lord, which the prophet referenced earlier as *the day of his coming* (3:2), is now given further definition. In each case, fire is associated with the warning of impending divine judgment. The purpose of the fire in the former is purification, especially of the Levites (3:2–4), while in the latter it is complete destruction of post-exilic Israel.

The burning *furnace* is probably 'a fixed or portable earthenware stove, used especially for baking bread'.[18] The expression has its closest parallel in Hosea 7:4, where the desires of the wicked *burn like an oven*. The imagery of a burning *furnace* (or 'oven', NAB, NJPS, NRSV) used as an incinerator for destroying wicked people in the day of YHWH's judgment is both graphic and frightening (cf. Ps. 21:9). Those who clamoured for the epiphany of the God of justice will get what they asked for in full measure (2:17).

The *wicked* (v. 18) are further identified as *arrogant* or 'insolent' (NAB; NJB, 'proud') and those who practise evil deeds (CEV, 'sinful people'; HCSB, 'those who commit wickedness'). The expression is not a reference to two separate categories of people, 'but is simply

---

15. Cf. Craigie (1985: 246): 'A society may decide to abandon the distinction between good and evil, but God never abandons it.'

16. Cf. Verhoef (1987: 324).

17. See *TDOT* 6: 31.

18. Andersen and Freedman (1980: 456).

a twofold description of all those who do not fear the Lord'.[19]
Malachi's use of the word *stubble* ('chaff', NEB; 'straw', NLT) repro-
duces the imagery of the Day of the Lord portrayed in Joel 2:5. The
linking of the terms *fire* and *stubble* (4:1) frequently connotes God's
judgment of the wicked (e.g. Isa. 5:24; 33:11; 47:14; Obad. 18; cf.
Exod. 15:7).

The destruction of the wicked with the Hebrew community is
absolute, reflected in the merism of *root and branch*, the extremities
of a plant signifying its entirety. The metaphor highlights 'the totality
of the coming destruction, with its completeness made more
evident through the burning even of the roots, which ordinarily do
not succumb to a flash fire, being protected by the earth'.[20]

2. The shift from third person (3:16) to second person in the
address to those who 'fear' (NAB, NJB) or 'honour' (CEV) God's name
personalizes the prophet's final declaration.[21] The reference to those
who fear YHWH also has liturgical implications, and designates a
group of people who have remained faithful to YHWH and stand in
readiness to serve as his agents in restoring covenant faith, righteous
behaviour and true worship in Judah.[22] Those who fear YHWH's
name are those who have repented and long to see his cause triumph
and right prevail.[23] The word *name* is a key theme in the prophet's
second disputation (1:6 – 2:9), and Malachi uses the term to represent the essence of God's being, especially his sovereignty, love and
faithfulness to Israel as revealed in his covenant name, YHWH.

The expression *sun of righteousness* is unique to Malachi in the OT.
The phrase may be a solar epithet for YHWH, given the association of God with the sun and light,[24] or it could be merely a figurative description of the Day of the Lord, the dawning of a new
day that ushers in an era of righteousness and brings about a reversal
of circumstances for the people of God (cf. NJPS, 'sun of

---

19. Verhoef (1987: 325).
20. Baker (2006: 297).
21. Cf. Baldwin (1972: 273).
22. Cf. Hanson (1986: 284).
23. Baldwin (1972: 273).
24. See Redditt (1995: 184).

victory').[25] The winged sun-disk of Ancient Near Eastern iconography is one possible source for Malachi's solar epithet. This icon depicting falcon or eagle wings against a full sun represented the guardianship and blessing of the deity for the rulers or people, overshadowed by the protecting wings of the god.[26]

Early Christian interpreters understood the word-picture as a messianic title fulfilled in Jesus the Messiah.[27] The EVV understand the phrase as a solar epithet for YHWH (or a Christological title) and render it '*the* sun of righteousness' (even though the phrase is indefinite; cf. KJV, 'the Sun of Righteousness'). The new day coming portrayed in the rising of the sun is characterized by *healing*. 'Rather than the fire of judgment, the balm of healing arrives by means of the "wings" of the sun of God.'[28]

The pastoral imagery of well-fed calves romping playfully in the pasture conveys a sense of joy and freedom for the righteous in the Day of the Lord – another picture of the reversal of fortunes awaiting those who fear YHWH ('And you will go free, leaping with joy like calves let out to pasture', NLT).

3. The verb *trample* ('tread down', NAB) is unique to Malachi 4:3 in the OT. The combination of the verb *trample* and the word *feet* signifies victory, perhaps evoking the image of a triumphant king with his foot planted on the chest or neck of the vanquished enemy – a common motif in the biblical world (cf. Josh. 10:24; 2 Sam. 22:39–40; 1 Kgs 5:3; Ps. 110:1; Isa. 51:23).[29] The expression may also be a veiled allusion to the covenant destiny of Israel as outlined in Deuteronomy 11:24 (the divine promise of possessing *every place where you set your foot*). The word *ashes* (Heb. *'ēper*) may also be rendered 'dust' (so NJPS, NLT), but the context of God's fiery judgment requires the former.

---

25. Cf. Stuart (1998: 1387–1388).

26. See the discussion in O'Brien (1990: 313); for examples of Assyrian and Persian representations of the icon, see *ZIBBCOT* 5: 233, 241.

27. See Ferreiro (2003: 307–311).

28. Baker (2006: 298); cf. Taylor and Clendenen (2004: 453); cf. NIV 2011, 'with healing in its rays'.

29. Cf. *TDOT* 13: 319–320; *ZIBBCOT* 5: 418.

Meaning

Malachi's prediction of 'the eventual rehabilitation of the pious and the shameful end of the "wicked" ... refutes the suggestion that to serve God is meaningless' (cf. 3:14).[30] In one sense, Malachi's final disputation is a most fitting conclusion to the prophet's message because of the 'amazing reversal' of fortunes for the righteous.[31] Such reversal serves as a climax to the literary motif of turnabout prominent throughout the book. This reversal or antithesis is not between the restored covenant people of Israel and the nations, as is often the case in prophetic discourse regarding the Day of the Lord (e.g. Isa. 11:14; Zeph. 2:9; Hag. 2:7; Zech. 14:12–14). Rather, the reversal takes places within the covenant people of Israel, between the righteous and the wicked.[32] The vindictive tone of Malachi's final sermon may provoke a disturbing uneasiness in the modern reader. Keil understands the trampling down of the wicked by the righteous as a symbol of liberation from all oppression.[33] Given this perspective, the gist of the message is one of the triumph of divine justice more than the victory of the righteous over the wicked. Nonetheless, any theophany of YHWH is awesome and terrible, and the reality of YHWH as a divine judge is terrifying, since he is a consuming fire (Deut. 7:21; Joel 2:11; Heb. 12:28–29). Such truths should be disturbing.[34]

---

30. Ogden and Deutsch (1987: 114).
31. Baldwin (1972: 274).
32. Verhoef (1987: 332).
33. Keil (1975: 467).
34. Ogden and Deutsch (1987: 111).

7. APPENDICES (4:4–6 [MT 3:22–24])

Context

The appendices to Malachi are an editorial conclusion containing two postscripts. The first references the ideal figure of Moses (4:4 [MT 3:22]) and the second the ideal figure of Elijah (4:5–6 [MT 3:23–24]). The epilogue serves double, perhaps even triple, duty as the ending to the book of Malachi, as well as concluding both the Book of the Twelve Prophets and the collection of Latter Prophets in the Hebrew Bible. The canon order of the English Bible (following that of the LXX) provides an appropriate segue to the NT, with the Gospel narratives opening the curtain on the preaching of John the Baptist, an Elijah figure preaching repentance (Matt. 3:1–12; cf. 11:11–15).

Early commentators such as Martin Luther and John Calvin assumed the unity of Malachi 4:4–6 [MT 3:2–24] with the rest of the book. More recent commentators also affirm the integrity of the closing verses of Malachi as a conclusion to the prophet's final disputation. The hortatory style and thematic unity of these verses with the message of the book, especially the fourth disputation (2:17 – 3:5), are cited as supporting evidence.[1]

The more clear purpose of the epilogue appears to be that of uniting the Book of the Twelve Prophets (or the Minor Prophets) with the Latter Prophets (Isaiah, Jeremiah, Ezekiel) and the Primary History (Torah or Pentateuch + the Former Prophets or Historical Books of Joshua through to Kings) by means of the two ideal figures representing these literary collections. The ideal figure of Moses represents the literary collection of the Torah in the Hebrew Bible, while Elijah represents the literary collection of the Latter Prophets. Thus, the association of the ideal figure of Elijah with the ideal figure of Moses serves to invest the Latter Prophets with the same divine authority accorded to the Torah and the Primary History of the Hebrew Bible.[2]

Comment

A. Charge to obey the law of Moses (4:4 [MT 3:22])

4. The combination of the words *remember* and *law* occurs only here in the OT (the close parallel is found in the prayer of Nehemiah, Neh. 1:8). To *remember* is more than memorializing the past by means of the intellectual activity of recalling YHWH's deeds in history. Rather, it is an exhortation to act upon that knowledge, by harnessing the will in obedience to God's commandments.

The *law* (Heb. *tôrâ*) of Moses refers to the stipulations of the covenant code enacted by YWHW and accepted by Israel first at

---

1. E.g. Baldwin (1972: 275) considers Mal. 4:4–6 to be original to Malachi and regards the passage as the conclusion to the book. Stuart (1998: 1391) and Sweeney (2000: 714) include the material as part of the prophet's sixth disputation, while Verhoef (1987: 337) understands the passage as an independent postscript to the book of Malachi (cf. R. L. Smith [1984: 340–342]).

2. See the discussion in Hill (1998: 363–365). The reference to the Torah in Malachi's epilogue also links the Latter Prophets with Ps. 1 (and *the law of the LORD*, v. 2), thus uniting all three divisions of the Hebrew Bible.

Mount Sinai (Exod. 19 – 24), and again in the region of Moab near Mount Nebo (Deut. 1:5–6; chs. 5 – 26). Later, the expression *law of Moses* will come to signify the entire Pentateuch (or Torah of the Hebrew Bible). The phrase *law of … Moses* is intentionally ambiguous here, since the greater purpose of the first postscript is to connect the collection of the Latter Prophets with the Torah of Moses (i.e. the whole Pentateuch comprising the covenant stipulations, civil and ethical instruction, and the narrative traditions associated with Moses as lawgiver). The covenant stipulations, or law regulating Israel's relationship with God, are summarized in the phrase variously rendered 'decrees and regulations' (NLT), or 'statutes and ordinances' (NJB, NRSV). 'Statues and ordinances' are more 'strictly the categorical law and case law' and 'a very common way of referring to the law of God in general' (Lev. 26:46; Deut. 4:1, 5).[3] Ancient Israel's identity was rooted in the exodus event (Exod. 12 – 14), and her existence and destiny were inseparably joined to the law of Moses (Deut. 30:15). For this reason, the Hebrews were commanded to remember *this day* [i.e. the Passover] for all time (Exod. 12:14). The same is no less true for the Christian church. Her identity and destiny are inextricably tied to the Christ event – the cross (1 Cor. 5:7, 'Christ, our Passover Lamb, has been sacrificed for us' [NLT]) – and remembered in Eucharistic re-enactment until the Lord's return (1 Cor. 11:26).

The word *servant* is an honorific title prominent in the Primary History (Genesis – 2 Kings), ascribed to Abraham (Gen. 26:24), Isaac (Exod. 32:13), Jacob (Deut. 9:27) and David (2 Sam. 3:18) among others. The ancient title describes 'the ideal role of the Israelite rule in intimate relationship to Yahweh's supremacy'.[4] The inclusion of the epithet for Moses in the first appendix accents the role assigned to him by Hebrew tradition as Israel's lawgiver, and specifically endows the Book of the Twelve, the Latter Prophets and the Former Prophets with the same divine authority accorded the Torah of Moses.

The place name *Horeb* functions synonymously at times as an

---

3. Baldwin (1972: 276).
4. Meyers and Meyers (1987: 68).

alternate name for Mount Sinai (cf. Exod. 33:6; 1 Kgs 19:8). In other
instances, Horeb refers to the desolate region bordering Mount Sinai
(e.g. Exod. 17:6; Deut. 1:19; Ps. 106:19). Here *Horeb* refers to Mount
Sinai and Israel's covenant experience with YHWH there mediated
by Moses (Exod. 19:1–2, 11).

B. Elijah and the Day of YHWH (4:5–6 [MT 3:23–24]

5. The interjection 'Look!' (*See*, NIV; 'Lo!', NAB, NRSV; 'Behold!',
KJV) introduces an exclamation of immediacy, and when coupled
with a participle *sending*, the exclamation has the 'nuance of vivid
immediacy'.[5] The clause has affinities to Malachi 3:1 ('Look! I am
sending my messenger', NLT), and both Malachi 3:1 and 4:5 [MT 3:22]
are recognized as an intentional reworking of Exodus 23:20 (*See, I
am sending an angel* [Heb. *mal'āk*, 'angel' or 'messenger'], NIV).[6] The
citation of Exodus 23:20 in the second postscript strengthens the
argument for understanding Malachi 4:4–6 [MT 3:22–24] as a coda,
forming a bridge between the Primary History (Torah + Former
Prophets) and the Latter Prophets in the HB. The name Elijah ('my
God is Yah[weh]') occurs only here in the Minor Prophets and the
Latter Prophets (Isaiah, Jeremiah, Ezekiel). This form of the
prophet's name is uncommon, and is found outside of Malachi in
2 Kings 1:3, 4, 8, 12. The LXX inserts 'the Tishbite' for the prophet,
a harmonization of the phraseology (*Elijah the Tishbite*) found in
Kings (e.g. 1 Kgs 17:1; 2 Kgs 1:3). The announcement of Elijah as
a forerunner prior to the 'Day of the Lord' may help clarify the identity, nature and character of the ministry of Malachi's *messenger of
the covenant* (Mal. 3:1).

Typologically, John the Baptist has been identified by Christian
interpreters as the iconoclastic preacher of repentance fulfilling this
prophecy (cf. Matt. 11:14), although it is entirely possible, as Wolf

---

5. On the 'exclamation of immediacy', see *IBHS* §40.2.1b, p. 675; cf. GKC
　§116p, pp. 359–360, the *futurum instans*. Meyers and Meyers (1987: 67)
　have observed this grammatical construction 'nearly always ... has an
　ominous force, indicating Yahweh's intended punitive actions'.

6. Petersen (1977: 42).

has noted, that the ministry of John the Baptist did not completely exhaust the full meaning of this prophecy.[7] The Gospel of Matthew hints that John was the Elijah figure in a limited way, and that Elijah both 'has come' and 'is coming' – perhaps in the form of one of the witnesses prior to the end of the age (Rev. 11:3; cf. Matt. 17:11).

The appositive construction, *the great and dreadful day*, signifies the categorization of quality or character of the lead word (in this case the phrase *day of the LORD*). The Lord's epiphany will be both *great and dreadful*, in that it will be awesome in magnitude and dreadful in outcome. Most EVV read the compound appositive adjectivally: *that great and dreadful day of YHWH* (so NIV, NRSV). The same expression is found in Joel 2:31b [MT 3:4b], and similar phraseology occurs in Joel 2:11. The citation of Joel 2:31b [MT 3:4b] in the second appendix of Malachi probably represents an example of Fishbane's 'mantological' exegesis: the revision and adaptation of earlier oracular materials by a later prophetic tradition.[8] The appeal to Joel's description of the Day of the Lord and the reference to Elijah the prophet ensure the authority of the continuity of the apocalyptic vision for Israel seen by the earlier prophets, despite the modifications of those oracles by Zechariah and Malachi (e.g. the shift from the restoration of Davidic rule envisioned by Haggai to the hierocratic rule of Malachi).

The prophet Malachi promised a day when God would act to distinguish between the righteous and the wicked (3:18). For him, the Day of the Lord was one of justice, in the form of vindication and restoration of the righteous, and judgment in the form of punishment and destruction of the wicked (4:1–3). The Christian church awaits that day when Jesus the Messiah will return 'to repay all according to their deeds' (Rev. 22:12, NLT), and *making everything new* (Rev. 21:5, NIV). *The Spirit and the bride say, 'Come! ... Amen. Come, Lord Jesus* (Rev. 22:17, 20).

6. Some Greek versions (e.g. A, B, Q) and the Arabic transpose Malachi 4:6 [MT 3:24] with Malachi 4:4 [MT 3:22], presumably

7. Wolf (1976: 124–125).

8. See Fishbane (1985: 506–524).

to avoid ending the book with the threat of a curse (although both the final disputation and the appendices conclude with the ominous spectre of divine judgment).[9]

The second postscript highlights a key theme prominent in Malachi and the entire OT prophetic corpus: the *turning* of hearts and the ministry of reconciliation (cf. NLT, 'His preaching will turn ...'). The word *turn* is the OT term for repentance, and indicates a complete reversal in loyalties or an 'about-face' in one's direction. Implicit in this act of repentance is turning towards God, as Malachi had exhorted his audience in his fifth sermon (Mal. 3:7).

The word *heart* is the most important term in all the vocabulary of OT anthropology, and should be understood synthetically as the locus of human feelings, desire, reason and volition. The idea conveyed by the verse is one of inter-generational reconciliation, the practical outcome of this repentance or turning of the parents and children to one another. Baldwin describes the ministry of the coming Elijah figure 'in terms of bridging the generation gap'.[10] The NIrV appropriately renders: 'Elijah will teach parents to love their children. He will also teach children how to honor their parents.' The postscript refers not so much to family discord as to covenant renewal with YHWH – the 'resolution of opposites' in the sense of faithful ancestors versus faithless descendants, or vice versa.[11] Although the reconciliation of family discord is not the focus of the postscript in context, that message is certainly relevant, given the breakdown of the nuclear family unit in Western society. The dissolution of the family is manifest in the rampant dysfunction seen in parents and children alike, in the form of abuse, addiction and obsessive behaviour patterns. What better word for a society disintegrating slowly due to its own self-absorption than *turn* – to God and to one another?

The verb *strike* has the sense of 'ruin, destroy or strike dead'. The Jews of post-exilic Jerusalem had already experienced this divine

---

9. See Baker (2006: 299); on the paraphrasing tendency of the LXX in Mal. 4:6, see Kruse-Blinkenberg (1967: 72).

10. Baldwin (1972: 276).

11. Cf. Petersen (1995: 231).

judgment in the form of natural disasters *striking* the land (Hag. 2:17).

The reference to *the land* signifies the land of Israel, the land of covenant promise (reduced to the confines of the province of Judah by Malachi's time). The word 'ban' (so NEB) or *curse* (so NIV, NLT, NRSV) is the term (Heb. *ḥerem*) used regarding how the Hebrews were to treat the conquered cities of Palestine (cf. Deut. 7:1–11; 20:18–20; Josh. 6:17; 10:1). In this context, the term is better understood as an object or person marked for 'doom' (NAB; 'put the land under a ban to destroy it', NEB) or even 'the curse of destruction' (NJB, following the LXX *anathema*). The combination of the verb *to strike* and the active noun *curse* specifies the nature and extent of the divine judgment – 'utter destruction' (NJPS).[12]

Meaning

The appendices to the sermons of Malachi emphasize two essential teachings. First, the vitality of the post-exilic Jewish community's religious life is dependent upon its capacity to re-identify with the past.[13] Israel's faith in the present tense and hope in the future tense are always conditioned by her ability to remember the words and deeds of YHWH in the past tense (cf. Exod. 13:3; 20:8; Deut. 5:15; Ps. 77:11).[14] The second is the centrality of the Torah of Moses to the life and mission of Israel. From Moses to Ezra and beyond, the law of God is 'life and death, blessing and curse' for Israel (cf. Deut. 30:15–20).

Craigie has further condensed the meaning of the postscripts of Malachi for post-exilic Judah into *retrospect* and *prospect*:[15] retrospect in the form of an exhortation to covenant faithfulness based upon an appeal to the ideal figure of Moses; and prospect in the form of an admonition, both threatening judgment and pledging restoration

---

12. Cf. *TDOT* 5: 186–187 notes that the curse applies primarily to the people of the land, not just the cultivated ground.
13. Isbell (1980: 77).
14. On the importance of remembrance in Hebrew education see Brueggemann (1982: 14–39).
15. Craigie (1985: 248).

based on an appeal to the ideal figure of Elijah. Together the post-scripts compose a type of credo verifying the Hebrew Scriptures of the Law and the Prophets as the source of authority and guidance, and the witness of divine presence for the Jewish restoration community.